Dis/Organization as Commu...........

This book accounts for the transformation of organizations in a post-bureaucratic era by bringing a communicational lens to the ontological discussion on organization/disorganization, offering a conceptual and methodological toolbox for studying dis/organization *as* communication.

Increasingly, scholars acknowledge that communication is *constitutive of* organization; because meaning is always indeterminate, communication also (and simultaneously) generates *dis*organization.

The book synthesizes the major theoretical trends and empirical studies in communication that engage with dis/organization. Drawing on dialectics, relational ontologies, critical theory, systems theory and affect thinking, the first part of the book offers communicational explanations of how dis/organization unfolds. The second part of the book grounds this theoretical reflection, providing empirical studies that mobilize diverse methodological and analytical frameworks (e.g., ethnography, situational, interactional and genre analysis) for studying the practices of dis/organization. Overall, the book exposes organizations (and organizing processes) as significantly messier, more irrational (or a-rational) and paradoxical than scholars of organization typically think. It also offers readers the conceptual and methodological tools to understand these complex processes *as* communication.

This book will be essential reading for scholars in organizational communication or management and organization studies, together with senior undergraduate and graduate students studying organizational communication, organizational discourse, discourse analysis (including rhetoric, semiotics, pragmatism and narratology) and courses in management studies. It will also be richly rewarding for organizational consultants, managers and executives.

Consuelo Vásquez is Associate Professor in the Département de Communication Sociale et Publique at the Université du Québec à Montréal, Canada. Her research interests include ethnography, project organizing, volunteering and the communication as constitutive of organizations. Her work appears in such venues as *Communication Theory*, *Human Relations* and *Qualitative Research in Organizations and Management*.

Timothy Kuhn is Professor in the Department of Communication at the University of Colorado Boulder, USA. His research addresses the constitution of authority and agency in organizational action, with particular attention to how knowledge, identities and conceptions of value emerge in sociomaterial, power-laden communication practices. His research has been published in *Organization Studies*, *Academy of Management Review*, *Academy of Management Annals*, *Organization*, *Management Communication Quarterly* and *Communication Monographs*, among others.

Routledge Studies in Communication, Organization, and Organizing

Series Editor:
François Cooren

The goal of this series is to publish original research in the field of organizational communication, with a particular—but not exclusive—focus on the constitutive or performative aspects of communication. In doing so, this series aims to be an outlet for cutting-edge research monographs, edited books, and handbooks that will redefine, refresh and redirect scholarship in this field.

The volumes published in this series address topics as varied as branding, spiritual organizing, collaboration, employee communication, corporate authority, organizational timing and spacing, organizational change, organizational sense making, organization membership, and disorganization. What unifies this diversity of themes is the authors' focus on communication, especially in its constitutive and performative dimensions. In other words, authors are encouraged to highlight the key role communication plays in all these processes.

Methodological and Ontological Principles of Observation and Analysis
Following and Analyzing Things and Beings in Our Everyday World
Edited by François Cooren and Fabienne Malbois

Dis/Organization as Communication
Exploring the Disordering, Disruptive and Chaotic Properties of Communication
Edited by Consuelo Vásquez and Timothy Kuhn

Dis/Organization as Communication

Exploring the Disordering, Disruptive and Chaotic Properties of Communication

Edited by Consuelo Vásquez and Timothy Kuhn

Routledge
Taylor & Francis Group

LONDON AND NEW YORK

First published 2019 by Routledge

2 Park Square, Milton Park, Abingdon, Oxfordshire OX14 4RN

52 Vanderbilt Avenue, New York, NY 10017

Routledge is an imprint of the Taylor & Francis Group, an informa business

First issued in paperback 2020

Library of Congress Cataloging-in-Publication Data
A catalog record for this book has been requested

ISBN: 978-1-138-58838-7 (hbk)
ISBN: 978-0-367-67162-4 (pbk)

Typeset in Sabon
by Apex CoVantage, LLC

Contents

vi *Contents*

Editors' Acknowledgments

The editors would like to thank all the contributors to this book for their adventurous spirit and groundbreaking work, as well as the participants at the Standing Working Group "Organization as Communication" at the European Group of Organizational Studies (EGOS) Colloquium 2016 in Naples (Italy), where the idea of this book emerged. A special thanks goes to Marie-Claude Plourde for her great assistance in editing the book.

Introduction

Consuelo Vásquez and Timothy Kuhn

No doubt there is something rather revealing, and disquieting, about the state of our world when people believe that the Muppets can explain it. Muppets are well known, at least among North Americans, as the felt- (and often fur-or feather-) covered puppets populating *Sesame Street*, the 50-year-old educational program on public television aimed at preschool viewers. They also appear on *The Muppet Show*, a TV variety program (accompanied by several films and other media appearances) that entertains slightly older viewers. In 2012, Dahlia Lithwick, writing in the online magazine *Slate*, argued that each Muppet character—as well as every human—can be categorized as either an Order Muppet or a Chaos Muppet (Lithwick, 2012). Chaos Muppets, as the name implies, sow disorder through their energy, emotionality and volatility. Order Muppets, on the other hand, tend to be "neurotic, highly regimented, averse to surprises and may sport monstrously large eyebrows. They sometimes resent the responsibility of the world weighing on their felt shoulders, but they secretly revel in the knowledge that they keep the show running" (¶ 4). Such a classification of persons, Lithwick argues, can explain a good deal of social life: "It's simply the case that the key to a happy marriage, a well-functioning family, and a productive place of work lies in carefully calibrating the ratio of Chaos Muppets to Order Muppets" (¶ 4). Lithwick's tone signals that this "theory" is offered mostly tongue in cheek, but other writers on social media praised what is essentially a dichotomous category scheme imposed on persons for being enormously revelatory (e.g., Hudson, 2012). And there are other somewhat more serious, or at least more scholarly, efforts to employ the same logic: Prominent psychologist Michelle Gelfand (2018) suggests that human cultures can be sorted as either tight or loose, based on the strength of their social norms and their tolerance for deviance—both of which result from the sorts of external threats the culture has faced. Gelfand argues that these differences "can explain global patterns of conflict, revolution, terrorism, and populism. Around the world, tight-loose operates as a universal fault line. . . . The rifts aren't just blared in headlines; *they surface in daily interactions*" (p. 4, emphasis added). Although Gelfand's scheme is somewhat more nuanced than the Muppet theory (it acknowledges that any given culture can harbor both tight and loose elements simultaneously), the thinking is similar: The units of analysis are stable entities—characters or human cultures—with determinate qualities, and those qualities bring about predictable outcomes.

There is good reason to be suspicious of such stark distinctions and all-encompassing conclusions, especially if one agrees with French poet Paul Valery: "*Deux dangers ne cessent de menacer le monde: l'ordre et le désordre*" ("Two dangers continually threaten the world: order and disorder"). The threat lies in the undermining of the difference that distinguishes them; order and disorder are not simply opposed to each other; they are mutually constitutive. Literature scholar Mária Brewer Minich aptly notes that Valery's epigraph was written in the midst of the two great world wars. His words are to be read as a concrete alert to remain vigilant of those narratives that "impose one order by eliminating what they claim to be disorder" (1995, p. 5). It is thus with suspicion and vigilance that in this book we propose to question the mutual constitution of order and chaos, and the threats they entail for our "organized" world.

Why Dis/Organization?

In *The Order of Things*, Foucault (1970) showed how the bases of knowledge about our world result not from some inexorable march toward greater rationality and timeless truth, but instead from social practices that make certain discourses (im)possible. In his early work, Foucault portrayed the apparatus (often presented as a discursive formation) that generates these conditions of possibility—what he called an *épistémè*—as singular and overarching, though shifting across epochs. As he noted, "in any given culture and at any given moment, there is always only one *épistémè* that defines the conditions of possibility of all knowledge, whether expressed in a theory or silently invested in a practice" (p. 168). Foucault's thinking on the *épistémè* was understood as a novel approach to the longstanding sociological problem of order, a central plank of social theory asking how stability can be wrought from the ever-present potential for conflict in a social system (Burrell & Morgan, 1979; Wrong, 1994). Later in his life, however, Foucault revised his thinking, concluding that there are multiple and intersecting systems shaping the social world at all times, such that order can never be complete or totalizing—a conclusion that echoes John Law's discussion on the modes or narratives of ordering: "Perhaps there is ordering, but there is certainly no order. This is because . . . orders are never complete. Instead they are more or less precarious and partial accomplishments that may be overturned" (1994, p. 1).

Foucault is but one entrant in the long line of thinkers who have sought to solve the problem of order. This book enters this theoretical stream not by presenting a more persuasive model of order, but with an alternative point of departure: that of excess. The organization studies field has, over its history, imported various responses to the problem of order, drawn from thinkers such as Marx, Weber and Parsons (as well as Foucault). From these assumptive grounds, scholars tend to assume that organizing is all about allocating and managing *scarce* resources—of time, attention, money, motivation, characteristics and the like. The division of labor, for instance, is a recognition of limitations to individuals' talents and productive capacities.

Andrew Abbott (2014), in contrast, argues that the key social (and thus organizational) problem is not scarcity, but *excess*. Excess occurs when we, individually or socially, have too many desires, choices, resources, influences, etc.; it can be too much of one thing (what he calls surfeit) or too many things (welter, in his terminology). Abbott argues that social theory has too long ignored abundance, and that examining how we manage excess can illuminate an array of social processes:

> many great problems of our era are problems of excess: massive pollution, sprawling suburbs, a glut of information. Yet our social theories and normative arguments focus mostly on scarcity. Budget constraints, tradeoffs, impoverishment: These are concepts of scarcity. Confronted with excess, we nevertheless make scarcity the center of our attention.
> (p. 1)

Abbott is arguing that excess is the source of many common organizing processes. For instance, when problems are too complex to grasp, or when action alternatives and sources of information seem infinite, individuals and groups often experience overload and paralysis. What becomes interesting for organization studies are the strategies Abbott identifies for managing excesses. Practices of organizing might include following fads and fashions, relying on entrenched habits and standard operating procedures, generating hierarchies and rankings, creating distinct spheres and responsibilities (e.g., relegating the expression of emotion to the private domain, or planning departments to interpret environmental complexity), or simply ignoring difference and multiplicity. For instance, crowdsourcing, where an organization puts a question or problem to a large and heterogeneous group of individuals (usually outside the organization's boundaries, and usually conducted via the Internet), can generate overwhelming sets of suggestions, ideas and opinions (see also Rehn & O'Doherty, 2007). Piezunka and Dahlander (2015) found that organizations deal with the glut by focusing attention on only the ideas aligned with management's existing thinking, which means that a practice designed to broaden insights accomplishes the opposite.

Returning to the sociological problem of order, Abbott's suggestion is that organizing often involves translating excess into scarcity, as can be seen when organizations mandate leadership turnover, rely on vitality

curves (i.e., "rank and yank" performance assessment systems), categorize employees by race, or create demand for a small set of consumer
goods amenable to the logic of the market. What is particularly interesting, for our purposes, is that activities that appear to be generating
order are born out of excess. Recognizing that excess gives rise to such
organizational practices suggests not only that analysts should recognize
the reduction of possibility involved in organizational practice, but also
that surfeit and welter are unlikely to be rooted out of organizational
practices for long. That point of departure we mentioned above, then,
is similar to Foucault's realization about epistemic multiplicity: Excess is
ever-present in social life, such that order and disorder are always two
sides of the same coin, both threatening our "organized" world.

An alternative engagement with the sociological problem of order
positions itself against the managerial emphasis (in both research and
practice) on structure and strategy. Munro (2001, 2003) argues that
what is interesting about this history of thinking along these lines is
that structure was, in classical management thinking, seen as a *supplement*, something that must be added to practices to control operations
and persons. Positioned not as a controlling incursion from the outside,
structure was understood to be a necessary element *inside* the practice
of organizing (think spans of control and hierarchical lines of authority). Contemporary management thinking, interestingly, inverts this
image, portraying order as an impediment to swift organizational action.
Management increasingly understands formal structure as a supplement
that interferes with the organization's need to adapt to the exigencies
of the omnipotent market, leading managers to dismantle and flatten
hierarchies—to *dis*/organize. Munro concludes that, following such dis-
mantling, "what remains of organizational structure are managerial processes for accumulating credit and divesting blame" (p. 292); authority
recedes from employees and accrues to management. Dis/organization,
in this telling, is less about mess than another chapter in the relations of
production, yet another attempt to translate excess into scarcity.

Why Communication?

Another way to address the sociological problem of order can be found in
Cooper's (1986) seminal paper "Organization/Disorganization." Briefly put,
Cooper sets the ground for an ontology of disorganization, as the counterpart of organization, by questioning the mutual relation between order and
disorder. In defining organization as a process through which order is appropriated out of disorder, he foregrounds disorganization as the motivation or
trigger for ordering, in his words "the call to order", showing the intrinsic
and intimate relation between organization and disorganization.

The question of excess is, we would argue, central to Cooper's conceptualization of disorganization. Introducing Marcel Mauss's concept of

zero degree, he defines disorganization as "an excess to order or meaning", "the overabundance of the signifier in contrast to the 'reduction' contained in the signified" (Cooper, 1986, p. 316). Cooper's explanation of zero degree is, we may agree, quite communicational: The excess of meaning derives from the undecidability of language. Drawing on Saussure's and Derrida's works, he compares the process of organization/disorganization to the play of difference that characterizes the relationship between the signifier and the signified. In language, Cooper notes, the sign as meaning is always incomplete. Therefore, it can never be fully grasped: It is always continually deferred by the multiple and potential meanings of the signifier. It follows that any attempt to fix meaning in the sign is a reduction, since the multiple other meanings are constantly haunting it. In other words, disorganization is the excess, the surplus and abundance of meaning, the "more than"; while organization, the "less than", is the attempt of reducing meaning, ordering it, controlling it.

Abbott's (and also Foucault's) argument regarding the subtle and yet pervasive presence of excess in social life is also shared by Cooper. His explanation to unsort the puzzle of the emergence of order-with-disorder is a first step to respond to the question at the beginning of this section: Why communication? The indeterminacy of meaning generates *at the same time* the call to order and disorder. In language lies both the capacity to fix meaning and open it: Communication has indeed dis/ordering properties (Kuhn, 2012; Vásquez, Schoeneborn & Sergi, 2016).

However, Cooper's reading slightly differs from Abbott when considering scarcity, since Cooper also associates disorganization to a condition of *no* meaning, of *no* form (1986, p. 321). Consequently, on the one hand, disorganization implies the *excess* of meaning and potentialities and, on the other hand (or should we say, at the same time), disorganization derives from the *lack* of meaning, scarcity. Again, Cooper's explanation for understanding this paradox advances the contribution of a communicative understanding of dis/organization. He turns to the notion of information, which he defines as a process "in which form is made out of non-form" (p. 305). Information, for Cooper, derives its value from impossibility: The more unexpected an event, the more information it carries. Said differently, the less information we have of the event—let's say a tornado or an earthquake, or if we enter the organizational realm, the arrival of a new CEO— the more (conflicting) meanings (thus more information) will this event trigger. Informing (i.e., giving form or matter) an unexpected event will thus necessarily bring a surplus or excess of meaning. To paraphrase Weick (1979), more equivocality inevitably brings more sensemaking. Organizing can certainly be understood as the reduction of equivocality; the risk is, however, reinforcing the assumption that excess (i.e., disorder) is dangerous and needs to be reduced. Yet this is precisely what most managers (and managerial perspectives on disorder) will say about excess: "To preserve order, we must eliminate disorder!" In the same vein, some managers have been taught to "thrive on chaos" (Peters, 1988), to disrupt convention, but this is typically understood either as a momentary deviation from a (desired) orderly state or a "new normal" that becomes its own version of order. Cooper, in contrast, reminds us that disorder is what we need to preserve (i.e., the excess of meaning). Without disorder, there is no ordering, no organizing; it is not a temporary malfunction or aberration, but an ontological claim.

One last insight we can take from Cooper's organization/disorganization perspective that enhances the contribution of a communication-centered approach lies in his reading of the excess/lack of meaning as an act of power. Power, he argues, is the forcible transformation of undecidability into decidability (p. 314). Reducing, fixing, ordering only happens through the exercise of power and authority, which in turn is made possible by the management and control of language. Following Marcuse he argues that the repression of the essentially ambiguous nature of communication is realized by "cleaning the undecidable" (p. 323). For Cooper, organization cannot be understood without (outside) of power: The process through which decidability is appropriated out of undecidability is a question of control, mastering and authority. Cooper's reflection on the management of language echoes Foucault's *épistémè*: Both acknowledge the power of discourse and language in shaping (i.e., ordering) the social world, while recognizing that this order is never fully completed, but rather always in the midst of becoming.

So, why communication? Cooper's reflection on organization/disorganization as the interplay of excess/lack of meaning and reduction/deduction of meaning offers interesting insights for developing a communicative explanation of dis/organization. To some extent, and even if this was not Cooper's intent, we could say that his ontology of organization/disorganization lies in communication. Communication, and this is a shared assumption between the authors of this book, is the locus of disorganization: That which explains the mutual, creative and co-constitutive relation between order and disorder. Cooper's attention to language and information, among others, resonates well with the current development of a communication-centered approach to dis/organization that emphasizes the disordered, irrational and chaotic features of organization by paying attention to the indeterminacy of meaning and to the negotiation and struggles for controlling and stabilizing it (Mumby, 2005; Trethewey & Ashcraft, 2004).

Overview of the Chapters

The first section of the book, consisting of Chapters 1 through 6, outlines the theoretical break involved in seeing dis/organization as communication. In line with Cooper and Abbott, these chapters sketch conceptual frameworks that engage in various ways with the organization/disorganization duality. Each highlights tensions, paradoxes and contradictions as central to how we should understand dis/organization. Some chapters foreground the systems that form in relation to these tensions (e.g., Grothe-Hammer and Schoeneborn's Chapter 3 and Fairhurst and Sheep's Chapter 4), whereas other contributions are less interested in systems than in the articulation and configuration of dis/organizing practices and processes (e.g., Putnam's Chapter 1, Cooren and Caïdor's Chapter 2, Ashcraft's Chapter 5 and Mumby's Chapter 6). Despite this axis of difference, these chapters stake two claims when considered as a set. First, they argue for the necessity of understanding dis/organization as a complex communicative practice (where communication is about struggles to shape meaning in the face of inherent indeterminacy). Second, they present models for how analysts might shift our units of analysis away from traditional "substances" (individuals, groups, texts and the like) and toward *practices*. Pursuing these claims, these first six chapters offer insights into organizing not available from conventional theoretical frames.

The second part of the book, composed of Chapters 7 to 11, presents empirical studies that take communication as the starting point of their inquiry into the practices of dis/organization. These studies were held in or respond to a variety of contexts, such as human right abuses in Morocco (Albu's Chapter 7), socio-technical system theory in Indian cotton mills (Banerjee and Bloomfield's Chapter 8), civic participation in a North American NGO (Porter and Jackson's Chapter 9), political Internet memes (Winkler and Seiffert-Brockmann's Chapter 10) and extreme humanitarian missions in the Democratic Republic of Congo (Matte's Chapter 11). Moreover, these chapters offer detailed descriptions of different types of methodology that are suitable for studying dis/organization from a communicative lens, such as shadowing (Albu's Chapter 7), longitudinal case study (Porter and Jackson's Chapter 9), organizational ethnography (Matte's Chapter 11), archival data collection (Banerjee and Bloomfield's Chapter 8) and qualitative-reconstructive analysis of visual online communication practices (Winkler and Seiffert-Brockmann's Chapter 10). Each chapter also describes the analytical lens used for interpreting the empirical material: thematic analysis (Albu's Chapter 7), textual analysis (Banerjee and Bloomfield's Chapter 8), situational analysis (Porter and Jackson's Chapter 9), analysis of styles (Winkler and Seiffert-Brockmann's Chapter 10), and interactional analysis (Matte's Chapter 11). Together they offer a rich and diverse methodological and analytical toolbox for exploring the organization/disorganization duality from a communication-centered perspective.

To complement these overviews of the contributions of the two sections, we also provide a more detailed description of each chapter, paying particular attention to how they consider one or more of three key issues raised by our engagement with dis/organization:

1. The questioning of the organization/disorganization duality (and our rejection of the relationship as a dualism)
2. The indeterminacy of meaning as triggering process for dis/ordering
3. The struggle and control over meaning as politics of dis/organization

Linda L. Putnam's Chapter 1 begins the book by examining the first and second questions. If communication constitutes dis/organization, Putnam argues, it becomes incumbent upon analysts to understand how this constitutive process operates. She starts by framing communication as triggering order and disorder, and then frames ordering and disordering as existing in a dialectical relationship. Drawing on Cooper (1986), she shows that what makes order-disorder dialectical tensions "go" are the contradictions associated with framing moves that enact binary distinctions between elements. She then draws attention to four features, or forces, of organizing that catalyze order-disorder dialectics. These are *working on boundaries*, the means by which logics of inclusion-exclusion, inside-outside and association-dissociation unfold; *struggling* over authority, recognition and rationality; *negotiating meaning* in the face of the linguistic excess and indeterminacy; and *re-presenting context*, such that meanings are situated in nested practices and, thus, are available for dislocation into new contexts. Importantly, for Putnam, these processes are not merely what *human* agents do; they implicate hybrid and multiple agencies, which leads her to usefully identify three types of agentic assemblages that carry contrasting implications for order-disorder dialectics.

Chapter 2, by François Cooren and Pascale Caïdor, addresses the first of our three guiding questions. Positioning the chapter as beginning in a dialogue with Karl Weick's model of organizing, Cooren and Caïdor argue for a model of organizing built on relationality, one in which all beings, organizations included, are literally built of relations. And those relations are also attachments or connections between the "organs" through which relations articulate themselves. Using an excerpt from a meeting drawn from data collected in a large Canadian organization, Cooren and Caïdor demonstrate how dis/organization can be understood as the modification or annihilation of organs, which occasions alterations in the organ *agencement* (assemblage) that comprises organization. Dis/organization, for these authors, occurs *in* observable communication processes (and nowhere else); framing conversation as the site where the organs speak and respond to one another shows how changes to the *agencement* are continual features of situated action and, consequently, analysts must develop approaches sophisticated enough to access the tensions characterizing the multiple agencies implicated in organizing.

Michael Grothe-Hammer and Dennis Schoeneborn, in Chapter 3, draw upon Luhmannian systems theory to take up the second guiding question. They portray project-based organizations (PBOs) as precarious, as always encountering communicative events that create disruptions because these systems outlive the projects that constitute them. Order, in a Luhmannian view, is about the selection of a meaning for action from the universe of potential meanings, such that the excess (and disordering possibility) of meaning is an ever-present shadow lurking in organizing practice. Decisions, as the foundations of organization, are thus paradoxical in that they call forth alternatives and revisions not chosen, but this decisional communication—which is always simultaneously organizing and disorganizing—constitutes an organization's history and future. Grothe-Hammer and Schoeneborn provide two cases of PBOs to exhibit this communication practice, demonstrating how practices both fix (or establish) and open up (or loosen) meanings as systems make decisions that respond to institutionalized structures that guide action. The chapter, then, provides a novel theoretical stance on the perpetual oscillation between ordering and disordering, one that frames information as emergent from communication events.

Chapter 4, by Gail T. Fairhurst and Mathew L. Sheep, aligns with Putnam's Chapter 1 in its concern with paradox. Grounding their thinking in complexity theory—a conceptually rich but under-utilized perspective in communicative thinking on dis/organization—they advance the notion of tensional knots as a vehicle to understand the presence of multiple tensions marking organizational problem setting. A case in which school systems in New York City and Los Angeles responded rather differently to identical terrorist threats allows Fairhurst and Sheep to examine how actors' discourse enacts a system of tensions, and how the resulting knots can evince a dynamic disequilibrium when under competing versions of reality. The framework emanating from this exploration is tremendously heuristic, resulting in five propositions that promise to drive future research. Focusing on the discursive and communicative forces that generate and manage these knots allows Fairhurst and Sheep to develop a compelling response to the second question about how the indeterminacy of meaning constitutes dis/organization, but they also generate insight into the third question as they draw attention to privileged actors' (and note that those actors could include both humans and texts) capacities to shape the context for problem-solving, suppress dissent and structure decisional responsibility. Fairhurst and Sheep show us that the notion of knots is a rich model for thinking about the pliability of, and struggle over, meaning in complex dis/organizing practices.

In Chapter 5, Karen Lee Ashcraft works against the grain of much organization studies literature, in which a relatively bounded system— *an* organization—is the site upon which phenomena unfold. In contrast, Ashcraft emphasizes practice as she examines hoarding as an interesting case of dis/organization. Arguing against accounts that situate it as a problem of deviant and defective individuals, she moves from defining to addressing hoarding to grasp the *happening* of the practice. From this vantage point, hoarding becomes deeply communicative in its capacity to dis/organize the flow of affect, and our attention is directed to the organizational killjoy as an interruption to the flow, embodied in the person of the hoarder. Illustrating this dis/organizing with her own experience of her mother and the affective shame accumulating around deeply personal hoarding leads Ashcraft to reflect on the first and third of our guiding questions, since constant threats of disorganization fuel fears that efforts to order might fail to regulate affect and, in turn, might fail to produce the subjectivities "appropriate" for advanced capitalism.

Dennis K. Mumby's Chapter 6 exposes brands (and branding processes) as key factors creating the indeterminacy of meaning in advanced capitalism, but which also shape contemporary valuation practices and enable new forms of capital accumulation. Pursuing a different sort of Communication as Constitutive of Organization (CCO) model—that between Communication, Capital and Organization—Mumby sees the (in)determinacy of, and struggles over, meaning as key to understanding dis/organization. Capitalism has become less about the economic question of capturing the surplus value of labor; it revolves increasingly around the indeterminacy and surplus of meaning created by brands— and which now characterizes everyday life. What creates an intersection between this vision of capitalism and dis/organization for Mumby is the neoliberal state of precarity. Under neoliberal capitalism, brands mediate our relation to the world and to others, construct the individual in terms of (human) capital and frame the microprocesses of everyday life as a key site for capital accumulation. Working through examples drawn from the gig economy and a bestselling book by Facebook's Sheryl Sandberg, Mumby shows how meaning construction has not simply shifted to a new type of order, but that it relies on an ongoing insecurity that prevents the possibility of stability in personal and organizational life. Dis/organization is the inevitable result, and it is that dis/organization that marshals subjects in new logics of capital accumulation.

In Chapter 7, Oana Brindusa Albu engages with our first guiding question by focusing on the role of information and communication technologies (ICTs) as dis/organizing devices. The political context of the study, a Moroccan civil society organization engaged in the protection of human rights, highlights the key role played by ICTs for working both in overt and covert ways. Drawing on a CCO approach, which considers the social and material dimensions of organizing, and accounts for nonhuman agencies, Albu shows how ICTs create organizational visibility and invisibility in paradoxical ways, which in turn can facilitate or disrupt the coordination of activities. Ordering and disordering are here triggered by what Albu coins as the "paradox of (in)visibility". Visibility creates order when, for example, ICTs bypass traditional media gatekeepers and publicly share government secrets. Yet this same visibility in social media or the Internet allows for governmental monitoring and policing that can obstruct the coordination of collective action and civic participation. Invisibility also creates order as ICTs' possibilities of encryption, conceal-ment and obfuscation avoid governmental surveillance and obstruction. Yet, this same secrecy leads to disorder through the exclusion, silencing and elusion of information that encryption entails, which, in turn, can disrupt the coordination of activities or the sharing of data. Albu's ethno-graphic study offers detailed and rich illustrations from the field, which demonstrate that ICTs are powerful agents for managing (in)visibilities in context where balancing overt and covert work is not only needed but key for (individual and organizational) survival. As dis/ordering devices, ICTs can both generate and avoid surveillance, aggregate and loose infor-mation, facilitating and disrupting coordination at the same time.

Anindita Banerjee and Brian Bloomfield (Chapter 8) explore the pro-cesses of dis/organization by paying attention to the dis/ordering prop-erties of texts. Texts, they argue, promote a given interpretation of organizational reality, which, at the same time, suppresses alternative accounts that nonetheless remain "haunting" the text and "threatening" its given meaning. To illustrate the political and organizational effects of this textual dynamic (guiding questions 2 and 3), Banerjee and Bloomfield revisit Rice's (1953) seminal *Human Relations* article, which set the basis for the generalization of the Tavistock Institute's socio-technical system theory. Drawing on Taylor and Van Every's (2000) text/conversation dia-lectic, the authors show how Rice's article brought order into the appar-ent "chaotic" work organization of the mills at Ahmedabad in India, where the experiments took place. Textual ordering was mostly realized by removing the cultural and political dimensions of work relations. This "decontextualization" was realized through the inscription of rationality in the use of diagrams and numbers, as well as the consultancy-type genre of Rice's text. To disrupt Rice's reading of the Ahmedabad mills, Banerjee and Bloomfield introduce documented conversations about labor union and worker resistance that were happening during the time of the experi-ments at the mills, and yet were excluded from Rice's account. This "recontextualization" is also informed by a postcolonial viewpoint, which draws attention to imposition of Western systems of knowledge about order/organization onto non-Western contexts. Hence this chapter can be seen as an invitation to disorder (i.e., opening up meaning) and disrupt normative texts to give voice to "Others".

In Chapter 9, Amanda J. Porter and Michele H. Jackson explore the mutual constitution of organization/disorganization by addressing the paradox of digital civic participation: Digital technologies transform traditional government decision-making to a more participatory and democratic process, while increasing participatory problems, such as the devaluation of citizen knowledge and the widening of the government-citizen divide. Combining a communication-centered perspective that highlights the indeterminacy of meaning (second guiding question) and the disordering properties of communication with object and practice based approaches, Porter and Jackson offer an answer to this paradox showing that digital civic participation is *multiple*, that is, across interconnected communication episodes, it allows for meanings to open and close in such a way as to interfere with one another and, in so doing, enact a paradoxical practice. The illustration of this paradoxical practice is based on the situational analysis of a digital civic participation project coordinated by an NGO. Porter and Jackson detail a controversial voting incident showing how this controversy emerged from enactments of digital civic participation across two different communication episodes. The consideration of multiple, distinct and overlapping communication episodes highlights the existence of a third dimension of dis/organization, which entails the push and pull for control over meaning negotiation.

In Chapter 10, Peter Winkler and Jens Seiffert-Brockmann introduce White's concept of styles to problematize the relation between organization and disorganization (first guiding question). Styles, they argue, represent a form of social organizing stemming from disorder that reproduces through irritating and subverting established meanings, role expectations and sociomaterial affordances. Following this definition, disorder is not only a trigger for ordering but can also be seen as a particular form of organizing in itself. Drawing on the example of two widely known Internet memes, the *Obama Hope* meme and the *Trump's First Order of Business* meme, the authors reveal recurring patterns of subverting established meaning, manipulating audience expectations, and outwitting affordances and algorithms of the Web as basis modes of reproduction of this digitally subversive style. The chapter applies a novel analytical qualitative approach for visual online communication practices that articulates three dimensions: meaning, audience and web affordances, and proposes three analytical steps based on documentary analysis that allows users to reconstruct the Internet meme as a subversive style.

The organization/disorganization duality is questioned in Frédérik Matte's chapter (Chapter 11) by studying an extreme context where disorder and chaos are experienced as "business as usual". The chapter focuses on a meeting in the Democratic Republic of Congo in which representatives of a humanitarian aid organization and local health collaborators discuss the organization of a large-scale vaccine campaign. Drawing on Cooren's ventriloqual theory, Matte shows how the contradictory yet complementary figures of extremeness and normalcy are mobilized as a discursive token to push forward a specific medical agenda. Those said-to-be extreme contexts, Matte argues, are always opened to negotiation, thus triggering organizing and disorganizing processes at the same time. The findings of this chapter suggest that this rhetoric of dis/organization is key in ensuring inter-organizational collaboration, particularly in settings where chaos and disorder are mundane and ordinary. The chapter also offers a rich description of the context of study and a detailed illustration of interactional analysis, showing the benefits of combining organizational ethnography with a focus on the analysis of meetings and conversations.

Concluding Note: Celebrating the Organizational Carnival

> [G]reat changes, even in the field of science, are always preceded by a certain carnival consciousness that prepares the way.
>
> (Bakhtin, 1984, p. 49)

In *Rabelais and His World*, Bakhtin (1984) discusses the style of carnival, what he names the carnivalesque, as characterizing Rabelais's novels. This representation comes with displays of excess in the form of "grotesque realism" in which grandiose and exaggerated imageries of the body, including eating, defecation, and sex, are communally performed through laughter and mockery (Rhodes, 2001). The attributes of exaggeration and hyperbolism that characterize the carnival style create the possibilities for transgressing norms, breaking down conventions and enabling genuine dialogue. "The carnival spirit", notes Bakhtin, "offers the chance to have a new outlook on the world, to realize the relative nature of all that exists, and to enter a completely new order of things" (1984, p. 34). Carnivals create an alternative social space characterized by freedom, playfulness and abundance, where hierarchies can be inversed, debased and profaned, thus opening to new orders and imaginaries (Robinson, 2011).

Reading this through the lens of dis/organization, we might say that carnival is the celebration of excess and abundance (of meaning): an invitation to dis/organize by creating spaces where silenced voices are heard and alternative interpretations and understanding are creatively performed. This book is our communal attempt to build a "carnival consciousness" that, we hope, will prepare the path to new potentialities in the study and practice of dis/organization.

Part I

Communicational Explanations of Dis/Organization

1 Constituting Order and Disorder

Embracing Tensions and Contradictions

Linda L. Putnam

Research in organizational studies has shifted away from focusing on stable and static entities to centering on networks, interactions and discourses as constituting dynamic features of organizing. This work highlights processes rather than outcomes, verbs instead of nouns, and complex, nonlinear dynamics rather than a steady state (Hassard, Kelemen & Cox, 2008). In challenging the very ontology of an organization as a "thing", scholars have questioned the false dualisms between individual and collective, local and global outcomes, and organization and disorganization (Thompson, 2008). All of these binaries become situated processes in which organizing emerges from chaos, flux and transformation (Jeffcutt & Thomas, 1998).

The questioning of binaries raises concerns about whether social systems are necessarily ordered structures. One consequence of this claim is what Bisel (2009, pp. 631–632) calls false dualisms that promote "an organizing bias" or a tendency for scholars to focus on coordinated actions that constitute order and ignore ones that create disorder. A second consequence of false dualisms is conceiving of order as a normative function, one that devalues disorder by treating it as a deviation or an abnormality (Tsoukas, 1998). This practice of devaluing disorder may contribute to the modicum of research on it in the organizational literature. A third consequence of this dualism, even among scholars who acknowledge the importance of disorganization, is a tendency to marginalize the role of communication in this process. This consequence leads to difficulty in accounting for how order and disorder emerge as interdependent processes.

One school of thought that situates communication as central to this interdependent process is "Communication as Constitutive of Organization" (CCO). Scholars in this tradition explore the communicative processes that constitute organizations as collective actors that are talked into existence (Cooren, Kuhn, Cornelissen & Clark, 2011). Rather than presuming that organizations are pre-existing entities in which communication occurs, CCO scholars examine how organizations come into being in and through communicative practices. Communication, then, is "the main force that creates, generates, and sustains—constitutes—what we consider to be organization and organizing practices" (Schoeneborn, Kuhn & Kärreman, In press, p. 2).

Most CCO research treats communication as creating order, but recent studies have begun to develop a view of CCO as destabilizing through constituting disorder. Based on this work, this chapter adopts the stance that communication constitutes organization and disorganization as interlocking and often simultaneous processes (Ashcraft & Mumby, 2004). Yet, the key question is how do these processes work? What communicative features trigger the connections and interchanges between order and disorder? How do they reveal different types of dialectical relationships? What are the implications of these relationships for a CCO approach to organizational complexity? Complexity focuses on the interweaving of multiple actors as they engage in constituting (dis)organization as contradictory forces. It focuses on the entanglements of multiple, hybrid actors and multiple tensions as they co-evolve in the communicative activities of constituting order and disorder.

These concerns also tie to the literature on contradictions and dialectics. *Contradiction* refers to opposites that are regarded as mutually exclusive, interdependent with each other and potentially negating each other (Putnam, Fairhurst & Banghart, 2016). They surface in the very nature and relationship between order and disorder and challenge the idea of logical consistency as a standard for organization (Thompson, 2008). *Dialectics* centers on the ongoing interplay of opposites or the push and pull between them in which each bi-polar pair implicates the other. Despite the fact that scholars treat organization/disorganization as opposites, no work has applied a dialectic lens to unpacking the order-disorder relationship.

This chapter undertakes this task through examining the role of dialectics and contradiction in the theoretical roots, assumptions and constructs that emerge in the organization/disorganization literature. It centers on the forces or salient triggers that activate the interplay between order and disorder based on a communicative approach that embraces a dialectical lens to the constitution of (dis)organization. In this chapter, organization is defined as the action of ordering, one that emphasizes predictability, stability and certainty while disorganization centers on disruptions, divergences and instability that surface from disorder. In this way, order and disorder are the processes that produce (dis)organization.

Much of the theoretical work on organization/disorganization draws on postmodernism as an alternative for rethinking institutions (Hassard et al., 2008; Thompson, 2008). Even though scholars acknowledge language as a key player in the order-disorder relationship, they do not focus directly on the discursive processes, practices and texts that enact this relationship. This chapter, then, draws attention to the tensions in this relationship as revealed in the communicative constitution of (dis)organizing (Cooren et al., 2011; Putnam, Nicotera & McPhee, 2009).

As such, I begin this chapter by reviewing the role of communication and contradiction in Cooper's (1986) work on organization/disorganization. Then I explore the CCO literature on the key features of the order-disorder relationship; namely, boundary work, struggle, meaning and context. This exploration calls for integrating these features into a CCO approach to (dis)organization, one that unpacks the interplay of oppositional roots. Through this integration, I build on an alternative way of depicting organizational complexity, one grounded in the tensions and arrangements among multiple hybrid agents in (dis)organization. Finally, this chapter sets forth directions for future studies that embrace this lens, centers on oppositions and treats order/disorder as grounded in the ongoing, situated and embodied processes in which multiple human and material actors come together (Ashcraft, Kuhn & Cooren, 2009).

Theoretical Foundation for Organization/Disorganization

Although a host of theorists introduce the notion of rupture, chaos and disjuncture as pivotal to organizational change (see for example, Benson, 1977; Marx, 1867/1906; Hegel, 1969), Cooper (1986) is one of the first to problematize how these features contribute to (dis)organization. For him, organization is a process of transforming ambiguous conditions into ordered states (p. 305); that is, organization is the appropriation of order out of disorder. Order, as previously noted, refers to making practices regular, stable and predictable, privileging unity of time and space, and fixing form and meaning, whereas disorder entails decentering unity, introducing surprise and flux, and disrupting the smooth entropic development of order. In disorder, objects and events blend into each other and lose their distinct identities. Even though disorder appears more threatening and difficult to engage, Cooper (1986) treats it as a normal and inevitable by-product of the quest for order. Ordering then does not eliminate disorder, nor does disorder reject the possibility of orderliness (Clegg, Kornberger & Rhodes, 2005).

Drawing from Derrida (1981) and Bateson (1972), Cooper (1986) shows how three key constructs—undecidability, differentiation and language/information—enact (dis)organization. Communication is pivotal to this process through differentiating between form and non-form (see the Introduction) and developing a boundary or a frame. Boundary in turn serves as a source of paradox through wedding opposites in ways that create the perception of something unitary. Thus, the concepts of binary structure and contradiction are pivotal to Cooper's (1986) thinking, but they remain underdeveloped in deciphering the ongoing interplay of opposites as discursive practices.

For Cooper (1986), *undecidability* refers to *zero degree* or the absence of form. This condition motivates or energizes a call to organization through a state of disorder or the absence of a preferred state (Bateson, 1972).

Undecidability then calls for creating a boundary or a frame in the gap between system-environment, inside-outside and order-disorder. In traditional social sciences, boundary functions as a static concept that holds a system together and detaches it from its environment. In this way, boundary creates order, or what Munro (2001) calls "the illusion of the edifice": the idea that structure privileges stability and marginalizes disorder. Thus, the system has the boundary not the environment, and what lies outside the frame is considered less ordered and less unitary than what is inside of it.

In contrast, Cooper (1986) casts boundary as an active process of *differentiation* which equally serves both the system and the environment. *Language* makes this happen through the communication of difference and *différance*. First, language is a system of differences comprised of a concept (sign), the meaning of the sign (signified) and the vehicle through which individuals exchange meaning (signifier) (de Saussure, 1974). In this process, signs have meaning only through their differences from other concepts. Language is also a system that is incomplete, with no beginning and end, and engaged in a continual deferral. This system of difference prompts a negation that motivates action through the need to select one state over another. Second, language functions as a system of *différance* that produces the illusion of presence (Derrida, 1981). As Cooper (1986, p. 312) states, "the sign is that which we put in place of the absent thing we wish to be present to us; in this way the sign represents the present in its absence". In a continual deferral of meaning, each sign is inscribed in a chain which refers to other concepts. Language, then, as a system of differences, enacts boundary as an indeterminate process and disorganization as zero degree or absence of form and meaning. In addition, messages take on a mediating role through their link to boundary, language and framing. Framing engages in boundary making through including certain messages while excluding others; hence, it becomes a process of ordering or selecting based on the principles of inclusion/exclusion (Cooper, 1986, p. 328). Thus, while Cooper (1986) clearly adopts a language-centered process view of organization and disorganization, he stops short of centering on the discursive practices that enact framing, boundary making and the ongoing interplay between order and disorder.

The key element in embracing this interplay is contradiction or the binary structure that mediates between form/non-form and order/disorder. Specifically, information becomes transformed through two processes: framing, in which "order is extracted as form and disorder refused as non-form" (Cooper, 1986, p. 328), and a binary structure rooted in distinction and division. Specifically, in traditional systems theory, polarities like inclusion-exclusion, night-day, man-woman, etc., are distinct terms. The act of separating them paradoxically creates the perception of something that is whole or "mutually parasitic" (p. 306). Yet, based on *différance*, the two cannot be separated because the presence of one implies the absence of its opposite.

Thus, a second way to view this binary is to focus on division or the boundary between polar terms. Boundary, then, serves as the loci of paradox through centering on the mutuality of opposites; thus, division both separates and joins. In this way, "one side of the opposite crosses into the other through an ever active play" (Cooper, 1986, p. 315); thus, it is the contradiction in framing or boundary in which the mutuality and interdependence of opposites conceals the paradox in the play. Embracing mutuality, Cooper (1990) readily notes that dissention counteracts consensus and inconsistencies keep an organization coherent, yet this reversibility of binaries is presumed rather than treated as discursively enacted. For Cooper (1986, p. 312), a language system reveals the binary structure of information, but it is not able to "bring out the essential play of differences" to show how mutuality develops discursively; hence, scholars need to focus on this agenda. Thus, the concepts of contradiction and paradox are pivotal to Cooper's (1986) notions of order/disorder; however, they remain underdeveloped in examining how ongoing communicative practices constitute the order-disorder relationship and the ways that opposites "play out" and develop mutuality.

Another explanation for why Cooper (1986, p. 328) stops short of unpacking this interplay of opposites may stem from the politics of (dis)organization. Politics entail who or what controls the transformation of undecidability into decidability and how this occurs through the management of language. For him, "Language as the object of conflict becomes the center of the struggle for power . . . [it is] the object to be appropriated". Power, then, stems from control of the textual representation or the authoritative text in the process of organization/disorganization.

In addition, Munro (2001) critiques Cooper's (1986) theoretical perspective for prioritizing disorganization over organization. In an effort to cast disorder as a normal and natural state rather than an anomaly, Cooper (1986) valorizes disorganization. Thus, scholars who draw on this orientation often focus on instability as engendering new webs of entanglement and shifts in equilibrium and control (Stacey, 1995). The valorizing of disorganizing, in Munro's (1998) view, has even become a common practice for new managers who develop "an almost pathological urge to disorder", through breaking up traditions, disrupting complacency and disparaging subordinates as "belonging to the past". As a form of control, the ambiguity that emerges from these change initiatives adds new procedures on top of old ones and de-stabilizes organizing. Intentional practices of disordering, as Munro (1998) contends, can become a means to gain power and control through manipulating disorder. Drawing from this overview, scholars need to embrace mutuality in the order-disorder relationship, privilege both disorganization/organization and avoid valorizing disorganization.

In summary, Cooper (1986) treats language as marking off decidability, developing a frame for inclusion/exclusion, deferring meaning through presence/absence and controlling textual representation. He centers contradiction at the core of binary structures and lays the foundation for examining the interplay of opposites in the order-disorder relationship through embracing a lens of communication as constitutive of organization.

Developing a CCO Approach to Order and Disorder

Communication scholars draw from Cooper's (1986) foundational work on organization/disorganization, but they center on discourse and interactions in addition to language as constituting organization (CCO). Even though the majority of CCO work focuses on creating order (Kuhn, 2012), research that adopts a CCO lens to the order-disorder relationship is now appearing in the literature. Developing a CCO approach to this relationship entails three assumptions.

First, organizing is a dynamic process that unfolds in ongoing communicative performances. This view of becoming differs from traditional process notions in which preexisting entities evolve and change over time (Kuhn, Ashcraft & Cooren, 2017). In effect, the locus of order/disorder centers in the communicative processes that set (dis)organization in motion (Kuhn, 2012). These processes embrace a variety of communicative features, for example, sign-signifier relationships à la Cooper (1986); framing à la Bateson (1972); multiple meanings à la Vásquez, Schoeneborn and Sergi (2016); and organizational texts à la Cooren (2004). A CCO lens might focus on one of these features, such as discourse or texts, but the key difference is centering the performative and contingent character of communication. A second key assumption that differs from Cooper's (1986) is that order and disorder are constituted through the dynamic interplay of tensions and contradictions in producing (dis)organization (Kuhn et al., 2017). As opposites, the two not only exert tension on one another, but they co-evolve in ways that define the nature of their interrelationship.

A third assumption embraces a relational ontology that captures the material dimensions of communicative performances. It posits that humans exert agency in relation to talk, bodies, objects and spaces that make a difference in (dis)organization. In CCO studies, different types of human and material agencies give voice and presence to the constitution of organization (Cooren, 2006). Specifically, bodies or the physical location of people in rooms, objects such as technological artifacts and spaces such as open offices may assume the role of agents to speak on behalf of the organization. CCO work on order/disorder reveals that these material features make a difference in constituting disorganization through engendering surprise, flux, uncertainty and disruption (Knox, O'Doherty, Vurdubakis & Westrup, 2015).

Key Forces That Trigger the Order-Disorder Relationship

Through embracing these three assumptions, CCO scholars have begun to investigate the motivators or triggers that energize the order-disorder relationship, ones that differ from Cooper's (1986) notion of forces that are grounded in a system/environment perspective. Four specific features—boundary work, struggle, meaning and context—emerge from the existing literature as triggers in which communication constitutes (dis)order through the interplays of opposites. These four emerged from the conceptual and empirical literature that explicitly employed a CCO lens to examine order/disorder (Bisel, 2009; Fassauer, 2017; Knox et al., 2015; Kuhn, 2012; Porter, 2013, 2014; Vásquez et al., 2016). To develop this review, I listed and consolidated the triggers that motivated shifts in the interplay between order and disorder and focused on these four. Boundary work centers on (in)decidability or the creating of a frame that marks off order/disorder; struggle refers to acts of conflict and crisis that disrupt modes of organization; meaning focuses on the difficulties of fixing or ordering interpretations and context deals with locating and dislocating meanings. These four features parallel the forces of (dis)organization that Cooper (1986) developed, yet communication scholars focus on the processes or the ways that the order-disorder relationships become constituted; they do not merely identify forces. Importantly, each of the four invokes different types of relationships among opposites.

Boundary Work as Developing Order From Disorder

Boundary work is an active process of differentiation, or what Cooper (1986) refers to as a *frame*. Specifically, boundaries are not static borders or walls; nor are they containers that determine fixed spaces. Rather they are fluid and fleeting processes that change in shape and form over time. They differentiate through marking off decidability, creating order and making something temporarily stable (Latour, 2013b). In particular, the intermingling of multiple human and nonhuman agencies produces difference that problematizes boundaries and triggers disorganization (Thompson, 2008). Nonhuman agencies introduce difference into an ordering process that can disrupt boundary practices and processes. Boundary work then functions as a source of dialectical tensions through identifying how inclusion-exclusion, outside-inside and association-disassociation engage in ordering/disordering.

Inclusion refers to people and practices that become immersed in organizing while *exclusion* designates the ones that fall outside the boundaries. For example, Porter (2013) examined the situated interactions of humans and technology in the emergence of a shelter during an evacuation caused by Hurricane Katrina. Focusing on both organization and disorganization, she observed how responsive volunteers became distant from reactive ones through continually creating and improving technologies. Thus, humans and technology became intertwined as hybrid agents actively involved in addressing problems, for example, developing a database for evacuee intake and creating online systems for locating relatives of shelter residents. Addressing these demands for technology also led to a dependence on the responsive volunteers. Over time, these practices resulted in a divided organization marked by inclusion and exclusion. Boundary work resulted in redefining both the *insiders* and *outsiders*; that is, city volunteers who came to assist at the shelter became the *insiders* who took control of the situation while actors from the healthcare organization who established the shelter became isolates through exhibiting reactive behaviors.

In this example, the tensions between inclusion/exclusion in boundary work demonstrate how order surfaces from disorder. Hybrids of interactions between humans and technology shape the organizing process, mark off borders and redefine the original insiders as outsiders. Thus, as Porter (2013) highlights, the inclusion of particular meanings always accompanies exclusion of alternative ones. Inclusion and exclusion function as contradictions in which order emerges from segmenting the poles and selecting one over the other at different points in time.

Boundary work also occurs through the relationship between *association* and *disassociation* among hybrid agents. Association focuses on how actors align their practices with other human and nonhuman actors while disassociation centers on distancing or separating from relevant others. In a different study, Porter (2014) showed how technology coordinators engaged in instructional practices that disassociated their work from the machine itself as well as from other technology personnel. In this way, they enacted order through boundary creation that distanced themselves from repair functions. Yet, in some circumstances, they violated this distinction through performing troubleshooting operations that aligned the software with the hardware of the machine and re-associated their roles with maintenance personnel. Thus, consultants created order by discursively distancing themselves from maintenance personnel while they shifted to disorder to address real material conditions when a problem occurred. In this way, communicating as boundary work constituted difference through aligning with the material conditions of the moment (Porter, 2014, p. 644).

As this discussion suggests, boundary work and the interplay of order and disorder occur through enacting contradictory relationships among opposites. Practices linked to inclusion-exclusion, outside-inside and association-disassociation become managed in different ways, but primarily through separating, reversing the poles or splitting them at different moments in time. Ordering marks off boundaries, and disruptions thrust boundary work into disorder. The two become intertwined through segmenting each pole at different points in time to create order and then disrupting this order at other times to trigger disorder. In the Porter (2013) article, actors segment or separate tensions and assign them to different organizational roles. The second example (Porter, 2014) shifts the emphasis on order and disorder to moments in time. Importantly, in boundary work, order and disorder are treated as separate and distinct concepts. In this treatment, boundary work privileges order through creating the notion of something unitary (Cooper, 1986), coordinating contradictory injunctions that lie at the foundation of organization (Latour, 2013b, p. 396), and showing how "organization . . . is constantly bound up with its contrary state of disorganization" (Cooper, 1986, p. 304).

Struggles Over Authoritative Texts as (Dis)Ordering Order

Unlike boundary work, struggle as an activity that triggers the interplay between order and disorder surfaces through acts of conflict, crises or unexpected events that disrupt established modes of organization; hence, it depicts a disorder-to-order relationship. Conflict, often viewed as endemic to organization, refers to a disjuncture that occurs when alternative logics clash with one another. Fassauer (2017) contends that these logics stem from a struggle for recognition, namely, personal integrity, respect and identity as basic dimensions of communication (Honneth, 1996, 1997). Misrecognition or feelings of personal harm, disrespect and exclusion trigger a struggle that de-stabilizes and makes disorder visible.

Moreover, ignoring violations of personal integrity in everyday conversations can also lead to a struggle for recognition. This occurs through condensing multiple interactional episodes into a collective identity or an authoritative text that legitimates certain practices and downgrades others (Kuhn, 2012; Taylor, 1999). These texts then embody a moral view of communication, one that extends through time and space in multiple texts and documents as well as past struggles for recognition, such as labor disputes.

The literature suggests that two dialectical relationships contribute to the struggle for recognition: *emotional-non-emotional* and *rational-irrational*. Privileging rationality, optimizing economic efficiency and disregarding the "irrational" aspects of organizational life trigger a struggle for recognition, especially between expression and mutual care that organizational members need. In effect, the ideology of instrumentality relegates emotions to the "unreasonable" (Fassauer, 2017). Moreover, these binaries often become blurred, which opens the way to resistance and new orders. Rationality also surfaces in relying on such texts as common standards of treatment or in devaluing individual skills, practices or accomplishments. For instance, labor disputes, as Fassauer (2017) suggests, are often as much about emotional and moral issues aimed at recognition as they are about income distribution. Conflict, then, makes instability and disorder visible in a struggle over the ethics of organizing (Cooren et al., 2011). This moral dimension de-stabilizes and produces disorganization through activities of struggle aimed to form a new order and to lay claims to the authority of a particular text (Fassauer, 2017, p. 36).

Communication during crises and chaotic situations also constitutes disorganization through highlighting the ambiguities and uncertainties of events. Crises demonstrate how order and disorder are momentary accomplishments that unmake each other as they become entangled with materiality in addressing routine problems. Specifically, Knox et al. (2015) examined performances of organization/disorganization in which a man threw a bag and cellphone onto the apron of a British airport (where aircraft parked as they were being loaded and unloaded). What occurred in-between and in responding to this "spatial happening" enacted disorder in which "objects appeared treacherous, spaces mutable, agencies ineffectual, and informants unreliable" (p. 1001). What unfolded was not a single order, but multiple overlapping orderings as competing authoritative texts arose in the shifting webs of associations among objects, spaces and agencies. These competing texts focused on who and what was a trustworthy and reliable source of knowledge, as evident in airport directional screens that "lost their authority" by instructing people to go to inaccessible areas and false projections of command authority, such as anyone who possessed a uniform, walkie-talkie or yellow jacket. As one person noted, "I wouldn't listen to her, she is just a cleaner" [a person who wears a yellow jacket]. In effect, the relationships among material and human agents became unstable and in flux. In this crisis, reorganization became a never-ending reconstruction of "both order and disorder and certainty and uncertainty" (Knox et al., p. 1013). Only with reconstructing the "authoritative order of events (i.e., discourses of authority) . . . could reorganization begin to gain its shape" (p. 1010).

Struggle, then, makes disorder visible through communicative acts of conflict and crisis aimed at recognition, addressing ethical problems and establishing a new order. Struggle over the authority of particular texts and the need for recognition constitute disorganization through a clash of logics that challenge order. Importantly, these struggles center on the moral dimension of communication and questions of integrity, respect and perceived harm. In struggle, discourse, materiality and historical texts become entangled and generate multiple orderings that destabilize, break and then enfold into new orders. Materiality plays a pivotal role in the destabilizing and disrupting of order as well as intermingling new and old orders.

(Dis)organization is also constituted through the interplay of dialectical tensions among such opposites as emotional/non-emotional, rational/irrational and uncertain/certainty. Interestingly, these dialectics become blurred or intermingled as multiple forms of ordering and disordering emerge. They often surface in inverse relationships, for example, rationality as triggering emotionality and uncertainty and irrationality as energizing non-emotional responses aimed at restoring certainty. As an example, Knox, O'Doherty, Vurdubakis and Westrup (2007) illustrate how information technology at airports leads to inverting oppositions linked to over-determined performances. In particular, information that directs the rational and orderly flow of people in airports, for example, screens and announcements of flight arrivals and departures, also inversely triggers anxiety and uncertainty through projecting flight delays, gate changes and security warnings. In effect, "airports are saturated with . . . the sense of danger of flight itself" (Knox et al., 2007, p. 277). The repetition of information and the regular patterns of synchronized flow, such as video surveillance, invert opposites, thus constituting both predictability and unpredictability in safety and danger of air flight. Thus, inversions of opposites "add to a giddy cocktail of promise and threat, excitement and danger, and desire and frustration" (Knox et al., 2007, p. 277) paradoxically linked to order and disorder in navigating airports.

In struggle, communication constitutes (dis)organization through vacillating between disorder and order, triggering inversions between poles and producing multiple orderings that often become blurred and reconstituted. Reconstruction becomes a process of moving from disorder to order through invoking difference. Thus, it is the disordering of the order that constitutes organization through actions and interactions that emerge and become reconstituted (Knox et al., 2015).

Negotiating Meaning as Enacting Order/Disorder

As features that trigger (dis)organization, both boundary work and struggle treat order and disorder as distinct concepts and then pull them together to show how one implicates the other. Closer to Cooper's (1986) view, boundary work emerges through appropriating order out of disorder while struggle privileges disorganization as the inception for reconstituting organization. Both develop the order-disorder relationship through privileging either organization or disorganization and then showing how they impinge on each other.

Negotiating meaning, however, enacts (dis)organization through a reciprocal, mutually intertwined relationship between order and disorder that draws on the indeterminacy and plurality of language. Order and disorder in this view are two strains that are interwoven and can be unwoven and then rewoven in constituting (dis)organization. The two embrace a mutuality in which they cannot be separated. Similar to Cooper (1986), the indeterminacy of language refers to the fragility or difficulty of fixing meaning, but building from this work, CCO scholars focus on how meaning emerges in actions and interactions that evolve over time (Vásquez et al., 2016). Thus, the indeterminacy and ambiguity inherent in all language makes communication a particularly viable approach for studying the enactment of the order-disorder relationship (Cooren et al., 2011).

Plurality or the inevitability of multiple meanings contributes to this process through introducing multiple interpretations. Efforts to select or fix meaning as an ordering practice are often countered by alternative meanings that destabilize and create disorder. To illustrate, Vásquez et al. (2016) examined the practices of ordering and disordering in three project teams. Ordering entailed selecting or trying to fix meanings while disordering emerged from the use of questions, omissions and assertions that interjected multiple interpretations and disrupted group members' understandings. Texts, such as documents, proposal forms and PowerPoint slides, that aimed to fix or formalize meanings shifted to new genres that destabilized and opened up meanings. Disordering practices also created the sharing of more narratives that fostered ambiguity and challenged the interpretation of activities. Thus, the presence of multiple plausible meanings introduced instability that interplayed with order in a continual process of negotiating (dis)organization.

This process ties directly to the dialectical tensions that surfaced in the negotiation of meaning in this study. First, the relationship between *stable* and *unstable* emerged in the ways that team members closed off interpretations and fixed meaning. Initiating alternative views, however, shifted meanings within the same text and drew on linguistic forms that challenged the stability of the organizing process. Second, the interplay between *formalizing* and *re-formalizing* texts constituted disorder through dislodging meanings that seemed stable and introducing new understandings (Vásquez et al., 2016). The continual interplay of dialectical tensions then laid the groundwork for fundamental shifts in organization/disorganization.

Negotiating meaning as a way of constituting (dis)organization works through a reciprocal process in which order/disorder become entangled to form a new whole. Selecting, fixing and stabilizing meanings interface reciprocally with introducing multiple interpretations, destabilizing understandings and reformulating meanings. Hence, opposites exist in a dialectical process in which they continually interplay to form a new whole. This continual, reciprocal interplay of opposites treats order and disorder as mutually intertwined rather than as discrete constructs that shift (boundary work) or vacillate back and forth (struggle). In effect, this way of embracing tensions and using them to form a new whole differs from selecting one pole over the other at different times or vacillating between them in a cyclical way. Importantly, the intertwining of order and disorder produces what dialectical scholars refer to as transformation or a radical change in formulating a new whole (Putnam et al., 2016). Yet, it differs from Hegelian (1969) notions of synthesis of opposites that often relinquishs the push and pull of tensions. Transformations or new wholes emerge through a co-creation that preserves tensions in the continual connection of opposites and that produce ideas, practices and activities as fundamentally novel understandings.

Re-Presenting Context as the Interplay of Order/Disorder

Inscribing meaning in context also triggers the communicative constitution of order/disorder as a reciprocal process, but one that reframes or transcends through shifting context-related meaning. Rather than viewing meaning as residing in individuals, a constitutive approach treats it as nested in situated practices that shape organizing over time. Specifically, as discourse patterns shift within or across contexts, language can decontextualize meaning, engender uncertainty and ambiguity, and constitute a different order-disorder process. Reframing draws on language features such as naming to form a new whole through shifting situational interpretations (Putnam et al., 2016). It functions from constituting opposites in different ways across circumstances or situations within the same general context. Re-presenting is a process that enacts the order-disorder relationship through developing a metalanguage that transcends as it crosses different contexts (Cooren et al., 2011). In addition, material objects, spaces and nonhuman actors play a pivotal role in these shifts within and across contexts.

To illustrate reframing and situational shifts within context, Porter (2014) showed how technology consultants constituted order with their clients through providing simplistic instructions that rendered technology helpless and harmless in pedagogical settings. Yet, when their egos felt threated, consultants shifted the meaning of their contextual circumstances, reframed the complexity of the machines and created disorder by rendering technology powerful and controlling. Importantly, this reframing increased the agency of the machine through casting technology as complex. In this example, communication constituted order and disorder through dialectical tensions that played out in the consultancy-client relationship, particularly *simple versus complex* computer operations and *reducing and increasing* agency of the technology. These practices enacted contradictory control in which decontextualizing hid the technology while contextualizing revealed its material power (Porter, 2014, p. 646). In this example, reframing dialectical tensions reformulated meaning through a naming process that enacted organizing as complex, simple, situationally adaptive and differential in roles of agency. Similar to negotiating meaning, the interplay between order and disorder works from formulating a new whole or novel perspective, but one that arises from inscribing meaning in different situations or circumstances.

Shifting contexts also triggers the interplay of order and disorder through dislocating and re-locating texts and other types of materiality (Cooren & Fairhurst, 2009). Texts such as documents, minutes of meetings and policies form a spatio-temporal context, one that travels across settings. In this way, the here and now of events become dislocated through simultaneously linking them to the past and the future (Vásquez et al., 2016). As actors draw on discourses or conversations that embody features of previous texts, they disrupt once stable meanings, create new genres and enact disorder. Texts, in this way, transcend contexts, become disconnected from an author's initial intent and develop meanings through links to other nonhuman actors (Cooren, 2004); thus, materiality can dislocate interactions through transcending contexts.

Re-presenting constitutes (dis)organization through the use of a metalanguage that transcends meaning. Similar to forming a new whole, a metalanguage represents through connecting the oppositional tensions, for example, between local-global, past-present and locating-dislocating. The interplay of these opposites, including ordering and disordering, works in circular and recursive ways; thus, the present reflects back on and alters the past and local practices draws on and simultaneously reconstitute global ones, and vice versa. Contextualizing and decontextualizing then move in circular ways to inscribe and reconstitute meanings and create disorder through ordering (or order through disordering). Transcending dialectical tensions, such as simple-complex and locate-dislocate, through contextualizing/decontextualizing enacts the order-disorder relationship as recursive and circular.

Integrating the Forces and Developing a CCO Perspective

Communication scholars bring a particular lens to the order-disorder relationship, one that focuses on the interfaces of language, meaning, materiality and contradictions. Specifically, a CCO lens treats ordering and disordering as dynamic, ongoing processes constituted through discourse, actions/interactions and texts that interface with materiality. Language and discourse become interwoven in the communicative performances that enact framing, reframing, transcending and re-presenting (dis)organization. Crossing these order-disorder relationships with materiality and meaning in each of these four triggers reveals the building blocks of a CCO perspective on (dis)organization.

Both boundary work and struggle enact order and disorder as distinct processes that implicate each other, but often privilege one pole over the other. In boundary work, ordering marks off, separates and distances while disordering disrupts, re-brackets and redefines differentiation. The two interface through segmenting the poles and locating them in different structural arrangements, units or time frames. This splitting de-couples interdependent concepts and often leads to privileging one over the other. Struggle makes disorder visible through vacillating between the two poles and creating multiple and blurred forms of order/disorder.

In contrast, the triggers of negotiating meanings and re-presenting contexts treat order and disorder as interdependent concepts that become mutually entangled. They enact the interplay of order and disorder through connecting them in recursive ways. Preserving mutual entanglements between opposites often leads to transforming, reframing and transcending dialectical relationships (Putnam et al., 2016).

Materiality plays a pivotal role in these relationships; specifically in differentiating and problematizing boundaries, accentuating and intensifying struggles, dislodging meanings, exercising control and locating/dislocating interactions. In these examples, materiality surfaces as the turning points or the shifts that emerge from the interplays of order/disorder. In a similar way, all four triggers focus on efforts to fix, close off or open up meanings through enacting borders that include and exclude understandings, clashing on the interpretations of moral and textual authority, negotiating the plurality of meanings and contextualizing and decontextualizing understandings. As Porter (2014, p. 640) points out, the relationship between communicative performances and hybrid agents reveals how "meaning and matter meet in the space between organization and disorganization".

Thus, in developing a CCO perspective for the study of (dis)organization, scholars need to pay particular attention to the types of dialectical relationships between order and disorder. The issue is not how one implicates the other, but rather how the communicative performances engage the two in a dialectical interplay. Specifically, the triggers linked to multiple meanings and re-presenting context hold the most promise for examining order/disorder as mutual entanglements. Researchers also need to explicate the assumptions that underlie different triggers and their orientations. Language, meaning and materiality are clearly the elements that are central to future CCO research on order-disorder.

Developing CCO Views of Complexity

A dialectical approach to order and disorder can also aid in deciphering complexity among hybrid agencies. A hybrid or plenum of agencies refers to multiple human and nonhuman actors with variable ontologies that mobilize the enactment of organization (Cooren, 2006). Past work suggests that hybrid agencies come together through imbrication or the layering of communicative practices (Taylor & Van Every, 2000) or through chains of agencies in the organizing process (Cooren, 2006). These approaches, though, are grounded in constituting order not disorder. Yet, how do these multiple agencies come together in constituting the interplay between order/disorder, not just order? A dialectical view of this process is deeply rooted in complexity or the interweaving, entangling and complicating of actions among hybrid agents as they constitute contradictory forces (Bouchikhi, 1998).

In the systems theory literature, complexity is equated with disorganization or disequilibrium (Cunha & Gomes, 2003). With a bias for order, systems scholars often recommend that organizations balance contingencies or find an equilibrium point between order and disorder (Cunha & Gomes, 2003). The issue for systems theorists, then, is how to enact contradictory forces in ways that create a balance between equilibrium and disequilibrium (Bouchikhi, 1998).

Conceptualizing complexity through relying on systems theory raises a number of concerns for CCO scholars. First, systems approaches often presume the existence of either order or disorder prior to the communicative constitution of their interplay. A CCO lens, in turn, treats language, meaning and communicative practices as enacting the essence of order/disorder as a mutually entangled process among hybrid agencies. Clearly, this critique does not apply to all treatments of systems theories (see Luhmann, 1995; Schoeneborn, 2011; Chapters 3 and 4, this volume, for exceptions), but it does to most approaches. A second concern is that balance as a goal for the interplay between opposites is problematic and rarely centers on the constitutive role of hybrid actors in the order-disorder relationship. Finally, only a few scholars (see, for example, Fairhurst and Sheep, Chapter 4, this volume; Sheep, Fairhurst & Khazanchi, 2017) incorporate dialectics and paradoxes into notions of complexity that align with the order-disorder relationship. CCO scholars, then, need to theorize complexity as constituted from communicative practices that become interwoven in contradictions and paradoxical tensions.

This chapter then contributes a CCO view of complexity through focusing on the assemblage of hybrid and often distributed agents as they deal with multiple tensions linked to order/disorder. Grounded in performativity, *assemblage* refers to the constellations or arrangements that emerge from multiple human and nonhuman actors that constitute organization (Latour, 1999, 2005). These different types of assemblages are both durable and fleeting and can amplify or attenuate complexity in a variety of ways. Thus, the concept of *assemblage* helps to decipher how multiple tensions among hybrid agents contribute to complexity in how they are assembled, disassembled and re-arranged. In relationships that become amplified, tensions grow in intensity and impact (i.e., increase in complexity), whereas in attenuating patterns, the force, amount and intensity of tensional relationships reduce complexity (Sheep et al., 2017).

Three types of assemblage surface from the four triggers in the dialectical interplay of order and disorder. These three differ in how they amplify or attenuate sets of tensions between order and disorder. The first type, *assemblage through association*, draws from Actor-Network Theory (Latour, 1999) to show how hybrid agents come together through connecting chains that align and/or separate actors. In boundary work, human and nonhuman agents become entangled through marking off borders among sets of opposites, such as inclusion-exclusion, integral-periphery and outside-inside the organization. Boundary work relies on segmentation, source splitting and connecting/disconnecting multiple tensions. In doing so, it separates the poles and splits them into different arenas, for example, isolating them in different moments, aligning each pole with different problems or privileging/marginalizing materiality. For example, boundary work in the emergency shelter for evacuees from Hurricane Katrina became entangled with technology through segmenting and splitting opposites that marginalized and shifted insiders and outsiders (Porter, 2013). Tensions developed between association and disassociation among hybrid agents that amplified and increased intensity, which added complexity.

In a similar way, struggles over authoritative texts increase complexity through amplifying tensions, for example, developing clashing logics among hybrid agents and forming overlapping interplays of multiple orderings and disorderings. These struggles illustrate *affective assemblage* (Deleuze & Guattari, 1987) that intensifies as multiple tensions become interwoven in cyclical and recursive ways, often resulting in complex knots (Fairhurst & Sheep, Chapter 4, this volume; Sheep et al., 2017). Knots are defined as multiple dynamic tensions that become recursive and self-referential over time as they affect each other (Sheep et al., 2017). Oscillating between poles can lead to a spiraling inversion in which tensions become knotted. This inversion of tensional poles exerts stress, evolves into twists and kinks and often produces new tensions that tighten the knot.

Specifically, in the airport crisis example (Knox et al., 2015), objects, spaces and bodies form an affective assemblage that intensifies in their relationship as the crisis becomes more pronounced. Opposites, such as true-false projections, certainty-uncertainty of announcements and rational-irrational scenes, become inverted and twisted in the interplay between order and disorder, contributing to an increase in complexity. Moreover, tensions that become aligned with morality and identity, as in struggles over authoritative texts or clashes of alternative logics, also emerge as knotted and likely amplify complexity.

The third type of assemblage, *metalanguage*, attenuates tensions through drawing on interactions among multiple hybrid agencies that transcend opposites and reduce complexity. Metalanguage is similar to meta-conversation in the CCO literature in which participants draw on the recursive property of communication to develop meta-narratives that enfold multiple actors in reframing (Robichaud, Giroux & Taylor, 2004), yet, it differs from this concept through reforming opposites into a new whole. Two of the four triggers, negotiating meaning and re-presenting context, develop metalanguage through communicative practices of reframing, introducing new genres and transcending context. The process of negotiating meanings triggers disordering through opening up interpretations, reconnecting opposites and forming a new whole through disentangling complexity. As an example, disordering practices in a project team connected opposites, such as present-absent, and orchestrated them into a new whole of executive summaries that simultaneously condensed and elaborated information (Vásquez et al., 2016).

In re-presenting context, texts that develop into a metalanguage transcend context through stretching opposites, such as local-global, past-present and locate-dislocate, to construct elasticity that reduces complexity. In this way, hybrid actors "expand the pie" through creating a metalanguage that transcends the here and now in spatio-temporal elasticity (Sheep et al., 2017). To illustrate, multiple trajectories in a Chilean outreach project became a metalanguage of "stories-so-far" that stretched boundaries and made hybrid actors fluid and mobile in disseminating knowledge throughout the country (Vásquez, 2016). Materiality plays a central role in constituting complexity in the communicative practices of hybrid actors. In particular, the moments when materiality gains or loses agency in discursive practices of ordering and disordering seem critical to increasing or reducing complexity. Porter's (2014) study of the role of technology in the client-consultancy relationship showed how shifts in the agency of computers attenuated complexity through inscribing meaning and constructing a new whole that embraced opposite tensions.

In effect, incorporating tensional relationships into CCO studies of order-disorder contributes to unpacking complexity. Complexity refers to how multiple human and nonhuman agents come together through assemblages or constellations of entanglements with each other and with contradictory forces. Actions and interactions in these dynamic assemblages amplify or attenuate complexity through ways that actors deal with tensions. In studies that adopt a CCO approach to order/disorder, assemblages of association and affect increase the intensity and amount of tensional relationships (amplify) while assemblages that develop a metalanguage reduce complexity through elasticity that stretches opposites and forms a new whole. Thus, rather than recommending a balance between equilibrium and disequilibrium, hybrid actors need to engage in communicative practices that stretch opposites, transcend tensions and develop a metalanguage.

Directions for Future Research

CCO work on the study of (dis)organization is in its infancy. It holds considerable promise to develop new conceptions of organizational complexity through focusing on the forces that trigger shifts in ordering and disordering and on the ways that scholars can enjoin these forces. It positions language, meaning, texts and genres in the foreground as constitutive players in (dis)organization and it shows how these communicative features produce different dialectical tensions that contribute to processes of order/disorder. In addition, it incorporates hybrid agencies as ways that humans and nonhumans intersect in developing multiple tensions, increasing the agency of materiality and shifting patterns of order/disorder.

Future research needs to cross combinations of the four triggers, such as negotiating meaning and boundary work, as ways to decipher how multiple tensions become entangled or dis-entangled in developing complexity. Selecting different contexts in which texts and meanings locate and dislocate might aid in deciphering these tensions. Future studies also need to incorporate a greater variety of hybrid agencies, including bodies, space and places, that may lead to different types of tensions in the interplay between order/disorder. In this way, scholars could problematize the hypothesis that materiality functions as a turning point between organization and disorganization. Finally, researchers need to examine the role of macro actors in speaking or acting on behalf of (dis)organization. Attending to the role of genre and metalanguage as formulations that develop new orders holds the potential to tie particular types of order-disorder processes to (dis)organization.

Finally, scholars need to apply the relationships between order/disorder to critical problems in post-bureaucratic organizational life. Specifically, which types of order-disorder relationships promote flexibility and adaptability and how can organizational members engage in practices such as reframing and transcending to embrace tensions and shift easily between the two. Researchers might also examine how particular communicative practices in boundary work and re-presenting context aid in navigating the rapid shifts in collaborations, joint ventures and co-sharing work that characterizes the new era. Alternatively, scholars might integrate identity work with studies of (dis)ordering to examine how negotiating meanings and engaging in identity struggles might be navigated more effectively through attenuating tensions that reduce complexity. In addressing these issues, organizations do not have to eliminate disorder, close off meanings or constrain contexts. Rather they need to work with the processes of ordering and disordering to understand how shifts occur and to embrace tensions as triggers for these shifts.

2 Communication as Dis/Organization

How to Analyze Tensions from a Relational Perspective

François Cooren and Pascale Caïdor

What is organizing? According to Karl Weick's (1979; Weick, Sutcliffe and Obstfeld, 2005) well-known definition, it is about reducing situations of high equivocality through interlocked behaviors, that is, behaviors by which people manage to make sense of a given situation by collectively selecting an appropriate response to make the world more orderly (Cooren & Robichaud, 2010). Although this definition certainly has had a profound and positive influence on organization studies for almost 50 years (as it encouraged us to study the details of interactional episodes to better understand how people get organized), we believe that one of its downsides is that it tends to reduce the emergence of organizations to sensemaking activities (Weick, 1995), with the consequence that the relational dimension of these activities is likely to be backgrounded.

Another way to address this question consists, more prosaically, of starting from the etymology and definition of the word "organizing". The verb "to organize" indeed literally means "to transform something into an organ" (the suffix *-ize* indeed means to render or to make), where organ etymologically comes from the Greek *organon* (instrument), which itself comes from the Indo-European root *werg* (to do, which also gave "to work") (Bencherki, 2009). According to this etymology, any activity of organizing thus consists of transforming things or persons into instruments, that is, intermediaries or means by which programs of action are supposed to be accomplished to fulfill specific ends. In other words, organizing, as we will see, is a special form of *relating* as it consists of linking people and artifacts to the accomplishment of specific tasks.

Bruno Latour (2013a, 2013b) echoes this definition by showing that organizing has something to do with the existence of *scripts* (Vásquez, 2013). When you create a to-do list, you are *organizing yourself* to the extent that by later following what this list indicates, you transform not only the list, but also yourself into instruments, media or means by which each specific action, which you previously defined, will be completed. Latour rightly notes that at some point, one has to be *above* the list, that is, define what it will consist of, while at another point, one is *under* the list, defined by what this list enjoins us to do. In some cases, the two persons (the one above and the one under) can be the same, while in other cases, they can be two different individuals.

As illustrated in this mundane example, organizing thus implies the production of ordering devices, which we propose to call *organs*, whether they are organizational charts, machines, protocols, procedures, job descriptions, statuses, orders, authorizations, etc., which define what people *must* or *may* do to complete various objectives. These organs do not have to be necessarily written down (they can just be spelled out in a face-to-face discussion), but they constitute the partial sources by which a form of *ordering*, *stability* and *systematicity* will be created or instituted, as ephemeral as this organizing might be (Cooren, 2000, 2010, 2015). We therefore understand why organizations in general tend to be defined by the existence of these devices as they constitute the very source of their relational existence.

This way of conceiving of organizing also leads us to acknowledge how *disorganizing* takes place (Vásquez et al., 2016). What constitutes a source of order for specific beings (e.g., lumberjacks following instructions to cut down trees in a forest area) can also become a source of disorder for others (e.g., animals being forced off their lands, ecosystems being annihilated, other competitors losing contracts). Organizing thus has to constantly deal with situations where specific programs of action appear to interfere with others, making the latter impossible or at least difficult to complete (Latour, 2013a). Any assemblage or *agencement* (Kuhn et al., 2017) thus has to constantly deal with these tensions where contradictions or incompatibilities appear between what two or more different ordering devices/organs/programs of action literally dictate.

Studying dis/organization from a relational perspective, which we propose to do in this chapter, thus amounts to studying the communicative constitution of dis/organizing, that is, examining the ways things and persons get positioned or position themselves as organs or instruments by which others articulate themselves (in both senses of the word "articulate": assemble and speak), creating an *agencement* that can also disappear or be altered when contradictions or incompatibilities occur (Ashcraft & Kuhn, 2017). It is the tensions inherent in these *agencements* that we will especially focus on in the context of this chapter.

In what follows, we will examine what a relational ontology consists of, especially regarding questions of materiality, performativity and existence. In dialogue with Karl Weick's (1979, 1995) notions of enactment, selection and retention, we will then show what this ontology has to tell us about this specific way of relating we call organizing and organization. Having defined the relational aspects of organizational processes, we will also explore why disorganizing is always at stake when organizing takes place, creating tensions that constitute an intractable aspect of organizational processes. This relational perspective will finally be mobilized to analyze a meeting excerpt during which two managers and two human resource advisors speak about a workforce diversity program in a large Canadian organization.

Relational Ontology

What does it mean to defend a relational perspective or ontology? It means that anything or anyone, whatever it/she/he is, should be conceived as literally *made of relations*. But relations—and this is a crucial point—are themselves beings or things that establish connections or links between other beings or things, which means that there is a priori no *absolute* difference between relations (what establishes the connection) and *relata* (the beings that are related to each other through these relations). In other words, *anything or anyone always is both a relation and a relatum*: a relation because it links other relata with each other and a relatum because it is related to other relata through other relations.

For instance, someone—let's call her Kathy—can be related to her grandfather, George, through her father, Paul. This means that Paul can be here conceived as the link through which Kathy happens to be related to George. One of the ways to define who Kathy is thus consists of saying that she is George's granddaughter, an identity that, as we see, is *relational*, that is, defined by the relation that links her to George *through* her father, Paul. But *Kathy is herself a relation* as she is also the link through which her daughter—let's call her Lucia— is related to her grandfather Paul and her great-grandfather George. Since a relational ontology insists on the relative or relational characters of beings, *there is no absolute starting point*, which means that nothing or no one can be considered *in itself/herself/himself* a relatum or a relation.

As we see through this simple illustration, another important feature of relations is that they are always *material*, which means that they are always *made of something or someone* (Cooren, 2018), which establishes a link or connection between other beings, called relata (James, 1912/1976). For instance, being an official member of an organization is an identity that is usually established through a contract that literally binds this person to the organization she is working for (Ashcraft, Kuhn & Cooren, 2009). The link that relates her to this organization thus materializes itself, among other things, through this contract that partly defines who she is: an employee working for this specific organization.

Another characteristic of relations consists in their *performative* dimension, that is, the fact that they have to be performed in order to be established (Cooren, 2000). While some relations are long-lasting (for instance, the link, materialized in a family tree, that relates a granddaughter to her grandfather, even beyond their respective deaths), others can be evanescent, such as a discussion that happens to bring together two strangers waiting for the bus. What matters in any case is that these relations have to be *produced* and *performed* in order to exist. But this also means that they make a difference in the way the relata are defined.

From a biological viewpoint, the relation that links Kathy to her father has been performed and established through the fertilization of her mother's egg by one of her father's spermatozoids, while from an institutional viewpoint, it has been performed through the creation of a birth certificate that is supposed to establish his paternity or filiation. What matters in these two cases is that what links or relates Kathy to her father has, by definition, to be *produced by* something or someone, otherwise it simply means that such a link or relation does not, for all practical matters, exist. Furthermore, there must be audiences/sources of authority that/who determine whether particular productions count, which adds to the relational character of what is supposed to exist.

This performativity is important as it creates/produces/generates specific identities. Karen Barad (2003, 2007) proposes, for instance, the neologism "intra-action" to acknowledge this creative/productive/generative nature of relations. While the word "interaction" presupposes the existence of beings that are then presented as interacting with each other, the word "intra-action" highlights that these beings should, in fact, be considered as *constituted* by the relations that define who they are and what they do. This is why any being can be said to be constituted by the relations that define it/her/him.

A good illustration of this phenomenon is the contract that links a person to her organization. This contract, when it is signed, creates/produces/generates at least two identities: She is now an employee of this organization, and this organization now is her employer. From a legal viewpoint, this person is an employee of this organization because there is somewhere a contract that certifies that she has indeed been hired by this company. This does not mean, of course, that this legal relation exhausts her status of employee, but from a legal viewpoint, this is how this identity is established and defined.

This transformation is possible because the contract, which materializes the relation that links her to her organization, literally *does or performs something* each time it is read or invoked. What does it do or perform? It defines her as an employee of her organization and it defines this organization as her employer, with all the rights and obligations that come with these new statuses. In other words—and this is a crucial point to understand what a relational ontology consists of—what relates beings and things with each other *always* consists in other beings and things that do something by *linking them to each other in a specific way*, creating new identities, sometimes permanent, sometimes ephemeral.

As we see, a relational ontology does not consist of calling into question matters of identity or even individuality; it just presents them as *constituted* by relations. *Nothing more, nothing less*. For instance, if you have a first name, a last name and a gender, it is because these names were usually given to you by your parents at your birth and because this specific gender was recognized after you were born, with all the consequences (negative or positive) that comes with such identification and institution (Butler, 1990, 1993). Furthermore, documents exist—a birth certificate, for instance—that attest that these are your names and gender. The same logic applies for nationalities, skin colors, reputations, etc. Beings are what they are because of the connections that link them to other beings.

But why should organizational communication scholars care about relational ontology? We think they should care precisely because communication consists, by definition, in establishing relations that have a constitutive power, especially (but not exclusively) regarding organizational forms (Cooren, 2012). When James R. Taylor (1988), the founder of the CCO perspective, insightfully declared, some 30 years ago, that an organization is nothing but a web of communication (*"une organisation n'est qu'un tissu de communications"*), he anticipated, without naming it, what a relational ontology consists of. Communication is constitutive of organizations (among other things) because what an organization is or does will always depend on the beings and things that speak and act on its behalf, hence its relational existence.

For instance, an organization can communicate with its environment by writing and releasing press releases. These press releases can be seen as *what relates this organization to* the journalists, who will then possibly comment on this announcement and make it known to the public. As we see in this illustration, an organization exists and does things *through* the beings and things that stand and act on its behalf, what we previously identified as its *organs*. These beings and things can be quite diverse: buildings, logos, websites, CEOs, spokespersons, employees, ledgers, policies, machines, products, operations, etc. What matters is that they presentify, i.e., make present, and materialize the organization they are *standing* and *acting* for. Through these various intra-actions (Barad, 2003, 2007), it is therefore specific versions of the organization that present themselves to us.

Relationally speaking, we thus understand that an organization is—in the strongest sense the verb "to be" can have—its buildings, logo, website, CEO, employees, ledger, policies, machines, products, operations, etc.—that is, all the organs that link it to whoever or whatever has to deal with it (clients, other organizations, administrations, citizens, etc.). They are all organs because they are all supposed to do things *for* the organization they represent. An organization therefore is polymorphous, a sort of

Leviathan, as Callon and Latour (1981) pointed out a long time ago. In other words, there is never one person or thing that exhausts what the organization is supposed to be all about.

Organizing, Organization and Relationality

Having presented what a relational perspective consists of, we think we are now in a good position to show how this approach can inform the way we conceive of organizing and organization, in the first place, and of disorganization and disorganizing, in the second. Since Karl Weick (1979), we know that organizing can be understood as "a consensually validated grammar for reducing equivocality by means of sensible inter-locked behaviors" (p. 3). A grammar, for Weick, is indeed "a systematic account of some rules and conventions" (p. 3), that is, "recipes for getting things done when one person alone can't do them and recipes for interpreting what has been done" (p. 4). Organizing is therefore a process by which organization is supposed to emerge (cf. p. 15).

As mentioned in the introduction to this chapter, if organizing etymologically means "to transform into an organ" (where organ means instrument, intermediaries or means), Weick (1979, 1995) reminds us that this transformation implies the construction of recipes, rules or conventions that will have the effect of reducing equivocality. When people are getting organized, they thus agree to subject themselves to what we called "ordering devices", that is organs such as organizational charts, machines, protocols, procedures, agreements, job descriptions, rules, statuses, orders, authorizations, etc., which will define what they have to and may do in order to achieve specific objectives.

Although Weick's (1979, 1995) reflection is essentially centered on people's sensemaking activities, a relational perspective invites us to acknowledge what these organs *also* do and how they do what they do once they have been produced. For instance, coming to an agreement about specific procedures certainly amounts to defining "recipes for getting things done" (Weick, 1979, p. 4), but this then means that these recipes make a difference, that is, that they literally *do something* once they have been created (Cooren, 2004; Kuhn, 2008). In other words, following a procedure or recipe means, whether we like it or not, that it is this procedure or recipe that also *leads us* to do what we are doing (Bencherki, 2016).

From a relational perspective, organizing certainly implies that people make sense of their environment, but *only if making sense is considered a two-way street*. In other words, sensemaking should also be understood as the way by which this environment manages to express itself through what people have to say about it. In this respect, the Weickian notion of *enactment*—which captures the "active role that we presume organizational members play in creating the environments which then impose on them" (Weick, 1979, p. 130)—echoes this relational character. If enacting an environment consists, among other things, in isolating what counts or matters in it, it means that what ends up mattering or counting will then be voiced in a discussion, that is, that a certain version of this environment will be *made present* and *materialize* in this conversation.

From a relational perspective, each person is potentially a medium/intermediary/means through which aspects of a situation will express themselves. But note that there is no absolute starting point: If somebody enacts an aspect of the environment, it is also because this aspect caught or is catching her attention (Kuhn et al., 2017). While Weick's (1979, 1995) perspective tends to be human-centered (after all, he is a social psychologist), a relational ontology invites us to acknowledge the *bidirectionality of enactment*. Enactment should be understood relationally, that is, as a type of intra-action (Barad, 2003, 2007).

When people get together—in a board meeting, for instance—to figure out what to do about a situation, what we also observe are multiple ways to voice what the situation not only looks like, but also dictates, what Mary Parker Follett (1926) would have called the "law of the situation" (p. 33). This multiplicity of versions should not be surprising as it precisely results from various ways of enacting the situation, that is, various ways of expressing *what should count or matter in it*. Each person around the table then potentially becomes the way/means/intermediary by which specific aspects of a situation express themselves and what should be done about them.

The sensemaking phase that Karl Weick (1979) calls *selection*, that is, the reduction of equivocality per se, can thus be reinterpreted, etymologically, as the *reduction of the potential equality of all these voices*, especially if they happen to contradict each other. To collectively make sense of a situation indeed amounts to constructing, as Taylor and Van Every (2000) would say, a voice among all these voices (Robichaud, Giroux & Taylor, 2004), that is, a collective version of what the situation dictates or commands. Whether this is achieved by consensus, vote or imposition, this reduction will consist in building a response that will correspond to which version or frame has been (consensually, democratically or dictatorially) selected to make sense of the situation.

Relationally speaking, this reduction of equivocality certainly implies the confrontation of voices, but it is then crucial to acknowledge the diversity of the (always partial) origin of these voices. If we definitely hear people speaking, we also realize that their speaking irremediably consists of *making other elements say things* (Cooren, 2010). Some people will stage facts that, according to them, speak for themselves; some will invoke rules, procedures or policies that, according to them, dictate what should be done about the situation; others will speak out of experience or will bring their expertise to bear on the issue. In other words, the reduction of equivocality will consist of *creating a sort of monophony out of this polyphony.*

From a relational perspective, selection à la Weick (1979) is about collectively selecting what *counts* or *matters* not only in what is supposed to be happening, but also in what might help people deal with this situation (principles, values, expertise, experience, procedures, rules, recipes, etc.). Identifying what the situation dictates thus consists of trying to articulate all these elements together, knowing that they have to be enacted or voiced in order to be identified. Relationally speaking, organizing a response is therefore about collectively identifying what aspects of a situation end up mattering and what courses of action should materialize to deal with them (which also means that some matters might also have to be sacrificed or silenced, whether we like it or not).

Whether it takes the form of an agreement, a procedure or a rule (what Kuhn (2008) would rightly call an authoritative text), this response will therefore commit people to these programs of action. Karl Weick (1979) calls this third phase of sensemaking *retention*, as it is these programs of action that are typically retained to embody or materialize the organization, i.e., what has been decided and organized. In other words, these agreements, procedures, rules, conventions, recipes can then be later mobilized to address what people perceive as similar situations. An organization thus is made, to a certain extent, of all of this retention, which precisely allows it to be what it is supposed to be, i.e., *organized*, i.e., transformed into the organs of a collective action.

Studying organizational communication therefore consists of keeping an eye on at least two dimensions: how people *get organized*, that is, how they manage to transform themselves and other things into organs *on the spot*, so to speak, but also how people *are organized*, that is, how they tend to be already organs, that is, means by which other elements or realities act and express themselves in specific circumstances. For instance, people participating in a board meeting are certainly trying to find ways to get organized, but they are also, of course, *already organized* to the extent that they each represent specific concerns, realities, sources of expertise or even other people or groups of interest, which usually explain why they are, in fact, present.

To a certain extent, Weick's (1979, 1995) entire career can be reinterpreted as an attempt to explore this *intractable tension between organization and organizing.* We need organization (understood as retention) because we have to be able to rely on past experiences, rules, procedures, protocols, recipes, decisions, etc. to deal with what appears to be "business as usual" (in other words, we should not have to reinvent the wheel each time we have to take care of something). However, we also need organizing (understood as enactment) because we also have to remain open to "what the situation dictates", especially when this situation does not appear as "business as usual" and can have disorganizing effects.

It is not by chance that the selection phase is where communication matters the most in Weick's (1979) model, as selection is precisely this process by which what is enacted will be confronted with what has been retained. In other words, this is where organization and organizing meet, as people become not only the voices of what they already know, represent or believe (retention), but also the voices of what they possibly observe, discover and learn (enactment). This is where iteration meets eventfulness, where something new can emerge from what is already known.

For good reasons, Weick (2001) is wary of organization because being organized can make us blind to what unusual situations dictate. We think we know what should be done, but we then realize, sometimes too late, that the situation was not what we thought it was (Weick, 1993). Being highly reliable, as an organization, thus means, according to Weick and Sutcliffe (2001), that we remain preoccupied with failure, reluctant to simplify, sensitive to operations, committed to resilience and deferent to expertise, five hallmarks that all remind us how crucial it is to remain mindful of what is to come, in all its eventfulness, that is, to what a new situation might dictate.

But what does this reflection on organization and organizing mean from a relational perspective? First, it means that communication becomes essential to understand both phenomena. Communication is indeed at the crossroads of iteration (retention/organization) and eventfulness (enacting/organizing), what Taylor and Van Every (2000) would respectively identify as text and conversation. Iteration because any act of communication is, whether we like it or not, an act of *re*-presentation/ *re*-production, that is, an act by which certain realities get *re*-presented or *re*-produced. Eventfulness because this act of re-*presentation*/re-*production* has to be enacted for another next first time, in its haecceity or uniqueness. In other words, it also constitutes, by definition, an act of *presentification* and *production*.

When people get organized, they usually are, as we already saw, already organized, that is, they are themselves the organs by which other elements will be able to materialize and act from a distance. Analyzing this process of organizing thus leads us to observe how this tension between organization and organizing is dealt with on the terra firma of interaction (Cooren, 2006). While some aspects of the discussion will mark an iteration (speaking out of experience, speaking as an expert, evoking a well-known procedure, etc.), others will mark a form of eventfulness, whether it is the voicing of something that had never been acknowledged before or a response that appears to depart from traditional procedures, rules or recipes.

If communication is about relating, linking or stitching together, organizing, as a special type of communication, is about the mobilization *and* creation of organs that are then supposed to help people deal with a given situation. Organs, according to a relational perspective, have agency because they are a source of enablement and constraint. Procedures or orders, for instance, will *guide* people regarding what the latter are supposed to do, but they will also *constrain* them in their action. Although they can be discarded or rejected, once they are followed, they organize the conduct of people, that is, they also transform them into organs of a collective action where each person is supposed to fulfill a specific role.

Communicating is organizing—it is also, as we will see in the next section, disorganizing—as it is the way through which people mobilize and create these organs that will link them to each other and the organizational form they end up working for: Orders are given, authorizations are extended, roles are distributed, commitments are voiced, pieces of information are transmitted, sanctions are pronounced, as many speech acts (Cooren, 2000) that, in turn, are supposed to transform their recipients into organs, that is, participants in the exploitation of their own actions to fulfill a collective end. As Latour (1996) points out, to do is causing to do, which means, from a relational viewpoint, that we always are, by definition, the organ of something or someone else.

This is why, as pointed out by Taylor and Van Every (2000), orga*nizing* is about *imbricating*, that is, the embedding of courses of action into other courses of action. Organiza*tion* is also about imbrication and embedment, but then it means that organs are already in place: People already have statuses, rights and responsibilities; procedures, protocols and rules already exist to guide and constrain their actions; tools, equipment and technologies are at people's disposal to allow them to go about their business. These *ready-made organs* are what gives organization their stability to the extent that their staying capacity—what Derrida (1988) would have called their *restance*—can be iteratively mobilized to re-produce routine ways to deal with what is coming.

Although organs can be ephemeral (for instance, we can momentarily be designated as the voice of a group, a status that disappears as soon as the group dissolves), what we tend to have in mind when we think about them is precisely a form of *restance* or staying capacity. The old word that sociologists tend to use to refer to this source of stability is "structure", even if this hodgepodge word does not really explain much (Cooren, 2018). By acknowledging the agency of rules, statuses and machines, we are, we believe, in a better position to understand where this source of stability comes from and how it can iteratively make a difference in various situations.

For instance, having a status (e.g., manager) means that a person X can iteratively rely on it to enjoin others (her supervisees Y and Z) to do what they are supposed to do, according to their job description. When these supervisees interact with her, they not only interact with X, they also, and maybe especially, interact with their supervisor, which usually makes, of course, a huge difference in their conduct. When X speaks to them, it is *also* and maybe especially their manager who is speaking, with all the rights and obligations that come with this title. Although this status can be rarely invoked by X (if it does, it usually is considered a bad sign for her authority), it iteratively and silently *makes a difference*, i.e., *it does something*, to the extent that it enjoins Y and Z to do what X asks them to do, as long as it fits with their job description (Kuhn et al., 2017).

Relationally speaking, X, Y and Z are then constituted by the relations that iteratively define who they are and what they do. But note that these relations are not made of thin air. They are organs we call statuses, job descriptions, organizational charts, etc. that keep *defining*, for another next first time, who they are and what they can do and cannot do. Communication is therefore not just about how people speak when they interact with each other, it is also about these forms of *silent communication* by which someone ends up been *intra-actively* seen as acting *as* a supervisor, without even having to mention it. The fact that Y and Z do comply can, in this regard, be seen as another embodiment of the agency of this status (see Benoit-Barné & Cooren, 2009).[1]

Because of their staying capacity, their *restance*, organs thus iteratively participate in the organizing of our world. For instance, a professor is an organ, whether she likes it or not, as her actions *as a professor* are supposed to embody the means by which the university acts through her when she teaches, supervises or does administrative work. Her job description is also an organ, as it tells/reminds her what she can do and cannot do, what she has to do and what she does not have to do. Although this job description and title fortunately do not exhaust who she is as well as her rights and obligations (we do not always act as members of the organizations we are working for, which means, fortunately, that we *never* are *just* organs), they can participate in the performance of what is happening in a given situation.

Disorganization and Disorganizing

Now that we have presented what it means to study organization and organizing from a relational perspective, it remains to be shown how this perspective can also help us understand their reversing states or processes: disorganization and disorganizing. Logically speaking, if organization and organizing are respectively related to the existence and creation of organs to achieve specific ends, disorganization and disorganizing should logically be related respectively to the lack and alteration/deterioration/ destruction of organs. Disorganization is indeed usually associated with the absence of means to achieve specific ends, while disorganizing is about actively participating in the alteration/deterioration/destruction of these means, whether intentionally or not.

While organizing and disorganizing could, at first sight, be seen as clear opposites of each other (that is, you either organize or disorganize, but you cannot be doing both at the same time), Latour (2013a) points out that this reassuring reality cannot be the case. Organizing can indeed have disorganizing consequences precisely because it can interfere with other plans, objectives, goals, aspirations, etc., creating a tension between them (Cooren, Matte, Benoit-Barné & Brummans, 2013; Putnam, Fairhurst & Banghart, 2016). In other words, scripts can pile up, creating the need to constantly reorganize what tends to be disorganized.

Anybody minimally familiar with the organizational world can have a sense of what is implied here. If we go back, for instance, to the example of our board meeting, we can see how getting organized can also be about disorganizing other courses of action, not only outside the organization per se, but also inside of it. In other words, what constitutes organs for specific programs of action—say, putting into place benchmarking indicators to measure nurses' performances in a hospital, a measure that is ultimately supposed to improve the efficiency of this institution—can end up contributing to the alteration/deterioration/destruction of other programs of action depending on their relative or absolute incompatibility—for instance, requiring an expenditure of time that prevents the nurses from taking care of their patients properly, which is supposed to be their primary professional responsibility.

From a relational viewpoint, disorganizing can thus be conceived as the alteration/deterioration/destruction of organs, knowing that organs can be as diverse as procedures, technologies or, of course, people, as they are supposed to each constitute the means by which specific objectives or ends will be iteratively completed. For instance, nurses used to have the time they thought they needed to take care of patients depending on their respective state of health. The nurses were following procedures that they thought allowed them to respond to these specific needs accordingly. Now that the benchmarking indicators have been put into place in their hospital, they are expected to spend no more than five minutes with each patient, which means that the usual procedures cannot be followed as strictly as they used to, especially for patients with severe conditions.

They feel that their working conditions are now deteriorating and their actions start not making sense anymore (Moreland & Apker, 2016). What seemed to be a good idea from an administrative viewpoint begins to have daring consequences for the quality of the care provided to the patients as well as the nurses' mental and physical health (Tunc, 2009). Organizing this new system of benchmarking thus amounts to disorganizing the nurses' work, that is, preventing them from reaching what should *also* be their objective, i.e., providing quality care to all the patients. What used to meaningfully link them to their patients—know how, procedures and usual caring activities—appears now threatened by the new procedures.

From a relational viewpoint, this deterioration of organs can have daring effects, as they amount to altering *relations that count or matter*, that is, relations that also define who people are, i.e., their identity. Weick (1993) famously invited us to wonder what firefighters become without their tools. This is because tools tend to represent essential means of their collective action—that is what relates them to what they are supposed to do, i.e., putting out fires. Similarly, is a nurse still a nurse when she cannot rely anymore on what is supposed to meaningfully relate her to her patients?

Any organization has to face this kind of situation, which also means that (dis)organizing is a never-ending story. Any assemblage or *agencement* (Kuhn et al., 2017) has to constantly deal with tensions where contradictions or incompatibilities (Putnam et al., 2016) appear between what various organs dictate or allow. Managing, in many respects, thus is ideally about dealing, on a daily basis, with these tensions, that is attempting, for another next first time, to render programs of action as compatible as possible with each other.

What remains to be shown, however, is precisely how these tensions are concretely dealt with on the terra firma of interaction. This is what we now propose to do by analyzing in detail the excerpt of a meeting.

Analysis of a Meeting Excerpt

In order to show how this relational perspective can inform the way we conceive of dis/organizing, we now propose to analyze an excerpt taken from fieldwork conducted by the second author. This fieldwork, which is currently completed in a large Canadian organization—fictitiously called EBF—which counts more than 20,000 employees, consists of studying the implementation of a professional mentoring program designed for immigrants who recently arrived in Canada. This program requires, among other things, the organization of discussions where managers can talk about the challenges they face in the context of this implementation. The excerpt we analyze is taken from the audio-recording of one of these discussions.

In 2016, the management board and the new CEO decided that cultural diversity had to be considered a critical business issue for the company. According to this CEO, the company was not as diverse as it was supposed to be, which led him to ask for recommendations regarding the implementation of various initiatives with the objective of correcting this situation. Following these recommendations, the management board endorsed 15 initiatives, all designed to improve the workforce diversity and inclusivity. Among these initiatives we find the program we are studying: a professional mentoring program designed for recent immigrants with no experience on Canadian soil.

In the context of this professional mentoring program, EBF is supposed to select and hire immigrants who recently arrived in Canada. These persons are then supposed to be sponsored by more experienced employees who are in charge of helping them not only do their work but also integrate their work teams. In order to facilitate this process, a project team was created to lead this project designed to produce the conditions of a more diversified and inclusive work environment. The excerpt that we propose to analyze is taken from the recording of a discussion where the members of this management team talk about how they are going to welcome these new workers coming from an immigrant background.

In this meeting, we find Jack, who, in addition to being a member of this committee, is also an important manager of the unit in which the program is implemented. His principal interlocutor, Janet, is a human resource advisor in charge of coordinating the program. A third person, Mary, is a colleague of Janet and also works for the human resource department. As the excerpt begins, Jack is expressing his viewpoint regarding the immigrants who are about to arrive in his unit, as well as the way they are going to be selected. To facilitate the reading, we decided to first reproduce this excerpt extensively. Most of the passages of this excerpt are then analyzed afterwards.

153	JACK:	A young student who arrives, who did his intern-
154		ship, who has never worked in a company, then you
155		give him responsibilities, he just arrived, he does not
156		know anything, this is also challenging. They [the
157		employees] are used to it, there are roughly 20 of
158		them [interns] per year.
159		
160	JANET:	But things have all the same to be named differently,
161		according to the two profiles.
162		
163	JACK:	Yes, but what I just mean is that my feeling, is it
164		more demanding? I don't think that our interns, not
165		our RCR—sorry ((speaking to Mary)), RCR are
166		external consultants. But honestly, when you hire
167		an intern for 20 weeks, you know, I have Sophia
168		who is going to be with us, I have to welcome her, I
169		have to sponsor her, she has a shock because she has
170		never really worked in a company. We have to get
171		her used to working in a company, have an office. I
172		have to take care of her logistics.
173		
174	JANET:	I'm not saying that in terms of energy calculation it
175		is more, but they are from elsewhere=
176		
177	JACK:	=Different colors

178	JANET:	Someone who has left his country, who has left his
179		family, who hasn't worked in his domain for three
180		years or five years, who has experienced war.
181		
182	MARY:	He has different needs.
183		
184	JANET:	It's not true that this is simple, it's really not sim-
185		ple. You can expect that he will deliver because the
186		diploma is there, the experience is there. But maybe
187		it won't be that easy.
188		
189	JACK:	Uh I—
190		
191	JANET:	I don't know how we are going to proceed, but
192		probably in the preparation.
193		
194	MARIE:	Maybe the sponsors' preparation.
195		
196	JACK:	You know, I'm gonna tell you, according to the pro-
197		cedures, there is going to be a selection process, I
198		imagine.
199		
200	JANET:	Yes, well yes.
201		
202	JACK:	In the selection process also, there is no denying that
203		when they are going to try to choose someone, they
204		are going to choose someone whose integration level
205		in the thing [the program] is going to be easier too.
206		
207	JANET:	On the other hand, to play—here I am going to be a
208		little bit the gatekeeper of the reason why this pro-
209		gram is being proposed. It's also that we adhere to
210		the principle that there are people who did not have
211		their chance, but you know, the ones who deserve it
212		and who have all the skills. Is it because integration
213		is going to be harder that we are going to put him
214		aside because, meanwhile, we have to keep the busi-
215		ness running and everything? I don't know where to
216		find the balance in there, but—
217		
218	JACK:	I am not helping him if I get him in the organization,
219		and then he has too big a curve to reach, I won't
220		help him either. EBF is not necessarily a company to
221		help him do so. I understand what you mean, Janet,
222		but he does not do either—The program objective is

223	to offer professional sponsors to people who have
224	experience and training from outside Quebec and
225	for whom it is the first job in Quebec. Our work is
226	to welcome these people, and then there is a win-
227	win at the end of the exercise. And then a win for
228	the person who arrives. And if the person arrives,
229	and then there is a big curve to get in EBF, you're
230	going to find this difficult. You know—

To what extent can relational aspects of organizing and disorganizing be identified in this excerpt? And especially, to what extent can a relational perspective help us understand how the tensions generated by these contradictory forces are dealt with on the terra firma of interaction? These are the two questions we will address in this section.

First, we note, in the beginning of this excerpt, how Jack evokes the case of young interns they routinely welcome in his unit, a situation he says they are used to as "there are roughly 20 of them per year" (lines 157–158) even if it is "challenging" (line 156). We understand that this situation is, for him, supposed to *speak to* the case of recent immigrants they are about to hire. Both immigrants and young interns are indeed new office workers in the company, which means that they are supposed to lack experience about how things get done at EBF. What is this case supposed to say, according to Jack? That he and his unit might actually be well prepared to welcome the immigrants hired as temporary employees, given that he and his colleagues are used to this type of situation.

Relationally speaking, we see how Jack implicitly positions himself as a representative of his unit. He is indeed speaking in the name of a reality that he and his colleagues are supposed to be quite familiar with: the case of young interns and how to deal with them. By comparing the two cases (immigrant workers vs. interns), he is also mobilizing a procedure or program they are used to (what to do with interns) in order to make sense of something they are not familiar with (what to do with immigrant workers). Intra-actively, his intervention not only positions/identifies him as the spokesperson of his unit in this meeting, but also makes a specific situation *present* to his interlocutors, a situation that is supposed to say something about the program they are talking about: They are, in fact, prepared for this new situation, which appears to be not that new, after all.

However, we see Janet responding, "But things have all the same to be named differently, according to the two profiles" (lines 160–161), which amounts to questioning the similarity Jack implicitly puts forward between the two situations. These two profiles that she mentions in her turn of talk are indeed supposed to show that the professional mentoring program has, in some aspects, to be distinguished from the intern program: They are not speaking about the same population (interns vs. immigrant workers). Relationally speaking, Janet thus implicitly positions herself as the spokesperson for another reality that, for her, *matters* in this situation: the fact that immigrants are not traditional interns.

By saying "But things *have* all the same *to* be named differently, according to the two profiles" (lines 160–161, our italics), we also observe how the aspect of the situation she highlights is supposed to *dictate*, according to her, the usage of two different names that are meant to describe (and possibly act on) two different realities. In terms of disorganizing, a *first tension* can therefore be identified here: While the intern program Jack is referring to is supposed to *dictate* how they should proceed vis-à-vis the immigrant workers, the distinction Janet makes appears to *contradict* this way of making sense of the situation. While the professional mentoring program is supposed to be compatible with the way units function, we therefore see how potentialities for *disorganizing* begin to materialize in this discussion.

This is confirmed by Jack's reaction just after, as he then asks whether it is "more demanding" (line 164), which implies that the professional mentoring program might consequently be too much of a burden for his unit. He then takes the example of an intern, called Sophia, who is going to work with them and enumerates all the things he and his colleagues will have to do to take care of her ("I have to welcome her, I have to sponsor her, she has a shock because she has never really worked in a company. We have to get her used to working in a company, have an office. I have to take care of her logistics" [lines 171–172]).

What is Sophia's case supposed to show? That welcoming interns already is an extra burden for his unit. In other words, if the professional mentoring program is even more demanding than the intern program, chances are that its implementation will constitute too much extra work for his unit. This is what Janet also seems to understand as she responds, "I'm not saying that in terms of energy calculation it is more, but they are from elsewhere" (lines 174–175), as to reassure Jack about the amount of extra work that the immigrant workers might require.

In other words, we see here an attempt, on Janet's part, to present the professional mentoring program as compatible with how Jack's unit functions: They are indeed talking about two different populations (interns vs. immigrants) and this difference has to be acknowledged in order to know their respective needs. However, this does not mean, according to her, that the immigrants will require more energy than the interns. While Jack appears worried about the dysfunctional/disorganizing aspects of this program, we see Janet trying to reassure him about its compatibility with the way his unit currently functions.

What we thus observe so far is two spokespersons, that is, two organs, speaking to each other about what respectively matters to them: on one side, Jack, who appears preoccupied by the functionality of the unit he is in charge of and, on the other side, Janet, who seems concerned about the functionality of the program she is supposed to implement. While Jack considers these two matters as potentially colliding with each other, Janet attempts to make them compatible even if she does not hesitate to insist on the unusual character of the immigrants' profile.

Both Jack and Janet can therefore be seen as the media/intermediaries/ means through which various aspects of a situation materialize themselves in this meeting. By getting together, they try to figure out what to do about a situation (the hiring of immigrant employees), which consists, as we saw, of identifying what the situation not only looks like, but also dictates. What we therefore observe is various ways of *enacting* the situation, that is, various ways of expressing *what should count or matter in it*. Each person around the table then potentially becomes the way/means/intermediary by which specific aspects of a situation express themselves and what should be done about them.

But let us now look at what happens just after Janet reminds Jack that "they are from elsewhere" (line 175). We see Jack saying, "Different colors" (line 177), which marks how he relates to what Janet has just said. The fact that these immigrants are from elsewhere becomes, through him, the fact that they just have a different skin color. Janet immediately corrects this reduction by specifying what she actually intended to say: "Someone who has left his country, who has left his family, who hasn't worked in his domain for three years or five years, who has experienced war" (lines 178–180). In other words, we see her again insisting on the specific profiles of the immigrants they are about to welcome, an information that is confirmed by Mary who adds, "He has different needs" (line 182).

This reality that Janet is depicting is thus supposed to show Jack that their difference cannot be reduced to the color of their skins. They have, as Mary points out, different needs, which requires, on the units' part, specific responses. Janet then adds, "It's not true that this is simple, it's really not simple. You can expect that he will deliver because the diploma is there, the experience is there. But maybe it won't be that easy" (lines 186–187). In other words, we see her marking what appears to be the ambiguous or equivocal character of the situation, at least for her: They have a diploma and experience, so Jack can expect them to deliver, but they are also coming from countries where they often lost everything, which means that they might have special needs.

While some aspects of the situation appear to be reassuring (the immigrants' diplomas and experiences), others are depicted by Janet as potentially worrisome (the traumatisms associated with their immigration, the fact that they might have not worked for a long time in their domain of expertise). Beyond what could be reduced to case of intra-group conflict, we thus observe how enacting the situation amounts to materializing certain of its aspects in the discussion, aspects that each time are supposed to *say something* about what could be done about it. The trouble here is that these varied aspects do not seem to say the same thing, hence the equivocal character of the situation.

The equivocality of the situation, indeed, comes here from a *tension* that the interlocutors appear to feel between two imperatives dictating two incompatible courses of action. On one side, the necessity to adequately respond to the immigrants' special needs (a concern put forward by Janet and Mary) and, on the other side, the necessity to allow EBF units to function optimally and effectively (a concern highlighted by Jack). We witness here a typical organizational situation: Both parties are, in many ways, *organized*, that is, they are talking and acting on behalf of specific programs of action they are in charge of completing. However, they also have to *get organized*, that is, identify programs of action that could allow them to harmonize, as much as possible, what appears so far incompatible.

This is what precisely takes place in the following lines when we see Janet responding to her own puzzlement: "I don't know how we are going to proceed, but probably in the preparation" (lines 191–192), a possibility that is echoed and completed by Mary: "Maybe the sponsors' preparation" (line 194). Implementing this program of preparation for the sponsors could maybe allow the units and professional mentoring program to cohabit with each other, that is, allow them *not to disorganize each other*. Preparing the sponsor is therefore presented as a program of action (a new procedure) that could possibly reconcile two logics of action that appear so far hard to reconcile, especially for Jack.

While we insisted so far on the way the three interlocutors enact aspects of the situation, that is, make them say something about what has to be done, we can now address what Karl Weick (1979) calls *selection*. Selection, as we know, is the reduction of equivocality, that is, the reduction of the potential equality of different voices, especially when they happen to contradict each other. To collectively make sense of a situation indeed amounts to building a voice that will give a collective version of what the situation dictates or commands, that is, *creating a sort of monophony out of this polyphony*.

What we see happening here is precisely this phenomenon, as Jack, Janet and Mary try to find a sort of common ground that could represent, i.e., make present, for all of them, the situation they are facing. Although we cannot identify any form of explicit agreement at this point, we can still observe that Jack's concerns appear to be acknowledged by Janet and Mary. Saying, "I don't know how we are going to proceed, but probably in the preparation" (lines 191–192) and "Maybe the sponsors' preparation" (line 194) is indeed a way for Janet and Mary to not only acknowledge the tension (and its potentially disorganizing character) that Jack has been highlighting so far, but also propose a solution in response to what this tension would require in terms of intervention.

However, Jack does not seem comfortable with this move, as we see him putting forward another solution. As he points out, "You know, I'm gonna tell you, according to the procedures, there is going to be a selection process, I imagine" (lines 197–198). As these procedures are confirmed by Janet ("Yes, well yes" (line 200)), he then presents what could be done about this situation: "In the selection process also, there is no denying that when they are going to try to choose someone, they are going to choose someone whose integration level in the thing [the program] is going to be easier too" (lines 204–205).

While Janet and Mary were proposing to create another procedure, Jack invokes an existing one (the selection process) that might, according to him, address their concerns. In other words, no need to implement a new procedure to prepare the sponsors to help the new employees (a solution that would probably have the disadvantage of adding more workload to the sponsors, even if this eventuality is never explicitly spelled out), as chances are that the selection process will end up selecting what Jack considers to be the right candidates, that is, the ones whose integration in the professional mentoring program will be easier.

In terms of retention this time, we therefore see how Jack's intervention consists of invoking a procedure that already exists, a procedure that is presented as responding and speaking to the situation they are facing. However, Janet does not seem comfortable with Jack's solution as we see her explicitly positioning herself as the "gatekeeper of the reason why this program is being proposed" (lines 208–209), a position that leads her to recall that they "adhere to the principle that there are people who did not have their chance, but you know, the ones who deserve it and who have all the skills" (lines 209–212).

In reaction to the existing procedure that Jack is invoking, Janet thus puts forward a principle that, according to her, *calls for* some revision in the way immigrant workers should be selected. As she asks, "Is it because integration is going to be harder that we are going to put him aside because, meanwhile, the business needs to be run and everything?" (lines 209–212). In other words, we see her calling into question the idea of a selection procedure that would run counter to (i.e., disorganize) the program she is in charge of. If the selection is indeed too strict, there is indeed no way immigrant workers will be hired, a situation that would thwart the raison d'être of the professional mentoring program.

The tensions between two logics of action are, once again, reaffirmed, as Janet explicitly stages their relative incompatibility: on one side, a principle that dictates that they give these newcomers a chance (lines 210–211), while in the other side, another principle according to which "we have to keep the business running" (lines 214–215). To these two principles that appear to clash with each other, Janet responds by acknowledging the difficulty she has in finding a way to reconcile them: "I don't know where to find the balance in there, but—" (lines 215–216).

We then see Jack interrupting her as he reaffirms, once again, his key concern (i.e., the effectiveness of his unit). However, it is noteworthy how he enacts the situation differently, as we see him taking, for the first time, the immigrant's perspective ("I am not helping him if I get him in the organization, and then he has too big a curve to reach, I won't help him either. EBF is not necessarily a company to help him do so" (lines 220–221)). While Janet has been, since the beginning, speaking on behalf of the immigrants' special needs, we see Jack taking up her positioning but by *making it say something else*.

These new workers indeed deserve to be helped properly (this is Jack's way of acknowledging what Janet has been saying so far), but, according to him, helping them *calls for* a selection process where candidates who have "too big a curve to reach" (line 229) end up being excluded. In other words, Jack marks that he, like Janet, has the immigrants' best interests in mind, but his caring takes another form in its conditionality: They have to minimally fit the expectations, otherwise, any help will be completely useless.

As he marks his understanding of Janet's viewpoint ("I understand what you mean, Janet" (line 221)), we see him recalling the program's objective ("to offer professional sponsors to people who have experience and training from outside Quebec and for whom it is the first job in Quebec" (lines 224–225)), which he presents by highlighting the sponsors' responsibilities vis-à-vis the immigrants. This is reaffirmed in what he says just after: "Our work is to welcome these people, and then there is a win-win at the end of the exercise. And then a win for the person who arrives. And if the person arrives, and then there is a big curve to get in EBF, you're going to find this difficult. You know—" (lines 229–230).

While Jack had been so far insisting on the importance of selecting the right candidates so that they fit with the units' expectations, we then see him taking Janet's perspective while giving it a key twist. For him, it is, in fact, in the immigrants' best interests to be selected properly as choosing someone who would not fit the bill would put him or her in a difficult situation. In other words, Jack positions himself as voicing the immigrants' interests, but by making them say what he has been saying so far: These interests call for a strict selection procedure.

Discussion

What did we learn from this relational analysis regarding the processes of organizing and disorganizing and to what extent this analysis helps us understand how the tensions generated by these contradictory forces are dealt with on the *terra firma* of interaction? Regarding the question of organizing, we can first note how our relational perspective helped us identify the three stages—enactment, selection and retention—identified by Weick (1979; Weick et al., 2005) while giving them a relational twist. While Karl Weick's (1979, 1995) anthropocentric perspective tends to focus on what people say and do, we saw how enactment, selection and retention are always, in fact, bidirectional. In other words, we saw that what is enacted, selected or retained also does and says things throughout the discussion.

By *enacting* a situation, participants are not only identifying which elements of this situation are supposed to matter to them, they are also giving them a way to *materialize themselves* in a given discussion. In other words, *what matters to the participants is also what tends to materialize in their conversations*. While Jack cares for the effectiveness of his unit, Janet cares for the success of her program. They thus both (most of the time, implicitly, once explicitly) position themselves as the organs (here, the spokespersons) of their respective unit and program. When Jack speaks, we saw that it is the interests of his unit that are also supposed to express themselves. Similarly, when Janet speaks, it is also the interests of her program that tend to materialize.

Enacting a situation is therefore a way to give some of its elements a way to *also exist* and *matter* in a given conversation. When something or someone starts to exist in a discussion, it also means that this thing or person can start to make a difference, as we saw in our analyses. According to Jack, his unit and its effectiveness *call for* a strict selection process capable of identifying the immigrants who will not have too big a learning curve. According to Janet, the professional sponsoring program and its success *call for* a certain openness in terms of who ends up being selected, as being too selective would, by definition, defeat the purpose of the program.

The tension that the participants feel and express in their conversation thus results from the fact that the interests of the unit *dictate* courses of action that appear to run against the interests of the program and vice versa. In other words, both interests appear to literally *contra-dict* each other, hence the equivocal character of the situation they are facing. The situation is equivocal because it does not say or dictate the same thing depending on which of its elements participants decide to focus on. This marks the bidirectionality of enactment, that is, its relational character.

In terms of *selection*, the second stage of sensemaking, we saw how this equivocality was concretely addressed in two very distinct ways: by invoking existing procedures—this is essentially Jack's moves when we see him invoking the procedures they use to welcome young interns or the selection process that is already in place—or by proposing new procedures—which is what Janet and Mary suggest (preparing the sponsors) after having explicitly highlighted the equivocal character of the situation. While Jack's moves essentially consist of relying on what Weick

(1979) would call *retention*, that is, rules, procedures, habits that have been organizationally retained to deal with various types of situations, Janet and Mary propose to innovate by finding a way to really deal with what they perceive as the unusual character of the situation.

As we saw, both selection and retention are bidirectional to the extent that the procedures that are identified or created are supposed to *speak to* the situation they are facing, that is, *respond to what it dictates*. What we also discovered throughout our analyses is the way Jack, Janet and Mary try to acknowledge each other's contributions. For instance, if Janet and Mary propose a new procedure to better prepare the sponsors, it is in response to Jack's concerns about the functionality of his unit. In other words, this new procedure is supposed to *speak to* the necessity for Jack's unit to operate as smoothly as possible.

Similarly, we also see how Jack acknowledges Janet and Mary's concerns when he starts speaking in the name of the immigrants' interests and the success of the program. Although this move could be considered artificial, it is still a way for him to show that the selection process *speaks to* what matters to his interlocutors. According to a relational perspective, the kind of meeting we just analyzed (and meetings in general) is not *only* about people talking to each other, it is *also*, and maybe especially, about various elements of a situation (procedures, principles, objectives, other people and their interests, etc.) speaking to each other *through* these persons.

These elements—whether they are created on the spot (e.g., the new procedure Janet and Mary proposed) or identified as already existing (i.e., the professional mentoring program, Jack's unit, the intern program or the selection procedure)—can be said to speak because they are *made to say things* by Jack, Janet and Mary, but also because they *make these three people say things* during the meeting. As already pointed out, it is because Jack *cares* for his unit that he speaks on behalf of its interests throughout the excerpt and the same thing can be said about Janet and Mary regarding the professional mentoring program they are in charge of.

Any conversation can therefore be seen as a *situation where elements of a situation are presented as speaking or responding to each other*. When Jack claims that the selection process speaks to the exigencies of the program, organizing is taking place to the extent that the selection process is implicitly presented as an organ or means by which the professional sponsoring program and his unit will be able to run effectively. Similarly, when Janet and Mary propose a new procedure, they implicitly suggest another organ or means by which their program and Jack's unit will be able to function as smoothly as possible.

Speaking and responding are about organizing precisely because they allow specific courses of action to articulate with each other. It is, however, about *disorganizing* because some disarticulations will always happen. This is precisely what Jack, Janet and Mary fear regarding the situation they are facing: Jack, when he points out that the program might disorganize his unit; Janet and Mary, when they point out that the selection process might disorganize their program. Although we saw how they tried to reach out to each other, they also realize that some compromise might have to be made, that is, that some disorganizing might take place on each side.

Communication is also about disorganizing precisely because of these alterations, deteriorations or destructions that are consciously or sometimes unconsciously enacted by the participants (in the name of a compromise, for instance). Tensions, according to a relational perspective, are therefore intractable because each participant is, by definition, *attached to* elements of a situation that will never say exactly the same thing about what should be done about it. This is the essence of management, as management precisely is about how to deal with these tensions on a daily basis, knowing that any organizing will always create, somehow, somewhere, somewhen, disorganizing.

Note

1. To be sure, we can imagine cases where titles do not signify rights and obligations, job descriptions are loose recommendations, identifications are weak or multiple, and organizational charts do not exist, but this then simply means that we are then dealing with a loose form of organization, which also means that organizing, i.e., the creation of organs, will be crucial to assure the functioning of the organization.

3 The Queen Bee Outlives Her Own Children

A Luhmannian Perspective on Project-Based Organizations (PBOs)

Michael Grothe-Hammer
and Dennis Schoeneborn

In a recent article, Vásquez, Schoeneborn and Sergi (2016) suggested conceptualizing organizations as processual phenomena that are constituted by an alternation of communicative processes of ordering (i.e., attempts to fix meanings and interpretations) and disordering (i.e., the opening of potential meanings and interpretations). As the authors demonstrated in a cross-case analysis of project work, organizational efforts of ordering are typically accompanied by the creation of disorder at the same time. By drawing on a "Communication as Constitutive of Organization" (CCO) perspective, Vásquez et al. (2016) thus argued that disorder is unavoidable in communicative attempts to accomplish order because "whenever language is used and texts are created and shared, meanings tend to multiply and escape the full control of single actors" (p. 630).

In this chapter, we put forth the argument that this conceptualization of organization—where organization is a processual and precarious phenomenon which needs to be reinstantiated recurrently through communication—can be further advanced by employing the theoretical vocabulary that German sociologist Niklas Luhmann (1995, 2018) developed in his sociology of organizations. On a more general level, the similarities of the North American tradition of CCO scholarship and Luhmann's sociology of organizations have been well-documented in various publications over the past years (e.g., Blaschke, 2015; Blaschke, Schoeneborn & Seidl, 2012; Brummans, Cooren, Robichaud & Taylor, 2014; Cooren, Kuhn, Cornelissen & Clark, 2011; Dobusch & Schoeneborn, 2015; Koch, 2017; Schoeneborn, 2011; Schoeneborn et al., 2014; Seidl & Schoeneborn, In press). However, in this chapter, we go beyond these prior works by highlighting that a Luhmannian perspective is particularly well suited to put forth a paradoxical understanding of communication as being constitutive of both ordering and disordering simultaneously in one and the same performative speech act, that is, decisional communication (cf. Nassehi, 2005; Schoeneborn, 2011). Importantly, Luhmann's theory provides us with a mechanism that can explain this perpetual oscillation between ordering and disordering (cf. Cooper, 1986), grounded in the inherent paradoxicality and undecidability of decisions (cf. von Foerster, 1992; see also Derrida, 2002) and the attempts of reaching (intermediary) order through decisions nevertheless.

To illustrate our argumentation, we draw on a comparative analysis of project-based organizations (PBOs) and the various projects as temporary organizations that (co-)constitute the PBO's existence. Because of their semi-temporariness, PBOs appear to be particularly suitable for inquiries into how organization as a precarious phenomenon necessitates continuous (re)constitution in and through communication. Specifically, we cross-compare two empirical studies in the context of film projects (Grothe-Hammer, 2015) as well as consulting projects (Schoeneborn, 2013a, 2013b). In a transversal analysis of both cases, we highlight that the temporary character of projects interrupts the possibilities to create the flow of order through interlinking with decision premises of past projects. As we will elaborate, the Luhmannian approach allows us to understand PBOs as a particular "species" of organization. Using a metaphor from fauna as a source domain, a PBO is like a "honeybee queen" that recurrently lays eggs and gives birth to multiple worker bees, i.e., the projects. However, it is characteristic that the queen bee outlives her own creations that have only a temporary existence—but that are nevertheless constitutive for the honeybee queen's existence.

In sum, our chapter adds to recent debates in CCO scholarship on the paradoxical constitution of organization (e.g., Cooren et al., 2013; Schoeneborn, Vásquez & Cornelissen, 2016) as well as on the communicative *deconstitution* of organization (e.g., Bean & Buikema, 2015; Hoffmann, 2018). We also contribute to the pertinent literatures on PBOs. For instance, our chapter highlights that while projects are broadly celebrated as an extremely flexible form of organizing (Manning, 2017), this high flexibility seems to be accompanied by a high degree of inflexibility, i.e., a tendency to order without disordering. Moreover, we emphasize that one insight to be drawn from this line of theorizing is that a PBO and its projects are mostly environments to each other. We finally elaborate on the explanatory potential of the Luhmannian approach for understanding problems of organizational learning in the context of PBOs.

A Luhmannian View on Communication and Organization

Creating Order and Disorder Through Meaning Making in Communication

The basic assumption of Luhmann's social systems theory is that the world is excessively and overly complex and disorderly, so it must be ordered in some way to reduce this complexity (Luhmann, 1993). In the social domain, this complexity reduction takes place in communication processes, and only in communication processes. For Luhmann (1995), everything social consists of the operational element of communication (see also Seidl, 2005; Seidl & Becker, 2006). However, it is important to note that Luhmann's theoretical framework suggests a co-constitutive understanding of the order-disorder relation. While communication has the potential to transform complexity/disorder into something more ordered at least temporarily, this ordered character is precarious, given that meanings can always be reinterpreted and contested, thus carrying the seed for new disorder to arise (see also Vásquez et al., 2016).

The notion of communication highlights the importance of relationality by pointing out that social phenomena need at least two (human) individuals as a basis to construct a meaning: a sender of an *utterance*—which is the equivalent to a social action—and a receiver providing an *understanding* (Luhmann, 1992). Only when both are given can *information* be established. This information is neither determined by the sender nor by the receiver nor is it congruent with the utterance or the understanding. It is a construction that needs both and therefore has its own emergent social characteristics. Communication processes, hence, have the tendency to create both order and disorder by producing and referring to meaning. Meaning in this sense is constituted by and resides within the communication events—and only there—however, the specific meaning actualized in one event always refers to some preceding events. Building on Edmund Husserl (1948), Luhmann (1993) defines meaning as the difference between actuality and potentiality, whereby "the actual is defined with view on a horizon of other possibilities" (Grothe-Hammer, 2017, p. 44). Hence, meaning making is the communication process in which the excessive complexity of the world is socially reduced by selecting (actualizing) certain possibilities in reference to other (potential) possibilities (Morgner, 2014). In this respect, Luhmann acknowledges Heinz von Foerster's "order from noise" principle (Luhmann, 1995, p. 214). To illustrate these rather abstract remarks let us cite David Seidl's example of a knife:

> The meaning of "knife", for example, is its reference to actions and experiences like cutting, stabbing, eating, operating, cooking etc. Thus, the knife is not only "knife" as such but "knife" with regard to something beyond the knife. . . . A knife is a knife and not a spoon, or fork.
>
> (Seidl, 2005, pp. 16–18)

Meaning making, therefore, is the process of constantly drawing distinctions—an ongoing and ever-changing selection of certain possibilities (i.e., the attempt of a fixation of one particular meaning) in distinction to other possibilities that remain unactualized. It is an ongoing process to be realized in every communication event that constantly oscillates between actuality and potentiality. It "lives off disturbances, is nourished by disorder, lets itself be carried by noise, and needs an 'excluded third'" (Luhmann, 1995, p. 83). In this sense, communication contributes to the "perpetual movement between order and disorder" (Cooper in Chia & Kallinikos, 1998, p. 154). Furthermore, communication always draws on previous events of communication and it always needs connection to subsequent communication—even if implicit—because otherwise it would just vanish in an instance. Through this recursivity, communication can build systems of operationally closed interconnected networks of communication (Blaschke et al., 2012). These communication systems are operationally closed in the sense that they constitute a boundary by constantly drawing distinctions that mark what is treated by the system as internal and what is excluded to the horizon of unactualized possibilities (Luhmann, 2006).[1] When there are distinctive communication processes that only connect to specific communications and exclude others, a system distinguishes itself from its environment. As we will elaborate in the following, the term "organization" denominates a specific type of such a communication-based system.

Order, Disorder and Organization

Organizations play an important role when it comes to creating order in our society (Apelt et al., 2017; Luhmann, 2018). While the existing literature uses the terms "order" and "organization" typically as largely interchangeable (see, for instance, Cooley, 1924; Fortes, 1955; Frank, 1944), for our purpose it is important to draw a clear distinction. Order, for us, is the selection of a certain meaning that always emerges out of and relies on disorder as a background of other possible meanings. In contrast, an organization is a social system that both produces and draws on such (dis)order. For Luhmann (2003, 2018), an organization is thereby a certain type of social system that is distinct from other social phenomena in that it consists of decisions. In the same context, it is important to note that Luhmann applies a notion of decision that differs significantly from the existing literature in organization studies as well as in sociology more generally. While the majority of the existing works defines a decision as "a choice between alternative courses of action or positions" (Luhman & Cunliffe, 2013, p. 45; see also Bruch & Feinberg, 2017), Luhmann (2003) discards such a rather cognitive view and instead defines *decision as communication*, and more specifically, as a certain type of communication:

> Decision is not understood as a psychological mechanism, but as a matter of communication, not as a psychological event in the form of an internally conscious definition of the self, but as a social event. That makes it impossible to state that decisions already taken still have to be communicated. Decisions are communications.
>
> (p. 32)

A decision is a particular form of communication that tends to visibilize its own contingency (Luhmann, 2018). While in Luhmann's view it is only communication that is the locus of a decision, individuals are relevant for decision-making nevertheless—in two main regards. First, as in all forms of communication, decisions rely on the participation of individual human beings as the necessary basis (Luhmann, 2002). Although humans cannot directly participate in communication in the sense that their thoughts cannot directly connect to words or texts or another one's thoughts, humans are a crucial precondition for the possibility of communication in this view. Communication, to keep going, of course needs the involvement of individual human beings to hear, read, speak or write. However, in this process, the thoughts and intentions of individuals can only "trigger" the occurrence of communication but, importantly, they cannot determine how communication plays out eventually (which is theorized here as a social system in its own right); even if this idea of the fundamental indeterminacy of the communication process may sound abstract at first, this insight is actually very intuitive; it matches with the practical experience many individuals have when engaging in communication, for instance, when an interaction with the spouse, a business meeting or an interview takes an unexpected turn that cannot fully be traced back to the intentions of those individuals who were involved in the communication event. In this sense, the individuals involved in communication remain "black boxes" for the communication and their involvement is constitutive of producing the necessary indeterminacy. Depending on which individuals participate in communication, certain expectations are possible on the likely course of events (but not predictions in a rather deterministic sense). By doing so, individuals also serve as "addresses" for communication, that is, as reference points (Dobusch & Schoeneborn, 2015) which couple communication events through time (see also Blaschke et al., 2012). Therefore, an organization needs humans (in its structurally coupled environment) to remember its decisions (Luhmann, 1996). The second reason for the relevance of individuals for processes of decision-making is that decisions produce the necessity to attribute human decision-makers as the authors of decisions (Luhmann, 2018).[2]

A decision not only communicates a certain possibility that has been selected, but also—explicitly or implicitly—that other alternatives could have been selected instead (Schoeneborn, 2008). In this respect, a decision differs from other kinds of communication. While, as outlined above, a communication always selects one possibility in reference to others, a decision always implies that other possibilities *could have been chosen*— or in other words, that these other possibilities were in fact alternatives. A sentence like "The sun is shining" is a good example for an ordinary assertion. What the sun is, is clear to us, in distinction to a moon, a human being or a tree. And what "shining" means is also largely clear to us, because we know the difference to darkness, etc. However, in this example it is also clear that it would not be possible to choose another possibility as an alternative. When the sun is shining, it is shining (in the words of Searle, 1995, this can be seen as a "brute fact"); in this sense, we cannot choose whether it is shining or not. A decision is fundamentally different from that. We borrow again an example from Seidl (2005, p. 38) to illustrate a typical organizational decision: "I am going to employ candidate A and not candidate B". In this sentence, it is clear that selecting candidate B was an alternative that could have been chosen instead. Therefore, in order to fix a meaning by selecting a certain option, a decision always also opens up meaning by communicating disregarded options as well.

As a consequence, decisions are inherently *paradoxical* in character (cf. von Foerster, 1992; see also Derrida, 2002). They provoke opposition, alternation, revision and rejection, i.e., by follow-up communication that questions why a particular alternative has been selected and not another (see Schoeneborn, 2011). Moreover, while in most contexts this characteristic means that communication can fail—if one rejects the chosen alternative—it is exactly this aspect that produces an organization's existence. Organizations totalize decisions as their mode of operation, making an organization *nothing but* decisions. As Luhmann (2018, p. 45) puts it, in an organization, even being late can be considered a decision (in follow-up communication). New decisions build on the organization's history and refer to earlier decisions, and even rejecting a decision needs a new decision. As a result, in organizations "one decision calls for ensuing decisions, resulting in a self-reproducing stream of decisions" (Ahrne, Brunsson & Seidl, 2016, p. 95). While in most contexts decisions are highly fragile, because rejecting a decision implies the possibility of just ignoring it, in an organization accepting as well as rejecting a decision produces the need for new decisions.

For instance, a multinational corporation's decision to enter the Chinese—and not the Japanese—market inevitably creates new contingencies and the need for follow-up decisions, such as where to base the local subsidiary, etc. (see the example discussed in Schoeneborn, 2011). The same decision could also produce rejection, however, only in the form of a follow-up decision, if, e.g., the multinational corporation's decision is revoked in the next board meeting. Therefore, totalizing decisions can be seen as a deparadoxification mechanism that reduces the fragility of decisions stemming from their inherently paradox character (see Andersen, 2003; Schoeneborn, 2011).

Organizations in this sense serve as the producers not only of decisions but also of their own "decision necessities" that, in turn, perpetuate their very existence (see Nassehi, 2005). In this sense, organizations simultaneously produce order and disorder through decisions—that is, they fix meanings (e.g., a firm's decision to enter the Chinese market and not the Japanese market) and at the same time call for opening up meanings (e.g., the need to execute follow-up decisions about *how* to enter the Chinese market, for instance, through a joint venture or other forms of business partnerships). It is this continuous dialectic between ordering and disordering that ensures an organization's existence. Since an organization only consists of decisions, it only exists in the actual decision events (Luhmann, 1996). The simultaneity of order and disorder (cf. Cooper, 1986) within a decision produces decision necessities and therefore makes it likely that follow-up decisions will occur. Hence, without decision necessities there would be most likely no new decisions and without new decisions there would be no continuation of the organization anymore.

Although organizations in this view are constituted by the simultaneity of order and disorder, they are capable of producing certain relatively stable elements of order, as well (Ahrne & Brunsson, 2011). As decision systems, organizations can decide on certain premises that serve as fixed reference points for further decisions—as for example memberships, rules or hierarchies (Luhmann, 2018; Ahrne et al., 2016). Decision premises then serve as the organization's structures and limit the possibilities of what is accepted as decisions in organizations (Luhmann, 2018). In this sense, decision premises are another mechanism of the deparadoxification of decisions. For example, a decision on membership regulates that only certain individuals have the right to participate in decision-making and therefore only decisions that involve members are accepted as organizational decisions (Luhmann, 1996). Decision premises persist in time by serving as potential bases for follow-up decisions. By deciding on decision premises, organizations are able to fix meanings through time and thus create order at least temporarily. In other words, by reducing complexity, decisions (paradoxically) allow for the production of new complexity.

Hence, in Luhmann's (2003) processual understanding, an organization continuously oscillates between stability and flexibility. On the one hand, it is flexible through the capacity to produce new decisions continuously, while on the other hand, it always relies on a (relatively stable) set of decision premises, which indeed are also a matter of decision and therefore inherently contingent. An organization needs both ongoing decision-making and decision premises to persist. It needs a stable set of at least some structures in order to achieve high degrees of complexity—which is only possible if not everything has to be decided and re-decided in every instance. However, it also needs the continuous and recursive production of follow-up decisions, because without follow-up decisions the self-reproducing process of organization just stops. If this happens, an organization either just vanishes (Grothe-Hammer, In press) or certain decision premises that were once decidable become institutionalized and taken-for-granted (Ahrne et al., 2016) and are not anymore treated as something that could be different.

Taken together, the Luhmannian view allows us to understand organization as an entitative, yet processual phenomenon. In this view, organizations are social systems that are constituted by recursively connected decisional communications that can also decide on premises for decisions. Accordingly, Luhmann's view invites us to study organization by focusing on how the *interconnectedness* of various decisional processes is accomplished. Hence, in the following, we draw on Luhmann's theoretical framework and vocabulary to examine a specific type of organization, that is, project-based organizations (PBOs), where the interconnectedness of decisions across projects is continuously at stake.

Empirical Illustration: Exploring Project-Based Organizations (PBOs)

To illustrate the fruitfulness of a Luhmannian approach, we locate our inquiry in the context of temporary forms of organization (Lundin & Söderholm, 1995). More specifically, we look at two project-based organizations (PBOs) and the various projects as temporary organizations that (co-)constitute the PBO's existence (Hobday, 2000). Projects can be defined as temporary organizational systems that are established to achieve specific purposes in a predetermined time frame. PBOs, in contrast, are permanent organizations that rely mainly on initiating and coordinating projects. PBOs provide essential elements of social order for the temporary organizations, which draw on this order as premises for accomplishing their own decisions (see also Manning, 2017). Such "semi-temporary" forms of organization like PBOs—as well as the organized project networks in which the PBOs are often embedded—have gained significant scholarly attention in the past years (e.g., Bakker, 2010; Starkey, Barnatt & Tempest, 2000; Manning, 2017). Bakker, De Fillippi, Schwab and Sydow (2016) emphasized the relation between the temporary and the permanent in temporary organizational settings as an interplay between processes and structures. This view corresponds to the aforementioned Luhmannian understanding of organization as a process of ongoing decision-making that continually fixes meanings (order) and opens meanings (disorder) through the interplay of decisions (processes) and decision premises (structure) (see also Seidl & Becker, 2006).

Those forms of organizations that are neither fully permanent nor fully temporary are particularly interesting for us here (Bakker et al., 2016 refer to them as either "semi-permanent" or "semi-temporary" forms of organization). Projects are by definition temporary in character and usually have a (more or less fixed) termination date. Accordingly, in projects the stream of decisions that would be usually constitutive for organizations by default gets disrupted eventually, that is, when the project reaches the end of its temporary existence. In the following, we want to take a look at how ordering and disordering takes place in the relation between projects and their PBOs. We selected two cases of partially permanent/temporary forms of organization, i.e., film projects (see also Grothe-Hammer, 2015)

Table 3.1 Locating Our Two Case Illustrations in the Typology of Temporary Forms of Organizing

Structure/Actor	Temporary	Permanent
Temporary	(1) Temporary, ephemeral or disposable organization	(2) Semi-temporary organization: The consulting projects (Case 2)
Permanent	(3) Semi-permanent organization with temporary employment: The film projects (Case 1)	(4) Permanent organization

Source: Adapted from Bakker et al. (2016)

and consulting projects (see also Schoeneborn, 2013a, 2013b). To select these cases, we followed the typology of temporary forms of organization as developed by Bakker et al. (2016), who suggested to distinguish four basic archetypes of organization (see Table 3.1): the conventional permanent form of organization; a fully temporary form of organization that can be understood as "disposable"; and two forms in between that mix partially temporary and permanent aspects of organizing, i.e., the type of the "semi-temporary organization" and of the "semi-permanent organization". Semi-temporary organization is characterized as relying on permanent employment while using mainly temporary structures in differing projects. This type is represented by our case of consulting projects. Semi-permanent organization is understood as applying more permanent organizational structures while relying mostly on temporary employment practices. This type is represented by our case of film projects. Both cases therefore feature different types of temporary organizing and have accordingly different characteristics. However, both cases share a great similarity in that their temporary character disrupts the organizational decision processes at certain points in time. As we will outline in the following, this disruption creates a discontinuation of the oscillation process between closing (ordering) and opening (disordering) at some point.

Case 1: The Film Projects Case

In the context of film projects, we draw on six qualitative interviews with filmmakers who worked for several PBOs at film projects on central positions. Interviewees were selected by approaching two prominent institutions for film production-related education in Germany. These institutions suggested highly experienced filmmakers with good insights into the industry. Additionally, we draw on 79 documents from different projects, the experience of one coauthor who worked at several projects and an extensive amount of professional literature (for an overview, see Grothe-Hammer, 2015).

Film production companies are PBOs that only employ very few managerial positions permanently. They mainly coordinate film projects for which 30 people or more are employed temporarily to produce a specific movie on the basis of a preselected script within a predefined time frame. The projects and the PBO are very loosely coupled with only limited interventions by the PBO into the certain project processes:

> If you draw a line between the factual production that is only concerned with the project and the firm, which has a permanent and ongoing structure, then there is the line producer [Herstellungsleitung] as the monitoring position for the single productions. The line producer sits in the firm and "floats" above the single productions . . . and always oversees several projects simultaneously. For this very reason the line producer is not governing the daily work. There are line producers who intervene, but these are just interventions. The day-to-day business is not theirs. The day-to-day business lies with the production. And the administrative head of the production is the production manager. From this position there is an interface to the production firm.
>
> (Interview, production manager)[3]

Film production companies and their projects are usually embedded in project network organizations (Manning, 2017)—which provide a relatively stable set of relations among actors—and an organizational field in the form of a particular film production region—in this case, the German-speaking countries (Manning & Sydow, 2007). Scholars have repeatedly highlighted that it is the project-based form of film production that allows for the flexibility and innovativeness needed for producing diverse and creative content (Grothe-Hammer, 2015; Robins, 1993; Storper, 1989; Sydow & Windeler, 2004). However, one aspect typically neglected in this context is that this flexibility is crucially enabled by highly standardized—yet very complex—organizational structures within each project (Grothe-Hammer, 2015). Film projects usually feature the same types of positions (e.g., dolly grip, best boy grip, gaffer, key grip), the same strong and detailed hierarchies, the same departments, communication channels, production checklist forms and monitoring instruments (see also Ebbers & Wijnberg, 2017). In other words, the technical core of every project is highly institutionalized and therefore an instance of persistent order which serves as the basis for the needed creative disorder for producing novel content (e.g., shooting, lighting, directing and playing scenes in creative ways). Even the digitalization of film production did not lead to significant changes (Gornostaeva & Pratt, 2005). This is also the case for German film productions. As one production manager puts it: "On each set there are 10 percent differences you have to get used to. Ninety percent is the same on each set".

However, since these highly institutionalized structures are limited to certain world regions, a comparison between those regions shows that film production design can vary significantly. For example, in German film projects several positions exist that you would not find in North America—like the German "Set-Aufnahmeleiter" (Set-AL), who is an administrative leader directly at the movie set—while the position of the First Assistant Director has very different tasks and responsibilities in the different regions (cf. Gumprecht, 2002; Interviews, 1st AD; production manager). Another striking example is the nonexistence of a sound-recording department on set in many Russian film projects (Interview; representative of a large Russian film production company). Therefore, the existing structures cannot be explained by functional necessities. Instead, they have historically evolved. In Germany, the structure of the film production industry changed during the 1980s and 1990s from a studio-based system with permanent employment to a project-based system with temporary employment (Wirth, 2010). Since then, the structure of film production in Germany has looked more or less the same. Our interviewees emphasized that these structures persist because they have proven to be functioning or successful. Accordingly, over the past decades, only smaller changes have taken place, like the disappearance of some assistant positions or technical innovations:

> You have to distinguish two things. Technical innovations. These are implemented often and happily—and it happens fast. But most technical innovations you can integrate into the existing processes without significant changes. . . . Even "high definition" did not cause a significant break. . . . There are only very few things that change—that really change personnel or processes.
>
> (Interview, production manager)

However, several interviewees suggested that there have been larger attempts to change structures. One of these attempts is the import of the so-called First Assistant Director (1st AD) system from North America to Germany (see Gumprecht, 2002). While in Germany there are the positions of the 1st AD supporting exclusively the director and of the "Set-AL" supporting the production manager, in North America or the Netherlands, for instance, the 1st AD combines both functions in one role (Ebbers & Wijnberg, 2017). However, so far these attempts have not been successful.

Moreover, another interviewee mentioned several occasions in which existing structures turned out to be dysfunctional in certain projects, and a significant organizational adjustment of existing project structures between projects within a certain PBO would have been useful. Nevertheless, as our interviews indicate, the PBOs to which the projects belong were not able to vary structures between projects significantly.

For seven years now, I know that always when this director makes a movie, they need a new assistant director after two and a half weeks, because he is exhausted. . . . I say: "But you know that he always needs two assistant directors. Why don't you start with two assistant directors?" But, as I learned, they now shoot again with one assistant director. That means the same is going to happen again. They do not learn. This about constants, yeah? This is something very striking.

(Interview, 1st AD)

The interviewee also reported on another example in which she successfully changed the structure of a film project. In this case the conventional departmental structure with a distinction between the 1st AD department and the production management department was dissolved. Instead the project relied on a downscaled production department and an upscaled 1st AD department with two 1st ADs occupying the same position. As the interviewed 1st AD explained, this allowed for a greater flexibility in managing the project:

And we just got it done. So, we ordered the busses we needed, we set up tents, and in this sense we just did it. . . . Why? The production manager was of course there. . . . And she was really glad that we just assumed all this.

While according to the interviewee this project design turned out to be successful, these changes were hardly ever carried on to further film projects. As she also told us, this seems also to be true for some other instances of attempted changes.

In sum, the interviewees confirmed that the structures of film projects tend to be highly standardized and that only small changes have taken place in the last decades, if any. Moreover, despite several attempts to change structures, none of these changes were successfully transferred from one project to another. This seems even to be true on occasions in which existing structures turned out to be dysfunctional in certain projects, and a significant organizational adjustment of existing project structures would have been useful. Indeed, the PBOs and projects extensively draw on highly institutionalized practices and structures within an organizational field. However, while we are aware that in the case of film projects institutional pressures might play a significant role, we argue that the inability to learn from experiences in one project and consequently adapt structures stems from the disconnection of processes between projects. While in permanent organizations institutionalized structures can be (and often are) adapted or implemented symbolically if useful or necessary (Meyer & Rowan, 1977; Bromley & Powell, 2012), the PBO is limited in its capability of doing so. In each new project, the same order tends to be reinstantiated with only minimal variances.

From a Luhmannian standpoint, the standardized structures of film production can be seen as highly complex forms of social order. In nearly every project the same fixed meaning tends to be actualized whether it is the crew positions, the set rules or the hierarchical structure. By drawing on this order, a film project can start working instantaneously without negotiating hierarchical orders, job descriptions or working tasks. Personnel are recruited for known project positions and—as a decision premise—usually know about their basic tasks and about what is expected from them and what to expect from the others. Accordingly, in the production stage of a film project (when the actual film shooting takes place), the majority of the crew starts immediately working on day one without further introduction. They just come and start working—many even without having read the script—and leave the project with the last take.

This is possible because the project structures they are drawing on are so highly institutionalized that they are taken for granted. It follows that for the communication process of the film project the meaning of these structures is so fixed that it is only actualized implicitly. The specificities of the structures of a film project are explicated only seldomly (Windeler, 2004). Meaning is constituted by using elements of order in the communication process without reflecting explicitly on these elements—for instance, by just using the concept of the position of a dolly grip without explicating what this position should do.

As our interviewees confirmed, this order is perceived as rather "natural". In other words, the very characteristic of a decision—the implication that it could be otherwise—is not given in this respect. Hence, usually the established structures are just used as they are. Although the order of the film project is not determined, it is thereby very restricted in terms of variety—"10 percent" according to the aforementioned interviewee. Disordering in regard to these structures—e.g., the possibility of deciding to use other structures for a film project—is limited.

Indeed, the project is able to make aspects of this order a matter of decision, that is, by explicating it in communication and creating the possibility of introducing alternatives. For example, the abovementioned 1st AD reported on instances in which she successfully made some aspects of the order a matter of decision in single projects. However, at a certain point in time the project ends and with it the project structures are dissolved. For the next project, the PBO typically hires newly assembled personnel and although some of them may have worked together in previous projects the project team composition is typically different every time. The new project has a new composition of individuals serving as addresses for communication and decision processes (cf. Luhmann, 1996). Hence, decisions in the new project cannot directly connect to decisions in the previous projects, because the coupling between these projects via individuals is minimal. It follows that the new project establishes a new decision history in its own right and cannot directly build on the decision history of previous projects. As mentioned above, although the projects are part of an overarching PBO, their basic operations are highly decoupled from the PBO. Decisions for the project are made within and for the project— they are "encapsulated" there (cf. Schoeneborn, 2013b). As a result, the decision process is disrupted between the projects instead. Obviously, a decision on a change in a previous project could be thematized in communication during the new project. However, such thematizing means that a new explication would be needed to make it a new decision within the new project—which seems improbable to us, because there is still no direct connection to the decision process history that led to the decision in the earlier project.

Consequently, an oscillating flow between ordering and disordering that persists beyond a single project cannot emerge in such organizational constellations. The decision process is disrupted between the projects. However, one could object that such disconnection of processes between projects would be in this case at least partly due to the temporary employment. Therefore, in the following, we are exploring whether we can identify a similar pattern also on another type of PBO, which relies on permanent employment instead.

Case 2: The Consulting Projects Case

In a next step, we cross-compare these findings with another PBO that is located in a different industry context. This second case is a multinational consulting company with a focus on providing IT-based solutions to its clients. While this company is also organized in the form of a PBO, it can be classified as what Bakker et al. (2016) refer to as the "semi-temporary" archetype, since its structures are rather temporary even though the employment relations of consultants with the PBO are usually of a more permanent character. For this shorter, contrasting case illustration, we draw on data from 14 qualitative interviews with consultants and other members of the firm's knowledge management (KM) division— as well as from a genre analysis of 565 project documents, drawn in a randomized sampling procedure from a company-wide cross-project learning database (for more extensive descriptions of the case and the data set, see Schoeneborn, 2008, 2013a, 2013b). In the specific company we investigated, the presentation software Microsoft PowerPoint plays a pivotal role: PowerPoint was used in this PBO not only as a key tool for presenting analyses to clients but also as a means of cross-project learning. As one interviewee, a consultant, put it: "There is almost no communication among consultants that does not involve PowerPoint in some form". In the aftermath of each project, project participants were required to make summaries of past projects, typically then based on PowerPoint slide decks, and to make those available for other consultants by uploading them to the PBO's company-wide KM database. The idea of the database was that new project teams could draw on the experiences from preceding projects—in the aim to prevent "reinventing the wheel" over and over again in these new projects. However, as the study's findings showed (see also Schoeneborn, 2013a, 2013b), the vast majority of these PowerPoint documents were rather densely written (e.g., 62 percent of the PowerPoint documents in the database consisted of one slide only) and focused primarily on summarizing the final project results (97 percent). According to one interviewee, a consultant, this is due to the common practice by the consultants to upload to the KM database "only final documents, not interim documents". Moreover, only a tiny fraction of the project documents from the cross-project learning database (3 percent) was concerned with revealing to some degree the inherent contingencies of the very project processes that led to the project's final outcomes. However, as several interviews revealed, the practice of conducting such past project reflections often was sacrificed in order to keep the consultants' "billability" on a high level.

> Writing down some lessons learned documents is simply not billable for us as consultants . . . and therefore is seen [in the case firm] as a waste of time. Strictly speaking, we are supposed to be at the client's site five days per week. So it's only the idealists among the consultants that would sit down and sum up such lessons learned. . . . But this is pure extra work that takes place on a voluntary basis.
> (Interview, senior consultant)

Based on our Luhmannian framework, we concluded that the consultants' ability to treat past project results as decision premises for the future is limited, since decision communication in Luhmann's sense (2018) would require that the inherent contingency and optionality of decisions gets "visibilized", at least to some degree. In this regard, each consulting project appeared to represent an operationally "closed" decisional system in its own right (for similar findings, see Mohe & Seidl, 2011). In this sense, the KM database fulfilled the function of an "organizational memory" (see also Langenmayr, 2016) on the level of the PBO only to a very limited degree. Accordingly, the PBO featured neither the emergence of a decided order that would interconnect the various projects on a horizontal level nor did project-inherent processes usually serve as decision premises for the overarching organization, since decisions were ultimately made for the project and not for the PBO. As in the case of film projects, the projects of the consulting firm tend to draw on the same (temporary) hierarchical structures (i.e., the teams typically split into partners, project leaders and consultants) and even the same pool of personnel from the PBO. Even if there were changes in single projects, PBOs have difficulties in transferring these changes to another project (see also Mohe & Seidl, 2011). After the disbandment of one project, the next project is reborn with a "borrowed" order that stems from the PBO but only to a limited degree from prior projects, i.e., the temporary "sibling" organizations. In this regard, we find a similar pattern across both the first case, the film projects as part of semi-permanent organizations, and this second case, the consulting projects as part of semi-temporary organizations. We further elaborate on transversal insights across the two cases in our final and concluding section.

Discussion and Conclusion

In this chapter, we have looked at two different cases of partially permanent/temporary organizations. Our selected cases featured two distinctive types of organization (Bakker et al., 2016), semi-permanent organizations (film production companies) and semi-temporary organizations (consulting firms). Semi-permanent organizations are characterized by relatively permanent structures and mainly temporary forms of employment, while semi-temporary organizations are characterized by a temporariness of structures and permanent employment. Despite the differences between these two types we find striking similarities on a general theoretical level. Both cases show a disconnection of recursive chains of decisional communication between the projects. In both cases we identify the PBO's inability to treat earlier projects as decision premises for follow-up decisions in further projects, thereby interrupting the very process of interconnecting the decisional processes (of ordering and disordering) that are constitutive of the organization from a Luhmannian viewpoint. The actual organizational processes are encapsulated within each project—although in different ways. In the case of the consulting projects, processes are encapsulated because the PBO's internal KM fails to make processes from foregoing projects sufficiently visible for new projects. The processuality of decision-making was invisibilized by the PowerPoint-based practices of cross-project learning at the case firm we studied. In the case of the film projects, the processes were mainly disrupted, because individuals were only employed for single projects and therefore could not couple decision processes from one project to processes in a new one. In both cases, the PBO continues to exist *despite* a recurrent discontinuation of the decision processes that usually constitute an organization (because those decision processes are undertaken on behalf of the temporary project and not on behalf of the PBO). In other words, by treating earlier projects as *fait accompli* and thus in a too ordered way, PBOs establish an asymmetric relation between past projects (where only the ordered side is highlighted/remembered and the disordered side is invisibilized/forgotten) and future projects. Consequently, the symmetrical perpetuation between ordering and disordering through interconnected episodes of decision-making that constitutes organization can hardly occur in PBOs across projects (see Schoeneborn, 2013b) but only for the project itself (see Mohe & Seidl, 2011).

As we furthermore demonstrated, in both cases, the projects can draw on highly institutionalized structural templates. The temporary character is possible by drawing on known elements of social order that allow for setting up and disbanding projects instantaneously. In both cases, however, the projects as temporary organizations are able to (seldomly) change these institutionalized structures. They can make the used order a matter of decision thereby transferring a taken for granted structure into a process of ordering and disordering. For example, in one case a film project decided to create an assistant director department that is very different from the usually used order. In Luhmannian terms: The project is able to both fix meanings (ordering) and open up meanings (disordering) in the very instance of *making a decision*—it can transform institutionalized order into its own decisions and newly decided decision premises. However, the overarching PBO does not seem to possess this ability and changes are usually limited to single projects. Hence, for both cases, we argue that this structural invariance emerges out of the temporariness of the single projects—regardless if this temporariness comes with temporary employment or not. Because of the temporariness of the projects, the PBO loses its ability to make certain elements of social order decidable.

Although the projects produce their own decision premises, these were not treated as decision premises within the overarching PBO as such—in other words, they did not serve as premises for decisions outside the single projects. Decisions within a project organization usually did not produce decision necessities within the PBO that go beyond the project. The projects and what happened in them, including possible changes, in most cases merely appear as a *fait accompli*—and neither as something that could be done differently anymore nor as decision premises facilitating subsequent decisions in further projects (except, for instance, in rare occasions, such as our second case where consultants made the effort to create "lessons learned" documents that could be picked up and serve as a decision premise for future projects). Therefore, on the level of the PBO, the decision process is disrupted—it usually stops with each project. This explains the invariance of the project structures, which are reset by the end of every project. As a result, the institutionalized structures upon which the projects and PBOs draw are reinforced every time. They remain order that can be disordered punctually in certain projects, but not permanently on the level of PBOs or Project Network Organizations, because on this level an ongoing stream of decision-making is not maintained. Think of the aforementioned example of the film director who always needs two assistant directors. In this example, several projects had learned this characteristic and decided to hire a second assistant director after a few weeks. However, none of these projects transferred this project decision into a premise for the overarching PBO. Each new project started with one assistant director again.

Therefore, we conclude that when organizations are restricted to a temporary existence, there is a discontinuation of the oscillation process between closing and opening of meaning that is constitutive of organization. PBOs thus run the risk of becoming overly ordered while losing the ability to change most elements of order. They discard the production of decision necessities and therefore their form of social order changes from organized to non-changeable. In other words, order loses its paradoxicality and therefore its balance with disorder. While a decision implies that it is principally undecidable (see von Foerster, 1992; Derrida, 2002), because choosing one alternative always implies other alternatives, a non-changeable order is overly fixed to one meaning losing its alternativeness. Accordingly, we conclude that temporary organizations cannot deterministically influence the elements of the PBO, while PBOs have difficulties to adopt changes and learn from the temporary organizations.

Indeed, in both cases we can think of ways to connect decision processes from one project to the other. Film projects could install a pre-stage in which structures could be explicitly designed for the project and in which experiences of previous projects could be thematized.[4] Consulting projects could make decision processes further visible in cross-project learning (see Schoeneborn, 2008). Nevertheless, an attempt to change the overall order would imply to unlimit the existence of the temporary organizations—which is a contradiction in itself.

Taken together, these findings provide us with the chance of a radical reformulation of what counts as a PBO from a Luhmannian viewpoint: The PBO itself can be described as a meta-organization (see Ahrne & Brunsson, 2008), that is, an organization which has other organizations as its members. However, the PBO deviates from conventional meta-organizations in that it has other temporary organizations, i.e., the projects, as its "members". At the same time, the Luhmannian approach yields the counterintuitive insight that the (permanent) PBO and the (temporary) projects are environmental to one another. They mostly observe each other "from the outside" so to speak, but, as we have argued above, the connectivity among decisional processes between the PBO and its projects is limited. In other words, the communicative process of ordering and disordering that is constitutive of organization (Vásquez et al., 2016) is bound and encapsulated within each project, but presenting to its outside only the "ordered" side (e.g., the attempts to fix meanings through polished PowerPoint slides, as made available in the cross-project database) tends to invisibilize the "disordered" and contingent side of decisional processes that, in turn, would be required to establish such cross-connectivity.

Even if these theoretical considerations may sound highly abstract on first sight (and by mobilizing Luhmann's theoretical vocabulary we certainly run that risk), they nevertheless yield rather concrete implica-tions. If the PBO, its projects and also the projects among each other are appropriately described as forming mutual environments, this view can provide an integrated theoretical explanation for why efforts of cross-project learning tend to fail (see Currie & Kerrin, 2004; Newell, Bresnen, Edelman, Scarbrough & Swan, 2006), why organizations exhibit diffi-culties to learn from their "own" past projects (Swan et al., 2010), and why consulting projects are limited in "transferring" knowledge to the client (see Mohe & Seidl, 2011). Furthermore, the Luhmannian approach offers a new vocabulary to account for PBOs as a particular "species" of organization. The PBO can be described here as a rather rudimentary and "stripped-down" exemplar of a (meta-)organization that lives "on the backs" of its own creations, so to speak. This allows us to return to our initial metaphor of the PBO as a "honeybee queen". Metaphorically speaking, the "honeybee queen" (i.e., the PBO) recurrently lays eggs and gives birth to multiple worker bees (i.e., the projects as separate temporary organizations). However, it is characteristic for the PBO queen bee that she outlives her own children, while the children's current and past lives are constitutive for her own existence. This metaphorical view of PBOs as "beehive" rather than an organization in the classical, formal sense can pave the way for reconsidering PBOs based on a relational ontology (see also Kuhn, Ashcraft & Cooren, 2017) and to account for different degrees of "(dis)organizationality" (cf. Dobusch & Schoeneborn, 2015; Schoeneborn & Dobusch, In press; Schoeneborn, Kuhn & Kärreman, In press) that are accomplished in relational-temporary rather than entita-tive-permanent constellations.

Notes

1. Luhmann (2018) builds his theory on the works of Spencer Brown (1972), who pointed out that the categories of internal and external are the product of a prior structuring process that implies that the one can only exist in reference to the other. For example, there can only be a "nothing" if we can distinguish it from a "something". In this respect he also builds on Derrida (although admit-ting that his reading of Derrida would probably have been unacceptable for Derrida himself) by emphasizing that the excluded is always taken into account by the internal: "Whatever is excluded is treated as present simply by the fact that it is excluded" (Luhmann, 2013, p. 195). Note also the similarities here to the work of Alfred North Whitehead, as elaborated by Tor Hernes (2008).
2. One further reaching implication of Luhmann's insistence on communication as *the* constitutive element of all social entities (or "social systems" in his termi-nology) is that human individuals are not considered as being an integral part of these systems (e.g., an organization). Instead, human individuals contribute to the very communication processes that constitute an organization as part of their environment. This decentering of the human agent in how the social world comes into being implies a particular form of nonhuman agency, even if not in a Latourian sense. For Luhmann, the communication process itself is an "animal" in its own right that is nearly impossible to control from the

outside, i.e., even for the human individuals that actively partake in it (see also Schoeneborn, 2011).

3. In most cases, our interview excerpts were translated from German.
4. One might think that permanent employment could be an option, too, for ensuring the connectivity between projects. If personnel are employed permanently, they would presumably be able to couple previous decision processes to new decision processes—as members of the PBO and not only of one project. However, the historical development shows that permanent employment leads to restrictions in producing creative and novel content (see Robins, 1993). In other words, permanent employment seems to hamper disorder in respect to the creative part of a film production, which seems to be a main reason for the historical change from permanent to temporary employment.

4 Rethinking Order and Disorder

Accounting for Disequilibrium in Knotted Systems of Paradoxical Tensions[1]

Gail T. Fairhurst and Mathew L. Sheep

On December 15, 2015, the New York City and Los Angeles school systems, the two biggest in the United States, each received a largely identical terrorist threat routed through the same server in Frankfurt, Germany. NYC reviewed the warning and dismissed it as a hoax. On the heels of the 2015 San Bernardino terrorist attack that killed 14 and injured 22, LA officials closed their 1,100 schools. They forced the district's 640,000 students home for the day, and only later did they arrive at the conclusion that it was likely a ruse (Nagourney, Perez-Pena & Goodman, 2015). While we do not know what happened behind the scenes, evidence suggests that the school administrations constructed the problem in different terms.[2]

The actual problem setting was likely marked by a topic we explore in this chapter, knotted tensions, which school officials would *make relevant* and potentially *related* in their conversational attempts to define the situation. More specifically, Schön (1983, p. 40) defines *problem setting* as "a process in which, interactively, we name the things to which we will attend and frame the context in which we will attend to them". Obviously, there would have been concerns, not only for student safety (suggestive of an experienced tension between safe vs. unsafe, along which people would locate and position themselves), but also for the economics of a shutdown (high cost vs. low cost). Issues would also arise regarding the adequacy of the risk management systems (risk averse vs. risk taking), logistical planning (strong vs. weak logistical shutdown plans) and anticipated reactions of the community (convenient vs. inconvenient; critical vs. praiseworthy), among others.

Delving further, a typical LA school official might have said something like the following, which we amend slightly to reflect the tensions and their emphases:

> Of course, student safety is paramount (**safe**–unsafe), especially after the recent San Bernardino terrorist attack (**past**–future). That's uppermost in everyone's minds, but it's really a case of "damned if you do, damned if you don't", isn't it? Consider the tremendous cost associated with a shutdown (**high**–low)—and possible unforeseen planning issues (predictable–**unpredictable**). It's not like we have the

routine snow days of the Midwest or East Coast. So this is very risky for us (**risk averse**–risk taking). Plus, can you imagine the second-guessing if this turns out to be a hoax? (**criticism**–praise).[3]

The formulations of complex problems involving multiple tensions are a major touchstone for this chapter because they suggest a paradox lens. *Paradox* refers to "contradictory yet interrelated elements—elements that seem logical in isolation but absurd and irrational when appearing simultaneously" (Lewis, 2000, p. 760). Typically, these "elements" are organizational *tensions*, "ubiquitous and persistent forces that challenge and fuel long-term success" (Lewis & Smith, 2014, p. 3).[4] This line of research is usually focused on categorizing *individual* tensions and their management strategies (Putnam, Fairhurst & Banghart, 2016). Yet, there is still much to learn, especially regarding the ways that multiple tensions interact with one another, much as the problem setting over school safety indicates.

In this chapter, we discuss how actors' construction of interweaving multiple paradoxical tensions produce *tensional knots*, based on our earlier work of actors' problem setting discourse in an innovation setting (Sheep, Fairhurst & Khazanchi, 2017). We discuss tensional knots as a source of disorder in organizations and show how the *marriage of order and disorder* is really the crux of a paradox lens. Finally, we extend and rethink one of the crucial elements of paradox—that of *dynamic equilibrium* (Sheremata, 2000). Dynamic equilibrium is a motor for organizational sustainability, where cyclical responses to paradoxical tensions coalesce to create peak performance (Smith & Lewis, 2011). In the setting of tensional knots, however, dynamic equilibrium manifests itself in a balance or trade-off among opposing forces operating in the moment. However, in such problem setting, opposed forces are *not* necessarily equal in magnitude, but can more often be pulled out of balance in one direction or another. For the organizational actors involved, these situations can be particularly difficult to manage, as their problem setting often justifies inaction or incorrect ways of responding. Thus, we extend findings from our previous empirical research (Sheep & Fairhurst, 2015; 2016; Sheep et al., 2017) to propose a more precise distinction between the concepts of dynamic equilibrium and disequilibrium. We further illustrate the propositions that our discussion generates with the above case study and others from the literature, and we conclude with the implications for future research and praxis.

Theoretical Background

Tensional Knots: Investigating Multiple Paradoxical Tensions Simultaneously

The role of organizational tensions in actors' sensemaking and coping are forcing analysts to reexamine their assumptions and approaches to them (e.g., Jarzabkowski, Lê & Van de Ven, 2013; Norton & Sadler,

2006). One recent effort to address multiple tensions involves the study of tensional knots by Sheep et al. (2017). *Tensional knots* involve actors' *simultaneous* construction of interweaving multiple tensions in problem setting formulations (Schön, 1983), thus distinguishing itself from the single tension empirical focus of most paradox research. While most analysts concern themselves with multiple tensions conceptually, they rarely do so empirically.

Were analysts to refrain from singling tensions out or, at least, if they would empirically verify that actors are exerting reductive tendencies, they would discover in actors' discourse an interweaving of multiple tensions as they narrate (and attempt to navigate) complex environments. The example at the start of this chapter mirrors what others and we have found in different contexts (Baxter, 2011; Norton & Sadler, 2006; Sacks, 1992). More specifically, Sheep et al. (2017) studied innovation and constraint in the context of a corporate spin-off in the print industry undergoing radical changes. In so doing, they introduced an extended approach to studying paradoxical tensions by focusing on actors' discursive problematizing of multiple simultaneous and interacting tensions, in short, a *discursive* lens to paradoxical tensions. Treated in this manner, knots delve deeply into actors' sensemaking formulations, articulated in communication and through their discourse—and thus the ways that actors may talk their paradoxical circumstances into being (Poole, 2013).

The analysis of knots in the Sheep et al. (2017) study also showed how multiple tensions can interact in *prismatic* ways, i.e., how tensions amplify one another, or in *anti-prismatic* ways, i.e., how tensions attenuate one another. Their research established the implications for individual innovative (in)action, depending on how the actor constructed the knot—with mutually amplifying (i.e., prismatic) tensions leading to pessimistic justifications of inaction or paralysis, or with mutually attenuating (anti-prismatic) tensions leading to optimistic justifications for innovative action. In the latter condition of an anti-prismatic knot, it is not that the tensions themselves or their complexity are unobservable in the discourse, but the ways in which they are managed in discourse (and with what effects) are differently constructed.

Where Do Paradoxical Tensions (Singular or Knotted) Reside?

The construction of tensional knots surfaces a key question already raised in the paradox literature: *Where do paradoxical tensions reside?* The answer to this question represents the beginnings of a theoretical framework for the study of tensional knots. In particular, Smith and Lewis (2011), among others, locate organizational tensions either in the external environment or in cognition, while Sheep et al. (2017) add discourse as a third, heretofore underdeveloped, lens that can inform and be informed by the other two. All three are interrelated, but their approaches to paradox vary.

Crucially, each of the three lenses (environmental, cognitive and discursive) works with the *marriage of order and disorder*, the crux of a paradox lens, in somewhat different ways. For example, analysts who use an environmental lens, or a combination of an environmental lens with a cognitive lens, capture disorder through vicious cycles of undesirable, repetitive and confounding behaviors (e.g., Lewis, 2000; Smith & Lewis, 2011). An example of a vicious cycle might be the NYC or LA school system that professes concern for student safety, but leaders frame the problem as an either-or choice between safety and resource constraints. Therefore, with each budget cycle, the system leaves itself vulnerable to outside attacks because funds are tight. It thus creates a sustained cycle of non-action and weak justification. The path to restoring order, i.e., moving from vicious to virtuous cycles, lies in *paradoxical thinking* in which a "both/and" orientation that addresses opposing poles in some fashion (e.g., exploring cost-effective ways to prepare for terrorist attacks) surpasses an "either/or" approach (Smith & Lewis, 2011).

A discursive lens gives us two different ways to capture order and disorder. For example, Vásquez et al. (2016) argue that order results from discourse that is relatively fixed in meaning vis-à-vis a unitary or single privileged account, while disorder stems from discourse that is open to multiple interpretations that can become contested/competing versions of reality. Acknowledging Vásquez et al., Sheep et al. (2017) also locate order and disorder in the number of intersecting tensions in tensional knots and, within the tensions themselves, the relative weighting of one pole over another as constructed in actors' discourse. By focusing on the system of tensions and their potential effects on one another, not to mention their open interpretability, tensional knots can inform us about equilibrium and disequilibrium in paradox.

To be clear, a discourse lens examines how organizational members both enact and respond to tensions in and through language and communication (Putnam et al., 2016). While knotting evidences itself in actors' problem setting discourse in which they name multiple and intertwined tensions, analysts are often able to piece together knots in the face of actors' sensemaking accounts that may be fragmented, lacking or incomplete (Fairhurst & Sheep, In press; Fairhurst & Putnam, 2018; Norton & Sadler, 2006). By implication, analysts can study (dis)order and (dis)equilibrium, especially when they have converging pieces of evidence garnered through ethnographic observation, archival data, textual analyses and so on.

Dynamic Equilibrium and Sources of Disequilibrium in Tensional Knots

Smith and Lewis (2011, p. 386) characterized paradox as a *dynamic equilibrium*, metaphorically represented from biology by cellular "homeostasis", and defined by Sheremata (2000, p. 390; cf. Andriopoulos & Lewis, 2009) as "forces (that) are equal in magnitude but opposite in direction". Although Smith and Lewis (2011, p. 386) added that dynamic equilibrium presupposes "constant motion across opposing forces", the idea of dynamism nevertheless assumes that equilibrium is maintained overall, and does not account for conditions of *disequilibrium* that would indicate that opposed forces are *not* necessarily equal in magnitude but can more often be pulled out of balance in one direction or another. Specifically, and as analyzed in the prismatic effects of actor problem setting (Kreiner, Hollensbe, Sheep, Smith & Kataria, 2015; Sheep et al., 2017), the poles of paradoxical tensions are not constructed as equal in magnitude or in "balance and equilibrium" (Sheremata, 2000, p. 391), even if in constant motion. There may be forces of order *and* disorder acting upon a system of tensions to weight one pole over another, which impacts other tensions differentially to move the system toward equilibrium or disequilibrium.

In the NYC and LA school system example, forces for order would consist of specific and standardized training protocols (a **planned–unplanned** tension) that administrations could introduce as they partner with police and fire authorities for a rapid response. Forces for disorder, however, might entail a recent (**past–present** tension), heightened (**specific–nonspecific** tension) threat like the knowledge that terrorists were targeting school systems or local colleges, as was discovered for LA with the San Bernardino attack. However, we could also envision a cost (**effective–ineffective**) tension as a source of disorder, impeding the extent and nature of the planning to mitigate the threat.

In dynamic equilibrium, we can account for a mechanism by which opposite poles of a paradoxical tension can be managed indefinitely without necessary resolution. In disequilibrium, we can account not only for the persistence and non-resolution of the tension, but also the question of "how much?" of one pole vis-à-vis the other—a matter of comparative degree of tension push-pull between poles, in which poles are rarely, if ever, discursively in balance or are equally privileged. Such imbalance may be having an effect on the other tensions in ways that tighten or loosen the knot.

However, none of this implies that disequilibrium negates the simultaneity of management of the poles of a tension, or their persistence. Again, from a discursive perspective, we emphasize that attributions of (dis)equilibrium are made relevant in and accomplished through problem setting discourse. For example, in their ten-year-long study of the Episcopal Church during organizational identity-related transitions, Kreiner et al. (2015, p. 994) found that:

> identity dualities/contradictions may be held indefinitely in the tensions that produce the push-pull "stretch" accomplished in members'

organizational identity work. The persistent—yet unbalanced and unequal—stretch and contraction of these tensional dualities constituted what we observed in our data as identity elasticity. . . . In the dynamics of identity elasticity, stability is only *momentary and fleeting*, at best. Rather, disequilibrium must be attended to creatively in an ongoing tension (without necessarily being synthesized or resolved) if the organization is to survive intact as a whole.

While the Kreiner et al. study finds a prevalence of disequilibrium in identity tensions, we do not claim that all discourse would be directed toward constructions of disequilibrium. There are discourses in which actors move a "version of reality" toward equilibrium, and there are competing versions in which actors would move it toward disequilibrium. *Thus, we seek to know what a discursive view of paradoxical tensions would look like whose goal did not assume or press for equilibrium (even if dynamic) or stable order, but also would account for ongoing disequilibrium in and among tensional knots.* Moreover, we are interested in the sources of disequilibrium, not just as caused in a single tension as if it existed apart from other tensions. Rather, we identify interrelated tensions that are difficult to untangle as tensional *knots*, as in the school safety example in which a safe–unsafe tension might be exacerbated by other tensions, such as cost effective–**ineffective**, the extent of the planning (planned–**unplanned**), threat specificity (**specific**–ambiguous) and so on. Tensions can perturb and produce increased disequilibrium among each other, thus having systemic effects in a knot of tensions as actors variously construct the qualitative relationships among those tensions. In the next section, we explicate these ideas further in terms of sources of disequilibrium.

(Dis)Order: Dynamic Disequilibrium in Knots Through Contested Versions of "Reality"

How do questions of (dis)equilibrium relate to questions of (dis)order? If we follow one communicative perspective of (dis)order, then order results from discourse that is relatively fixed in meaning vis-à-vis a unitary or single privileged account, while disorder stems from discourse that is open to multiple interpretations that can become contested/competing versions of "reality" (Vásquez et al., 2016).

In terms of what Sheep et al. (2017) call tensional knots, analyzed through a discursive lens, contested versions of reality involve actors' constructions of which tensions impact other tensions in prismatic or anti-prismatic ways. Importantly, these accounts can vary widely from actor to actor. For example, interviewees in the sample of Sheep et al.'s study variously constructed some of the same tensions (e.g., culture of risk versus efficiency, creativity versus constraint, mechanistic versus organic) in interdependently entangled ways (knots). Others constructed them as relatively independent or singular. Even if considering only those constructions that are knot-like, some interviewees managed those tensions very differently. As indicated above, some applied either-or choices and double binds that produced negative (pessimistic) discursive transformations, justifying a course of inaction or paralysis. However, others who managed those *same tensions* applying a more ambidextrous approach produced positive (optimistic) discursive transformations justifying innovative action. The underlying discursive mechanisms for the former transformation involved actors constructing the entwined tensions as having mutually amplifying (prismatic) impacts on one another to increase disorder/disequilibrium. In contrast, the latter transformation involved actors constructing the entwined tensions as having attenuating (anti-prismatic) effects on one another, thereby reducing disorder/disequilibrium overall among the interdependent system of tensions.

Thus, what counts as the "real" explanation for "the situation here and now" (or as the legitimated version of reality) is very differently constructed by different actors, even though they are naming and describing some of the very same tensions in their talk. These divergent versions of reality then often *generate new tensions* that entangle with the ones that produced them—between a positive versus negative transformation of discourse, between justifications for action versus inaction. In short, *multiple versions of tensional knots, reflected in communication and through discourse*, produce disorder, but so does the *addition of new tensions*. For example, knots surrounding school safety issues in LA might have seen additional tensions added to them through heightened emotional (**emotion**–reason) constructions of the knot, due to the San Bernardino attack, or the weak (**low**–high) credibility assessments of school administrations. Moreover, all may not construct these tensions as equally relevant or as having the same relationships to one another.

In embracing multiple over unitary readings of tensional constructions, we also gain an understanding of just how unsettled and contested both individual and knotted paradoxical tensions can become. Taken collectively, they can produce a state of wildly unbalanced pushes and pulls both within and between tensions. Divergently constructed versions of organizational reality (whether it be identity-related tensions, paradoxes of innovation or other contexts) reveal an ongoing discursive struggle among organizational actors to include and contain, while *simultaneously* to predominate and contest, the varying ways in which paradoxical tensions are being constructed for the organization. The persistent—yet *unbalanced* and *unequal*—stretch and contraction of the *system* of tensional dualities constitute *dynamic disequilibrium*.

But how, precisely, are stretch and contraction epistemologically knowable or observable in discourse? As actors individually construct tensional knots, they name multiple tensions, position them in terms of relevance or importance and designate moderating roles. For "unbalanced and unequal" to happen in a tensional knot, one tension (more specifically, one of its poles) needs to be undiminished or increased in intensity concurrently with other tension(s) being constructed as increasing or more central. The whole of the system of tensions, as constructed by multiple actors, reaches a more unstable state the more that they cannot be "balanced" by trade-offs (e.g., some other tensions becoming reduced or less relevant).

In the school safety example, consider the threat of successive attacks on school systems in NY or LA communities whose external support systems (e.g., police, fire) are weak or unreliable. The safe–unsafe tension, exacerbated by school systems that lack the budgets (cost effective–**ineffective**) for planning (planned–**unplanned**), cannot be offset by community support services that would make up for school system inefficiencies, thus creating a state of disequilibrium among the tensions.

Recall, however, that the intertwined, multiple tensions we call "knots" are not only in a dynamic interplay *within themselves* but also *between themselves*, being marked by uneven and unsettled pushes and pulls caused by competing discursive constructions and the struggles that ensue. These multivocal renderings or "versions of reality" set forth by different individuals or groups produce not simple dichotomies but varying continua of positions (addressing the question of "how much?", i.e., location along the continuum of a tension or tensions) among different actors. The more divergent or polarized the positions that have to be negotiated among contested versions of reality in the system, as well as the greater the number of intersecting tensions, the more likely that conditions are created that could only be described as "far from equilibrium" (as in complexity theory—see below) (e.g., McKelvey, 1999; Plowman et al., 2007, p. 343).[5]

Speaking in terms of paradox, varying discursive constructions by actors, individually or collectively, can elevate the emphasis of order over disorder, such as in "trade-off talk". Discourse can also be directed at a more paradoxical view that understands order as continually emerging from disorder (or vice versa) in a "marriage of order and disorder", in which there are (potentially unequal) discursive forces for both. Thus, increasing disorder (competing, contested meaning and/or increased numbers of tensions) is seen to increase disequilibrium, as competing views on tensional constructions and their relationships defy a consensus on how tensions should be viewed or managed. Thus, we propose two sources of increasing disequilibrium in knots:

Proposition 1: As competing versions (constructions) of tensional knots diverge rather than converge, disequilibrium both within and between paradoxical tensions in a knot increases.

>   *Proposition 2: As competing versions (constructions) of tensional knots increase in number of tensions, disequilibrium both within and between paradoxical tensions in a knot increases.*

However, is increasing disequilibrium necessarily to be viewed as a negative condition to be avoided? We address this issue in the next section, which is also our third proposed source of disequilibrium in tensions—systemic effects.

Dynamic Disequilibrium Through Systemic Effects in Tensional Knots

In this section, we apply a systems perspective of complexity theory (e.g., McKelvey, 1999) in order to better understand tensions in their co-occurrence, interdependence and *unsettling effects* on one another, to produce tensional systems marked by disequilibrium. We have proposed above that a balanced equilibrium in paradoxical tensions is likely to be momentary and fleeting (in individual and collective discourses) when analyzing simultaneous, interrelated tensions that we call knots. As such, uneven forces, or disequilibrium, must be attended to creatively if the knot is to be managed with beneficial outcomes.

A somewhat loosely conceived analogy here might be the swing of the pendulum (a mechanical system). In one sense, if one looks only at the potential (or kinetic) energy in the system, then only when the pendulum is at its midpoint can it be said to be in a state of equilibrium, where potential energy to disrupt equilibrium is zero at that point on the arc. However, the force of kinetic energy (and momentum) carries it immediately to another state of unequal magnitude of forces—disequilibrium—as "potential energy" increases as the pendulum moves further toward its limits. Similarly, rather than equilibrium being punctuated by moments of disequilibrium and change (e.g., Romanelli & Tushman, 1994), we propose that in systems of tensional knots, disequilibrium can be the norm (but without the predictable periodicity of pendulums because communication is involved), punctuated only by brief, if not illusory, occurrences of equilibrium.

"Without the periodicity of pendulums" suggests yet another way to look at the analogy. That is, a pendulum can be viewed as in dynamic *equilibrium* if one looks only at the *total* of potential and kinetic energy in the system. The total is conserved, remaining constant—as one increases, the other is proportionally decreased, as the pendulum swings—as long as there are no further perturbations of the system. However, the analogy breaks down if one could continually increase or decrease the arc (degree of swing) of the pendulum. In that case, it would be continually necessary to increase (or decrease) potential energy *disproportionately* with kinetic energy, and we would characterize that system as in disequilibrium.[6] In other words, if the limits of the arc (or system) are being stretched (or contracted) continually, then disequilibrium is necessary to accomplish that boundary change.

Thus, we propose that knotted tensions can be both *indicative of* and *productive of* the uneven forces of disequilibrium—especially when a tensional knot is viewed as an interdependent, mutually amplifying or attenuating system of tensions. We can theorize such a system as multiple actors variously constructing interdependent relationships among tensions in and through their discourse as competing versions of reality. Such a perspective accounts for the agency of individuals in purposefully asserting their (sometimes competing) versions of reality in everyday discourse through naming tensional constraints. *We thus advance our understanding of "knots" as interdependently connected (mutually affecting or generative) systems of entangled tensions, given substance through communicative processes.*

When we conceive of a knot as a system of interdependent paradoxical tensions that may be close to or "far from" equilibrium as constructed variously in and through discourse, a useful theoretical frame becomes that of *complexity theory* (e.g., Dawkins & Barker, 2018; McKelvey, 1999; Plowman et al., 2007), in which "far from equilibrium" describes a system in which even small perturbations can cause large effects (whether ordering or disordering). The (dis)ordering is not an objective reality, but a discursive construction that can vary considerably in the way the "system" of tensions is intertwined, and in whether such relationships among tensions increase equilibrium or disequilibrium (through prismatic or anti-prismatic effects; cf. Sheep et al., 2017). By way of example, consider the contagion effects of one or two influential NYC or LA school administrators who are optimistic about their ability to confront school safety threats (Barsade, 2002). However, if such optimism spreads too much, it could lead to complacency and inertia (Weick, Sutcliffe & Obstfeld, 1999).

Therefore, we maintain that it is problematic to assume that disequilibrium *should be* reduced for improved outcomes. Newtonian or traditional management principles have long been premised on a teleological equilibrium and order (seeking simplicity rather than complexity). For example, while arguing for the advantages of accepting the complexity of the wholeness of a system, Wheatley (1999, p. 13) writes of the "order we crave" as individuals in organizations. Weick (1979) writes of reducing the equivocality of meaning (thus increasing the order) within a system. By contrast, the findings of Vásquez et al. (2016) suggest that increased *disordering* may have the more beneficial results for organizations. Moreover, increased *disequilibrium* as it relates to the disorder can be beneficial in its outcomes, as reflected by Margaret Wheatley (1999, p. 7) that "disorder can be a source of new order, and . . . growth appears from disequilibrium, not balance".[7]

Such reasoning raises a crucial debate in the literature regarding assumptions about the effects of disordering and disequilibrium in the discursive aims of individual actors, i.e., whether order or disorder, equilibrium or disequilibrium, ought to be viewed as the *favored* strategic aim of paradox. Whatever the "ought", we still must deal with the "is". As Sheep et al. (2017) found, when viewed systemically, individual actors can discursively interweave multiple paradoxical tensions such that tensions are overlapping and mutually impactful with each other as well as generative of new tensions. When one tension is made worse by the presence of a related tension, or produced by another tension or knot of tensions, then equilibrium of tensional "forces"[8] within the system becomes only a fleeting possibility. Disequilibrium, both within single tensions and systems of tensions (knots), increases as a result of the complexity of tensions—with individual actors not knowing which to attend to first, or how to approach all of them at once. Thus, we propose:

> *Proposition 3: When multiple actors construct tensional knots as prismatic (amplifying) rather than anti-prismatic (attenuating), disequilibrium both within and between paradoxical tensions in knots increases, also increasing the complexity of managing the "system" of knotted tensions simultaneously.*

Dynamic Disequilibrium and System Elasticity

The crucial aspect of understanding how disequilibrium can nevertheless be accommodated beneficially is that of the system's "elasticity" (Kreiner et al., 2015). As actors construct multiple tensions as knotted, do they also construct a boundary or limit to the degree of disequilibrium that the tensional knot can withstand—and still retain the systemic unity or "integrity" of the organization itself without its fragmenting into multiple and relatively independent subsystems? Such limits can be heard when actors invoke categories in their talk that they will "stretch" (in terms of category features) in order to include a new member of a category, or they will restrict such features to ensure that a member does not qualify for that category (Jayyusi, 1984; Sacks, 1992). Such category work constructs the extent of "elasticity" in their version of the knotted system of tensions because such tensions are always premised on categories of "this versus that", or as a category versus its opposite.

For example, in the Kreiner et al. (2015) study, organizational identity was theorized as a set of six tensions such as embracing vs. eschewing external trends and problematizing vs. normalizing internal identity controversies. Constructions of how one interlinked these internal and external tensions, and how far they could be "stretched" without fragmenting the organization, determined the degree of elasticity. Put more generally, how much can a system (or knot) be "stretched" as a result of disordering and disequilibrium-producing (unbalanced and uneven) forces without resulting in fragmentation and dissolution, i.e., a "giving up", if you will, of trying to manage the knotted system of tensions any longer?

Crucial to understanding the limits of disequilibrium is that it is *not a zero-sum game*, as would ultimately be an assumption of dynamic equilibrium. For example, to explain the notion of dynamic equilibrium, Smith and Lewis (2011, p. 386) usefully apply an analogy from biology—that of a cell membrane. As they put it:

> In biological terms, cells achieve a dynamic equilibrium state of homeostasis when molecules flow in and out of the cell at an equal rate. . . . In a dynamic organizational system the role of leadership is to support opposing forces and harness the constant tension between them, enabling the system to not only survive but continuously improve.

In this analogy, the cell illustrates "a dynamic equilibrium state of homeostasis when molecules flow in and out of the cell at an equal rate" (Smith & Lewis, 2011, p. 386). That is, if something flows in, something else must flow out (zero-sum) so that equilibrium is maintained, even though liquid is continually flowing in and out (constant motion).

Dynamic equilibrium necessarily assumes that pressure within the cell membrane must remain equal to that outside of the membrane in order for its boundaries to remain intact. However, what about the possibility that the membrane's boundaries might actually be elastic (changeable, stretchable)? *Only disequilibrium would then account for any stretch or elasticity* of the cellular membrane—allowing for that membrane to expand to a certain point—requiring unequal forces to act on it. Volume of materials flowing out would *not* have to equal materials flowing in (non-zero sum), but outward flow could actually remain steady while inward flow *increased*, thus expanding the membrane's boundary (if its elasticity could accommodate an uneven flow). Moreover, there is no necessary resolution in which the system would need to return to an equilibrium state, but could remain "stretched" indefinitely, perhaps even to expand further if additional elasticity was then possible.

Thus, how a non-zero-sum process occurs in a system without fragmenting or dissolving it is again made comprehensible by the notion of *system elasticity* and how the degree of elasticity is constituted in actors' discourse. That is, just because one pole (or set of poles in a tensional knot) may have greater momentary "pull" than the opposite(s), it does not necessarily mean that there is any less "pull" from the opposite pole. In the Kreiner et al. (2015) study of organizational identity work in the Episcopal Church, just because some members emphasized a need for greater inclusiveness or expansion of identity, it was not necessarily constructed *at the expense of* a more restrictive (e.g., scriptural, authoritative) orthodoxy. Many interviewees in that study voiced that it is *possible to expand both*, or at least to increase one without decreasing the other.

In terms of more commonly researched paradoxes such as that of exploration versus exploitation (e.g., Andriopoulos & Lewis, 2009), an elastic approach would assume that these may be expanded simultaneously (resulting in disequilibrium and expansion), or that one pole (e.g., exploration) might be expanded without reducing the other (e.g., exploitation). Elasticity would be indicated to the extent that organizational members can discursively pull off this "version of reality".

Organizations may produce disequilibrium in service to "new normals" that presumably preserve elastic choices. In the school safety scenario, for instance, NYC and LA community partners like police and fire-fighting units might schedule regular readiness tests (e.g., mock drills) for school systems under their jurisdiction to expand the elasticity of the system. That is, schools do not typically consider themselves to be high reliability organizations (HROs), but could (elastically) adopt such a stance for safety issues precisely because they require coordination with other HRO organizations like police and fire units whose mission it is to train through (disequilibrium) testing. Again, this would be manifest discursively in the category work of actors as they begin to describe their schools in HRO-like terms (e.g., "mission-talk", concerns expressed for reliable performances through a preoccupation with failure or reluctance to simplify complex contingencies, and so on [Weick et al., 1999]).

To summarize, unequal forces *expand* the boundaries of what is constructed as possible by exerting uneven "pulls" on the system (stretching its boundaries). *Put simply, zero-sum equilibrium (where emphasis on one pole presumes a balancing de-emphasis on the other to maintain overall equilibrium of the system) cannot "expand the pie", whereas disequilibrium does exactly that.* Thus, regarding knots, how much can the prismatic interaction of tensions produce exacerbating or perturbing effects on one another (thus expanding the tensional forces both within and between tensions in the knot in a non-zero-sum game), without causing such a "far from equilibrium" state of affairs that it is destructive of the individual and organizational endeavors that the knot constrains?

As McKelvey (1999) found, there can be a point reached that becomes "catastrophic" due to *too much* interdependent complexity within a system (as constructed by individual actors), or extending *too far* beyond an equilibrium condition. The system can become treated as fully chaotic rather than at the "edge of chaos" where self-organizing structures can emerge. Actors' discourse will reveal the extent of systemic elasticity and thus the boundary conditions for what might constitute *too much* or *too far* (Kreiner et al., 2015).[9] Indeed, McKelvey's (1999) work supports "optimum levels of complexity" (meaning that there can be too little or too much) that account for systemic viability and adaptability.

Additionally, optimal complexity is evidence that an optimal level of disequilibrium can be accommodated and contained within a system beneficially and without resulting in its fragmentation or dissolution as a system. In complexity theory, disequilibrium is brought about by energy *differentials* (in the case of paradox, ostensibly opposing "forces") that must be contained or dissipated (in how they are managed) in order for the system to remain whole. In more specific terms, what is the configuration of tensional poles? When poles are held in tension indefinitely, they exist in a both-and fashion (e.g., change and stability co-occur in both productive and potentially unproductive ways). When poles *dissipate*, they have been integrated or transcended in some way (e.g., the more things change, the more things remain the same). When poles *fragment*, one has been selected over another (e.g., stability over change). System elasticity marks the boundary of these outcomes. Thus,

> *Proposition 4: Actors construct system elasticity as the boundary at which disequilibrium of opposing forces within a tensional knot can be held in tension indefinitely (in an unresolved, both-and approach), dissipated (resolved in an integrative, synthetic approach) or result in systemic fragmentation (resolved in an either-or choice or mandate).*

Forces Impacting Constructions of (Dis)Equilibrium

Thus far, we have tried to advance an understanding of "knots" as interdependently connected (mutually affecting or generative) systems of intertwined tensions, given substance in and through communicative processes such as problem setting. To operationalize this stance in the NYC and LA school safety example, we would ideally like to have observed and interviewed relevant personnel and conditions in both school systems, for example, to understand 1) various tensions and if actors view them differently, 2) how tensions intersected in NYC versus LA, 3) whether different kinds of knots formed based on the power of one (or more) tensions to exacerbate or diminish others, 4) whether specific formulations added more tensions to the knots, 5) whether school systems differed in terms of how they were addressed (i.e., shutdown or not) based on the elasticity of tensional categories, 6) how much consensus or dissensus existed within and between school administrations and 7) how the above combination of factors was used to justify (in)action.

Such problem setting would likely generate a wide variety of forces impacting the construction of (dis)equilibrium. For example, consider contextual issues such as the perceived *specificity* versus *ambiguity* of the threat, which would heighten the threat–safety tension because specific threats tend to be seen as more credible. The nature of the planning, such as *generalized* best practices (versus *localized* community-dependent plans), could impose a certain level of order via uniformity, although best practices could be overstated in their efficacy across contexts.

Time can be a construction and a constraint on other tensions, not simply a linear variable. The passing of time is essential for the concept of equilibrium to make any sense because "equilibrium represents a dynamic 'state' and not a static position" (Ciote, 2012, p. 462). However, equilibrium is only possible when actions are coherent within the same plan of action. Equilibrium could easily shift to disequilibrium through "any change in the relevant knowledge of an individual" that resulted in that individual changing a course of action over time (Ciote, 2012, p. 462).[10] A prevalent time tension might thus be voiced in the opposed ordering of whether to *assess* the threat first or to *act* first, to impact the potential outcome of threat. *Severe* time constraints (vs. *lax* ones) could exacerbate other tensions, e.g., the best ways to train crisis teams or action that must be specifically timed. Likewise, issues of temporal legitimacy and power also often intersect, such as when the *past* is used to legitimate the status quo, while the promise of the *future* is used to legitimate change.

Important questions to address vis-à-vis power relations are: Who gets to set the context? Whose interests are privileged, and why? Power relationships would become apparent in the problem setting of contextual parameters as either relevant or irrelevant to the threat at hand. In our school safety example, parents, the public, superintendents, school boards and the media set up a tension between *internal* and *external* stakeholders impacting such momentous decisions as to whether or not to arm teachers. School leaders could deploy both power and persuasion to reduce disequilibrium in the search for equilibrium through one or more forms of discursive closure (*open-closed* meaning), defined as interaction that reduces the possibilities of genuine conversation and suppresses conflict (Deetz, 1992). Although it is typically a form of systematically distorted communication in which those with power suppress dissent (Deetz, 1992), the means by which it may do so is to reduce complexity or, in our terms, untie the knot (of tensions). For example, *disqualification* occurs when not everybody has an equal say (e.g., the school board's voice is privileged over parents); *naturalization* occurs when things are made to appear as "that's just the way it is" (e.g., "That has always been school policy"); *neutralization* occurs when biased information is made to appear objective (e.g., when a minority of parents assume a majority); or *topic avoidance* in which certain topics become undiscussable (e.g., school systems' failed history to address problems) (Deetz, 1992, pp. 187–198). Independently or in tandem, these forms of discursive closure can untie the knot.

However, power could also be exercised both by individuals (who "makes the call" on what course of action to take) and texts (e.g., verbalized routines or written procedures), whose mere presence can demonstrate a nonhuman form of agency (Cooren, 2004). However, the power of texts is itself a paradoxical tension: *Standard protocols* (texts as a nonhuman agent) are contrary to having *flexibility* (enacted through empowerment of human agency) to deviate in non-routine situations (e.g., new kinds of threat). Moreover, texts have *staying* power, but their meanings can *shift* because they can be (re)interpreted based on who reads the text (Derrida, 1988) and how they combine with other texts to layer and interweave (i.e., their intertextuality). Especially in the case of social media, texts' open interpretability and intertextuality can be quite disequilibrium producing. As such,

> *Proposition 5: Actors and nonhuman agents such as texts increase disequilibrium in a tensional knot as they heighten or attenuate contextual, temporal and power-laced contingencies and their combinations.*

Discussion and Conclusion

This chapter began with an illustrative case of a recent event of simultaneous school shooting threats in New York and California to expand existing understanding of dynamic equilibrium in paradox. Following complexity theory (e.g., McKelvey, 1999), we examined factors leading to increased systemic disequilibrium in paradoxical tensions as well as knots of multiple tensions. Knots delve deeply into actors' sensemaking formulations, articulated in and through actors' problem setting discourse. Following Sheep et al. (2017), knotted tensions might have amplifying effects on one another (prismatic tensions) or attenuating effects (anti-prismatic tensions), depending largely on discursive constructions of how the tension should be managed (either as simple choices, double binds or ambidextrous strategies).

Building on extant literature to advance our understanding of paradox beyond a system in "dynamic equilibrium", we proposed sources of disequilibrium in knots that include 1) divergence in competing versions of constructed reality, which were linked to disorder that led to "far from equilibrium" states postulated by complexity theory, allowing for human and nonhuman agency; and 2) systemic effects within and between tensions that comprise knots.

Moreover, we conceptualize increasing disequilibrium as an inequality of "forces" in a tensional opposition of poles, or in a tensional knot as an interdependent set of poles as variously constructed across multiple actors. Following complexity theory (e.g., McKelvey, 1999), we postulate that there can be an optimally beneficial degree of complexity or disequilibrium in a system of tensions. There can be too little or too much. The limit of what constitutes "too much" is a discursive construction, but so is its boundary condition—that of system elasticity. Elasticity defines the limit at which disequilibrium has stretched the system of tensions (and the organization in whose context they are variously constructed) as too "far from equilibrium" in order for them to be managed in a viable way (e.g., in a transcendent or ambidextrous manner). Actors discursively construct elasticity as the limit beyond which stretching (further expansion due to uneven pull of forces) will result in system fragmentation or dissolution.

Thus, a certain amount of disequilibrium is necessary for the system to be viable and to adapt/change/grow (Wheatley, 1999), but too much disequilibrium (McKelvey, 1999) can cause a knotted tensional system to become destructive of the very group or organizational systems in which it is embedded and which it enables/constrains. The system of tensions (knot), of course, is embedded in organizational systems and serves to enable/constrain the organization's adaptability/viability/integrity as a system.

In this chapter, we also demonstrate how knotted tensions and their management could be deeply affected by issues of context (and, specifically, threat specificity or planning), time and power, as well as possible interactions between them. However, it is important in future research to take constructions of (and positions toward) context, time and power into account when investigating dynamic *disequilibrium* within and among paradoxical tensions. In other words, it is not enough simply to know the forces prompting disequilibrium, but one must also query 1) the multiplicity of contexts that are destabilizing tensional forces; 2) the orientations toward time that are either privileging past/extant power arrangements or challenging/resisting them; 3) the presence or absence of power and persuasion (of both human and nonhuman agents) to reduce or increase the number of choices (and contexts) that are in play; and 4) the "play" itself, i.e., how tensional knots are produced by communication but also instigate communication with others who wish to contest or confirm the versions of reality set forth.

Theoretically, this moves us well beyond simple metaphors of equilibrium or disequilibrium in paradoxes (such as biological cellular equilibrium [Sheremata, 2000] or quantum physics disequilibrium [Kreiner et al., 2015]). Rather, we have provided propositions that both enable and call upon future research to investigate (discursive) *forces* prompting disequilibrium when actors construct multiple tensions as paradoxical systems, as well as the factors that are driving *increased or decreased* disequilibrium (a close investigation of constructions of context, time and power, as well as their interactions). In doing so, we have provided a vehicle to understand how social actors talk their paradoxical circumstances into being and justify (in)action in the process.

In terms of practical implications, we see many possibilities for practicing managers and leaders to take into consideration these findings. For example, when managers must manage knotted systems of paradoxical tensions, it is necessary but not sufficient merely to identify the tensions with which they are dealing. Additionally, they must understand and address (in words and actions) the forces that are either increasing the equilibrium or disequilibrium in those tensions, for example, those of 1) *context* (how dependent are action plans on the variation in contexts?); 2) *time* (do we have a past→present orientation or are we focusing on an emerging future→present scenario?); and 3) *power* (how effective are human and nonhuman agents of power and persuasion in producing consensus and reduction in complexity?). Moreover, managers can better predict (and perhaps manage discursively in their communication) whether to expect increased equilibrium or disequilibrium in their interdependent "system" of tensions in the problem—depending on how they make sense of and construct those three aspects differentially and interactively to change disequilibrium dynamics.

We close with a cautionary quote by H.L. Mencken: "For every complex problem, there is a solution that is simple, neat, and wrong" (quoted in Woodside, 2014, p. 2495). We contend that a better understanding of forces and drivers of disequilibrium in paradox can mitigate such over-simplistic and potentially "wrong" solutions as scholars attempt to theorize, and practitioners attempt to navigate, increasingly complex problems/solutions in organizational environments.

Notes

1. Previous versions of this chapter were presented at the 2015 and 2016 European Group and Organization Studies Conference.
2. For this chapter, we drew from a publicly available transcript of *The Diane Rehm Show* (NPR, 2015), which aired originally on December 17, 2015, on National Public Radio (NPR) in the United States. The transcript comprised 32 pages of text in which host Diane Rehm interviewed five guests with various perspectives regarding school threat incidents.
3. A question might be raised as to why a tension (e.g., safe–unsafe) is implicated if one or more actors only mention one side of the continuum (e.g., "Student safety is paramount"). Because issues of school safety typically reside within a system of tensions (e.g., involving cost, planning, community reactions and so on), the situation takes on a dialectical character for the actors involved as soon as they communicate about multiple tensions and make their case for how they intersect (Norton & Sadler, 2006). When someone problematizes issues of cost, for example, it automatically renders various plans as more or less safe, hence the articulation of a tension.
4. Tensions may or may not be contradictory because they can combine in unusual ways to produce ironic outcomes (Putnam et al., 2016).
5. In a sense, this is consistent with Weick's (1979) notion of equivocality and his organizing model, which includes assembly rules and communication cycles needed to reduce equivocality. That is, the higher the equivocality with fewer rules, the more assembly cycles that are necessary to reduce equivocality (toward equilibrium, if you will).
6. There are limits to the disequilibrium (extent of the arc) before the pendulum would either break or arc back on itself, but it is nevertheless in disequilibrium

up to a point of systemic fragmentation. This is consistent with "optimal complexity" and "elasticity" in our subsequent discussion.

7. In terms of organizational change, analogous processes are found in studies such as that of Abdallah, Denis and Langley (2011, p. 333), where the positive effects of even ambidextrous tension management strategies can have deleterious effects over time. What they refer to as "transcendence" (or "a rationale that creatively bridges opposite poles of a dilemma") is similar to a discursive attempt to manage tensions (including those in disequilibrium) in an ambidextrous way. However, "inherent contradictions tend to resurface over time, suggesting that while transcendence offers a powerful stimulus for change, its range and lifetime may be transitory". Moreover, the acceptance of transcendent ideas "may sow the seeds of their eventual re-evaluation and dissolution". Thus, ordering and equilibrium may result in deleterious effects, while disordering and disequilibrium can stimulate beneficial effects.

8. When discussing paradoxical tensions from a discursive analytic perspective, "forces" are understood as discursive constructions by individuals as they categorize, describe and interrelate the push and pull (in magnitude, direction and relation) of tensional oppositions in their talk. These are not to be understood as objective or absolute forces at play in the "real world", but only as constructions.

9. As an example of disequilibrium with inelasticity, consider also how Middle East conflicts are intractably knotted because each side's identity is rooted in the destruction and negation of the other. There is little or no elasticity from which to negotiate a productive change. Disequilibrium based on conflict escalation and no elasticity on either side is their "normal", although it is "far from equilibrium".

10. Another Austrian economist, Ludwig Lachmann, took these ideas further by developing a disequilibrium framework that sought "independence from conventional equilibrium-based reasoning". Lachmann pointed to "the mutual incompatibility and incommensurability of these disparate plans" as "the ultimate source of disequilibrium within which all firms are forced to conduct their affairs" (Mathews, 2010, pp. 219–220). In short, disequilibrium increases with the extent of variation among plans of action among actors. For Lachmann, disequilibrium in the form of incommensurable (contradictory) plans—giving rise to increased multiplicity of paradoxical tensions—is the norm for firms, not the anomaly. As such, managers can and must learn to strategize effectively in conditions of disequilibrium.

5 Feeling Things, Making Waste

Hoarding and the Dis/Organization of Affect

Karen Lee Ashcraft

Disorganization is a thing of shame, at least as a mode of living in contemporary capitalist societies. Professional organizers, from management and productivity consultants to home storage advisors, monetize its threat. Countless self-help tools extol the virtue of getting our proverbial houses in order and teach us tricks toward a well-managed life. The imperative to re-arrange and de-clutter governs work and home alike. To do otherwise—to dare embrace disorganization—means surrender to the forces of inefficiency, incoherence, anarchy, derangement and demise. Or so says the thesaurus at my disposal. In a profoundly animating way, disorganization is the adverse partner of organization, the devil to its angel. Disorganization is an unholy mess, *a disorder*, a disease that expresses deep dis-ease with chaos.

If you doubt this, consider the surge of interest in *hoarding* (Frost & Steketee, 2010), a psychiatric condition involving "the compulsive urge to acquire unusually large amounts of possessions and an inability to voluntarily get rid of those possessions, even when they have no practical usefulness or monetary value" (ElementsBehavioralHealth, 2013). In the last decade, hoarding has become a sensation where mental health education meets gruesome spectacle. In the US, for example, it is the subject of popular books and a wave of news coverage, television shows and spinoffs, and dedicated conferences and resources. It is a trend I could not overlook because my mother is a diagnosed hoarder (and I am a scholar of organization—go figure).

Hoarding may appear to be all about stuff, but it is also about *affect*, by which I broadly mean feeling. Feeling can range from fleeting sensation to durable emotion, and this chapter includes that range. Specifically, I approach affect as relations that are materially expressed and felt through contact (Ashcraft & Kuhn, 2017). Affect is thus a sociomaterial force: the ebb and flow of sensory encounter that continually brings bodies into distinction through relation (Seigworth & Gregg, 2010; Stewart, 2007). The central question at stake in hoarding is whether affect is flowing "properly". Some say hoarding is affect out of order, aimed at the wrong objects. Others say hoarding is marked as a transgression because it breaks capitalist rules for allocating affect. Still others say hoarding is a human response to the affective pull of nonhuman matter.

This chapter works across available narratives of hoarding, toward the argument that *addressing hoarding is a communicative practice which enacts and circulates the affective boundary between human and nonhuman bodies.* In this view, the question is not which narrative is right or better but, rather, what lines of difference are drawn in the act of orienting to hoarding in certain ways. Simply put, how are relations between *people* and *things* evolving and imminent in concrete practices of addressing hoarding?

More precisely, I draw on Ahmed's (2006, 2010b, 2010c, 2014) conception of feminist killjoys and queer object orientation to cast the hoarder as *organizational killjoy*—a short circuit that interrupts the normative flow of affect through object circulation. To address hoarding, I suggest, is to communicate with this disruptive figure. I demonstrate the proposed approach with a performative encounter that seeks to know/do hoarding provisionally, through multiple modes of address. I conclude with the implications of this approach for re-orienting to hoarding and, especially, for theorizing communication and dis/organization. Ultimately, I contend that 1) the eternal threat of disorganization is a fear of difference gone wild, and 2) the attendant quest for organization is a mandate to produce and control difference through the regulation of affect. Such an argument suggests that relations of difference are even more, and differently, constitutive of capitalist organizing practices than previously considered.

What's Her Problem? Orienting to Hoarding

I begin by introducing available narratives of hoarding today: three versions I distill as *psychiatric, critical-cultural* and *posthumanist/new materialist.* The first identifies hoarding as a psychological disorder and holds public sway, while the latter two could be called minor theoretical alternatives. The second stems from cultural studies of the popular cable show *Hoarders* and emphasizes dynamics of late capitalism and difference—especially gender, race, class and (sexual) deviance—contributing to the contemporary rise of hoarding. The third, meanwhile, entertains hoarding as an expression of material agencies.

1. Too Attached: The Hoarder Has a Mental Disorder

Without a doubt, the dominant narrative of hoarding has become a psychiatric one. This version depicts hoarders as people afflicted by a mental condition that causes unhealthy attachment to worthless stuff. The idea that hoarding is an individual pathology of chronic disorganization—as opposed to an eccentric social practice of gathering curiosities, or a gluttonous habit of stockpiling private fortune—arrived on the public register in the mid-1900s (Herring, 2011b). Psychological research concerned with hoarding did not gain steam until the 1990s, however (Frost & Steketee, 2010); and Hoarding Disorder (HD) only appeared as a separate entry in the DSM-5[1] as recently as 2013.

Today, tell-tale signs of HD include "the acquisition of, and failure to discard, a large number of possessions that appear to be useless or of limited value; living spaces are sufficiently cluttered so as to preclude activities for which those spaces were designed", generating "significant distress or impairment in functioning" (Claes, Muller & Luyckx, 2016, p. 65). HD is widely known as a convergence of four mental health problems, for which cognitive behavioral therapy is the primary advised treatment: 1) behavioral avoidance (a defense mechanism where one persistently ignores a pattern despite mounting evidence and consequences); 2) information-processing deficits (cognitive difficulties with sorting, inability to distinguish items to keep or discard); 3) distorted beliefs regarding the nature and importance of possessions (unrealistic object value assessment); and 4) excessive emotional attachment to possessions (detrimental degree of affinity with objects) (Frost & Hartl, 1996).

By most accounts today, the fourth problem, abbreviated as "hyper-sentimentality", is especially critical to the distinctiveness and treatment of HD (Frost, Hartl, Christian & Williams, 1995). Experts broadly agree that hoarders' affinity for stuff remains poorly understood yet holds the key to improving clinical interventions (e.g., Kellett & Holden, 2014; Kings, Moulding & Knight, 2017; Timpano & Shaw, 2013). Research thus far points to three modes of emotional relation between hoarder and hoard. First, hoarders tend to *derive comfort and security*, or signals of safety and assurance, from their possessions. According to much consumer psychology, the urge to control one's stuff is normal and even indispensable to a sense of well-being. HD involves extreme manifestations of this urge, paired with a compulsion to save things for projected future use (Roster, 2015).

Second, hoarders commonly *derive identity* from possessions. They lean heavily on stuff to develop, extend and rework notions of self in the past, present and future. Some research differentiates between autonomous and affiliated identity-seeking, since hoarders vary in the extent to which they use stuff to build selves apart from or by association with other people (Kings et al., 2017). In either case, a key marker of HD is that possessions come to substitute for human boundaries and connections in debilitating ways. Here again, HD is distinguished only by abnormal degree. While many use stuff to enhance self, hoarders demonstrate a troubling "fusion" of persons and possessions, a failure to recognize an ultimate line between who we are and what we own (Kellett, Greenhalgh, Beail & Ridgway, 2010, p. 150).

The first two modes of emotional attachment reveal that HD involves enjoyable sensations like "affection, connection, pleasure, love, security, pride, and comfort" (Kellett & Holden, 2014, p. 136). Hoarders exhibit "a positive preference and emotion for an object that serves no apparently practical function", frustrating family, friends and observers with their "nonsensical" feeling (p. 122). This good feeling underscores the major clinical challenge of HD: It is egosyntonic, or mostly consistent with actual or aspirational identity. Hoarders often experience the therapeutic imperative to recalibrate "overvalued beliefs regarding objects" as excruciating, for it requires them to sever rewarding emotional connections with treasured things and realign their attachments with people and social relations instead (Kings et al., 2017, p. 56). Toward this daunting end, therapists are advised to discern and adapt to the specific mode(s) of attachment patients present (Roster, 2015).

A third mode of attachment has drawn empirical attention only recently. Many hoarders *anthropomorphize* possessions, or "see human-like qualities in non-human entities" (Timpano & Shaw, 2013, p. 383). Some psychologists explain this proclivity—to regard things not merely as objects of affection, but as having feelings of their own—as an effect of heightened sensitivity to anthropomorphism in advertising, which generates value by stoking emotional investment in commodities (e.g., Timpano & Shaw, 2013). So far, however, it seems that humanization in HD involves sympathy for items with *little* value: those discarded by others or acquired for free.

Women hoarders appear to show a stronger tendency toward anthropomorphic relations with things (Neave, Jackson, Saxton & Hönekopp, 2015), and those with anxious or avoidant orientations to human attachment seem to experience greater attachment to possessions (Neave, Tyson, McInnes & Hamilton, 2016). While we are on the topic, it is worth noting that the universal subject of hoarding is feminized, such that "she" is regularly used as a generic pronoun. Although more women than men seek treatment, there is some debate as to whether hoarding is actually more prevalent among women, or whether the trend reflects cultural gender norms (Frost & Steketee, 2010). Women are more likely to be held accountable, and thus to hold themselves accountable, for messy domestic space, whereas men appear more likely to resist the hoarder label and minimize the problem, for example, by declaring themselves collectors.

In any case, affinity not just for but *with* possessions can entail "negative indicated affects" like inflated responsibility, anxiety, guilt and grief (Kellett & Holden, 2014, p. 136). When stuff feels too, it is difficult to dispose of it without a sense of violation and loss. The extra burden of worrying for things is not the only bad feeling associated with HD. Shame, self-loathing, marginalization, isolation and abandonment are among other frequently cited sensations (Kellett & Holden, 2014). Of course, these can be read to follow widespread societal responses to hoarding, like morbid fascination, disgust, stigmatization, alienation and rejection. The hoarder's disorder elicits many social reactions, and empathy is rarely one. Arguably, the psychiatric narrative of hoarding counteracts this tide of judgment by treating hoarders as beset by illness instead of morally impaired.

2. Perverted: The Social Organization of Hoarding as Depraved Disorganization

A handful of scholars reframe this dominant tale as one of many ways we might have come to know the material practices now called hoarding. Of interest here is mental illness as a historical and cultural formation, or when and why the narrative of disorder *as* disorder arose. Questioning the timelessness implied by the reigning account—as if HD were there all along but only now discovered through scientific advance—such critical inquiry investigates the rise of hoarding as a phenomenon in both senses of the term: something taken to exist and something that excites interest. Put simply, how did hoarding become "a thing"?

What critical-cultural studies of HD lack in volume they make up for in provocation. The television series *Hoarders*, which began airing on the A&E network in 2009, appears to be the central text that galvanized their attention. One stream of critique positions the show and its popularity within the context of *advanced capitalism*. Lepselter (2011), for example, interrogates the hoarder's emergence as a figure of fascination in the early 21st century. What can the sudden fame of this "ultimate 'subject made of objects'", and our "increasing collective fetish for the hoarder's fetishes", tell us about the cultural anxieties of the time (p. 922)? To answer, she treats HD as a cross-breed of two familiar discourses: expert intervention in compulsive behaviors and "phantasmagoric consumption in neoliberal capitalism" (p. 921). The offspring of this merger, HD is a circulating narrative about a pathological failure of circulation "that multiplies even as it rots" (p. 921). Specifically, the narrative works to diffuse twin threats posed by the practices it names. First, the practice of accumulating decaying stuff evokes adjacent historical terms that exposed excesses in industrial capitalism,[2] raising the risk that systemic forces may be faulted for today's consumption woes. Second, attachment to junk muddies economic and affective value, violating their "natural" separation and respective targets (i.e., commodities, people). HD neutralizes both threats by reconstituting the retention of "obvious" waste as individual deviance, a dangerous personal addiction. In this way, HD erases socioeconomic history and re-naturalizes "proper" capitalist consumption.

To illuminate how this works, Lepselter zooms in on the *Hoarders* series. Each episode follows a three-step formula of spectacle, cause and negotiation with an expert. In the spectacle phase, we are called to witness the hoarder's disturbing material world as a manifestation of her mental world. The camera's gaze lingers on the mess itself, "fascinating and low. It is like being serenaded by Kristeva's (1984) chora, that infantile sexual space of limitless, purely material, pre-linguistic disorder" (Lepselter, 2011, p. 928). Random items congeal with no apparent logic, refusing to move through that obligatory cycle whereby consumed things become trash. As hoarder and expert tour the chaos, an urgency to organize builds: "There is a sense that language must develop out of babble to create a dominant symbolic order . . . the hoarder must speak *rationally*" about things in order to bring the mess "quite literally up to 'code'" (p. 928, original emphasis). In arresting images of one unruly domestic space after another, "The disorder itself pulses with its freak's body of a room" (p. 928). The link between sick homes and minds is often made explicit. The hoarder is encouraged to step outside her own mess in order to see it, and therefore herself, "as a freakish spectacle" in the eyes of others (p. 928). Like this, the feminized hoard becomes "a putrid, dark part of the embodied self that needs to be cleansed. . . . The disorder of clutter feels like, and discursively becomes, an embodied medical disorder or illness" (p. 926).

Freak exposed, the show takes a second step, seeking the cause of her symptoms. Usually, the answer follows the trope of the hole-inside-me, and past personal loss or trauma is revealed to make disorderly signs legible. It is here that the hoarder's tragic misstep becomes clear: replacing people with things, using stuff to cope with human troubles or more pointedly, *mistaking* attachment to possessions as a substitute for human connection and, thereby, confusing economic and affective value. In this way, HD reframes late capitalist contradictions that actually promote such confusion[3] as individual error, a sad and twisted reaction to trauma.

HD thus draws an absolute "line between things and people" and enforces personal responsibility to maintain "the proper boundary: while things must be exchanged and substituted for each other (and to circulate), things must not be mistaken as interchangeable with emotions or relationships" (Lepselter, 2011, p. 931). Indeed, the third step in the show's formula is all about honoring that line, coaching the hoarder toward the appropriate boundary. Ultimately, Lepselter reads *Hoarders* as a warning about consumption run amok and a forceful reminder of our individual burden to keep things in order. In other words, HD deems normative consumption prosocial *against* the hoarder's catastrophic inability to uphold a proper divide between affect and object, people and things, human and nonhuman.

Likewise, Eddy (2014) treats *Hoarders* as a late capitalist phenomenon, offering greater precision about the moment to which it speaks. For Eddy, the series reflects a recent spike in the longer quest to shore up the subject of consumer culture by requiring things to play commodity objects. Evidence of this spike can be seen in the surge of cable shows and even networks (e.g., HGTV) addressed to property ownership and proper object consumption, which flood contemporary television with a return of the real. *Hoarders* takes a new twist, however: the creation of a hyper-real deviant who serves to affirm the existence of "normal" consumption. The show's meteoric popularity in the wake of the 2008 financial crisis is no coincidence, she says. Its HD refrain joins a chorus of discourses that pin the crisis on the reckless behavior of individuals—especially ordinary consumers—and, thus, recuperate capitalist consumption as a legitimate practice perverted by abnormal people. In short, the hoarder is "an object lesson in a fictive allegory of normative consumption" (p. 11).

Eddy concurs with Lepselter that HD enforces the divide of human from nonhuman: "*Hoarders* capitalizes on the disjuncture between people and things . . . acquisition and retention of objects threatens personal relationships, since the value placed on objects is understood as displacing the value placed on interpersonal and family relations" (Eddy, 2014, p. 15). Like Lepselter, she identifies a three-step script to the show, wherein the hoarder confronts the mandate to "make waste" (p. 5), struggles to apply the correct valuation hierarchy and finally confesses to hoarder identity. Viewers, meanwhile, are trained in suitable response: rapt revulsion that turns to pardon for the self, pity for the other and hope for their rehabilitation.

Critical-cultural accounts of hoarding as an effect of advanced capitalism overlap with the dominant psychiatric narrative. Both recognize the human–nonhuman boundary as a central component of normative consumption; both cite excessive affective attachments between people and things in which the latter come to replace the former; both acknowledge anthropomorphism in advertising; and so on. And yet, where HD *finds* an individual problem with an eye toward pragmatic ways to solve it, cultural critics see HD as a discursive formation that *produces* the very affliction *and* patient it purports to treat. Thereby, it deflects attention from other possible narratives and excludes historical, social, economic and political forces that may well contribute to the material practices in question. In sum, critical-cultural studies regard the HD narrative *not* as some innocent first responder, but as a highly partial staging of the crisis—one entirely compatible, indeed in cahoots, with the political trajectory of late capitalist relations.

A second strain of cultural critique picks up on HD as a tale of *queer deviance*. Here, hoarding is a form of material non-normativity which stands to make prescribed material relations strange. Herring (2011b), for example, puts studies of material culture in conversation with queer theory. Although there are historical references to excessive accumulation as a sexual perversion,[4] the point of this conversation is *not* to argue that hoarding *is* a sexual practice, or that hoarders *are* sexual deviants but, rather, that hoarders and hoarding are usefully *analogous* to queer sexual orientations and practices. Resisting the usual assumption that objects are made to support culture, Herring entices us toward objects that fail to perform their designated function. It is precisely in going rogue, he claims, that stuff exudes thing power.

As the quintessential practice in which objects misbehave, hoarding is a perfect site for such investigation.[5] Attracted to things gone wild, hoarders inhabit queer bodies. Herring calls for sustained inquiry into how thing conduct "pathologizes as well as normalizes individuals as having proper and improper social relations". "Why is one material life commended while another is reviled?" he asks. "What queer pleasures and desires might be found" amid non-normative object orientations (p. 7)? Not surprisingly, Herring illustrates the potential of such inquiry through analysis of *Hoarders*, which he reveals as a failed home make-over series that succeeded only by embracing the genre of confessional addiction—a spectacle of deviance that demands correction even as it titillates the horrified senses. His queer analytic vocabulary is evocative. As we peer into straight object culture "botched" (p. 8) by "a material queer whose deviance can be cleaned up with the right DSM category" (p. 9), we cannot help but recall that, not so long ago, the DSM classified homosexuality as a disorder too. We read of a woman dreamily anthropomorphizing a decomposing pumpkin. We meet hoarders clinging to the pleasures of material perversion, refusing the psychological and professional organizing expertise that Herring implies is akin to conversion therapy. The upshot is a novel take on the hoarder's error: not exactly the substitution of things for people but, rather, unyielding attraction to and affection for the wrong bodies—nonhuman rather than human.

Reaching further back than most critics, Herring (2011a) delves into the archives of the first modern hoarding case featured in the psychiatric literature: the Collyer brothers and their Harlem mansion. In initial formulations, HD was actually dubbed Collyer Brothers' Syndrome,[6] since hoarding already referred to the practice of squirreling money away. In fact, it was the Collyer case that launched the transition of meaning from hoarding as secretly stowing wealth to accumulating worthless stuff. Sons of a once-prominent New York couple, the Collyer brothers stayed in their inherited Harlem home as the demographic composition of the neighborhood changed dramatically and the Harlem Renaissance came and went. Regarded for many years as curiosities, eccentrics, hermits and nuisances, the brothers were eventually found dead in their home in 1947, buried under a mountain of things. Herring traces how, almost overnight, their presumed wealth transformed in the public eye into "filthy riches"—a pathetic, revolting and therefore endlessly captivating mass of rubbish.

By foregrounding relations of difference—especially *race, class, place* and *(sexual) deviance*—in the Collyer case, Herring aims to recover "historical confluences that enabled hoarding to emerge as a disorder about disorganization in the twentieth century", forces entirely purged by today's HD narrative (p. 162). The short version is that cultural anxieties about race-class contamination accompanying a mass influx of outsiders became encoded in scientific theories of "social disorganization" (p. 164). This concept captured the decline in traditional forms of community that purportedly follows such infusions; and it soon morphed into deviance and disease associated with dark, immigrant or otherwise foreign bodies (read: not "white", in the ever-shifting boundaries of that category). As "black" working class people increasingly populated Harlem and its identity changed accordingly, the neighborhood became a focal point for accounts of social disorganization. The Collyers tried to distance themselves from the stain, but they could not shake guilt by association—not only because they remained in place, but also because they were already marked queer by reports of their odd (if not incestuous) lives and mysterious hoard. In the aftermath of the Collyers' death and ensuing clean-up, their "Harlem mystery house" came to epitomize the inevitability and consequences of urban disarray (p. 168). Supposedly, the brothers fell prey to "Harlemitis" (pp. 162–171), an infectious ailment that corrodes not only social order but mental organization as well.

It was this convergence of forces that shifted hoarding "from eccentric accumulation to pathological pile-up", such that "a messy domestic interior" became synonymous with "a messy psychological interiority" (p. 178). Herring traces specific aspects of the clinical definition back to the Collyer case. To be clear, though, the titanic claim proffered here is that *today's* concerns over chronic disorganization are tinged with race-class contamination anxiety: HD as we know it is caught up in tales of urban blight that continue to haunt the "scientific unconscious" (p. 183).

In sum, critical-cultural approaches situate the psychiatric narrative as a discursive formation arising in response to social and political exigencies. In particular, they shed light on how HD 1) shores up contemporary capitalism with fearsome images of feminized chaos, 2) enforces material normativity by pathologizing material deviance, and 3) enshrines fears of race-class contagion in benign medicalized discourse. One gets the impression that organization is venerated, and disorganization vilified, as a means of controlling relations of difference and keeping "them" in place. Put bluntly, the demand to de-clutter looks more like a quest to regulate difference in the service of capitalism.

3. Possessed: Hoarding as Attunement to the Call of Things

A third version of hoarding mines the critical-cultural narrative, namely its observation that HD enforces the human–nonhuman divide. It then veers posthuman, redirecting the spotlight from hoarder to hoard. In this view, human agency—individual (as in narrative #1) and discursive (as in #2)—is decentered in favor of a new focus: how the materiality of the hoard participates in disorder. Here, the human hoarder is no longer in full charge of mess and clean-up. She is, instead, a vessel uniquely attuned to the bidding of things. She does not so much possess stuff as she is possessed *by* it. This is her curse . . . *and* blessing?

The preceding critical-cultural review teems with allusions to stuff as active, not inert. Objects fail, even refuse, to perform as directed, exceeding their assigned meaning, function and place. Things fall "out of order", stop working and grow disruptive. Recall Lepselter's (2011) portrayal of the hoard as *chora*, pulsing with chaos and daring attempts at organization. She describes how things radiate value beyond that allotted, even as HD insists that this is the hoarder's mistake, not the hoard's fault: "hidden memory and a seed of potential are still subsumed into and expressed by the object. The hoarded, fetishized thing, still standing for a relationship between people, continues to animate itself" (p. 943). Eddy (2014) also claims that things assert themselves between psychologist and hoarder. The hoarder ventriloquizes their call (e.g., this pumpkin belongs here!), stipulating an egalitarian thingness, or even an anti-consumerist appreciation. Similarly, Herring (2011b) attends to things that fail to toe the line, thereby queering those who love them. On the whole, such critiques seem enraptured with the ways hoarders *and* hoards team up to resist the psychological narrative.

A leading voice in new materialist approaches, Jane Bennett (2012) goes the furthest to theorize hoard as active participant. She observes that, against the avid protests of many hoarders, the HD narrative rejects outright any possibility of a material practice that attests to the vibrant call of matter. Turning again to *Hoarders*, she notes how the featured patients regularly insist that the experts have it wrong. Stuff *does* beckon and congregate beyond human control; things *can* be vital members of ourselves and not mere objects of possession; nonhuman bodies *will* express themselves too. Their dissent is routinely subsumed into the illness as anticipated symptoms. The hoarder cannot sense what is there (i.e., make reasonable value judgments), yet she senses what is not there (i.e., feeling things). In this way, dualisms endemic to Western thinking, such as human–nonhuman and subject–object, are preserved. People act, whereas stuff does not; things are inert material, opportunity and constraint to be manipulated by humans. But at what cost are such dualisms maintained? And what if the threat of hoarding is precisely this: a direct strike at bifurcations that keep self-contained humans intact and alone on the throne of agency? No wonder we seek to tame it.

Specifically, Bennett asks us to consider whether hoarders may be ventriloquists for the power of things. Preparing for this exercise, she says, requires moving the nonhuman bodies of the hoard front and center, featured as primary actants on the stage, while the human hoarder recedes into the background. Bracketing the hoarder's plight allows us to address the hoard as an agentic assembling *by* greeting "the people, the hoarders, not as bearers of mental illness but as differently abled bodies that might have special sensory access to the call of things". We can "resist the frame of psychopathology, in order to better hear what the hoarder might have discerned about her objects' thing-powers" (p. 244).

Bennett thus attempts to heed how the hoarders of *Hoarders* talk about their things. Lest you balk at her choice to foreground talk in a study of material agencies, it is worth underscoring that she is *not* treating talk as a linguistic representation which stands apart from and mediates human knowledge of thingness. Instead, she treats talk as an *enactment* of thing power, one practice by which the force of stuff can be materially trans- lated (in the ANT sense), expressed or re-presented among bodies:

> Word-workers can best keep faith with things, I think, if they approach language as rhetoric, as word-sounds for tuning the human body, for rendering it more susceptible to the frequencies of the mate- rial agencies inside and around it. The goal: to use words to make whatever communications already at work between vibrant bodies more audible, more detectable, more *senseable*.
>
> (p. 242, original emphasis)

Listening to people in order to learn about things, Bennett detects three "hoarding intelligences". First, hoarders are in closer contact with the *slowness of things*, the durable and gradual quality of nonhuman bodies that renders them less erratic than human. Second, hoarders feel *inter- corporeality*—porosity of and contagion among bodies—more intensely than those without hoards. Their descriptions of discarding stuff as akin to severing limbs, excising organs, suffering rape and other forms of physical violence and loss attest to this sharper awareness. Stuff is not reduced to object, tool, device or instrument apart from human bodies, but is a vital participant in living. The first intelligence challenges HD's claim that hoarders mistake things as substitutes for human connection, arguing instead that hoarders value slowness compared with the variabil- ity of human relations. The second intelligence confronts HD's assertion of distorted beliefs about and attachment to possessions. It holds that hoarders acutely experience human–nonhuman hybridities that charac- terize everyone but remain muted (distorted?) for most.

The third hoarding intelligence entails a distinctive mode of relational- ity that she calls *inorganic sympathy*. Neither utilitarian nor aesthetic— two touted forms of relation to materiality that accentuate human agency—inorganic sympathy is distinguished by heightened sensitivity to the human inorganic, or the "its" of humanity, as well as to the call of nonhuman things (p. 258). Her reliance on the term *call* is crucial here: "I'm not willing to go so far as to project purposiveness onto things and say that *they* are using the hoarder" (pp. 259–260, original emphasis). Bennett does not reverse the subject–object relation between people and things; rather, she seeks to render things participants in and on their own terms. Whereas reference to the *will* or *feeling* of things animates stuff through humanization, reference to the *call* or *bidding* of things resuscitates the notion of "advenience" as "a presence that we can sense but not know", "a making-present to human sense-perception, a jutting or intruding into the 'regime of the sensible'" (p. 262). This final intelligence reinterprets anthropomorphizing as a human response to the affective summons of things in the only terms yet available.

Bennett delivers a provocative demonstration of Herring's (2011b) call to explore material deviance more appreciatively. As she listens to non-normativity speak for itself, she hears alternative r(el)ationalities that question the fundamental split of human from nonhuman and gesture toward other ways in which bodies of all kinds might make worlds together.

Addressing Hoarding as a Communicative Practice: Organization, Meet Your Killjoy

Thus far, we have encountered three articulations of hoarding, which broadly agree on the material practices involved. However, 1) the psychiatric version assembles these practices into a mental health disorder, whereas 2) the critical-cultural version charges HD with obscuring the cultural politics of hoarding. Meanwhile, 3) the posthumanist/new materialist version speculates what the hoarder might reveal about the vibrancy of things, if we relinquish certainty about her illness long enough to listen. Before proposing a fourth narrative below, I compare what the first three versions have to say about affect and its relation to agency, loosely defined as making a difference. I am particularly concerned with how the narratives make a difference to the urgent dilemmas entailed in hoarding, for practical and ethico-political reasons (i.e., as the implicated daughter of a hoarder *and* a critical scholar with an applied streak).

Across Articulations: What's Happening With Affect and Agency?

Affect, agency and their relation are central to all three articulations. Clearly, the psychiatric version rests on individual human agency, treating "people entrapped in massively cluttered physical environments *of their own making*" (Kellett et al., 2010, p. 121, emphasis added). The hoarder gathers and cannot discard; she is anti-social in her pro-materiality. But with professional help, she can retrain this compulsion toward healthier habits. Most importantly, she can get her affective house in order, choosing emotional attachments to friends and family over neurotic connections with rubbish. Through better object valuation, she can rebuild prosocial relations with the material world.

In the critical-cultural version, agency remains human but shifts to the discursive sphere and, specifically, to the rise of HD as *the* way to know extreme domestic clutter. As it produces docile bodies in need of psychological help, this knowledge-power regime eclipses questions about capitalist excess and related disciplines of difference (see Foucault, 1979a). It does so by enforcing participation in a circumscribed affective economy as a matter of psychological well-being. Here, a foundational ability to divide human from nonhuman, social from material, valuable from disposable—to feel only for the former and circulate objects accordingly—becomes a requirement for healthy living. HD normalizes these affective differentiations *through* the hoarder's patent aberration. With thinly veiled relish, several critics observe how some bodies and things resist normalization anyway.

The posthumanist/new materialist version of hoarding riffs on the latter observation, suggesting that hoarders are exceptionally vulnerable to material agency. The idea is not to invest stuff with intentional acting, nor to reverse presumed agency from people to things. Rather, the point is to weigh an alternative relationality in which humans share the driver's seat with other participants; human and nonhuman bodies are more entangled than we like to think; and agency transpires in practices of entanglement (see Kuhn, Ashcraft & Cooren, 2017). Hence the emphasis on the vitality of things: The ongoing call-and-response among bodies brings them into felt relation. In a word, agency here *is* affect.

Beyond their arguments *about* affect and agency, the three narratives also *perform* diverse affective stances toward the human hoarder, with varied capacities for agency as constructive assistance. My initial take on this surprised me, given my critical, new materialist leanings as a scholar. I experienced the first version as rife with empathy for her plight, whereas the second and third show little regard for her palpable struggles. As they call into question, or at least suspend, the realness of HD, they seem to exonerate and even celebrate her as a resistant figure. Living with a hoard, this is hardly a welcome liberation. It is difficult to deny the concrete problems of hoarding when you are enclosed in piles of stuff and the plumbing is about to fail. Emancipation from the looming material disaster sounds better. Can you sense how the worried daughter wrestles with the academic?

Upon further reflection, I would say that the three narratives care for the hoarder differently. The first approach does empathy through *expert assistance*. Exemplified in the best-seller *Stuff* (Frost & Steketee, 2010), and striking in the psychiatric literature and clinical communities I encountered, is a quest to better understand and help people who hoard. In two years of attending the annual Hoarding and Cluttering Conference in San Francisco, for example, I experienced only non-judgmental concern and tangible help from a devoted group of researchers, therapists and organizers. Repeatedly, they showed openness to any consideration that might enhance sympathy and intervention, including those that fell outside their expertise, like cultural and political factors.

In some contrast, the critical-cultural version does empathy through *ideological emancipation*. Here, the hoarder's shame can be lifted along with the veil of individualization that shrouds cultural and economic formations as mental health problems. The help offered here is more ideational than practical: "Without losing sight of the suffering involved, it is still possible to imagine a different range of stories, in which all cases now called 'hoarding' might not be contained within a single unifying frame" (Lepselter, 2011, p. 923). Experiments in reframing can relieve the pressure and solitude of personal madness by exposing the social and political trajectories whereby madness comes to be. An important line of comfort that opens horizons of thought, to be sure, but *not* one that opens space in the room.

Finally, the posthumanist/new materialist version enacts empathy through *uncommon listening*, trying to hear the hoarder as she channels thing power. As Bennett (2012, p. 267) puts it, "Hoarding is of interest to me because it is one site where the appearance of the call of things seems particularly insistent, and I've turned to hoarders for help in the admittedly paradoxical task of trying to enunciate the nonlinguistic expressivity of things". In this rendition, the hoarder harbors special insight because she is attuned where most tune out. She may not *have* a disorder after all. Nonetheless, she *lives* with disorder so extraordinary it threatens her very life. In a world where the call of things is soundly rejected, if regularly experienced, there are evident limits on the extent to which bracketing her plight for intellectual exercise can help her cope with the mountains of stuff in front of her. If she is differently abled, it is also in disabling ways.

The point I am working toward is this: If the second and third versions are on to something, they need not remain philosophical musing held apart from the hoarder's predicament. They can instead make contact with pressing dilemmas of living, such that their empathies become more tangible and accountable. But how to facilitate such an encounter in the absence of mechanisms parallel to the clinical apparatus of psychiatry? How can awareness of cultural politics and vibrant matter address the vexing human challenges of hoarding, helping hoarders to reasonably persist? In this light, my own mixed reaction to the three renditions of hoarding—as scholar of organization *and* daughter of disorganization—is more than a personal response. It stems from a lived hybridity that might prove generative for addressing these questions, because it approaches hoarding from all three versions, traversing them.

The Turn to Address: A Fourth Articulation

To make good on this potential, and to facilitate sustained encounter between abstract narratives and concrete dilemmas of hoarding, I propose *addressing hoarding as a communicative practice that enacts and circulates the affective boundary between human and nonhuman bodies.*

Several features of this proposal merit exposition, beginning with the shift from hoarding itself to *addressing* hoarding, which redirects focus from what hoarding *is* to *what* is *happening*, or what forms of relation are emerging, as hoarding is variously addressed.

The former question—what is hoarding?—hosts a debate among contenders for ontological origin, as if to authorize one. Is it a mental disorder, a discursive formation, an act of resistance *or* a symptom of material agency? As long as this is the occupying question, hoarding is a phenomenon whose existence seems independent of efforts to know and intervene in it. Matters of accuracy, of correspondence, stay central. In contrast, the latter question—what (else) is happening as hoarding is addressed?—recognizes that the activity called hoarding is already caught up and co-evolving with efforts to grasp and deal with "it". These efforts are themselves ways of (re-)doing hoarding. *Addressing hoarding* is performative, in other words—an ontological practice that ushers something, which is definitely happening but indefinite in nature, into certain modes of being *through* certain modes of address. From this vantage point, hoarding can only be known in relation (i.e., through address). It has no independent ontology—as disease, capitalist symptom or anything else—awaiting discovery. Hoarding *is*, or becomes, *as* it is addressed, because addressing enacts the relations that allow some*thing* to be a certain way. The question becomes what relational worlds come into view, what connections and configurations find traction, as hoarding is addressed. The question is also what we might *make* of these worlds, in the interpretive, evaluative and creative senses of the phrase.

Repositioned as the phenomenon of interest, then, addressing hoarding is an unfolding set of practices, an ongoing event, a reconfiguring that abandons ontological resolution in favor of multiple ontologies: *How does hoarding become through address, and what is becoming along with "it"?* Specifically, the turn to addressing hoarding points to *multiple, loosely connected scenes of ontological practice*—domestic and intimate, public and popular, academic and clinical, embodied and textual, grand and mundane. It calls for leveling, as in flattening, these scenes, rather than assuming some (e.g., clinical protocol) stand over others (e.g., hoarders gathering, plumbing failing, daughters pleading). Hoarding is addressed as much through popular television shows and published scholarly work (like this) as it is through counseling, home organizing, concealing curtains, closed doors, air fresheners, deafening silence and family screaming matches. There is no reason to presume *a priori* that these operate in separate registers or can be sifted neatly into micro, meso and macro planes. Any such differences can only be identified as they are made in situated practice and, even then, provisionally.

While the above examples of ontological practice may appear to privilege human bodies engaged in willful conduct, a closer look is warranted. Addressing hoarding is at once social *and* material, or *sociomaterial*, and invariably involves so-called human *and* nonhuman participants. The breakdown of plumbing collides with daughters pleading and stalls a hoarder's gathering, for example. Clearly, social and material relations are entangling here, as are human and nonhuman bodies. Noteworthy, however, is the impossibility of *dis*entangling them, much less achieving certainty regarding the direction of address. Did the bursting pipes and ailing toilets—events that manifested in growing leaks, dysfunctional appliances, physiological markers of anxiety and shame and escalating whispers of desperation—snap us all to attention? Who (or what) is addressing whom? Like this, addressing hoarding stays open to the call of things as much as the purposeful (and derailed) actor.

But why the particular term *address*? If, as hinted earlier, the term is meant to signal the relationality of hoarding—that "it" is bound up with attempts to know and wrestle with it—then what is the utility of address *per se*? My answer is that 1) the ontological practice of hoarding is necessarily *communicative*, and 2) "address" not only highlights this point, it compels us to conceive of communication in a novel way that accommodates the features outlined so far: multiple ontologies as well as sociomaterial and human-nonhuman entanglements.

When hoarding is *addressed*, someone or something is hailed, summoned, identified, spoken to and called out for response. This communicative gesture is not only social, however. Address is not a discursive *as opposed to* material mode of attention. Enduring notions of "public address", for instance, acknowledge the materiality of the social: embodied oratory, supporting props like stages and podiums or devices of amplification, situational and environmental details that affect reception, the "movement" of an audience. In its very definition, address is sociomaterial, spanning speech, directions to the physical location of an intended recipient and even a golfer's stance in relation to the ball. To be addressed is also to be physically oriented to, pointed toward and contended with—wrangled and tackled in various senses. Committing to address some problem, for instance, obliges more than conversation; it obliges *doing something* about it, taking *matters* into *hands*. Further, the meaning of address includes identifying someone or something in a specified way, as with an honorific. Address in this sense is also performative: It enacts the relation it names. Finally, to be addressed is to *feel* addressed, to sense—or register affectively—a summons to the body from another source. In this way, address not only incorporates affect as a vital communicative force, it opens to the possibility of human and nonhuman call-and-response. For all of these reasons, *address* enables us to recognize the communicative character of hoarding in a usefully multi-faceted way.

Of course, this discussion raises the matter of who or what, more precisely, is addressed by ontological practices of hoarding—a query that brings us to the final phrase of my proposal: a communicative practice *that enacts and circulates the affective boundary between human and nonhuman bodies*. As the first three narratives demonstrate, addressing hoarding generally entails *re*dressing a problematic breakdown of the human–nonhuman split and associated bifurcations like person–thing, social–material, and subject–object. Such demarcations rise and fall, succeed and fail, through the *dis/organization of affect*—the production and maintenance *as well as* interruption and malfunction of orderly circuits of feeling. To address hoarding is thus to acknowledge shorts in the affective motherboard, so to speak, and to perform some kind of repair work. But what exactly disrupts orderly flow in the first place, and what do efforts to restore that flow yield? I conclude my proposal for a fourth articulation by taking these matters in turn.

The Figure Addressed: Organizational Killjoy as Affective Short Circuit

The usual addressee of hoarding's ontological practice is the human hoarder, variously hailed as responsible yet ailing subject, hapless object of discursive discipline or ventriloquist for material agency. Yet if, as conceived above, addressing hoarding entails the dis/organization of affect, we need a way of approaching the hoarder beyond that of afflicted person or individual vessel for discursive and material agencies. We need a more *relational* account of the hoarder as a glitch in the "proper" flow of affect—a component in the circuitry that has stopped working and, therefore, threatens to frustrate or fry its operations. For this, I borrow on Ahmed's feminist killjoy (2010b, 2010c, 2014) in tandem with her queer phenomenology of objects (2006).

Spoilsport. Wet blanket. Party pooper. Sourpuss. These are but a few colloquialisms that disgrace the killjoy, one who dampens the mood. Ahmed's use of killjoy begins with this familiar figure but puts it to political use and casts a curious, sympathetic, even loving gaze in its direction. In brief, a feminist killjoy is a buzzkill to the normative flow of happiness—a flow fueled by the circulation of certain objects, "happy objects" (Ahmed, 2010a), to which the promise of happiness comes to stick over time. Perpetually passing these objects around keeps the fantasies they host alive and kicking, such that any*body* who drops the ball, as it were, ruins the mood. They kill joy by calling attention to elusive, partial and painful qualities within the fantasies—that is, the *un*happiness undergirding normative happiness.

Oddly, bodies who drop the ball become marked as the *source* of unhappiness, akin to blaming a caller who reports the fire *for* the fire itself. Queer and feminist bodies may interrupt happiness by refusing to mate and breed, or to laugh at heterosexist jokes. Melancholic migrants may disrupt its flow by declining to melt into the national pot. As these killjoy examples suggest, *objects* for Ahmed take many and flexible forms; they encompass whatever helps to distribute happiness as a possible yet intangible promise attached to particular things.

In parallel fashion, but taking objects more literally and materially, I suggest approaching the human hoarder as an embodiment of the Organizational Killjoy—a creature who curbs the buzz of normative capitalist relations between people and things with her rampant disorganization. The capitalization here is meant to signal a composite figure rather than the concrete body performing it, drawing focus to the affective short circuit, and not so much the person, hailed for repair in the communicative practice of addressing hoarding.

While this move may seem to de-humanize the hoarder, it does so *not* in order to degrade, but precisely to avoid taking the human for granted, and to emphasize instead the affective circuitry by which the human is produced in distinction from the nonhuman. Put another way, the Organizational Killjoy halts the normative flow of human–nonhuman relations because she cannot keep affect—and, therefore, any*thing*—in order. She does not feel, or rather *stifle* feeling, as required in the face of objectification. She is a problem that must be addressed, lest we have to examine the *un*happiness on which happy consumption proceeds. Lest we be tempted to ask what relations of difference, what *thingifications* (Barad, 2003, p. 812), must be swallowed, or *un*felt, in order to stomach the usual order of things. To be clear, then, in the spirit of Ahmed's formulation, I ask the reader to feel with and for the Organizational Killjoy *through* a kind of qualified and temporary de-humanization, which is *not* meant to diminish her dignity.

The final matter posed at the end of the prior section—what it is that efforts to repair the Organizational Killjoy might yield—can only be answered provisionally, from within particular ontological practices. I thus advocate an "inhabited" approach to analysis (see Ashcraft, 2017), one that dwells in the flow of events, staying right in the middle of things rather than reaching (for) firm conclusions. Such an approach is guided by an ethos of curiosity and vigilance over certainty and critique. It seeks to discern what might be blooming, and to cultivate potentially promising developments, *while* remaining mired in the mess and resisting the urge for disembodied distance. An inhabited analysis thus addresses hoarding tentatively and by feel, from the middle of its happening rather than through analytic abstraction.

In sum, the question posed by the fourth articulation is not which narrative is closer to correct or more productive but, rather, what lines of difference are becoming in communication with the Organizational Killjoy. Next, and with a decided shift in tone, I demonstrate how such an account might proceed. Addressing hoarding: Take one. [Insert audible throat-clearing.]

Mending the Motherboard: An Encounter With the Organizational Killjoy

My sister and I always joke, though not entirely in jest, that we can spot a hoarder a mile away. It's not fair to say, but something about her look, her vibe—her *affect*, that energy she brings into the room—feels so distinctive. Is it the layers? Like one too many perky clips in the hair, clothing that billows? How she carries her flesh, moving heavily, swaying or lurching slightly? She surveys the scene, aware of her steps, looking back and double- and triple-checking her stuff. Her speech is somehow literal (or is that earnest)—her stories, comprehensive. If she's lucky enough to have one, the state of her car can be a sign. No science supports these impressions, and no words do them justice. It's just a sense that comes from hanging around hoarding, and it stops me short every time. I wonder; I wince; I worry. I tune in and get agitated. She too is someone's Organizational Killjoy.

***

Growing up, I had to learn it was strange. Nothing becomes garbage too quickly. Think about it; think again; and shake the trash can three times to be sure. I look around the halls, now the living spaces—oh no—dad's den, the bed, my room . . . is nothing sacred? Piles everywhere, more like random hills rising toward mountains. They're trying to shut us in, shut us off from the world. Would she even notice if I throw a few things away so I can breathe, and maybe have a friend over?

The answer is almost always: yes. Her powers of observation are detective. *She cares about things no one else does.*

Years later, her watchful eye long behind me, I still empty the trash just so. Just in case.

***

There we are, my father, sister and me forever complaining, her own parents needling, everyone knowing: Your mom is a mess. Holidays are the worst. We frantically shove things behind closed doors, with her permission of course. We stage for company one bright and shiny scene that hides the hours of screaming hell it took to create. We force the flow of happy family feeling, but it keeps stopping short from all the seething. People whisper about her "problem", and she hangs her head. But when she's in its throes, watch out. The Killjoy rises.

Her rule is: Stuff rules. When it can be touched, moved, used and how is always a delicate and explosive negotiation. Stuff has its own rights in this house; it belongs. It is as or more important than you and me. Or so we lamented.

And yet, she saved everything I did. I had hoped this habit was a motherly tribute, until she saved a scab when I had chicken pox. That's when it got creepy. By the age of seven, I knew we were not normal or, rather, I knew *she* was off. I thought she was freakish, then scary. I began to despise her. I clung to my sister and father in fear, loathing and mockery. Only now can I see she too was drowning.

* * *

In our interview, she recalls watching college friends pack up to go home for the summer, and wondering how they did it so blithely when it took her forever. She explains that many of the things she saves materialize relationships, remind her of precious people and times, and keep those links alive and safe, even if she can no longer find them. There are too many things, yes. But she must find good homes for them, or they might feel bad. It pricks her to imagine rejected stuff *de*jected. She cringes with embarrassment at even these confessions. The whole mess is a shame. She longs to be normal for a day.

I relish being normal when it comes to my stuff. Once we were free of that rotting home, I cannot express the flood of relief. Finally *I* was the master of things. I rehearsed how to rule them well, how to keep them in line so they behave nicely and perform for others. I love organization so much I chose to study it; I cannot relax or function in a messy physical space.

Still, now, the house visits me in dreams. I float through the cramped hallways and marvel at the mausoleum to lives gone by. Every cobweb pays its respects. Each item of décor the same as in 1988. What Dad left behind still hangs there, fading. I am, for some reason, in awe of it all.

* * *

Next to no one entered that house for years. We gave up on our Killjoy. My sister and I looked away and agreed to host the holidays without a word. My grandfather drew a line. The Killjoy shielded visitors from her (not so) secret. By the time she let my sister and I back in, it might have been 20 years.

But let us in she did, and the courage of her "yes" still blows my mind. The fear was palpable, rejection lurking around each corner, patched dams sure to burst. She must have warned us a hundred times: *It will kill me if I kill your joy again.* The problem was that the Hoard itself threatened our Killjoy. All the bodies involved—house, human, food, technologies, random objects—were not only aging but tangled in a relation that defied outside help. Her "problem" was a disaster that would not wait long to happen. So after all of the disclaimers, she opened the door. That she had to doesn't make it less bold.

The first thing that struck me was the smell. Awful, too sweet and stale, and also a familiar, endearing odor I had missed for 20 years. So many of the very things that raised me still lived there: a barrette I had left on the windowsill in the early 1980s, empty bottles—of soap, hair spray, pills—dating back to the 1970s. These things had grown up as I had, and they too were living their own life and finding new friends.

Every possible surface—counter, tabletop, floor, you name it—was covered. Pathways through the piles grew hard to discern. The double ovens were now full of papers, the stovetop buried in flammable text. Light fixtures long burned out but unreachable, abject filth everywhere. An occasional swarm of bugs greets us from a hidden bag of festering fruit, so don't you dare open the pantry or even the freezer.

What *is* all this stuff, anyway? Lightly used Kleenex and paper towels, empty containers of all types, free "gifts" from church or that hotel, years of mail, bags upon bags, fading linens, endless clothes. Memorabilia unsorted and only vaguely laying claim to the category; any scribbling from someone might be meaningful. Years of voicemail on tape. Room upon room of wonders. Sticky name badges from countless functions attended declare, "Hello, my name is . . . !" Scores of them lazily adhere to the wall, as if to prove the Killjoy exists.

That's when I lose it. Duck behind a mound to *compose myself*, and that idiom takes on new meaning.

This is no sensationalized episode of *Hoarders*. This is the real thing, and it *is* sensational. It *is* like Kristeva's (1984) chora. The Hoard is flagrant, breathtaking in every sense of the term. It dares order to take a crack at it, and even the most organized among us cannot help but bow to its power. It *is* a thing to behold. It is my heritage and, worse, her daily life.

* * *

Two years later—after the travel to mental health conferences and once the professionals were involved—we would visit and rifle through a corner of a room together. She would fund our wine like cheap therapy, and the three of us would howl our way through decision and disposal. "What were you *thinking* when you bought this dress, a future in the cabaret?" This time, she was in on the joke. I once counted 34 bags of clothes in the garage awaiting removal—a hard day's work. Would they ever leave was the question. That garage is more like a holding pattern: Things move around but are rarely released. The psychologists call it "churning".

* * *

In the opening session of our first Hoarding and Cluttering conference, my sister and I meet the Collyer brothers, hailed as the Killjoy's forefathers from the early to mid-20th century. Faded images of their hoard grace the screen. But at the mention of their home in Harlem, we exchange a puzzled glance: What were rich white boys doing in Harlem at that time? Little did we know we weren't the first to wonder, but their race-class story is nowhere to be told. When we inquire about other factors, like gender and capitalism, the psychologists perk up. This is possible, they say, but we don't yet know enough. What we *do* know is that hoarding crosses time, place, culture, sex, even species. So there must be something about the gray matter.

Faulty wiring: This comforts our Killjoy, as does the idea that trauma caused it. This she can work with, because this she can work *on* (or appear to). When we regale her with our magnificent theoretical alternatives, she feigns interest but her body slumps. How does that help me, girls? I don't *want* to feel better about this.

At the conferences, we meet ourselves too. We learn that children of hoarders, especially women, are far more likely not to have children. Well, isn't that more than hypothetically interesting (we don't have kids)? The Organizational Killjoy, like her queer counterpart, disrupts happy circuits of breeding too. We are told to feel proud of our escape to the land of normalcy, our firm grip on our possessions, our perspective on *things*—and we do. We can only help her so far, they say. You must take care of yourselves.

* * *

We learned these boundaries anew some years later, when the Hoard returned better than ever and the plumbing went unfixed. The Killjoy receded into the shadows in favor of other ways of relating, which was fine by frustrated us. Screw conversion therapy and run with who she can be. This is why some psychologists push for "harm reduction" rather than healing: If you can't quit the habit, make it safer to live by. We never quite got there either, though. Not yet. Nor are we actively trying.

* * *

What relations are made by addressing hoarding in these ways? A way through, always and only for now. Human connection that makes space for strange attractions to nonhuman stuff. The Hoard brings us into relation, and we conspire against it together, armed with professional expertise, practical tips, intellectual escapes and tireless humor. There is the minor glee of making her giggle: ask if she sees the hotel housekeeping cart, full of tiny soaps and bottles for the taking, shudder when she walks by. And then there is the Killjoy, basking in the sun of our normative order, bragging about her daughters' lives to strangers. The sheer fact that we persist in relating at all is something: the best we've ever been at doing family. We are no match for the Hoard's power, to be sure. Nor can it kill our joy: We navigate a mutual pleasure that has been hard to come by over the years.

No, our Killjoy cannot host visits or holidays, and we are in some real sense displaced by her things. But neither is stuff a substitute for people here. Rather, people and their relations are emerging out of an imperative to "take care of *things*", to "get our *house* in order". This is not to say that stuff is causing those relations, or that it is *well* cared for in the process—by the Killjoy or her normative daughters—but it is most certainly involved. And I have come to orient differently to nonhuman things along the way. For example . . .

What must I mute to separate these things from myself, to keep them in their place? I get a small glimpse when, every now and then, I still work hard to swallow that feeling I knew as a child: that an object does not deserve to be discarded after all the good times we had together, even if it is used up. I *still* have to remind myself on occasion that *a thing is disposable.*

How different this is from the work that lets me feed on a battered animal carcass just after cuddling a pet, or helps me normalize sexual harassment and objectify my own body, or stokes that sense of white entitlement which renders brown bodies expendable, I cannot say. But the line between human and nonhuman doesn't look as sharp as it used to. It takes affective work, including the suppression of affect, to keep drawing it "right". This line is the *difference* continually made in the act of addressing hoarding.

***

As part of this project, she let me visit her home and record the conversation as we walked around and tripped over things. My partner stayed outside until, unexpectedly, she let him in. The generosity of that gesture, for all bodies involved, should not be understated. I was struck by the nervously proud tour she gave him of the home's former grandeur—what it used to be, what it could have been, its resale value if she could only clean it up, what a sweet piece of real estate and conspicuous consumption it was and stands to be.

She cares about things like everyone else does. Or so she needed him to know, I think. And I was touched by our Killjoy's normal imaginary, despite everything I know to be wrong with it, and even as we all stood there dying to burn the place down.

But *no matter*. I have already inherited it, in more ways than one.

Speculations: Addressing the Study of Communication and Dis/Organization

As evident in this imperfect illustration, the fourth articulation ponders what relational worlds emerge as hoarding is variously addressed. Concrete dilemmas of hoarding make contact with and alternate among each of the three narratives, sometimes merging them. A scholar-daughter becomes in relation to the Organizational Killjoy and is tied up with other bodies in the surround, as they tussle over appropriate distinctions (how to address stuff: human or not? creaturely? a thing with feelings and/or to feel for? object-ified, or *just* a thing?). No clear conclusions arise, but some connections come into view.

For one, the capacity for agency, or making a difference, does not reside in the hoarder, therapist, discourse or hoard. It emanates from the practice of addressing hoarding, which entails trying, and often failing, to fix the status of participants as human or nonhuman. It is worth underscoring the dual meaning of *making a difference* here: not only coming to matter, but *be*coming a particular *kind* of matter in relation (distinction) to other kinds. Addressing the Organizational Killjoy, in other words, upholds a human duty to produce and control such fundamental divides, and thereby *become* more fully human, by "feeling right"—humming along as an operative node on the affective motherboard of capitalist relations. To hum along joyfully is to sense without pause the sharp difference between persons and things, valuable and disposable. Because she feels things differently, the Organizational Killjoy miscarries the mandate to make waste happily. Yet imminent in her floundering is a potential: to stop blaming her for the fire and, instead, *trace more carefully how and which bodies get burned in the act of feeling right*. More on this in a moment.

Whereas the psychiatric narrative enacts empathy through expert assistance, critical-cultural through ideological emancipation and post-humanist/new materialist through uncommon listening, addressing hoarding performs empathy through *perceptive inhabitation*. It cannot "fix" either hoarder or hoard, but neither does it wash its hands of *the matter*. It offers help by noticing moments of promise and alarm that arise in attempted acts of repair. For this illustration, that meant snuggling up to the Organizational Killjoy and losing my self in joint attempts to tame the hoard. The goal was to sense more fully what is required to mend the motherboard—to demarcate deviant "her" and rebellious "things" from normal "us"—and to start discerning what sorts of consequences are cast down the line. This is *not* to say that the fourth narrative requires personal encounters with hoarding; any mode of address can be known through inhabitation.

As demonstrated in the preceding account, addressing hoarding reworks the first three narratives as parallel modes of address, on par with confronting the aging plumbing confronting you, ducking behind the hoard to weep at its power, the passivity and utter exhaustion with which she carves out a tiny space to watch television or writing this chapter. Flattened as comparable modes of address, these practices are multiple ontologies of hoarding. Thus, while it is tempting to see the fourth articulation as a meta-narrative, it refuses any privileged place. It cannot vie for ontological authority, because it already abandoned that quest(ion). It cannot address hoarding from some mythical higher level because it disputes the possibility of a perch outside of practice. In short, the turn to address proposed here is itself a mode of address, albeit one occupied by the rich array of addressings.

Returning to the matter marked above—the promise of tracing how and which bodies get burned—this is my ultimate contention: Addressing hoarding is a struggle over a bodily reflex, one that makes a body human by closing its affective valves toward any*thing* deemed less than fully human. Certainly inorganic things, but also organic matter, "nature" severed from "culture", creature bodies of all kinds and bodies veering toward the "animal", variously stigmatized and objectified, for example, by race, class, gender, sexuality, immigration and citizenship status, religion and the list of possibilities goes on. Boiled down to blunt terms, the mandate to organize things vis-à-vis people compels a physical, sensory ability to stomach the forceful stratification and regulation of difference functional to capitalist societies. Repairing the Organizational Killjoy is an ontological practice that circulates this obligatory complicity, a cultural and economic urgency that seeps into automatic bodily response.

For communication scholars, the turn to address provides a concrete illustration of how we can approach communication as an affective ontological practice, wherein the human and nonhuman as well as social and material are invariably entangled *and* made to appear distinct. Theorizing communication in ways that take sociomateriality seriously and decenter human agency is no easy task, as it unsettles the grounds of much current communication inquiry (see Kuhn et al., 2017). Social problems like hoarding, I suggest, oblige us to try.

Far more unsettling, however, are the implications of this project for the study of organization. For if I hope one of my speculations will stick, it is this: The relentless threat of disorganization stokes a fear of difference out of control, and the frantic quest for organization circulates a promise that difference can be handled, kept in its place, through the "correct" regulation of affect. If so, we are called to consider the possibility that relations of difference such as race, gender, sexuality, class and more do not merely help to constitute occupational and organizational worlds (e.g., Acker, 1990; Ashcraft, 2013). Rather, consenting to replicate these and affiliated divisions and rankings—without incapacitating qualms—may be the ticket to becoming a fuller human subject in advanced capitalism, where it pays to know by feel, yet somehow devoid of feeling, the difference between valuable bodies and expendable Others. To readily calculate the more and less human, or object; to sense correctly the order of "things". The impulse to organization itself becomes politically and morally ambiguous, a *thing* in question, to question.

Notes

1. This is the acronym for the latest edition of the *Diagnostic and Statistical Manual of Mental Disorders*.
2. For example, older definitions of "consumption" as a disease that ravages bodies with rot and "hoarding" as greedily stashing money.

3. Consider, for instance, advertising that beckons us to feel for even discarded things (e.g., the despondent old mop replaced by the Swiffer), or dating sites that urge us to commodify and market ourselves in affective economies (Illouz, 2007).
4. See Baudrillard (1996), for example, as cited in Herring (2011b).
5. It may help to recall that even the clinical definition cited at the outset hints at material defiance: "living spaces are sufficiently cluttered *so as to preclude activities for which those spaces were designed*" (Claes et al., 2016, p. 65, emphasis added).
6. Despite explicit association with the Collyer Brothers, hoarding became feminized as psychiatric studies picked up steam in the late 1990s and garnered public attention in the 2000s, in part because illustrative cases predominantly featured women.

6 Communication Constitutes Capital

Branding and the Politics of Neoliberal Dis/Organization

Dennis K. Mumby

"Communication constitutes organization." This claim has, in many ways, become a defining (one might even say "constitutive!") feature of the field of organizational communication (Boivin, Brummans & Barker, 2017). The mainstreaming of this so-called "linguistic turn" (Deetz, 2003) over the last 30 years has elevated communication from its hand-maiden role in the early years of the field (i.e., communication viewed as an epiphenomenal feature of already extant organizational structures and processes) to its current place as enabling the very ontological possibility of organizing. Everyone in the field—bar the most unreconstructed of neopositivists—accepts the basic truth of this idea and, indeed, many pages of books and journals have been devoted to exploring its implications (Ashcraft, Kuhn & Cooren, 2009; Cooren, 2015; Deetz, 2003; Kuhn, Ashcraft & Cooren, 2017; Putnam & Pacanowsky, 1983).

Now, I have no desire to challenge this claim or its generative capacity; it has significantly transformed our field—both theoretically and empirically—and has enabled researchers to develop a significantly more nuanced and complex understanding of organizational life. I do want to suggest, however, that this claim has directed our attention in ways that have not always been productive. In particular, I would argue that while this "constitutive" model of organizing has directed our attention to important questions of sensemaking, meaning construction, identity management and so forth, it has also resulted in a number of blind spots among researchers in the field. In this chapter, I want to address two of those blind spots.

First, it is clear that communication not only constitutes organization but also *dis*organization or, perhaps more accurately, dis/organization (Cooper, 1986; Knox, O'Doherty, Vurdubakis & Westrup, 2015; Kuhn, 2012; Trethewey & Ashcraft, 2004). For 30 years or more the constitutive model has focused predominantly on how organizing creates coherence, stability and shared organizational realities. This has been true regardless of theoretical perspective. For example, critical organization scholars have focused largely on the processes through which stable relations of power are constructed in the workplace (Burawoy, 1979;

Clegg, 1975; Collinson, 1992; Mumby, 1988). Interpretive scholars, on the other hand, have focused on the social construction of organizational reality(-ies) (Keyton, 2011; Martin, Feldman, Hatch & Sitkin, 1983). Even Karl Weick, for all his focus on nonrational sensemaking processes, sees organizing as an exercise in equivocality reduction (Weick, 1969, 1995). The focus, then, has been on how organizational stability and coherence are maintained in the face of challenges to that stability (e.g., resistance to the dominant power relations in the case of critical studies; alternative sensemaking processes in the case of interpretive studies). I am not saying that these perspectives ignore change, instability or disorganization. Rather, I am suggesting that their default position is to assume organization and stability as the optimal condition of everyday organizational life. While in recent years constitutive approaches to the study of paradoxes, tensions and contradictions have become *de rigueur* in organization studies (see Putnam, Fairhurst & Banghart, 2016, for an overview), this research focuses almost exclusively on how such phenomena are dynamic elements of, and integral to, organizing. Such research may view organizing as tension filled, tenuous and existing only in the moment to moment of everyday communication processes, but the "moment to moment" is extended indefinitely into the "*longue durée*" of institutionalized organizational forms (Giddens, 1979).

I want to operate from a different "default" in this chapter. I assume that *dis*organization is the lifeblood of everyday organizing and that, moreover, disorganization is both medium and outcome of work and identity under neoliberalism. Indeed, I would go further and suggest that disorganization, insecurity and precarity are necessary and constitutive features of organizing within post-Fordism and neoliberal capitalism. Disorganization and precarity are political processes and conditions that function as forms of governmentality (Foucault, 1979b; Miller & Rose, 2008), managing the dialectic between freedom and insecurity within neoliberalism (Lorey, 2015; Neilson & Rossiter, 2008). Disorganization, then, can be read as a form of neoliberal governmentality that promotes a particular kind of "free subject" who accepts precarity and "precarization" (Lorey, 2015) as a normal state of affairs. In this sense, a state of insecurity is an increasingly routine feature of subject formation under neoliberal capitalism.

Second, and related, I want to address the blind spot that enables organizational communication scholars to focus on the for-profit organization as the default organizational context, and yet consistently neglect the ways in which organizing and economic value production intersect. In other words, organizational communication scholars have generally ignored the communicative dimensions of dis/organization as a capital generation process. In this chapter I will address the relationship between communication and capital, arguing that communication constitutes capital, largely through the intersection of branding, the so-called "social factory" (Gill & Pratt, 2008; Lazzarato, 2009) and processes of "pre-carization" (Lorey, 2015). These links are not simple or causal, but speak rather to how value production in neoliberal capitalism has become less about struggles between capital and labor over the indeterminacy of labor power (as was the case under Fordist capitalism) and increasingly about struggles between capital and everyday life over the indeterminacy of meaning (Mumby, 2016).

My goals in this chapter, then, are as follows. First, I want to make a case for the historical centrality of communication to the capital accumulation process—a necessary move in making the case that "communication constitutes capital". Far from being peripheral, communication processes have always been central to, and constitutive of, capital accumulation processes. Second, I will address the emergence of the brand as a principal dis/organizing process in contemporary neoliberal capitalism. Third, I will explore the relationship between branding and the emergence of neoliberal governmentality, particularly in terms of their relationship to precarity, insecurity and disorganization. Finally, I will outline some elements of a CCC (Communication Constitutes Capital) model of organizing.

Communication, Capital and Organization

An alternative "CCO" perspective examines the relationships among Communication, Capital and Organization. The received view in the field is that communication was not taken seriously as constitutive of the organizing process until the late 1970s/early 1980s with the linguistic turn in social theory (Deetz, 2003; Putnam & Pacanowsky, 1983). However, this view belies the degree to which communication processes have been central to (and, indeed, constitutive of) capitalist organization from its very inception. As Virno (2004) has indicated, relations with others have always been a driving feature of the capital accumulation process, and thus one of the constitutive elements of the 20th century development and transformations of capitalism has been the evolving character and definitions of those "relations with others". Thus, rather than address the communicative production of organization (our default analytic position in the field), I want to explore the communicative organization of capitalist production via a "communicative imagination" (Kuhn, 2017).

In the early 20th century, scientific management (Taylor, 1911/1934) was not simply a set of management principles, but also embodied an incipient "transmission" model of communication that produced and reproduced particular social and political relations between management and labor. While our field typically thinks of the transmission model of communication as antithetical to constitutive views of the communication-organization relationship, this model is indeed constitutive of particular forms of organizing (Kuhn et al., 2017) and, indeed, capitalism (Miller & Rose, 1995).

On the one hand, Taylor's hierarchical model of organization embodied a transmission model of communication that constituted a particular subject/management–object/worker relationship. Taylor knew that the social and affectively solidary relations among workers in pre- and early capitalist industries had to be overcome in order to wrest control of the labor process from workers. The fact that—prior to Taylorism—workers knew more about the labor process than managers rendered the labor process indeterminate for capital and unnecessarily restricted (from capital's point of view) the creation of surplus value. Thus, as Braverman (1974) has shown, the Taylorization process was not intended primarily to make work more efficient (although it certainly did this) but to separate the conception of work from its execution, and hence provide management with a monopoly over knowledge about the labor process, rendering the erstwhile indeterminate more determinate.

On the other hand, Taylor's principles can be read as an important element of the burgeoning early 20th century Progressive movement which, in part, addressed concerns about the concentration of power in the hands of business executives and its effects on democracy and the public good. Taylor's development of a scientifically based system of rationalized work and its attendant system of communication substituted the arbitrary and capricious authority of late 19th-/early-20th-century capitalists with systematized managerial expertise (Miller & O'Leary, 1987; Miller & Rose, 1995). Thus, the systematization of communication processes under Taylorism can be read as part of the effort to mitigate early 20th century capitalism's legitimation crisis.

The legacy of Taylor's model of communication is thus complex in the sense that while it undermined the social aspect of work, individualizing the worker and instituting a subject–object, manager–worker relation, it simultaneously created the possibility for a more democratic workplace that reduced the need for state intervention to deal with the unchecked power of capitalism (Miller & Rose, 1995, p. 432). Of course, as Braverman has shown, it is this separation of the conception of work from its execution (previously unified in the worker) that enabled monopoly capital to deskill workers and essentially render hand and brain not only disconnected entities, but hostile to one another. In Taylor's system, communication functions as the information-based reification of this system (sometimes, for example, through the use of daily written work instructions).

The model of organizational bureaucracy that was dominant for much of the 20th century further inscribes this Taylorist model of communication. While Taylor focused on the micro-practices of work, the Weberian bureaucratic model institutionalizes written, impersonal rules of conduct that in many ways reify the transmission model of communication as a fundamental element of the organizational form. In terms of the relationships among communication, capitalism and organization, bureaucracy represents an important effort beyond Taylorism to stabilize capitalism after the turbulence of the late 19th--/early-20th-century period of "primitive" capitalism. As Boltanski and Chiapello (2005) show, this bureaucratic phase represents a second "spirit" of capitalism, with the figure of the rational manager as central to efforts to bring stability to the capital accumulation process. The figure of the rational manager also helps to further obviate the critique of capitalism as an exploitive system that creates massive inequalities in society; bureaucracy creates the possibilities for a meritocratic system of advancement in which, theoretically at least, all can participate. As Edwards (1979) has shown, moreover, the formalization of communication processes through a bureaucratic administrative apparatus helped to neutralize the contested relations between workers and managers by creating a legal-rational decision-making system that obscured asymmetric power relations. The production of surplus value, then, was framed as a natural consequence of a rationalized system of communication rooted in long-term decision-making. Thus, the locus of organizational control was shifted from capitalists to technocrats who used the rhetoric of science, rationality and the general welfare to establish their authority (Illouz, 2007, p. 11).

Of course, Taylorist and bureaucratic efforts to communicatively construct the capital accumulation process as the inevitable outcome of efficiency and rational planning could not completely eliminate the social and affective elements of organizing. Indeed, one could argue that these systems still *depended* on the social and affective for their continued reproduction. Bureaucracy, for example, has historically been dependent on a form of sociality that privileges white males and excludes minority groups. As Acker has shown, bureaucratic structures are not gender, race or class neutral but are structured on "inequality regimes" that both obscure the embodied and social character of work while simultaneously presuming an abstract and disembodied worker as the norm (Acker, 1990, 2006). Moreover, efforts to resist bureaucratic forms (e.g., Fordist corporations) have often included tactics that involve "working to rule" and "Svejkism" (Fleming & Sewell, 2002); that is, enthusiastically following bureaucratic rules to the letter such that the system comes grinding to a halt.

The emergence of the "human relations" movement in the 1950s and 1960s, then, was in part an effort to systematize the place of the social and affective in the capital accumulation process (Hassard, 2012). Technocrats teamed up with psychologists to explore the individual and irrational/emotional dimension of work. Elton Mayo is key to this transformation, recognizing as he did the fundamentally alienating experience of work in industrial capitalism, and comparing it to the "shell shock" experienced by the Australian soldiers he counseled during World War I (Smith, 1998). Mayo's introduction of a psychoanalytic approach to work (particularly, for example, with the deployment of "ventilation interviews" in the workplace) created a strong connection between the language of emotion (employees expressing their feelings about their work) and productivity. Alienation from work was thus conceived as the effect of unresolved psychological and emotional conflicts in workers (rather than fundamental structural contradictions within capitalist relations of production) that could be resolved through therapeutic communication. Fritz Roethlisberger's (1953) analysis of a workplace communication breakdown, for example, positions the manager in a quasi-therapeutic role, as someone who needs to be in touch with and deal with his or her own feelings in interactions with workers. As Miller and Rose (1995) state, Mayo and the Human Relations Movement's intervention meant that, "The plant was now understood as pervaded by an attitudinal and communicative atmosphere, a socio-psychological overlay to the actual organization of the productive process itself" (p. 435).

Thus, in terms of the connection between work and productivity we see a shift from a conception of communication as directive and instructive under scientific management and bureaucracy, to a conception of communication as therapeutic and relational. As Illouz has suggested, under human relations theory a continuity emerges between the family and the workplace whereby the blurring of public and private life occurs as emotional life becomes more central to work (Illouz, 2007, pp. 14–15). Illouz claims that the popular management psychology guidebooks from the 1930s to 1970s (when the model of Fordist industrial capitalism was at its most powerful) converged around the "cultural model" of communication as a new episteme (in Foucault's sense) that served as a "new object of knowledge that generate[d] new instruments and practices of management" (p. 18). Central to this object of knowledge, she argues, is a workplace self that must be taught to "perform its authentic interiority" (p. 21) as a way of demonstrating social competence and empathy. Professional competence is thus redefined not in rational terms, but in emotional terms, as the ability to empathize with others.

Illouz thus argues convincingly that "Emotional capitalism is a culture in which emotional and economic discourses and practices mutually shape each other, thus producing . . . a broad, sweeping movement in which affect is made an essential aspect of economic behavior and in which emotional life . . . follows the logic of economic relations and exchange" (2007, p. 5). And communication (or a particular conception thereof) is a constitutive feature of this relationship, perhaps peaking in the 1980s with the emergence of the corporate culture movement.

In many respects, this movement was the next logical step in the codification of emotion and affect into everyday organizing, with explicit connections to productivity and capital accumulation (particularly given the newly emergent specter of Japanese competition for global US market share). The corporate culture movement responded to this economic threat by making advances in the colonization of the employee's self-identity. While the adoption of a therapeutic model of communication was important in this regard, the corporate culture movement transformed this from a psychoanalytic focus on empathy and worker sentiment to a focus on the larger systems of meaning and sensemaking in which employees participated. The goal, then, was to "engineer culture" (Kunda, 1992) such that the employee's very sense of self was colonized by the corporation (Deetz, 1992). Work and identity thus became intrinsically linked.

One of the most interesting things about the corporate culture movement is that it reflects an effort to respond not only to the emergence of Japan as an economic power, but also to worker resistance against the increasingly alienating character of Fordist work. As Ross (2003) points out, quoting the 1973 US Department of Health, Education and Welfare report, *Work in America*, "Dull, repetitive, seemingly meaningless tasks, offering little challenge or autonomy, are causing discontent among workers at all occupational levels. . . . [H]aving an interesting job is now as important as having a job that pays well" (2003, p. 6). The emergence of the corporate culture movement, then, can be read as an adaptation of capitalism to the increasing disaffection of employees with Fordist work regimes, and an important part of this response was not only an effort to make work more meaningful, but also to actively and communicatively construct meanings about work.

It is therefore no accident that the corporate culture movement discovers narratives, metaphors, symbols, rituals and so forth, as the communicative structures through which the idea of work as meaningful is constructed. In effect, a new episteme emerged in which the object of knowledge is not simply a self that must "perform its authentic interiority", but rather a self that must perceive work and enterprise as intrinsic to the very definition of what it means to be a human being in the late 20th century. Communication becomes constitutive of the capital accumulation process in that it constructs organizational realities and meaning systems that function as a form of employee identity regulation (Alvesson & Willmott, 2002), in which each employee's sense of self is tied to a culture of enterprise (Du Gay, 1996). The regulation of employee identities creates workers who engage in processes of "self-disciplining" (Willmott, 1993) such that their exercise of "autonomy" is consistent with the core values of the corporate culture. If, under human relations, managerial competence was defined through empathy with the alienated, emotional worker, under the corporate culture movement every worker becomes a manager whose very sense of (authentic, non-alienated, enterprising) self involves internalizing an organizational, entrepreneurial reality.

Importantly, however, this discourse of enterprise was not limited to the corporate context. As Vallas and Cummins (2015) point out, beginning in the 1980s "the audience for popular business books began to expand in two directions at once: downward in the organizational and class hierarchy, and outward, encompassing new markets of young (and mid-career) job seekers and job changers" (p. 301). This is an important discursive (in the Foucauldian sense of the creation of subjects and forms of knowledge) and cultural shift in that it helps to lay the groundwork for the idea that "enterprise" and the "entrepreneurial self" are defining features of everyday life in the dis/organizing processes that constitute social actors as "human capital" (Becker, 1976) under 21st century neoliberalism, or what Foucault (2008) refers to in its US form as "anarcho-liberalism".

The turn to corporate culture, then, represents not an effort to eliminate the nonrational, affective aspects of organizing (as under Taylorism and bureaucracy) or to patronize it (as under human relations and human resource management), but to colonize it and govern it by engaging in "governance of the employee's soul" as a means to competitive advantage (see also Rose, 1999; Willmott, 1993, p. 517). The use of the term "soul" here is particularly apposite given that the corporate culture movement is seen as key to capitalism's economic and *moral* recovery in the wake of the collapse of Fordism during the 1970s. The corporate culture movement is thus a response to the legitimation crisis that the 1970s posed, articulating a new conception of work and organizations rooted in work as meaningful, value-driven and tied to employee self-identity— what Boltanski and Chiapello (2005) describe as the third (and current) "spirit" of capitalism.

This shift to corporate culture in the 1980s is also consistent with the rise of neoliberalism and post-Fordism during that time. With the global restructuring of capital, product markets and labor, we see a shift to a more flexible and contingent model of capital accumulation that requires parallel transformations in the nature of organizing. The corporate culture model gets employees to internalize the values of quality, flexibility and "value-added" (i.e., the idea that there is a close connection between individual behavior and capital accumulation—a connection that was much more indirect under Fordism). As Harvey (1989) has suggested, the transformation from Fordism to post-Fordism involves increased efforts to manage "the fleeting, the ephemeral, the fugitive, and the contingent in modern life" (p. 171). The corporate culture movement enables this through its emphasis on meaning and sensemaking, and stressing each individual employee's responsibility to autonomously manage their relationship with corporate values.

An important element of the corporate culture movement, however, was the idea of a corporate monoculture with which all employees strongly identify and which provides the resources for collective sensemaking (Peters & Waterman, 1982; Sathe, 1983). In this sense, we are still in the realm of common organizing properties, the point of which is to provide a shared affective experience that helps to minimize indeterminacy and ambiguity. Employee obedience, in this sense, is not about following orders or rules but about exercising autonomy within a shared set of core values. In the next section, however, our attention shifts to the dis/organizing processes that have, to a considerable degree, assigned the corporate culture movement and the idea of an organizational monoculture to the trash heap of management history.

Communication, Branding and Dis/Organizing

In addressing the relationships among communication, capital and organization in the previous section, I assumed the employment relationship as the unit of analysis. I explored how each of the constitutive conceptions of communication constructed a particular relationship between capital and labor. Within this framework, the question is how communication mediates and constructs the capital-labor relationship, and hence renders the indeterminacy of labor power more determinate in the production of surplus value. In this section I want to move beyond this conception and examine the dis/organizing properties of branding processes as a way to conceptualize the shift from Fordism to post-Fordism and neoliberalism. This shift, I argue, moves "organizing beyond organization" (Mumby, 2016) and transforms the locus of the capital accumulation process from the struggle between capital and labor "at the point of production" (Burawoy, 1979; Gramsci, 1971) to that between capital and everyday life. As several scholars of work have argued, the consequence of this shift is the transformation of life itself into living labor (Fleming, 2014; Zwick, Bonsu & Darmody, 2008). In this sense, my unit of analysis is no longer the employment relationship (i.e., the relationship between capital and labor in the narrow sense), but the relationship between capital and everyday life (Fleming, 2014), as it is mediated by the brand as institutional form (Arvidsson, 2006).

Central to this development was capital's recognition (sometime in the mid-1980s) that the production of goods was no longer the defining element of the capital accumulation process. Instead, capital increasingly relies on the meaning creation processes of communication itself as a central and constitutive feature of capital accumulation. As Lazzarato (2004) has famously argued, "Contemporary capitalism does not first arrive with factories; these follow, if they follow at all. It arrives with words, signs, and images" (p. 190). In this sense, one can argue that over the last 30 years the process of capital accumulation has shifted from a struggle over the indeterminacy of *labor* to a struggle over the indeterminacy of *meaning*. Capital thus harnesses communication as its principal mode of production. Of course, this does not mean that the actual production by workers of material goods is no longer an important part of the capital accumulation process. Rather, I am suggesting that the changing demands of capital have fundamentally reshaped the ways in which corporations pursue the profit motive and have, in effect, led to the rethinking of the very concept of the corporation.

Weil (2014) coined the term "fissured workplace" to describe this new corporate form. Stated aphoristically, the fissured workplace is described as follows: "Find your distinctive niche and stick to it. Then shed everything else" (p. 50). As he indicates, this development is not simply the product of the latest management fad, but rather is a response to the increasing demands of capital for ever-increasing returns on investment:

> Facing ever greater pressures from public and private capital markets to improve returns, companies who adopt fissured employment strategies aim to improve profitability by focusing attention and controlling the most profitable aspects of firm value while shedding the actual production of goods or provision of services.
>
> (Weil, 2014, p. 25)

The demands of capital have thus resulted in the growth of private equity models of investment in which private equity firms buy up corporations and restructure them and/or strip them of their assets. The goal here, of course, is to provide maximum shareholder yields, typically with a short-term investment horizon of five to seven years—a huge change from the Fordist strategy of long-term, multi-decade organizational planning. In this context, the principal role of management is to maximize a business's value to shareholders, resulting in such phenomena as incentive pay systems for CEOs, a shift from defined benefits (under Fordism) to defined contributions (under post-Fordism) for employees (which are subject to the vagaries of the market), and most importantly (at least for our purposes here), the pursuit of core competencies by the organization. Under this system, the product is less important than a company's flexibility and adaptability to changing market forces.

As such, the identification of "core competencies" (i.e., a company's distinctive niche in the market) is heavily defined by a company's brand which, over the last 30 years, has emerged as the principal means of capital accumulation for corporations. As Weil indicates, the actual production of the goods they purport to sell is a peripheral or even irrelevant feature of many organizations. In this sense, one can argue that organizations do not create brands; rather, brands create organizations (Kornberger, 2010). Organizations figure out and develop their brand—what they "stand for"—and then structure themselves around the core competencies that enable them to create and maintain that brand—a process, of course, that is fundamentally communicative in character in its continuous management of image, meaning and identity, along with customers' affective responses to those meaning management processes. In other words, the brand is "boss" (Endrissat, Kärreman & Noppeny,

2017) in contemporary organizational life. An example here might help clarify this point.

Brand "guru" Wally Olins (2000) quotes a Ford company executive as stating, "The manufacture of cars will be a declining part of Ford's business. They will concentrate in the future on design, branding, marketing, sales, and service operations" (p. 51). This is quite an astonishing statement given the status of Ford in the US cultural imagination as perhaps *the* icon of 20th century manufacturing prowess. However, it exemplifies the recognition of many companies that value production lies not in the manufacture of products per se, but in the management of image, meaning and identity around those products. Concomitantly, actual production processes become peripheral to the core corporate mission and their costs can be externalized through outsourcing, leaving a core group of knowledge workers to execute the real business of the company. It is not too hyperbolic, then, to claim that the brand is not an extension of the company; rather, the company is an extension of the brand, and hence communicatively constituted through the branded management of meaning.

The centrality of the branding process to contemporary capitalism is perhaps best summed up by former Coca-Cola CMO Sergio Zyman's (2002) statement that "everything communicates". On the face of it this is a fairly bland restatement of a truism that every student learns in Communication 101: "One cannot not communicate". However, the statement is key to the shift in the capital accumulation process mentioned above, whereby the central struggle over value production has shifted from the struggle between capital and labor to that between capital and everyday life and, in particular, the struggle over the indeterminacy of meaning. "Everything communicates" thus speaks to the infinite potential for everyday life to be captured and placed in the service of economic value production, mediated through branding processes.

Brands therefore operate at the epicenter of neoliberal dis/organization processes in that they are premised on (in)determinacy. This is true in at least two senses. First, brands thrive on a surplus of meaning that is never fully determinate. A brand whose meaning becomes fixed eventually dies. Sears, for example, has been unable to adapt to the new, Amazon-dominated retail world, and has lost its brand coherence, hence endangering its very existence (in 2018 the company announced two rounds of closures of more than 100 stores). Brands cultivate a dialogue with their publics, constantly engaging in efforts to exploit the various ways that brand consumers appropriate and extend brands. In this sense, brands thrive on resistance and "causing trouble" (Holt, 2002). Second, brands engage in a "politics of ambivalence" (Banet-Weiser, 2012) in which they constantly mediate the tension-filled relationship between the neoliberal privileging of the (entrepreneurial) self and the formation of collective communities around political and social issues (in which the self is defined in relationship to a broader identity community). Brands are aimed at individual selves; in many respects, they stand in for the loss of institutional and social moorings—family, religion, social group—that grounded the modern self. At the same time, however, the self must feel part of a larger "brand public" that enables connection and belonging (Arvidsson & Peitersen, 2013).

One might argue, then, that branding processes operate at the intersection of organization and disorganization. Via the indeterminacy of meaning, brands under neoliberal capitalism make possible the accumulation of capital by functioning as medium and outcome of the (in)determinacy of the dis/organization process (Mumby, 2018). Thus, under neoliberal capitalism the notion that "everything communicates" is a shorthand way to connect the production and management of meaning to the production of economic surplus value. Capitalism today is less about creating surplus value by making the indeterminacy of labor more determinate, and more about managing and mediating the indeterminacy and surplus of meaning within branded contexts. As such, all of everyday life has the potential to create surplus value if it is subject to corporate capture through branding processes.

Contemporary branding is not confined to corporate efforts to sell to consumers; employees, too, are an integral part of the corporate branding effort. Indeed, as several scholars have suggested (e.g., Fleming, 2014; Land & Taylor, 2010), corporations have widely adopted "neo-normative" forms of control where the goal is not to shape employees to the dictates of the organizational norms, but rather to "build their brand outside-in by incorporating identities that are already in play" (Endrissat et al., 2017, pp. 491–492). In this sense, corporations mobilize and incorporate extant sub-cultures to provide employees with the "freedom" to be themselves. Moreover, the distinctions among employees, consumers and branded organizations are increasingly breaking down as spheres of capital accumulation and everyday life become more indistinguishable, and domains of life formerly considered private become grist for value production as part of the so-called "attention economy" (Duffy, 2015; Duffy & Hund, 2015; Marwick, 2015). Thus, the relationship between capital and everyday life suggests that brands and branding processes are an endemic and ubiquitous feature of "communicative capitalism" (Dean, 2009, 2014), in which value production "doesn't depend on the commodity-thing. It directly exploits the social relation at the heart of [economic] value" (Dean, 2012, p. 129).

Lest this argument is perceived as somewhat hyperbolic, it is worth pointing out that the very architecture of what Srnicek (2017) refers to as "platform capitalism" (i.e., the development within the digital economy of infrastructures that function as intermediaries between different groups—consumers, advertisers, service providers, etc.) depends on the recording, extraction and analysis of everyday behaviors. As an economic model, the digital economy has an inevitable tendency to ever greater extraction of data about everyday human behavior as a means to revenue generation. For example, in the context of the so-called "internet of things" (IoT), "Google's investment in Nest, a heating system for residential homes, makes much more sense when it is understood as the extension of data extraction" (Srnicek, 2017, p. 99). In other words, Google has little interest in home heating as a business, but lots of interest in the consumer behavior data generated by a "smart" heating system. Similarly, the Amazon Echo not only interacts with consumers, but also records their activities, thus providing Amazon with useful information about consumer preferences. My point here is that the vampiric relationship of capitalism to everyday life is fundamental to the growth and vitality of the 21st century capitalist mode of production. Within this mode of production, brands and branding processes are the articulatory mechanisms through which this extractive process is made meaningful and turned into value.

Brand as "Vitalpolitik" in Dis/Organizing Processes

How, then, do branding, precarity and disorganizing intersect? And, what might a communication perspective on this intersection look like? Following Lorey (2015) and others (e.g., McRobbie, 2016; Neilson & Rossiter, 2008), I want to suggest that precarity and insecurity are necessary and constitutive elements of neoliberalism, and that branding functions as one important way in which neoliberalism both constitutes and mediates this insecurity and precarity. In this sense, brands are at the center of dis/organizing processes, managing the indeterminacy of meaning and mediating in the politics of ambivalence, providing (momentary) points of coherence within an ever-shifting and often chaotic economic and political terrain. Although Lorey does not address branding per se, one can argue that a focus on branding enables us to understand "how we are governed and keep ourselves governable specifically through precarization" (Lorey, 2015, p. 2).

Brands, I want to suggest, are capitalist institutions (Arvidsson, 2006) that function as a form of "Vitalpolitik" in 21st-century neoliberalism. "Vitalpolitik" is a term I borrow—via Foucault (2008)—from the German Ordoliberal group of economists of the early-/mid-20th century. The term refers to the Ordoliberal recognition that the capitalist economic sphere itself cannot provide a stable mode of social integration for a free market enterprise system. As Habermas (1987) might say, there can be no "system" without a Lifeworld. Thus, the Ordoliberals rejected a "laissez-faire" market model (in part because they argued that it led to the development of monopolies) in favor of a system of state "Vitalpolitik" that mediated and limited the market's excesses and maintained a form of social and moral integration. Foucault (2008) puts this in the following manner:

138 Dennis K. Mumby

The return to the enterprise is therefore at once an economic policy or a policy of the economization of the entire social field, of an extension of the economy to the entire social field, but at the same time a policy which presents itself or seeks to be a kind of *Vitalpolitik* with the function of compensating for what is cold, impassive, calculating, rational, and mechanical in the strictly economic game of competition. The enterprise society imagined by the *ordoliberals* is therefore a society for the market and a society against the market, a society oriented towards the market and a society that compensates for the effects of the market in the realms of values and existence.

(p. 242, emphasis in original)

"Vitalpolitik", then, is the means by which, under (ordo)liberal capitalism, the state ensures that the "Lifeworld" is not fragmented, and ensures "cooperation between men who are 'naturally rooted and socially integrated'" (2008, p. 243).

Under neoliberalism, however, Foucault (2008) argues that this relationship is reversed; rather than the market being under the supervision of the state, the state is under the supervision of the market. As Foucault (2008) suggests, under this logic the market itself becomes the site of truth. Indeed, under "anarcho-liberalism", neoliberalism "is a whole way of being and thinking", not just a form of government (p. 218). It is "a general style of thought, analysis and imagination" (pp. 218–219). American "anarcho-liberalism" is thus more radical than German Ordoliberalism in that it involves "the generalization of the economic form of the market . . . throughout the social body and including the whole of the social system not usually conducted through or sanctioned by monetary exchanges" (p. 243).

Given that US neoliberalism uses "market economy and the typical analyses of the market economy to decipher nonmarket relationships" (p. 240), what happens to the mediating function of the state in compensating for what is "cold, impassive, calculating, rational, and mechanical in the strictly economic game of competition?" If the state can no longer engage in Vitalpolitik (supervised and defined, as it is, by the "cold, impassive" market itself), what functions to maintain social integration and cooperation among social actors? How is the Lifeworld made meaningful? In other words, how does neoliberalism negotiate and manage the reduction of everything to an economic calculus?

In 21st-century neoliberalism, the brand and branding processes have emerged as a principal mediatory mechanism—what Arvidsson (2006) refers to as a "mediatic ambience"—through which the market manages nonmarket relationships. That is, the brand is the means by which human sociality can be constructed, made sense of, negotiated and translated into economic value within a market economy. If, within neoliberalism, the market economy is a "grid of intelligibility" that is applied to everything, including nonmarket relations, then the brand is the key, the legend, that enables that grid to become meaningful on an everyday level. It is the mechanism through which the non-economic can be analyzed economically (i.e., assigned value), but also assigned meaning within that system of value.

However, this neoliberal reversal of the state–economy relationship also involves a reversal of Marx's concept of labor. Rather than, like Marx, viewing labor in its abstract form as labor power and time that is sold as a commodity to capitalists, the neoliberal model views labor power itself as embodied capital—human capital—that can produce income. In this model, labor power is no longer a commodity to be bought and sold, but a form of enterprise that can itself accumulate value. Thus, humans are, under neoliberalism, forms of capital invested in (self)enterprises. In this sense, as Foucault argues, neoliberalism is a return to the model of "homo economicus" from classical liberalism, but instead of the individual being seen as a partner in exchange, he or she is seen as an "entrepreneur of him[or her]self" (Foucault, 2008, p. 226). Moreover, according to Du Gay (1996), "the character of the entrepreneur can no longer be seen as just one among a plurality of ethical personalities but must rather be seen as assuming an ontological priority" (p. 181). The enterprise self, then, becomes a part of the human condition, the way in which freedom is practiced under neoliberalism. For example, my own analysis of "Alex from Target" (Mumby, 2018) illustrates how even 16-year-old boys working part-time at Target can be subject to processes of "corporate capture" and transformed into enterprise selves. With one teenage girl's tweet of a photograph of him working at Target, Alex Lee went from an anonymous kid with fewer than 100 Twitter followers to "Alex from Target" with over 700,000 Twitter followers and appearances on *Ellen* and CNBC's *Fast Money* show, and a subsequent tour with a promotional company called Digitour. He had, in other words, become a branded commodity. This is perhaps an extreme, though by no means rare, example of the principle that "everything communicates" (potential economic value).

Thus, if we return to my argument in the first section of this chapter regarding the constitutive role of communication in the organization–capital relationship, we can now see that this particular CCO relationship (Communication, Capital, Organization) has changed in at least two ways under neoliberalism. First, rather than communication constituting and mediating the relationship between capital and labor (and hence playing a central role in determining the indeterminacy of labor power), it now constitutes capital directly by virtue of the (re)construction of the social actor as human capital (Becker, 1976) via the market logic of neoliberalism. Communication constitutes capital under neoliberalism in that the social actor is directed to be a communicative/performative being as an entrepreneur of the self. Second, and related, the sphere of capital accumulation has moved beyond the "point of production" such that the whole of everyday life is transformed into a "social factory" (Böhm & Land, 2012; Gill & Pratt, 2008; Lazzarato, 2004). We have thus shifted from capital–labor relationships to capital–life relationships; everything in the sphere of the social can be potentially transformed into human capital.

Therefore, within the neoliberal theory of human capital an economic calculus is brought to bear on everything (i.e., seeing and measuring everything in terms of its contribution to human capital) via a communicative process that enables social actors to make sense of it as meaningful. (Branded) communication processes mediate and constitute the relationship between human identity and sociality, enabling the capital accumulation process to be understood as a form of meaning making. One might argue that brands embody *both* system and Lifeworld, articulating together capital, power and sociality in a single institutional form. However, the brand as neoliberal Vitalpolitik functions as part of a broader set of political relations and conditions that are key to understanding 21st-century dis/organizing processes. I unpack these below.

Brand, Risk and Precarity

With the emergence of human capital as central to the neoliberal model, risk and precarity become defining features of social and economic life. Under Fordism and Keynesianism, risk was deliberately mitigated via the social safety net and companies provided security as compensation for "salarial subordination" (Lazzarato, 2009, p. 122). Under post-Fordism and neoliberalism, risk is spread increasingly downward, marking a shift from "venture capital" under Fordism to "venture labor" under post-Fordism (Neff, 2012). In this sense, the implicit separation of labor and capital under Fordism is eliminated under neoliberalism. Everyone is a venture capitalist, but of their own human capital. As Lazzarato, via Foucault, argues, the neoliberal focus of social policy on individuals rather than groups or society (recall Margaret Thatcher's claim that there is "no such thing as society, only individuals") "does not aim to ensure individuals against risk, but to constitute an economic space in which individuals *individually* take upon themselves and confront risks" (2009, p. 118).

However, neoliberalism also articulates risk together with precarity. While under Fordism precarity was a condition only of marginality, under neoliberalism precarity is not only the "new normal" but also an actual instrument of governance through insecurity. As Lorey (2015) argues, "In neoliberalism precarization becomes 'democratized'" (p. 11). If precarity is the norm, then there is no longer a separation between free subjects (in the classic liberal sense) and the precarious; those who are free are also precarious. Thus, for Lorey, the function of what she terms "governmental precarization" is to create subjects who accept precarity as the norm, an inevitable and necessary feature of self-governance within neoliberalism. Moreover, Lorey argues, this normalization of precarity protects the state of insecurity, which has become a constitutive feature of neoliberal subject formation. As Lorey states:

> Understanding precarization as *governmental* makes it possible to problematize the complex interactions between an instrument of governing and the conditions of economic exploitation and modes of subjectivation, in their ambivalence between subjugation and self-empowerment.
>
> (2015, p. 13, emphasis in original)

Extending Lorey's argument, one might suggest that the brand functions at the intersection of subjugation and self-empowerment within neoliberal governmentality. It is a mode of dis/organization that simultaneously subjugates and empowers entrepreneurial subjects, aiding in the normalization of precarity and insecurity.

We can see this process at work in the so-called "gig" economy—a term that refers to alternative, temporary work arrangements. "Gig" workers are generally "independent contractors" who work "only to complete a particular task or for [a] defined time and with no more connection with their employer than there might be between a consumer and a particular brand of soap or potato chips" (Friedman, 2014, p. 171). While the size of the labor force employed in such "non-traditional" work arrangements is still relatively low, comprising (as of 2013) less than 15% of the US workforce, Friedman points out that in the period from 2005 to 2013 fully 85% of employment growth was in "alternative work arrangements". The term "gig" itself brands the relationship between work and precarity in a particular way, with its connotations of a "rock and roll", independent lifestyle that rejects the old Fordist career model in favor of freedom from the nine-to-five daily grind.

In many respects, however, this branding belies the realities of work and life under neoliberalism. For example, the highest areas of gig employment are typically in those industries that have weak labor organizing. Moreover, a widely practiced corporate strategy is to fire permanent workers and then rehire them as independent contract workers at a lower salary and with no benefits. As Weil (2014) has indicated, the last thing companies want to do is to actually hire permanent employees when "gig" workers can perform the same tasks, especially in a context where corporate culture is subordinated to the brand. In addition, to function effectively a gig economy requires a large reserve army of unemployed or underemployed, hence keeping wages low and maintaining access to experienced workers looking for work—a labor pool that disappears under low levels of unemployment (Friedman, 2014).

But it is not only in the gig economy that workers experience such instability and precarity. Many service and retail jobs, for example, have a massive degree of unpredictability in terms of hours worked and pay from month to month (Cohen, 2017). Workers are often given extremely short notice about weekly shifts and shift changes, as companies try to maintain maximum flexibility to meet shifting consumer demands. Lack of income predictability from month to month increases stress and anxiety levels to such a degree that a recent report (Mas & Pallais, 2016) suggests that the average employee would give up 20 percent of their income in exchange for stable employment and a predictable income stream.

It is important, of course, that the economic reality of the gig economy is mitigated by the meaning making that occurs in and around it. Brand as Vitalpolitik performs this function by constructing the gig worker as empowered, doing exciting, fulfilling work, and economically successful (Sullivan & Delaney, 2017). Indeed, as Vallas and Prener (2012) show, the popular business press and media representations tend to construct precarity in a positive manner, generally idealizing "the uncertainties that have come to grip the labor market, defining the latter as a site on which individual agency can freely unfold" (p. 331). As such, a relationship that is defined by the market as the "site of truth"—in which the traditional ties of affect and solidarity among workers (and employers) have disappeared—is imbued with meaning and affect. Tolentino (2017) provides a good example of this process:

> Last September, a very twenty-first-century type of story appeared on the company blog of the ride-sharing app Lyft: "Long-time Lyft driver and mentor, Mary, was nine months pregnant when she picked up a passenger the night of July 21st," the post began. "About a week away from her due date, Mary decided to drive for a few hours after a day of mentoring."
>
> Mary, who was driving in Chicago, picked up a few riders, and then started having contractions. "Since she was still a week away from her due date," Lyft wrote, "she assumed they were simply a false alarm and continued driving." As the contractions continued, Mary decided to drive to the hospital. "Since she didn't believe she was going into labor yet," Lyft went on, "she stayed in driver mode, and sure enough—ping!—she received a ride request en route to the hospital."
>
> "Luckily," as Lyft put it, the passenger requested a short trip. After completing it, Mary went to the hospital, where she was informed that she was in labor. She gave birth to a daughter, whose picture appears in the post. (She's wearing a "Little Miss Lyft" onesie.) The post concludes with a call for similar stories: "Do you have an exciting Lyft story you'd love to share? Tweet us your story at @lyft_CHI!"

Lyft presents Mary's "adventure" as a human interest story that embodies the entrepreneurial spirit that the gig economy celebrates. Lyft "employees" go above and beyond to serve their clients, even when experiencing labor pains! The fact that Lyft viewed this story as an "exciting" one that reflects positively on its brand speaks to the degree to which the performative, entrepreneurial logic of the human capital model has become part of "commonsense neoliberalism" (Hall & O'Shea, 2013). Here, precarity is normalized as the lone(ly) driver plies her trade, anxious not to miss out on revenue even as she experiences contractions. Indeed, the experience of work as isolating seems to be a common experience of gig workers. As Heller indicates in describing the experience of a worker for TaskRabbit, "He rarely met other taskers, he said; there were no colleagues in his life with whom he could share experiences and struggles. The flexibility was great, if you had something to be flexible for. 'The gig economy is such a lonely economy', he told me" (Heller, 2017).

In many respects, this story and the comment by the TaskRabbit worker illustrate the paradox at the heart of the precarization process; that is, under neoliberalism the worker-subject is promised the freedom to self-actualize and fully realize their enterprise self, while simultaneously being subjugated to the normalization and privatization of risk and uncertainty. Moreover, they speak to the individualization of work that lies at the heart of the capital–labor relationship within neoliberalism. It is to this individualization process (and its connection to branding as Vitalpolitik) that I now turn.

Branding and the Individualization of Work

One of the features of the Fordist organizational form was the ability of employees to connect work and politics in the context of the often highly visible structural antagonisms of the labor–capital relationship (Ackroyd & Thompson, 1999; Beynon, 1973; Collinson, 1992, 1994). Work was a collective rather than individual enterprise, and leant itself to employees organizing for a common purpose. Indeed, the successes of the labor movement in the 20th century are premised at least in part on the labor process being tied to specific sites that enabled the political organization of workers and the recognition of their own class interests (Tronti, 2012).

On the other hand, work under post-Fordism is "fissured" (Weil, 2014) with an underlying politics of disorganization and what Fleming (2017) calls the "radical responsibilization" of work rooted in the conception of workers as individual human capital (see above), each responsible for their own economic success or failure. Indeed, one might argue that neoliberalism has transformed politics by collapsing the market–politics distinction. That is, while under a liberal, social democratic form of government, politics is about the development of a common purpose around shared interests and the market is about economic exchange among individuals, neoliberalism has—via branding processes—reframed the discernment of a common purpose through the grid of intelligibility of the market. Or, to put it another way, branding turns exchange into a form of disorganized, individualized, "radically responsibilized" politics, and politics into a form of exchange in which the strongest brand wins by accruing the most attention (and hence economic value), à la Alex from Target.

For example, Sheryl Sandberg's (2013) highly successful *Lean In: Women, Work and the Will to Lead* articulates a neoliberal, individualized feminism that situates the principal barrier to women's lack of entrée into the upper echelons of corporate life as rooted in women's psychology and their lack of will in speaking up in meetings, asking for raises, and so forth. Sandberg thus presents an individualized, aspirational politics in which women's individual perseverance is more central to success than the development of political coalitions that can overcome systemic exclusions and structural inequalities. Politics, then, is relevant only as an expression of individual freedom and self-empowerment. Indeed, one might argue that Sandberg's thesis is rooted firmly in a view of working women as undervalued human capital, largely by virtue of women's self-imposed limitations and inability to fully see themselves as entrepreneurial subjects who need to fully develop their brands.

Authors such as McRobbie (2016) and Duffy (2017) have each in different ways explored the ways in which branding and the individualization of work intersect. Duffy examines "aspirational labor", arguing that the political economy of insecurity has led to a growing cultural shift in which being passionate about one's work has become a central trope of neoliberalism. Duffy defines aspirational labor as "a mode of (mostly) uncompensated, independent work that is propelled by the much-venerated ideal of *getting paid to do what you love*. As both a practice and a worker ideology, aspirational labor shifts content creators' focus from the present to the future, dangling the prospect of a career where labor and leisure coexist" (2017, p. 4, emphasis in original). Duffy's analysis focuses on digital labor, exploring how (mostly female) fashion bloggers and vloggers adhere to a "post-feminist logic of visibility and individual expression" (p. 9) as a means to financial empowerment. Central to this is the development of an individual self-brand that is perceived as authentic. As Duffy indicates, there is a strong commercial appeal to authenticity, but the women in her study must constantly reconcile the apparent contradiction between the principle of authenticity and the goal of profit-making in their public expressions of their brand identity (p. 104).

McRobbie's (2016) study focuses on what she describes as the *dispositif* (Foucault, 1980) of "creativity"; that is, a broad and dispersed apparatus of policies, institutional norms, worldviews and aspirations that cohere as a set of principles and practices around "being creative" as a means to success within the precarious work environment of neoliberalism. Focusing on recent graduates of media and fashion design programs, McRobbie explores how creativity functions biopolitically within the so-called "creative economy" (Florida, 2003) to inculcate in new graduates a strong sense of self-entrepreneurship and career advancement. McRobbie argues, following Lorey (2015), that this celebratory elevation of creativity has both normalized precarity and displaced work in the traditional sense. As such, there is no workplace per se at the center of this *dispositif*, but rather a hierarchical economy of creative competition characterized by informal networks of young people pursuing highly individual freelance career paths. Thus, a collective workplace politics is difficult because 1) there is no clearly defined site of work, and 2) the principal political activity is self-production and self-marketing.

Captured in different ways in both Duffy's and McRobbie's study, then, is a politics of individual freedom and self-empowerment in which the precarity and insecurity of work under neoliberalism is made up for with the celebration of creativity and a passion for work that *may* lead to financial success and (micro) celebrity (Marwick, 2013a). But underlying this aspirational view of work and self is a pervasive and disorganizing anxiety that propels continual efforts to renew the individual brand through networking, increased digital media presence and a constant investment in new skill training. Ironically, and as Neff's (2012) study has shown, participants don't make sense of failure in terms of the structural problems endemic to neoliberalism, but rather as driven by their own inabilities to make good decisions as "venture laborers" within a risk-driven economy.

In all of these examples we are confronted with what Lorey (2015) refers to as "virtuoso labor"; that is, labor "that demands the whole person, [and] is primarily based on communication, knowledge and affect" (p. 5). Virtuoso labor is in part a product of the creation under neoliberalism of subjects who are both free and precarious. The participants in Duffy's, McRobbie's and Neff's studies accept the conditions of normalized precarization as a necessary and defining feature of the ongoing conduct of a (destabilized) life. As Lorey suggests, governing through precarization has created modes of subjectivation that create anxiety and foment individualization. Under neoliberal governmentality, the exposure to existential vulnerability produces a (never-ending) race for individual security that overshadows the possibility for communal solidarity and collective political action.

In this context, the brand as Vitalpolitik is an important means by which existential security is managed and created. In the absence of social democratic institutions and possibilities for communal solidarity, the brand works to create stable systems of meaning and affect in which social actors can invest. "Virtuoso labor" is, at least in part, a process of self-branding that enables the creative worker to construct a stable, enduring and authentic self that is both a buttress against precarity and a system of meaning and affective registers in which others are willing to invest.

Conclusion: Branding, Communication as Capital and Democracy

I have attempted to do several things in this chapter in developing what I have called the "CCC" (Communication Constitutes Capital) model of organizational communication. First, I have argued for the focus on dis/organizing processes as central to our understanding of contemporary organization life. Second, I suggested that organizational scholars have rather overlooked the constitutive relationship between communication and capital accumulation processes; that, in fact, communication and capital have been intimately tied together throughout 20th- and 21st-century capitalism, although that relation has been transformed several times. Third, I have argued that one of the principal (and most important) recent changes in the communication–capital relationship has been in enabling the shift from a focus on the indeterminacy of labor as the source of capital accumulation to a focus under neoliberal capitalism on the indeterminacy of meaning as the source of capital accumulation. As such, the defining relationship in neoliberal capitalism is not the capital–labor relationship, but the capital–life relationship, which is mediated through branded processes of communication, as corporate branding efforts seek to capture and monetize everyday life. Finally, I made a case for the brand as Vitalpolitik within neoliberal capitalism. That is, it is the mechanism by which the market as the principal grid of intelligibility under neoliberal capitalism is translated into a system of meanings and sensemaking processes that provide temporary moments of existential stability within a social, political and economic terrain of insecurity and precarity. If, as Lorey (2015) argues, precarization has become the principal mode of governmentality, then branding is one of the means by which precarization becomes normalized and central to "common sense neoliberalism" (Hall & O'Shea, 2013).

One might argue, then, that we are in an era where dis/organization, instability, anxiety and precarity is a central, defining feature of contemporary life. Indeed, the presidency of Donald Trump might be seen as the normalization and institutionalization of dis/organization, a kind of "frenetic hyperactivism" in which "chaos is the productive and strategic ground for at least some of the political trajectories and projects at work today" (Grossberg, 2018, p. 4). As the personification of the neoliberal id run rampant, Trump strategically courts chaos while branding himself as a populist strong man who rejects elitist political correctness and knows how to get things done. His success is rooted in disorganization—create chaos and distraction, foment anxiety and anger, challenge the very concept of truth and its role in argument and decision-making, and in the meantime quietly transform the very foundations of the democratic institutions that shape society.

My point is that processes of dis/organization have profound implications for the practice of democracy. The shift to neoliberalism has replaced "homo politicus" with "homo economicus", at the same time enshrining precarization as a system of governance in which individualism and self-entrepreneurship eclipse the social. It is in this context that the brand comes rushing in to provide succor to the self within an ontological condition of existential insecurity that our unstable and precarious times have normalized. But this succor is not neutral and apolitical. As Gorz (2010) states, "the brand . . . effects a seizure of power by immaterial fixed capital over public space, the culture of everyday life and the social imaginary" (p. 100). The consumer thus eclipses the citizen, and exchange is replaced with inequality and precarity as the normalized condition of a grid of intelligibility ruled by the market. Thus, "If we fail to understand precarization, then we understand neither the politics nor the economy of the present" (Lorey, 2015, p. 1). Understanding how "(branded) communication constitutes capital" is an important step in understanding these precarization processes and the dis/organized systems of inequality that they maintain and reproduce.

Part II

Methodological Toolbox for Studying Dis/Organization

7 Dis/Ordering

The Use of Information and Communication Technologies by Human Rights Civil Society Organizations

Oana Brindusa Albu

Information and communication technologies (ICTs) such as social media platforms, VoIP tools, encrypted voice, video streaming and instant messaging applications, etc., provide means with which individuals can organize collectively to bring about social change (Apprich, Slater, Iles & Schultz, 2014). However, the various ways in which ICTs undermine the abilities of partly formalized collectives such as civil society organizations (CSOs) to engage in protests and hold corporations and governments to account has received little attention (for a notable exception, see Uldam, 2018). Studies typically show that ICTs enable *order*, i.e., communication-based processes that facilitate the coordination of collective action (linking different sites, actors and conversations), specifying of actions (accessing targets, recruiting and gathering for sit-ins at specific locations) and framing of conversations (regulating or persuading public opinion, Kavada, 2016). However, research indicates that ICTs simultaneously introduce *disorder*, i.e., communication-based disorganizing processes that are caused by technological disruption and the destruction of multimedia interactions when data are traced, monitored and stored (Brunton & Nissenbaum, 2015). These different forms of visibility[1] created by ICTs can foster negative effects such as exclusion or demotion of dissent, polarization and the confirmation of bias through creating so-called echo chambers (Bennett & Segerberg, 2013). Nevertheless, the ways in which ICTs produce visibilities and invisibilities, thereby generating (dis)order in organizations, are relatively underexplored (Flyverbom, Leonardi, Stohl, & Stohl, 2016). As a result, studies on the agency of ICTs as (dis)organizing devices are scarce (see for an exception, Leonardi, Nardi, & Kallinikos, 2012). The aim of this chapter is to investigate how ICTs act to produce (in)visibilities that shape organizations in both ordering and disordering ways.

An established strand of research has indeed shown that both order and disorder occur simultaneously in any instance of organizing (cf. Cooren & Fairhurst, 2009). This continuum recognizes that order comes in various degrees, which means that disorder and messiness is inherent to organizational processes while also being concurrent with order (Chia

& Tsoukas, 2003). Accordingly, this chapter does not assume a dichotomy between order and disorder but treats them as two interdependent dimensions that intersect. In every situation where organization emerges from efforts to order action around particular rules and principles, disorder occurs in the form of struggles, negotiations and misunderstandings (Chia & Tsoukas, 2003). Disorganization is thus inherent to every effort of collective organizing due to the disordering properties of communication (Vásquez, Schoeneborn & Sergi, 2016). Yet the role of ICTs in producing technological disruptions and (dis)ordering dynamics is relatively little understood (Salge & Karahanna, 2016). In the case of civil society groups, for example, ICTs have been examined solely as tools used to create visibility and to bring the corrupt practices of corporations and government into the limelight (Den Hond & De Bakker, 2007). Both research and practice have demonstrated the ways in which governments, often working in tandem with corporations, respond with online and offline surveillance of activists (see Singh, 2017). In both organization and communication research, however, there is still a tendency to view ICTs as a means used to ensure a two-way communication flow (Rane & Salem, 2012). As a result, the ways in which ICTs create (dis)order dynamics and work, often counterintuitively, to disrupt, restrict and constrain activists, remain less explored.

Even less well understood, though yet more consequential, is the impact of ICTs on CSOs working in regions of political turmoil such as the Middle East and North Africa region (MENA) (Hänska Ahy, 2014). Whereas for Western CSOs disorder might entail a loss of financial resources and a struggle to improve integrative legislation, in MENA regions, when ICTs facilitate the tracing and monitoring of CSOs' texts and conversations, disorder can lead to surveillance, imprisonment and torture (FPU, 2016). There is a vital interest, therefore, both from an academic and a socially responsible standpoint, to explore how ICTs can destroy, alter, reshape and stabilize interactions in ways that either help or impede the ability of CSOs to organize. When ICTs gain such momentum, important questions about (dis)organization processes and dispersed agency take center stage: What role do ICTs have in shaping, facilitating and disrupting organizational processes? For example, can ICTs have the capacity to rally actors in the midst of a demonstration and enable them to debrief or plan for subsequent events at later stages, and simultaneously act as tracking mechanisms that disturb collective organizing?

Theoretically this chapter draws on the "Communication as Constitutive of Organization" (CCO) tradition, since this approach allows for seeing organizational interactions as multi-layered intermixes between social dynamics and materiality (Ashcraft et al., 2009). A CCO lens is important here because it enables an examination of how ICTs have agency and alter (while being altered by) organizational texts and conversations in (dis)ordering ways. To this extent the chapter contributes to disorganization studies, since it provides analytical tools to study ICTs as (dis)organizing devices. The chapter's findings will also serve as a springboard for future research into ICTs, visibility and surveillance studies.

The chapter proceeds as follows. The first section discusses the way that ICTs are conceptualized in predominant research vis-à-vis their positive impact on organizational processes and their ability to generate visibility. More insight is needed concerning the capacity of ICTs to create (in)visibility and (dis)order, and a CCO approach is introduced that allows such study to be undertaken. The methodology and analysis sections follow, depicting how ICTs have the capacity to create different forms of visibility and invisibility, that introduce both order and disorder for organizational activities. Finally, the findings are presented in the conclusion section and the limitations of the study are discussed briefly as a springboard for future research.

ICTs and the (Dis)Organization of CSOs

ICTs are widely regarded as facilitating vital information-sharing practices for the organization of social collectives that instill social change (Bennett & Segerberg, 2013). Usually it is argued that what is needed for CSOs to operate, recruit members and instill public policy transformation is essentially an informational infrastructure that provides connective and visible means of interaction (Apprich et al., 2014). Despite growing skepticism as to the supposedly straightforward manner in which these technologies are used to accomplish organizational and societal goals (Morozov, 2009), a tendency prevails in organization studies to focus only on human agency. In social media studies, for example, human beings are considered to be the only actors that connect with each other through meaningful ties (Obar, Zube & Lampe, 2012). The networks of connections of which activist groups are comprised is theorized to be constituted of humans who disseminate information among each other and work together, for example, to expose human rights abuses (see Rane & Salem, 2012). Such information-sharing and visibility, generated by individuals using social media, has been found to have influenced public debate and led to the recognition of crimes committed by authoritarian regimes in the Arab Spring (Dahlgren, 2013). Likewise, studies of activist groups have found that the main component that makes collective action effective is the human factor, since individuals ensure the four "WUNC" characteristics, i.e., Worthiness, Unity, Numbers and Commitment (Tilly, 2005). In this respect, collective actors are mainly studied as human "entities" appearing on a public stage by using ICTs to address other actors, while the processes through which this happens "remain essentially a black box" (Van de Donk, Loader, Nixon & Rucht, 2004, p. 10). Some organization and communication studies hold a similar human-centered focus wherein individuals are seen to have agency and to use ICTs for increasing mobilization and participation in protests (Kavada, 2016). An optimistic stance can arguably be detected in claims concerning the order that ICTs introduce to collective organizing and the ways in which individuals rely on such technologies to protest against authoritarian regimes (Mercea, Iannelli & Loader, 2016).

The focus on human agency does indeed offer valuable insights into how individuals can use ICTs for organizational purposes (Neumayer & Svensson, 2014). However, there is relatively little in-depth understanding of how ICTs exhibit agency and have (dis)organizing properties. Recent studies show that ICTs can facilitate more decentralized, dispersed, temporary and individualized forms of collective organizing that subvert the notion of the collective as a unified, homogeneous, coherent, mass of individuals (Kavada, 2016). Furthermore, these technologies are thought to bring disparate individuals together without the need for a coherent collective identity or formal organization, arguing for "connective" instead of "collective" action (Bennett & Segerberg, 2013). Still, the ways in which ICTs simultaneously ensure and disrupt connectivity, visibility and organizing are not yet fully understood. For instance, bots, trolls and algorithms have been shown to have both positive and negative influences in changing activists' behavior through the creation of different types of visibility, often including detrimental types as a result of the dissemination of inaccurate and fake information (Salge & Karahanna, 2016). Similarly, hashtags and live video streams have been found to create visibilities for some and invisibilities for others by re-arranging interactions in time and space with both positive and constraining implications for collective action (Schradie, 2018). In this respect, the next section discusses briefly how ICTs produce visibility and invisibility thereby causing both order and disorder for CSOs' organizational activities.

ICTs and (In)Visibility

The degree to which an organization is visible or invisible is typically assessed on the basis of three factors (Scott, 2015): organizational visibility, member identification and relevant audience. Organizational visibility can vary from "highly visible", where ICTs are used to promote advertisements, logos and slogans, to "highly hidden", where dissemination is limited and ICTs are used to encrypt, obfuscate or destroy communicative interactions (Brunton & Nissenbaum, 2015). Member identification refers to the extent to which organizational members actively express a sense of connection and affiliation with the organization. Concealing members' identification is an important factor in protecting organizational members, especially in dangerous situations. In the case of CSOs working to hold governments and corporate actors to account, for example, activists can face the risk of imprisonment, often construed in terms of "national security" and "predictive policing" (Costanza-Chock, 2004, p. 274). Maintaining the anonymity of affiliations between members and keeping the organization hidden is thus imperative for such organizations' survival. Lastly, relevant audiences need to be heeded due to the link between organizational visibility and affiliation. To ensure the safety of individuals and organizations, certain organizations might have to limit the access of specific stakeholders and carefully select which audiences they interact with. For example, the climate justice movement in Europe has had to ensure secured stakeholder communication practices in response to undercover officers from London's Metropolitan Police infiltrating peaceful demonstrations in order to detain the organizers of such protests (see Uldam, 2018).

ICTs thus enable ordering through bypassing mass media gatekeepers, and sometimes accessing traditional mass media, thus potentially helping CSOs to bring government or corporate secrets to the public domain (e.g., Wikileaks, 2016). This is a double-edged sword, however, since these technologies can have unintended implications through facilitating government and corporate monitoring, and sometimes the censoring of dissenting views (Uldam, 2018). Thompson's (2005) notion of mediated visibility captures how ICTs produce (in)visibility with uncontrollable consequences. In stressing the role of ICTs as being key to the relation between visibility and power, Thompson (2005) builds upon Foucault's notion of the panopticon and the idea that the "visibility of the many" and "invisibility of the few" works as a means of control. On the one hand, ICTs grant visibility to (media-savvy) activists and corporate or political actors independent of spatial-temporal locales. On the other hand, ICTs make invisible the conduct of surveillance by governments, corporations or activists. This development is made increasingly complex by the proliferation of ICTs as they render corporations and governmental authorities increasingly vulnerable to the scrutiny of CSOs and vice versa (Thompson, 2005). The visibilities and invisibilities produced by ICTs can therefore have unintended consequences, and little is known about the (dis)organizing properties of these devices because their workings are infused with market logics and post-political forms of governance (Flyverbom, 2016).

In the case of CSOs specifically, the visibility and invisibility created by ICTs introduces a paradox: ICTs create order by rendering visible conversations, information, connections, data, etc. At the same time, ICTs create disorder (through ellipsis) by rendering invisible some information, connections, events, etc. Furthermore, in the Moroccan context, which is the context of this study, visibility is required for coordination but has also negative implications, since data aggregation, tracing and community policing obstruct individuals from collective action. This is because activists' coordination practices are subject to monitoring where the content posted by individuals online is subject to data collection and aggregation. This typically includes risk assessments and sentiment analyses of different aggregated types of information, ranging from big data collected on the basis of click patterns and search terms, to Facebook and Twitter interactions such as favorites, likes, hashtags and updates (e.g., Andrejevic, 2014).

For instance, a Signal[2] application on my smartphone during fieldwork had the capacity to encrypt and instantly destroy messages after reading, generating both visibility and invisibility that lead in turn to both order and disorder. Namely, the Signal interaction created visibility for those who held private encryption keys, introducing order and being constitutive of collective action by allowing CSO members (and myself) to coordinate future tasks across three different regions (Denmark, Morocco and the UK), enabling visible conversations for designated users and specifying actions (the distribution of financial resources). At the same time, the Signal interaction caused disorder, since it disappeared after reading to avoid monitoring or interception by third parties. By becoming invisible, the Signal communicative interaction did not allow retrospective coordination and acted to disrupt unanimity and prevented the achievement of a future task (Lindebaum & Gabriel, 2016). In this respect, the locus of (dis)order lies in the multimedia interaction itself. This is because the agency of ICTs is based on a linguistic syntax that embodies a command structure to enable multiple visibilities and invisibilities to happen at the same time (Goffey, 2008).

In short, this chapter proposes that one way to understand how ICTs function as (dis)ordering devices is to focus on (in)visibility dynamics. The chapter adopts a CCO perspective in order to provide a richer view of the way ICTs create (in)visibilities that frequently clash with each other, thus creating the experience of disruptions (Cooren & Fairhurst, 2009). The point here is neither to assume a deterministic position regarding humans or ICTs, nor to assume that order and disorder are mutually exclusive (Farjoun, 2010). Instead, the underlying rationale of a (dis)ordering interplay is the acceptance of hybrid association, multiplicity, incompletion and heterogeneity as fundamental features of social life (Cooren, 2015). In this respect, this chapter regards human and nonhuman entanglements that make collective organizing possible as inseparable. It then becomes clear that "perhaps there is ordering, but there is certainly no order" (Law, 1994, p. 1), and order is never complete but rather "more or less precarious and partial accomplishments that may be overturned" (Law, 1994, pp. 1–2). Issues related to ICTs and (dis)order are then important to understand because this interplay affects how activists and CSOs organize since ICTs are embedded in unequal power relations that privilege some at the expense of others (Curran, Fenton & Freedman, 2012; Dahlgren, 2013). For a more comprehensive understanding of how ICTs generate a wide-ranging transformation of organizational and social structures, the chapter investigates the following research question:

> *RQ: How do ICTs exercise agency, introducing (in)visibilities and (dis)order for a Morocco-based CSO?*

Methodology: Longitudinal Case Study and Multi-Sited Fieldwork

Activists and ICTs cluster together in sociomaterial arrangements that have the potential to effect change (Apprich et al., 2014). This chapter provides a rare ethnographic study of the (dis)ordering agency of ICTs in the case of an international CSO ("Z"[3]) that relies on visibility management to work in both overt and covert ways in documenting human rights violations in Morocco. The chapter focuses on Morocco because this context provides invaluable insights into the underexplored (dis)ordering role of ICTs for organizations working in a non-Western area where visibility and invisibility are key constitutive features of organizing (Dalhuisen, 2015). The Z CSO was selected because it is an organization that uses ICTs as central resources in its campaign against human rights abuses, making it a relevant investigation site since it provides a rich variety of indicators from non-Western societies that are often neglected in predominant research. The chapter builds on a unique methodology that consisted of shadowing (Lindlof & Taylor, 2010) Z managers in both physical and virtual settings and which allowed for the identification of how ICTs act and shape collective action. The data set builds on multi-sited fieldwork undertaken over a period of two years (2015–2017) in locations across Morocco, Tunisia, Denmark, Lebanon, the UK and the US where Z managers conducted their work. The data set consists of:

1. 253 single-spaced pages of fieldnotes from observations, and 129 minutes of voice recordings based on the shadowing of one Z manager through different locations in Morocco (taking part in overt and covert operational activities in Rabat, Marrakech, Sidi Ifni) and other locations, including Lebanon (participating in staff meetings at the MENA regional office in Beirut), the US (participating in staff meetings at the headquarters in New York), Denmark, the UK and Tunisia (planning, coordinating and conducting digital security workshops in designated locations).
2. 280 minutes of video-recorded meetings with volunteers and permanent staff of Z.
3. 456 digital interactions on encrypted and non-encrypted technologies (Facebook, Twitter, Signal, Appear.In).

4. 19 interviews with Z managers.
5. 210 pages of annual reports, mission reports, etc., indicative of Z's tactics and strategies.

Importantly, the focus of this chapter is to go beyond the traditional idea that communication only involves humans and to show how human interactions also include specific nonhuman elements such as ICTs that constitute part of the fabric of everyday organizational life in the field. Thus, notes were taken while shadowing Z managers in both physical and virtual settings (Lindlof & Taylor, 2010), which allowed for the identification of ICTs interactions that shaped collective action. The unit of analysis was one communicative event or interaction. Data was analyzed based on a two-step thematic analysis. The first step involved open coding (e.g., encrypted interactions of Signal or Appear.In technologies that self-destruct coded for causing inability to communicate retroactively). The second step amounted to theoretical sampling, and was thus more explicitly analyst-driven as I paid attention to any themes that previous research on the topic of invisibility and disorder have identified (Dobusch & Schoeneborn, 2015; Brunton & Nissenbaum, 2015). In so doing, I individually compared and contrasted interactions while repeatedly reading through transcripts, online interactions and fieldwork journal entries. These methods provided a measure of triangulation, as most of the data were evaluated in relation to at least one other data source.

For example, codes that played an ordering organizational role were identified on the basis of a recurrent iterative process in the recorded interactions from both online and offline settings. Hashtags such as #justiceformorocco and Facebook events that acted as geo-location devices for recruiting volunteers at peaceful demonstrations that I participated in as well were coded for ICTs generating order and increasing the visibility of advocacy strategies ("the event got many activists to participate", staff meeting, Z manager). Interactions that led to data aggregation ("having the police on your tracks", interview, manager Z) were coded as visible interactions that had negative effects. Encrypted text messages indicating the distribution of financial resources ("we received the transfer and will buy the smartphones in Tunis tomorrow", Signal message sent to me, Z volunteer) were coded for invisibility practices that had an organizational role. Hidden interactions that created confusion ("@Z where does the sit-in against the WhatsApp Ban take place? I'm @ geo-location alone", DM tweet via VPN, volunteer) or exclusion ("two of our volunteers couldn't decrypt Veracrypt partitions on the new hard drives and because they had no access to the briefings they couldn't participate in the staff meeting today", staff meeting, Z manager) were coded for invisibility practices that created disorder. The recurring substantive codes in the data were clustered into two meta-themes indicative of interrelated (dis)organizing processes, each with three sub-themes, i.e., *visibility as order*, with sub-themes of data aggregation, monitoring and policing, and, *invisibility as disorder*, with the sub-themes of encryption, concealment and obfuscation.

The data offered a much wider range of findings than can be presented and discussed here, and therefore only those relating to the use of ICTs in Z in the specific time frame of the study are described in the next section. A translator from Arabic to English and French was used in situations where interactions occurred in Arabic. Due to space limitations in the present chapter, I will not be addressing the dilemmas concerning the data collection methods, even though these were central to the broader research project (i.e., Western-financed research and the controversial impacts of Western foreign aid, see Paragi, 2017). Furthermore, participant observation within social movement research, and at protests in particular, presents a very real danger of getting caught up in the moment and losing track of one's research purpose as protests can be intense, exhilarating and even dangerous environments (McCurdy & Uldam, 2014). Nevertheless, at the end of every fieldwork day I reflected, cross-examined and questioned my experiences. I did so in order to achieve the "critical distance" (McCurdy & Uldam, 2014, p. 48) necessary for the shifts between my status (e.g., insider, outsider, overt and covert white female European researcher) when present at demonstrations or team meetings at Z headquarters, for instance. The data is presented in the next section along two themes based on thick description (Paragi, 2017) in order to describe and explain the (dis)ordering role of ICTs for Z's organizational activities.

(In)Visibility and (Dis)Order for CSOs in Morocco

The Moroccan authorities created the three "red lines" (that is, "the Monarchy and its institutions, God and the Western Sahara", manager interview) that are interrelated discourses designed to control the organizational activities of CSOs. The red lines are inscribed in a powerful text with indisputable agency, i.e., Article 41 of the Moroccan Constitution, which stipulates that anyone who "offends" the institution of the monarchy, king and the royal princes and princesses, Islam and territorial integrity will be fined and imprisoned for three to five years (Zaid, 2016). As the following fieldnote excerpt illustrates, the visibility created by Facebook events reminds CSOs members of the need to obfuscate or remove any traces when treading over the "red lines":

I first met Nordin[4] (the Z manager in charge of Morocco and Western Sahara region) in front of the loud and crowded Rabat Ville train station on a hot Moroccan April afternoon. He was only a few minutes late and wearing strong cologne. We shook hands, greeted, and started walking briskly among the crowded streets, the hot air and honking cars towards a café. As we made our way through the mêlée, he said, while lighting up a cigarette, "on this street here, they make protests". "How often do people gather here?", I asked. Nordin answered decisively, with a short attempt to shade away from the sun by covering his forehead with his hand, "Every day! You *can see the events on Facebook sometimes* [chuckles]. We use that if we want to do public sit-ins and get media attention. *But it [Facebook event] attracts more than that* [he pauses and points with his head at a police guard to our right]. They start from over there . . ." he added, while exhaling tobacco smoke and pointing with his hand into the air behind us towards Avenue Mohammed V, "the parliament is situated here, that is why". With a trace of doubt in my voice, I asked Nordin: "But does that change anything in the parliament?". He stopped walking, looked at me perplexed, and asked rhetorically, "The parliament?". He paused briefly and retorted laconically, "Theater. In fact, dramatic comedy. . . . The parliament *does not control Morocco, those behind it do*," he said. It was my turn to look back at Nordin, puzzled. He *said nothing but pointed with his finger to a billboard*. On it, a huge portrait of *King Mohammed VI was looming above us*.

(Fieldnote, Rabat, Morocco, April 2015, emphasis added)

As shown in the above fragment, the discursively (re)constructed red lines shape Z's organizational activities (i.e., are situated "behind", "control"), since activists investigate human rights violations that are mostly caused by the monarchy's governance, the enforcement of Islamic law and the approach to the Western Sahara region. In order to achieve organizational tasks (e.g., making phone calls, writing emails and reports, gathering information, documenting human rights abuses and coordinating awareness campaigns), Z representatives rely on different ICTs to generate visibility for coordination of collective action. As described above, the visibility of the Facebook event (increased by the EdgeRank algorithm, Gillespie, 2014) provides Z with the ability to recruit volunteers and bring them together to a specific location. The event introduces order as it stabilizes organizational relationships and materializes Z as an organization. At the same time, the event introduces unintended consequences for Z since the visibility of the event "attracts unwanted attention" from police forces who monitor online activity and who are disruptive of Z's efforts to organize collectively.

In order to cope with such challenges, Z reduces its organizational visibility by engaging in covert work which amounts to conducting investigative reporting ("missions") where activists "research" human rights violations in a manner that cannot be detected by local authorities. To maintain the invisibility of member identification, Z provides its members only with a badge, an email address and a laptop with different encryption software installed. No office or other operational infrastructure is available, since the Moroccan authorities have retracted Z's authorization to operate. In this situation, visibility and invisibility are key organizing features because they condition which activities are allowed, possible or achievable to begin with. In order to obtain a preliminary understanding of the role of ICTs for Z's organizational processes, I followed the development of two of Nordin's reports over a period of one year from the moment he took the missions until these were completed. The sociopolitical context that Z activists are faced with is briefly presented below in order to provide a wider perspective on the ways in which Z's ability to organize is a relational and precarious accomplishment depending also on the agency of technological devices.

Nordin's reports disclosing human rights abuses in Morocco are published on Z's website without any identification details of his authorship, in contrast to reports from other regions, which all include the names of their Z managers. The only identifier in Nordin's report is the geolocation that shows the location where Z's MENA headquarters are based, which is Tunisia and not Morocco. When I asked Nordin during a team meeting in Rabat what prompted the need to hide his organizational identification, he responded by underlining the "problems" introduced by visibility:

> I used to have my name on it [the online report] but since we received *the letter* to stop all of our activity until further notice I cannot do that anymore. I want to stay away from having problems, you know. This is why we list only our H[ead]Q[quarters] as a location in it [the report].
>
> (Nordin, team meeting, emphasis added)

The letter was written by Mustapha Khalfi, communication minister and spokesperson of the Moroccan government, and was published on Morocco's state-owned news agency website as well as in a one-page ad in the *Wall Street Journal* of October 2, 2015. The websites where the letter was published created a high degree of visibility and an image of Z as an organization that has a "complete lack of neutrality and objectivity" (Agence Maghreb Arab Presse, 2015). In order to discredit Z and undermine its legitimacy, the letter was addressed directly to Z's CEO and positions values such as the kingdom's "hospitality" and "goodwill" to constitute a world view where attempts to conduct investigations and unveil human rights abuses stand in opposition to such values:

> Morocco's goodwill has consistently been faced with what appears to be a premeditated, systematic and unjustified policy of denigration and depreciation of the significant reforms undertaken, despite the fact that those reforms have been widely recognized and saluted by

others. Indeed, your [Z's] investigation and experts used and abused Morocco's open policy and well-known hospitality for no other purpose than to tarnish the image of its institutions and its democratic achievements, resorting to ready-made judgments.

(Agence Maghreb Arab Presse, 2015)

As a result, activists had to shift toward invisibility through covert procedures and encryption protocols in order to be able to continue to work. As the manager indicates in the next account, ICTs create visibility that is not only conducive of organizing but also potentially disruptive for all actors involved, both governmental authorities and their critics. When ICTs exhibit agency to "get activists to participate" and help recruitment, these technologies increase risks of deportation and arrest. This shows that not only mainstream ICTs such as social media platforms affect how people and information are associated and share knowledge (Leonardi et al., 2012). But equally when new ICTs such as Storymaker share encrypted data issues concerning agency, control and audiences (for whom is information rendered visible) become highly important. In this case, such technologies create visibility for targeted stakeholders and in so doing they affect foreign policy and "create pressure" by constituting Moroccan institutions in "certain" ways internationally, which is disturbing as it can be detrimental for economic and political relations:

What's going on is not new. It happened to W[5] last year when the police arrested and expelled two of their researchers. It was because they did a training on Storymaker, which is an app[lication] that is encouraging people to spread information that is not controlled by the state. The event got many activists to participate. But because of that, all the people that were involved in doing training are either deported, have lost their authorization to function, or are now facing a trial in two weeks. All this happens because often times our reports *create pressure*, and they [the authorities] don't like it when international CSOs like Z that have a lot of resources and global outreach *create certain images* of Morocco on the international scene. CSOs that are being backed by international funding are automatically considered to have *contradictory interests* to that of Morocco. So now they have started to pick on them and activists.

(Nordin, interview, emphasis added)

"[C]ontradictory interests" is a powerful state-narrated discourse, which is however not striking in an Arab country with a colonial history such as Morocco. Although in the course of my limited observations I saw that Z activists use a strict methodology in reporting and have built a positive reputation for impartiality over decades, a conspiratorial mindset is pervasive. Two Z foreign volunteers were deported on the grounds of undermining the stability of the regime, since these "associations and entities work under the cover of defending human rights, but are in fact trying to drive some of the international organizations to take hostile positions towards Morocco's interests" (Dalhuisen, 2015). In such a socio-political context, the visibility of Z's organizational activities introduces order while invisibility generates disorder, as the next sections show.

Visibility as Order: Data Aggregation, Monitoring and Policing

As frequently observed in informal conversations and interview data, ICTs are devices that both empower and make vulnerable. For Z activists, Twitter and Facebook and email and VoiP technologies create visibility that is essential in recruitment, mobilizing resources and creating awareness campaigns (Trottier & Fuchs, 2015). However, this visibility also enables data aggregation, monitoring and policing. Data aggregation is the practice of compiling information about particular groups for achieving specific objectives, enabling authorities to collect intelligence and to predict the behavior and movements of civil society activists and volunteers (Couldry & Turow, 2014). In this respect, ICTs generate unequal power relations and act as devices that impede coordination of action. The following excerpt is indicative of the organizational challenges that arise from "being watched" as experienced by Z representatives. The conversation happened while Nordin and I were on our way to meet with a Z volunteer. While walking across the labyrinthine streets of the Marrakech medina, I asked him about Z's main "research" activities, which consist of gathering information about human rights abuses:

ME: How do you work together with volunteers?
NORDIN: Doing the researcher's work isn't easy. You need to go and meet the people that were subject to abuses. Often they don't have time and do not react immediately, so you need to be flexible and *spend all your time covering your tracks*. Often times people just go on and on about "oh in Morocco *the police* are just beating people and are so bad and so on" and I am actually interested in one specific case, and I need to be very careful how I document all this, stick to our methodology, make sure all evidence and reports are encrypted, so I ask them to tell me *what did the police do to you*, but they keep on saying, "yes but you know in Morocco the police beats people and treats them bad", so you need a lot of stamina and perseverance to get people to talk about it while *avoiding having the police on your tracks*. This is why volunteers are of great help to help with spreading the different tasks across many locations.

ME: Why [do you need to] avoid the police?
NORDIN: We are not allowed to work on anything that is perceived as
           undermining the authorities, and *Baltajya* [police] violence is
           one of those very sensitive topics. We have formally made a
           request to obtain an authorization to function but never re-
           ceived a response from the authorities. They keep us in limbo,
           so meanwhile we need to find different ways to get work done.
           I got detained once a few years back for having notes in my
           pocket after I interviewed an informant. So I don't leave any
           trace either online or offline anymore. I don't carry any notes.
           I don't have my real name on the Facebook profile I use for
           work. *When we are being watched, our work becomes slower,*
           sometimes impossible.
                   (Fieldnote, February 2016, Marrakech, emphasis added)

Monitoring is a practice of continuous systematic observation of organizational activities triggered by visibility. Unintended implications of visibility here amount to censorship, expulsion, fines and imprisonment for
members of CSOs (Dalhuisen, 2015). Visible multimedia interactions
enable government forces (often referred to as "Makhzen") to monitor
the physical and digital traces of Z activists. Makhzen (المخزن,) was the
governing institution in the French protectorate of Morocco and in pre-
1957 Tunisia, centered on the king and consisting of top-ranking military
personnel and security service superiors. Now the terms "Makhzen" and
"baltajya" [lit. hooligans] are also popularly used as words referring to
"'thugs' hired by the 'State' that are sent to intimidate us" (Z volunteer,
interview). As one Z volunteer indicates, the visibility generated by ICTs
counterintuitively legitimates and normalizes such monitoring practices:

> Every time we organize a peaceful protest via Facebook or an event
> concerning the abuse of power in state institutions and unfair trials,
> they [the authorities] would have the same *baltajya* people show-
> ing up and storming the room. Once I noticed that the guy who
> showed up was the same who followed me once when I was going
> to the slums to do an interview, so I went and I said to him "Oh,
> Mohammed, take a seat, do you want any coffee?"
>   (Z volunteer, interview)

The visibility of the Z representatives (the many) who are monitored
constantly by the governmental authorities (the few) reflect the dystopian
Moroccan society built on the panopticon principle whereby individuals
do not know how much is observed and by whom (Brighenti, 2010). As
in Foucauldian panopticism, ICTs are disciplinary devices that enable the
panoptic visibility of the many. Activists internalize monitoring practices
and police themselves for fear of punishment: "their [Makhzen's]

behavior is very unpredictable, you know, so that you can't see a pattern and are afraid that they are following you—to discourage you from taking any action" (Z volunteer, interview).

Policing in its contemporary preemptive technological form can be defined as "a strategic, future-oriented and targeted approach to crime control, focusing upon the identification, analysis and 'management' of persisting and developing 'problems' or 'risks', which may be particular people, activities or areas" (Maguire, 2000, p. 315). In this respect, Foucault's notion of disciplinary power through the visibility of the many still bears relevance (Uldam & Hansen, 2017). ICTs simultaneously provide experiences of order but create discomfort for Z because the Moroccans' state monitoring of the Internet is invisible. The looming tower has been replaced by someone potentially watching every URL typed by activists in real time on a screen. To achieve this all-encompassing, intangible and omniscient online tracking apparatus, the Moroccan authorities rely on technologies provided by Hacking Team, an Italian software company (Kushner, 2016). Based on my observations, the intrusive spyware allegedly used by the Moroccan government, RCS (remote control system), had infected the smartphones and computers of five Z activists. These technologies act as a "man-in-the-middle" by intercepting and monitoring communications, deciphering encrypted files and emails, recording Skype and other VoiP communications, and remotely activating microphones and camera on computers (Wikileaks, 2016). The mass monitoring activities made possible by ICTs are considered necessary or proportionate by Moroccan authorities in a context of heightened security and a potential threat of terrorist attacks and cyber warfare. Hacking Team technologies respond to such needs by framing monitoring as certainty. In a twist of irony, it is not the user who decides on the very consequential categorization of the person but the algorithms that do this: "Innocent civilian or insurgent? Not certain? Our systems are" (Greenberg, 2015). Such forms of visibility, which allow coordination and collective action, also work to eliminate any form of privacy and are internalized as preemptive policing, as the MENA region manager suggests:

> I can no longer live a normal life for fear of being arrested at any time, so I became exiled in my own country. The simplest of everyday tasks for us [Z] require great caution, we can no longer use social media because they [the authorities] look for the smallest smudge to send you to prison. You no longer feel safe.
>
> (Z manager, interview)

In this case, ICTs become powerful and all-seeing Argusian[6] devices that introduce new conditions of visibility specific to digital panopticism (Taekke, 2011) in the day-to-day organizational practices of those

observed. In order to cope with such visibility, Z activists resort to practices of encryption, concealment and obfuscation that inadvertently
introduce disorder. These are presented in the following section.

Invisibility as Disorder: Encryption, Concealment and Obfuscation

Invisibility is not something that can be replaced by visibility; rather the
two exist in symbiosis (see Costas & Grey, 2014, for an understanding of secrecy and invisibility as a social process). The question is thus
not whether organizational processes are visible or invisible but to what
degree (Dobusch & Schoeneborn, 2015). Encryption, concealment and
obfuscation are invisibility practices that provide the ability to circumvent surveillance and allow Z activists to organize in a less visible manner.
At the same time, invisibility creates disorder because decisions cannot
be made effectively due to the inability to archive data for future organizational activities. Equally, the incapacity to communicate due to failure
in encrypting/decrypting processes, and the impossibility of identifying
which organizational decisions are genuine and which are attempts to
confuse the authorities, have disordering implications.

Encryption is a practice through which multimedia interactions become
inaccessible to various third parties, such as government or corporate
surveillance. Using Signal, Appear.In and Jitsi for secure text messaging
and voice/video calls was a regular practice for daily briefings and team
meetings between Z activists ("Sorry, I am late. Open this in chrome
pr firefox: https://meet.jit.si/TightDucksCodeAnywhere", email from Z
manager for setting up a meeting). However, disorder occurred when
their encrypted interactions disappeared. In many observed instances,
Z volunteers and managers could not keep track of past organizational
developments, leading to their exclusion from various tasks due to the
disappearance of Signal or Jitsi interactions.

Concealment is a practice through which individuals attempt to make
conversations invisible to those who might source their information from
social media platforms (such as Facebook, if activists are using Facebook
Messenger, or Google, if one is using Google Talk). Tor and Orbot are
VPN technologies that Z activists use to allow them anonymous Internet
use ("We give all our volunteers a P[rivate]I[nternet]A[ccess] subscription
to keep all our communications secure. We also have a policy of no selfies or hashtags for personal use during work", Z manager, workshop).
To conceal the locations of protest debriefing that may be made visible
by smartphones that act as tracking devices and provide location coor-
dinates through global positioning (GPS) and radio frequency identification (RFID) systems, Z activists store their smartphones in "pouches",
i.e., anti-tracking devices that are used to blocks the tags used to identify
objects/people based on the emitted signal. Disruption is introduced by

invisibility since ICTs typically fail in decrypting communicative interactions and leave activists unable to coordinate collective action ("I lost the USB stick on which my passphrase from my public keys was stored that day and I couldn't decrypt the email, so I was left out of the meeting", interview, Z volunteer).

Obfuscation is a practice that amounts to the deliberate use of ambiguous, confusing or misleading information to interfere with monitoring and data aggregation projects (Brunton & Nissenbaum, 2015). Z activists' practices amounted to using multiple fake Facebook accounts to disseminate different inconsistent messages about meeting points, reports or participants' identities in order to interfere with potential monitoring ("I try to shrug this fake sense of security I sometimes have. So I use one Facebook account to talk with contacts on the ground, and about four different accounts to share different sit-in locations, and I always tag myself in other places than I actually am", interview, Z manager). Such obfuscation practices introduced disorder when members were unable to identify which of the activities were authentic and which were aimed at misleading authorities, as I observed on many occasions. Disorder was also caused by user regulations of platforms such as Facebook or Twitter, since not using a real identity on an account means noncompliance with existing guidelines and leads to the suspension of the account.

Z's invisibility practices are of course heavily intertwined with face-to-face interactions in which any technological interaction is avoided to ensure privacy (Costas & Grey, 2014): "Sometimes we avoid using phones, and just meet to talk in person in a safe location. But in an emergency situation we might use a stupid phone, you know, an analog phone instead of a smartphone to avoid being targeted by spyware" (Z staff meeting, manager). In alternating between online and offline (in) visibilities, Z representatives are creating, maintaining, destructing and/ or transforming their communicative interactions, which are axial—not peripheral (Ashcraft et al., 2009)—to their existence, as Nordin says:

> We do yearly holistic security workshops with all our activists because *encrypting our communications* is *essential for our survival* as an association. We use both offline and online measures not only to protect ourselves but also the family and network of our informants who often risk their lives by coming to us.
>
> (Interview, emphasis added)

Visibility management enables Z activists to organize collectively in the region and to achieve their central task of reporting human rights violations. Reporting is a controversial activity because the monarchy's preoccupation with the way the international press constitutes the image of Morocco is "the only force that can give pause to the regime's repressive tactics" (Z manager, interview). One such instance is Z's advocacy work on behalf of seven activists who face judicial proceedings for their investigative reporting of allegations of corruption in state institutions. Along with traditional advocacy methods (sit-ins, peaceful protests, etc.), Z members relied on ICTs to document the way the trial was proceeding. In doing so, Z activists used Twitter and Facebook to share hashtags with hyperlinks to reports and tags to other CSOs in an attempt to increase the visibility dynamics of their actions ("Trial of 7 human rights defenders resumes in Morocco tomorrow. R[e]T[weet] to support ow.ly/ DURc305tlkU #justiceformorocco #Morocco @Z", Z tweet). Such practices allowed Z to increase awareness of their advocacy activities, as the manager indicates "[t]hrough retweeting ('RT to support') *we* could mobilize support and show that *we stand* with them" (Z manager, interview, emphasis added). Nevertheless, such technologies exhibit disordering properties despite the fact that ICTs are often considered to ensure collective action (Bennett & Segerberg, 2013). For instance, in order to gather international support for the trial of the seven activists, a Z activist created an online petition that she shared with the #justiceformorocco hashtag on social media platforms, along with hyperlinks to statements from international news outlets, and emailed it to an existing network of connections. Although the petition gained traction (shared on Facebook 95 times, tweeted 25 times and emailed 20 times), the number of signatures needed at that stage was not met (only 423 of the needed 500 were gathered). Z volunteers stated on many occasions that they were unable to keep track of immediate developments across multiple technologies. No intended tangible outcomes were identified in terms of influencing the way the juridical proceedings advanced on the specific case as a result of Z's organizational efforts (interview, manager). However, reflecting on the success (and lack thereof) of Z's advocacy strategies, the manager alluded to the (dis)organizing properties of ICTs for driving social change:

> The current state of affairs hasn't changed drastically, but the *language has changed*, and this is a tremendous step as *it does change realities*. You hear them talking now about reforms, aiding minorities, efficiency, etc., which was unheard of in 2008 for instance. Sometimes different international stakeholders can start pressuring here and there because of our *reports*, and then there is a big *media* debate about something, then the *government must take action*.
>
> (N, interview, emphasis added)

In sum, struggles for (in)visibility play a key role in the constitution of contemporary organizations working in socio-political contexts where hidden organizing is required (Scott, 2013). In a broader sense, the (in)visibility afforded by ICTs not only enables organizations and institutions to exercise panoptic power through the surveillance of their critics, but also to conceal from the public important aspects of conflicts between various institutions, organizations and their critics (see also Uldam & Hansen, 2017). This suggests that the processes of managing (in)visibility and their (dis)ordering dynamics are intrinsically related to power, control and legitimacy, and as such are inseparable from questions concerning agency, politics and the ethics of ICTs.

Conclusion and Future Directions

This chapter has explored the agency of nonhumans, i.e., ICTs, in a very specific context in which organizing is intimately related to questions of visibility/invisibility. The study undertaken for this chapter used a communicative approach and an ethnographic methodology to study the role of ICTs as (dis)organizing devices. The chapter indicates two interrelated processes that create the *paradox of (in)visibility*: 1) visibility creates *order* and enables coordination but has negative consequences because it is conducive of data aggregation, monitoring and preemptive policing that serve to obstruct individuals from collective action; and 2) invisibility facilitates coordination because encryption, concealment and obfuscation allow individuals to organize, but at the same time leads to *disorder* through ellipsis, exclusion and silencing. The findings show that ICTs are powerful surveillance devices that operate on different time–space infrastructures and are appropriated by other actors for managing (in)visibilities across different sites. The chapter contributes to the literature on organization/disorganization due to its communicational orientation that can be found both in the object of study (ICTs) and in the CCO approach mobilized to study it. Secondly, the chapter contributes to the ICTs and CSO literature by detecting that ICTs are not only tools used to exercise control over subjects through surveillance in delimited settings. The chapter also shows that ICTs have the capacity to be appropriated by other actors for managing (in)visibilities across different sites. In this respect, the findings of the chapter can be transferred also to organizational contexts that share similarities (Lincoln & Guba, 1986). This is the case in the Global North where ICTs are responsible for organizing, mobilizing and ordering and at the same time for disordering and creating chaos (as is the case with the Internet Research Agency, the "troll farm" and their interference in the 2016 US presidential election; see Matamoros, 2018). Other important implications of the mass digitization of information facilitated by ICTs are new surveillance practices that are relevant not only for law (right to privacy, ethics, etc.), but also for social inequality. The computational analysis of massive and diverse data sets by predictive analytics is shown to have the potential to technologically reify bias and deepen existing patterns of inequality (Brayne, 2017).

This chapter highlights the benefits of using an ethnographic approach to study new ICTs and (dis)organization. The observation of different members of the same community, both in their offline and online settings, as well as conducting face-to-face interviews with informants, allows one to achieve a deep understanding of the meanings of various artifacts and the properties individuals assign to them (see Muñiz & Schau, 2005). On a methodological level, ethnography facilitates mapping how ICTs configure themselves as work environments that provide the ethnographer with an array of preset tools that actually organize the space and flow of interaction (e.g., Twitter's retweets and hashtags; see also Albu & Etter, 2016). Ethnographic inquiries are thus very fruitful for exploring disorganization dynamics especially when a big proportion of the activities of contemporary organizations take place in the complex landscape of Web 2.0, mainly populated by social media platforms, which is a much more fluid and dispersed sociocultural context than virtual communities (Rheingold, 1994). For understanding how assemblages of human and nonhuman elements are involved in disorganizing the daily flow of interaction, the ethnographer has to deal with the fact that social media tend to structure online interactions across very fluid, ephemeral and dispersed social forms—a condition that pushes toward radically rethinking the classical ethnographic categories such as field, community, identity, participant, ethics, etc. (Postill, 2008). In this respect, a multi-sited fieldwork approach is useful in the preliminary phases of fieldwork, for mapping the organizational context in which participants are situated (Hine, 2015). Furthermore, fieldwork is also useful in advanced phases, when the ethnographer has to shadow the (dis)ordering practices of different human and nonhuman elements, which more and more frequently are taking place online (Dirksen, Huizing & Smit, 2010).

This study nevertheless has some shortcomings given the specific geopolitical context analyzed, and the limited breadth of multimedia interactions sourced. Furthermore, the organizational use of ICTs is difficult to explore due to the challenges specific to mapping the multidimensional relationship between technologies and actors and how that relationship offers possible (and actual) outcomes (i.e., what emerges from actors' interactions with technologies, Leonardi, 2017). Future research could thus use multiple methods to explore when and to what extent ICTs partake in communication processes (see Rennstam, 2012). At present, organization studies lack a vocabulary that would make it possible to talk about "speaking" objects or technologies other than human beings, and CCO scholarship clearly needs such vocabulary (Schoeneborn, Kuhn & Kärreman, In press). Future research could then investigate the way in which agency is distributed between technologies, humans and spaces in relation to power and politics in organizations, since agency is unpredictable and takes counterintuitive forms (Kuhn, Ashcraft & Cooren, 2017).

The findings of this chapter are also relevant for future research on visibility and (dis)organizing (Dobusch & Schoeneborn, 2015; Scott, 2013). In the case of whistleblowers and human rights activists, for example, ICTs are typically considered to facilitate "digital data inundation" (Beer

& Burrows, 2013, p. 47). However, more complex practical and conceptual issues revolve around the two-way visibility afforded by ICTs. Since these technologies are embedded in power relations that privilege government and corporate elites and their possibilities for monitoring the many (Curran et al., 2012), relevant questions could include: How far can ICTs increase or undermine revelations of abuse? What are the limits of strategic visualizations? Given that ICTs obscure and make visible organizational processes, what are the consequences for the observed entities? Such aspects are important since research on the bases and logics that underlie mass monitoring facilitated by ICTs in different institutional and organizational settings remains scarce (Brighenti, 2010).

Lastly, the findings of the chapter are also useful for prospective research on alternative forms of organizing and invisibility/visibility, thus mapping avenues for future studies that cross-fertilize these bodies of work (Cruz, 2017). Relevant questions could include: What types of visible and hidden practices do members resort to? When and by whom are invisibility practices more likely to be enacted and with what technologies? What structural and cultural elements (size of organization, fluid collectives or multinational associations, presence or lack of leadership, traditional media), in addition to digital factors, are enabling or constraining organizational processes?

Notes

1. Organizational visibility is defined here as "how identifiable or recognizable an organization's identity is . . . ranging from highly recognizable to highly anonymous" to outsiders (Scott, 2013, p. 84). Conversely, invisibility amounts to how unrecognizable a given organization is on the same spectrum. Invisibility and visibility are about how "known" an organization is (Cruz, 2017).
2. Signal uses standard cellular mobile numbers as identifiers, and uses end-to-end encryption to secure all communications to other Signal users. The applications include mechanisms by which users can independently verify the identity of their messaging correspondents and the integrity of the data channel (see signal.org).
3. Pseudonym used to protect the identity of the organization.
4. Pseudonym used to protect the identity of the informant.
5. *Ibid.*
6. Argus Panoptes is a many-eyed giant in Greek mythology. The figure is used to describe being subject to strict scrutiny in one's actions to an invasive, distressing degree.

8 Disorganizing Through Texts

The Case of A.K. Rice's Account of Socio-technical Systems Theory

Anindita Banerjee and Brian Bloomfield

Introduction

This chapter contributes to the understanding of how organizational texts can serve as key resources in the constitution of organization by defining and mediating practices through which organizing and organization are realized. More specifically, we argue that texts can promote a given interpretation or reading of organizational reality whilst at the same time suppressing alternative accounts that nonetheless remain as possible meanings that "haunt" that reading and threaten to destabilize it. The chapter revisits the Tavistock Institute of Human Relations' (TIHR) contribution to the evolution of organization theory in the post-WWII era: namely, socio-technical systems (STS) theory. Initially developed from observations of work structure in British coal mines (Trist & Bamforth, 1951), STS was a pre-cursor to neo-Human Relations theories of organization. In particular, the chapter examines the earliest textual account of the "experiments" led by A.K. Rice (later joined by Eric Miller, both staff at the TIHR at the time) and carried out during the 1950s in the weaving sheds of the Calico Mills at Ahmedabad in India. In these mills, owned by the renowned Indian business family, the Sarabhais, and situated in a very different economic and cultural setting to the British coal industry, the principles of socio-technical organization were applied to try and restore orderly and productive operations following the introduction of new technology. Subsequently the "experiment" became understood as an exemplar of the generalization of STS theory (Rice, 1953).

Within the field of organization studies (OS), Rice's consultancy-oriented text offers an image of organizational redesign at Ahmedabad that is rational, orderly and participative, a harmony of machinery and labor as a consequence of the application of STS. However, given that the new work design at the Indian mills experienced mixed fortunes following its apparent initial success (Miller, 1975), we have revisited the experiment to try and understand some of the contextual background. Our investigation, including archival research in conjunction with the examination of the use of particular analytical inscriptions (diagrammatic representations), reveals certain absences in Rice's (1953) account of STS theory. These absences destabilize or open up the intended or fixed meanings pertaining to the claimed success of the experiments in India and thereby the generalization of the theory as a means of managing technological change in work organizations (Rice, 1953, 1958, 1963). In particular, they suggest a difference between the democratic/emancipatory rationale of the initial principles of STS theory as developed in the British coal mines and the empirical details of its enactment at Ahmedabad.

The inherent interpretive flexibility or polysemicity of any text offers the potential for multiple readings that escape the author's initial intention (Cooren, 2004). This (dis)ordering property of textual communication (Vásquez, Schoeneborn & Sergi, 2016) is enhanced when texts are dislocated (Cooren & Fairhurst, 2009), i.e., extended beyond the temporal and locational contexts of their creation. Indeed, the idea of managing change around the conception of the socio-technical reorganization of work was first documented in Trist and Bamforth's (1951) *Human Relations* journal article. Deployed in other Tavistock projects at that time (e.g., Rice, Hill & Trist, 1950) in a specific British political and economic post-war context, this knowledge was transposed and applied to a completely different cultural setting in India, a major former colony of Britain. This "dislocation" of the initial communications of the coal mine studies led to the production of a general theory of organization through Rice's text. Our research, however, provides opportunities for yet another kind of dislocation. "Accidental" absent features we have found in re-reading Rice (e.g., omissions in the text pertaining to the nature of labor relations, alongside the contemporaneous observations of other commentators) have the potential to substantially destabilize its original meaning (Rorty, 1995) and thereby challenge claims about the general applicability of STS.

The chapter adopts a communication-centered perspective to examine the role of texts and conversation (Taylor, Cooren, Giroux & Robichaud, 1996) in organizing—specifically in this case, the power of Rice's journal article (1953) in shaping STS theory and its wider understanding. Inspired by the Montreal School's theorization of "communication as *the* essential modality for organizing", we analyze Rice's account to see how organization is "*accomplished* (or 'real-ized') and *experienced* in conversation, *identified* and *described* through text" (Ashcraft, Kuhn & Cooren, 2009, 20). In analyzing Rice's experiment, we trace the "conversation" (dynamic exchanges) that negotiated the existing or imagined tensions in the mills to understand how socio-technical organization is represented in the "text". These tensions that appear concealed in Rice's text—the absences—indicate and reinforce asymmetries of power in the prevailing organizational and cultural context within which the experiment took place. Arguably, they might be said to stem from a postcolonial sensibility of control and superiority of the West vis-à-vis the former colony.

Our research centers around a story of Western knowledge transfer in the context of organizational restructuring that happens to be located largely in a postcolonial[1] time frame. It is a story situated in the context of independent India's development drive geared toward increasing industrial productivity through modernization of industry and various organizational structures relevant to the purpose. Our political stance is inspired by the conviction that "[t]he construction of the modern organization, and control systems it has fostered, is inextricably linked to the construction of the discourse of modernity, a discourse that owes its primacy to the process of colonialism" (Mir, Mir & Upadhyaya, 2003, p. 48). The study of texts and conversation presented here is therefore informed by a postcolonial viewpoint that draws attention to the tendency of Western epistemology to theorize "its particular-organic empirical reality into a cognitive-epistemic formula on behalf of the entire world" (Radhakrishnan, 1994, p. 308). This Western perspective finds expression in various ways, including the imposition of its systems of knowledge about order/organization onto its "other", the non-West; places where disorder is seen to reign supreme. This is often aided by a tendency for postcolonial elites to reinforce such Western hegemony in the pursuit of modernization.

Following this introduction, we provide a brief overview of the history of Tavistock's STS theory before situating our argument within the literature on the "Communication as Constitutive of Organization" (CCO) perspective (Ashcraft et al., 2009) and outlining our method of analysis of Rice's text. Subsequently, we discuss the "Ahmedabad Experiment" (Rice, 1953), focusing on Rice's representation of the problem at the mills as well as the uptake of his recommended solution. Taken together, the problem of managing technological change and its solution indicate the power of the account (1953) to prescribe "organizing" and thereby fix meanings intended through it. However, in contrast to the "ordering" activity of Rice's account, other evidence helps us reveal absences, thereby opening up an alternative meaning or reading of the text and thus its "disordering" properties (Vásquez et al., 2016, p. 2). Finally, we discuss the findings of our study and the implications with regards to the trajectory and generalization of Tavistock's STS theory.

Tavistock's STS Theory

Socio-technical systems thinking developed initially out of a study by the Tavistock researchers Eric Trist and Ken Bamforth in British coal mines in post-war Britain. Trist and Bamforth aimed to understand the impact of new technology implementation on social aspects of the workplace and found that contrary to the technologically deterministic ways of organizing work prevalent at the time, and in the context of a need for greater industrial productivity in the economy, it was possible to respect human desires and goals in organizing work around technology. The researchers observed and claimed that multiple task structures depending on human needs were possible in an organization, even around fixed characteristics of machinery, because close and indeterminate connections between the technical and social subsystems existed. They thus suggested that in order to become effective, an organization needed to optimize the social and technical subsystems *jointly* (Trist & Bamforth, 1951). Within this newly observed way of organizing people around machinery, small autonomous work groups were discovered as having been a socio-technical unit for effective organizing.

Socio-technical principles of organization were applied in various projects that the TIHR undertook in the decades following the coal mine studies. In Ahmedabad, in the first run of the experiment in the automatic weaving shed, application of socio-technical principles of restructuring of work away from individualistic modes of production to a "group system", led to higher efficiency in production, lower rates of damage in manufacturing and a decrease in hierarchy in the work structure (Rice, 1953). Consequently, over the next few years these principles of work organization were further applied throughout other departments of the mills, and other industries of the Sarabhais (Rice, 1963). Complementary changes in the structure of management were also called for. This entire "experiment" of work and management restructuring in a different land, culture and industry, heralded a new age of success and popularity for socio-technical methods of organizing work. The apparent accomplishment of the experiment in India gave STS theory a universal appeal.[2] The prevailing account of a "generalized" STS theory by Rice (1953, 1958, 1963) is the description of Tavistock's consultancy in Ahmedabad.

In the 1960s and 70s, STS theory gained in popularity as a design approach. With increasing emphasis on the quality of working life, the concept of the autonomous work group gained in importance in the context of democratization of the workplace. It became popular in Scandinavia and in the US, and in the West generally, seeking to improve the quality of working life as well as using it as a job-redesign tool (Burnes & Cooke, 2012). Later, the socio-technical approach became popular in several fields in the context of work design, e.g., ergonomics, psychology, management and organizational theory. Moreover, the field of social networking uses socio-technical concepts (e.g., *Handbook of Research on Socio-Technical Design and Social Networking Systems* [Whitworth & de Moor, 2009]). However, Doherty (2014) argues that in the process of diffusion, the origins of concepts (in this case STS theory) often get forgotten. The theory itself has been reduced to a mere "cypher" and a "banner" under which various domains have flourished whilst often sharing little in terms of conceptual roots (Eason, 2014).

Texts and (Dis)Organization

Within the field of organization studies, the literature on the role of communication in organizing is largely clustered under the "Communication as Constitutive of Organization" (CCO) perspective (Ashcraft et al., 2009). In a nutshell, this perspective defines communication as "the means by which organizations are established, composed, designed, and sustained" (Cooren, Kuhn, Cornelissen & Clark, 2011, p. 1150), and is made possible through repetitive application and articulation of texts and conversations (Taylor & Van Every, 2000). These texts and conversations help "organize" by 1) orientating organizational actors to act in particular ways depending on what is described in texts; and 2) realizing their actions through conversation, i.e., interaction based on activities and processes of meaning negotiation (Taylor & Van Every, 2000). Drawing on the CCO perspective, this chapter uses a communication lens to further the idea that texts are more than mere representations of social reality. Texts also have a performative character (Searle, 1995). Additionally, a communication lens shows that the meaning of texts is context dependent, it is dynamic and may keep shifting depending on the changing nature of the conversations pertaining to it (Taylor & Van Every, 2000). As articulated by Taylor et al. (1996, p. 4):

> It is in th[e] dialectic of conversation and text that . . . organizing occurs. . . . [C]onversation is mediated by text, the text by conversation. There is what we call a double translation: from the text to the conversation and the conversation to the text.

Considerable literature in the CCO perspective focuses on the idea of how communication creates (social) order (e.g., Cooren, 2000). For example, texts often create order by helping in planning and coordinating or even by prescribing action (e.g., Callon, 2002). While order has been prominent in much of the literature in the CCO perspective, the acknowledgement of a "disorderly" dimension of communication (e.g., Weick, 1993) has proved rather less topical. Exceptions include Cooren et al. (2011), who have argued that communication is equally capable of disordering, destroying or transforming meanings and thereby can lead to the destruction of organizations. However, while acknowledging the disordering capability of communication, Vásquez et al. (2016) paint a more positive picture. They emphasize communication's capability to open avenues of negotiation and its power to improvise and innovate in the context of organization once a text is put to use. This opening up is possible because texts are intertwined with the social context of their use (Kuhn, 2008; Orlikowski, 2007). Indeed, through our empirical case we show that given our research-specific context of revisiting Rice's account—tracing its postcolonial background as well as the extant labor-management tensions—communication simultaneously implies the existence of absent meanings that can potentially be opened up depending on the context and the interpretive horizon of the audience.

The notion of the organizing/disorganizing potential of texts finds resonance with processual ideas on order and disorder in the field of organization studies. When it comes to mainstream OS that largely follows a rational perspective, order, as opposed to disorder, is usually considered to be the desired outcome and measure of success in any effort at organizing (Vásquez et al., 2016). In contrast, we start from the assumption that processes of organization and disorganization are inextricably interconnected, mutually parasitical. In this processual perspective the creation of order involves simultaneous efforts at the suppression of disorder (Cooper, 1986). But because the latter cannot be removed without remainder, disorder poses a continuing threat of de-stabilization. Borrowing an insight from de Certeau (1986), we might say that the ongoing pursuit or performance of organization may be confounded by the reassertion of that which has been repressed.

Following Vásquez et al. (2016), the chapter seeks to demonstrate *how* Rice's (1953) consultancy-style text contributed to the formalization of particular ideas and practices of organizing by bringing "order" into an existing problematic work organization whilst nonetheless remaining subject to the "disordering" possibilities of textual communication. We thus seek to contribute to the literature on the ordering and disordering properties of communication through a number of ways. We do this, first, by considering the inscriptions (the textual and diagrammatical tools) Rice used to capture and describe the organizational disorder at the mills as well as to facilitate its process of removal. Second, we trace the movements of "texts" and "conversations" (Taylor & Van Every, 2000) in Rice's existing account that in effect sought to fix meanings as regards the general applicability of the socio-technical theory of organization. Given that the social context that made way for these texts and conversations is of paramount importance in making sense of how communication can shape organization in any particular way, and aware of critiques of Rice's account, we treat the received understanding of his text with skepticism. In tracing the trajectory of the text-conversation dynamic, our premise takes inspiration from the argument that most of our knowledge about social relations, events, and power structures arises from "socially organized practices of reporting and recording" rather than from an "actuality . . . not directly accessible" (Smith,1974, p. 257). Of course, additionally, we know by Rice's own admission that the account that he wrote (and which has prevailed) was based on "facts" he was informed of: for in the main he was not present at the site of the experiment. Not only were Rice and the senior management not involved in any discussion with the mill supervisors or workers regarding the reorganization, they did not visit the loom shed until the reorganization had been implemented. Rice returned to London after spending just seven days at Ahmedabad and the results presented in his subsequent journal paper had "been sent to him by the Works Manager" (Rice, 1953, p. 298). Third, inspired by the idea that absent meanings "haunt" a text (Cooren, 2009; Vásquez et al., 2016), we aim to address gaps that are left hidden and unaddressed in the original account(s). In particular, we are interested to consider how the mill workers and the labor union at Ahmedabad are represented within Rice's text and thus what is *not* written about them. By revealing the potential for disordering opened up by these absences the chapter engages with the ordering-disordering properties of an organizational text (Vásquez et al., 2016). These properties, that always go hand-in-hand, show how revised interpretations can be harnessed to negotiate and rework the mainstream understanding of socio-technical systems theory still largely prevalent today. Finally, the chapter also seeks to show that although the disorderly nature of communication facilitates negotiations and improvisations, the outcome is largely dependent on context, on the prevalent power and hierarchy of the workplace as well as the audience in question.

Analysis: Decontextualization and Recontextualization

Our empirical inquiry into the (dis)ordering properties of Rice's text began with a thorough reading of his initial write up of the experimental socio-technical reorganization of work at the weaving sheds in Ahmedabad. This, along with his later book (1958) was then juxtaposed alongside the reevaluation of the experiment at the site 17 years later (Miller, 1975) together with the very few existing critiques (e.g., Roy, 1969). Our reading of Miller and Roy reveals both an element of failure (of the group method) and absences respectively in Rice's account, acting as catalysts in our engagement of archival work. We contend that the absences and failure shed light on the decontextualized character of Rice's orderly documentary account. To understand this further we analyze Rice's (1953) text from two angles.

First, we analyze it as a specific genre, i.e., a consultancy report, focusing on the use of "textual and graphical constructs—inscriptions" (Bloomfield & Vurdubakis, 1994, p. 456). As outlined in the previous section, we examine Rice's definition of the problem and the recommended solution at the mills in relation to these "inscriptions". From our postcolonial viewpoint, we consider how inscription devices like maps or diagrams may be drawn up by a "center" for purposes of convenient calculations or administration and used in efforts to control social practices in a "periphery" (Latour, 1987). In particular, they help to scale down phenomena in the periphery into controllable categories amenable to generalized analysis by the center. Such inscriptions can be understood as a form of representational practice, they serve to organize vision— a particular way of seeing—according to a particular vision of how an organization ought to be organized (Bloomfield & Vurdubakis, 1997). Such organizations of vision are inevitably partial, abstracted from the actual context, and so intricacies of the actual phenomena tend to be lost.

Second, we analyze Rice's account as a communication event centered around text-conversation movements (Ashcraft et al., 2009) that dislocates (Cooren & Fairhurst, 2009) a local understanding of STS theory (as initially developed in the British coal mines) and universalizes (decontextualizes) it. The process of organizing that the miners in the British coal mine studies had *themselves* come up with was based on democratic principles. This organization was observed by the Tavistock researchers and embodied in the text (i.e., Trist & Bamforth, 1951) written by them. At Ahmedabad the text was (re)produced through conversations between elites (an evolving communication between management and consultants). Decision-making never involved conversations between management, consultants and workers. This non-participative conversation, made possible by the postcolonial social, political and cultural context of the Indian experimental site, differs from the nature of conversations around the reorganization of work between the miners and management in the British coal mines. The selective nature of conversations in Ahmedabad carefully avoided the existing tensions and came to constitute Rice's (decontextualized) text, which in turn brought to life the STS theory of organization.

In analyzing the critiques of Rice's account, we discover something about the location- and culture-specific context of the experiment. In particular, alongside Rice's claim of voluntary and spontaneous participation of workers in the experiment (Rice, 1958) we are confronted by Roy's (1969) questioning of the running of the experiment without any monetary incentives being handed to workers. In addition, Miller's (1975) analysis of the failure of the Group System in the mills in the longer term (after the consultancy was completed) reveals a culture-specific hierarchy among Indian workers that worked against the principles of equal status of small group membership. These follow-up studies that prompted our skepticism about Rice's account beg questions about the workers' spontaneous or voluntary participation. Indeed, research into the existing situation at the mills leading up to Rice's experiment reveals several key factors in existing tensions. From the workers' perspectives these mainly involved discontent around pay structures (Wolcott, 1994) and the deplorable working conditions (Murphy, 1953). From management's perspective the tensions clustered around the realization of the need for new technology and proposals for rationalization.

Encompassing all of the labor-management tensions were management interests in tapping into a postcolonial nationalistic quest for industrialization, one driven by the political elites of the country and supported by big business. In this, the owners were convinced that superior expert knowledge from the West (the center) was essential in guiding the process of industrialization and management of change around technology and people in the underdeveloped former colony (the periphery). Hence the Tavistock, with which the chairman and his family had existing connections as students in Cambridge and at the Tavistock itself (Banerjee, 2015), was called in to steer the management of change in the mills.

Our research, juxtaposed with the background or prior context (Hassard, 2012) of Rice's experiments, offers a recontextualization of the received wisdom of STS theory by restoring the written-out tensions. Thus, when taken together, the sequential decontextualization and recontextualization of text that we pursue here tell Rice's story of organization and is underpinned by our suggestion that a postcolonial ideology helped set the context of the experiment. By themselves neither Rice's text, nor the conversations mentioned in the text, show *how* organizing occurs through communication. They are a-contextual. Informed by CCO research, our engagement from a postcolonial analytical perspective revolves around the idea that contexts define the meaning of texts and differ depending on the conversations that transpire (Taylor & Van Every, 2000). In the remainder of the chapter we therefore focus on studying the contexts—their removal (decontextualization) and their reinstatement (recontextualization).

Decontextualization and the Ahmedabad Experiment: (Re)Ordering in Rice's Account

At the very beginning, the consultancy was conceived in relation to the main problem presented by the chairman of the Calico Mills to Tavistock staff—namely, in spite of claimed harmonious labor-management relations there was falling productivity in the wake of the implementation of new machinery. This had also caused social and psychological discomfort among workers. In contrast, following an analysis based on his own preliminary observations as well as from conversations with senior managers of the mills, Rice communicated the problem, through inscriptions, as two-fold. First, although Rice perceived that all tasks in the experimental shed were interdependent, he contended that there was a lack of group structure among employees working with the looms. This led to the individualization of work and a lack of community-feeling among these workers which in turn hampered productivity. Second, he suggested that a confused pattern of authority and relationships among workers and supervisors led to poor communication and hence more time was being spent engaged in supervisory control by managers from outside the weaving shed. This restricted the efficient and productive use of the supervisory time of these senior managers. As a solution Rice proposed a restructuring of work around small (internal) groups to replace the individualized work structure: a small "group of workers for a group of looms" (Rice, 1953, p. 317).

To develop this picture of work reorganization in more detail we now focus on Rice's representation of the problem and recommended solution through 1) his use of textual and graphical constructs; and 2) our understanding of the text-conversation translations in his account.

Inscriptions

In order to grasp and to convey the details and indeed complexity of production, Rice drew up a number of tables and figures (diagrammatic representations) itemizing the work tasks, occupational designations, loom groupings, governance structure, the temporal sequencing of tasks and of course the allocation of workers/occupational roles according to the reorganization of production around small working groups. These inscription devices helped to represent the situation in the weaving shed and to offer the solution.

In contrast to a single loom, where production followed a cyclic pattern, in the experimental loom shed the production followed a continuous process involving multiple weaving looms in which production depended on carrying out many activities simultaneously. At the time of Rice's experiment, the shed contained some 224 looms which were divided into 19 different groupings (see Table 8.1). The five broad activities were weaving, loading and unloading, loom maintenance, cleaning and humidifying. Each activity was associated with specific tasks. Workers carried out these tasks as well as taking on occupational roles. The activities of the shed had been broken down into small components; the number of workers required to perform these tasks around the machine had been calculated by "the normal production engineering corollary of job-breakdown and work study" (Rice, 1953, p. 304) of the different components. Depending on their occupational role, each group of workers was thus allocated work, and depending on their skill the number of looms to be allocated to each group was decided.

There were two work shifts a day which were supervised by a "Top Supervisor". For each shift, a "Work Supervisor" was responsible to him. Working for the supervisors were 12 different occupational roles. Other than the humidification fitter (reporting to the Top Supervisor) every other worker reported to the Work Supervisor. Within the activity of weaving, the associated tasks of weaving, knotting broken yarn and battery filling (i.e., supplying full bobbins for the looms and removing empty bobbins) were carried out by eight "weavers" and three "smash hands", and five "battery fillers" respectively. In addition, there were two "bobbin carriers", two "gaters" whose work was to replace empty beams (the cylinders onto which bobbins were loaded) and one "cloth carrier" who removed woven cloth. In addition, two "jobbers" worked toward maintaining and adjusting the loom. They supervised two "assistant jobbers", but also directed all other workers to some extent. Alongside the

Table 8.1 Differentiation of Experimental Automatic Loom Shed into Loom Groups

Kind of Loom Group	Number of Loom Groups	Number of Tasks in Each Loom Group	Number of Workers in Kind of Loom Group	Occupational Roles
I (24–32)	8	1	8	Weaver
II (40–50)	5	1	5	Battery Filler
III (60–80)	3	1	3	Smash Hand
IV (112)	2	4	8	Gater Cloth Carrier Jobber Assistant Jobber
V (224)	1	5	5	Bobbin Carrier Feeler Motion Fitter Oiler Sweeper Humidification Fitter
Totals	19	12	29	

Source: Rice (1953, p. 304)

jobbers and assistant jobbers one "feeler motion fitter" and one "oiler" carried out the activity of loom maintenance. Finally, one "sweeper" swept and cleaned whilst a "humidification fitter" was responsible for activity related to humidification. Thus, 12 tasks were allocated to 12 occupational groups (one each) involving 29 workers. Further, there were 19 overlapping loom groups of 5 different kinds. This description communicates something of the complexity of the weaving operation and demands not insignificant attention for it to be assimilated. But presented in the form of Table 8.1 arguably it is grasped much more readily.

Although Rice noted that all the tasks in the shed were interdependent, he claimed that some workers (e.g., the feeler motion fitter) were more independent in that they were only connected to the Work Supervisor. Other workers had more interdependent relationships with different degrees of interdependence across overlapping loom groups. The intricacies of the relationships in production can be further exemplified by considering how some tasks/workers depended on others. For instance, amongst other things the activity of weaving depended on a ready supply of bobbins (the task of battery fillers) and someone to intervene and repair yarn when it became broken in the machinery (the task of a smash hand). There were five battery fillers and three smash hands serving eight weavers. Furthermore, some sorts of cloth demanded more work from certain groups of workers. This resulted in, for instance, one battery filler's time being completely used up in serving the looms of two weavers. In some cases this resulted in an opportunity for the two weavers to build up an interdependent relationship with the battery filler. This relationship would then be consistent with the interdependent nature of the tasks. Rice noted however that this was not a common occurrence.

Through his analysis Rice concluded that the task relationships were too complicated and confused to allow for any "stable, cohesive relationships between the members of the total work group" to develop (Rice, 1953, p. 309). Also, he felt that the confused loom groups hampered the possibility of the development of "small, internally structured and internally led work-groups consistent with task relatedness" (Rice, 1953, p. 309). Additionally, because of the different kind of loom groups and consequent allocation of one component task per occupational role, the workers could not be neatly organized for efficient supervision.

The work organization and management hierarchy of the shed prior to re-organization as presented by Rice is shown in Figure 8.1. Although he claims through this figure that the authority relationship among workers and supervisors was confused and chaotic, he found it intriguing that in spite of this confused and "broken-down" hierarchy, there were "no overt relationship difficulties". He felt this might partly be because of "the high quality of the [existing] relationships" (Rice, 1953, p. 308). We contend that as an external agent, a consultant from a different culture and country, it is exceptional to imagine that Rice could have grasped the social and cultural systems local to Ahmedabad

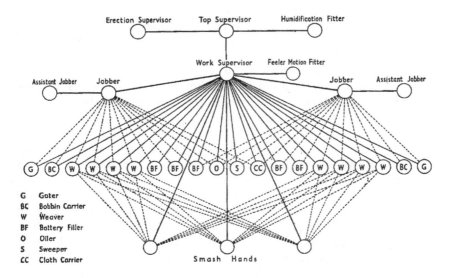

Figure 8.1 Management Hierarchy of the Experimental Automatic Loom Shed
Source: Rice (1953, p. 307)

184 *Anindita Banerjee and Brian Bloomfield*

that defined these relationships or led to what seemed to him a confused authority structure. Some 8,000 workers (none of whom Rice ever met) worked in the mills having moved into Ahmedabad from different regions of India and speaking multiple languages (Rice, 1958). If as reported by the chairman, there was any social or psychological problem affecting the workers and their relationships at work, it is difficult to imagine that these intricacies would ever be grasped completely by Rice, much less represented diagrammatically. In fact, by Rice's own admission many relationships were not represented[3] in Figure 8.1. Hence, we suggest that the diagram obscures subtleties that are crucial for a deeper understanding or communication of the problem in the mills. To be fair, Rice was well aware of the limitations of his study, as one of his concluding points makes clear:

> These results could not, in the time available, be related to the general ecological background of economic, industrial or cultural conditions in India, nor because of language difficulties could any direct evidence of the workers' attitudes and feelings be obtained. The only evidence of "goodness of fit" was the spontaneous acceptance, implementation, and continuation by the workers, and the withdrawal from the governing system of the shed by higher management.
>
> (Rice, 1953, p. 218)

But while Rice admits omitting certain relationships in depicting the authority structure in Figure 8.1, we might speculate whether certain categories of workers, particularly the "spinners"—the resisting group of workers (Murphy, 1953)—were deliberately left out from the story of the experiment. In many ways the work structure at the mills in Ahmedabad was based on a hierarchy defined by caste and religion in which the spinners belonged to the lowliest of castes (the so-called "untouchables") and had been resenting rationalization and the dire conditions of work (Wolcott, 1994). Accordingly, perhaps the experimental shed was purposefully set up in a department where spinners did not work in order to improve the prospects for a successful redesign of production. Expressed differently, the source of disorder represented by the spinners was left out of the initial experiment only to return (as we shall see later) when efforts were made to extend the experiment beyond the weaving shed.

The importance of social (discriminatory) boundaries in the context of production were evident in research conducted prior to Rice's experiment at Ahmedabad. For instance, Murphy (1953) relates an example in which "bubble fountains" were fitted by a mill owner in order to provide workers with drinking water but remained unused due to caste differences, other workers refusing to drink from a source shared by "untouchables". Against such a backdrop, Rice's laudable vision of removing hierarchy in work and management organization seems ambitious to us. It hinges on emancipating workers at the lower levels first and foremost, something requiring a fundamental reform of a caste-religion-based unequal work structure. Evidently, such problems of work organization would appear more intricate and complex than might be captured or even suggested in Rice's diagrammatic representations. The glossing over of caste-religious differences implied by democratic small group formation would appear as not particularly sensitive to the cultural context of mill operations in India at that time. Rice's diagrammatic inscriptions represent work tasks and occupational roles pertaining to the organization and use of machinery. Despite the intended commitment to understanding the whole system, including the "social dimensions" (Rice, 1953, p. 297), not to mention his understanding of the human/psychological dimensions of work, it was nonetheless a machine metaphor or perspective on production that would seem to have predominated at the expense of a detailed understanding of the social relations at Ahmedabad. The complexity of work and authority relationships became reified in the process of depicting the activities of the weaving shed. Rice's deployment of inscription devices served to highlight certain features of confusion and messiness (disorder) in the context of work organization in the mills so as to assist their eradication through the socio-technical redesign of production. However, as we have argued, at the same time this representation of the sources of disorder was partial due to the neglect of other important contextual aspects of the specific setting in which Rice found himself. Accordingly, we suggest that despite a seemingly formidable attention to detail in terms of the orchestration of work tasks involved in weaving, his inscriptions nonetheless decontextualize (Vásquez et al., 2016) the experiment whilst offering a prescriptive solution to organize and manage change (re-ordering).

The location specificity of the experiment is equally important when we talk about decontextualization of the text. With uptake of STS theory development having failed in Britain in the early 1950s (Trist, 1981), Tavistock looked for opportunities for funding and experimenting outside of the country (Dicks, 1970). The opportunity to apply the theory to the problem at the Calico Mills as presented by the Sarabhais offered the prospect of furthering the Tavistock agenda of theory development. Rice was on a (Tavistock) mission to promote and popularize the relevance of "small group" organization of work toward the attainment of efficiency as well as democracy in an organization. To show efficiency in production through restructuring of control mechanisms, any resistance toward the new form of organization (the experiment, in our case) needed to be avoided or held in check. Indeed, Rice argued against a possible reorganization of work through increased *external* control, cautioning that to do so would run the risk of workers feeling confused, "coerced and policed" which might further instigate them to "increase their resistance to greater effort and productivity" (Rice, 1953, p. 308). Instead he frames his recommendation of work reorganization along the lines of increasing *internal* control through formation of small work groups. The highlighting of confusion depicted in Figure 8.1 and the subsequent proposal for reorganization to remove chaos and restore order needs to be understood in this context. This echoes Smith's (1974) argument that documents (see Figure 8.1; Table 8.1 in our case) can shape the order of social practices by transforming actual phenomena into forms suitable for administrative purposes. They become instruments of governing and control for those who rule others. The practice of framing knowledge in a particular way through these documents (text) fixes meaning in a manner that promises the space for bringing the organization back into an orderly state. These reified representations reflect the orderly side of communication (Vásquez et al., 2016). Arguably, the use of representations that gloss over social complexities was aimed for use by consultants engaged in working for busy managers, not for the benefit of workers.

Text-Conversation Translations

Rice made his initial analysis of the problems at the mills in consultation with a "development group" consisting of the chairman, the mill manager and the works manager (a direct executive subordinate of the mill manager) of the company. This analysis was reported to other senior management members of the Ahmedabad Manufacturing and Calico Printing Company. "The decision to initiate the reorganization was taken by the Chairman at a meeting which was attended by all Senior Managers" (Rice, 1953, p. 298). Together, these collaborations and meetings can be understood to represent a series of conversations that were mediated by the initial "text" of STS principles (drawn from e.g. the British coal mine study). These conversations, a set of discursive social interactions in which the principles were interpreted and the decision for reorganization formalized, constituted a translation of that text (Taylor et al., 1996; Ashcraft et al., 2009). Only at this stage was the weaving master, a member from a lower rank of workers (perhaps from among the weavers or from a level in the hierarchy between the weavers and the jobbers in Figure 8.1) called in to participate. Rice reports that the idea of reorganization of workers (into small groups around a group of looms) was favorably and enthusiastically *accepted* by the weaving master. The works manager subsequently discussed the proposals with the Top Supervisor of the experimental automatic loom shed.

> Thereafter the supervisors and workers in the loom shed took over the proposals as their own; and within a few hours, to the surprise of management, the workers had organized their own working groups.
> (Rice, 1953, p. 298)

The success of the first set of experiments (in the experimental automatic loom shed) that resulted in Rice's journal article (1953) depended crucially on this apparent uptake by the workers.

We understand Rice's capacity to secure compliance with his redesigned work system from two broad angles: 1) his authority as an "expert" in change management (working in a postcolonial context); and 2) his perception of the power of the labor union and worker rights in Ahmedabad. For the former, we draw on the suggestion that the role of consultants can be understood in the light of strategies they use in i) making themselves indispensable to the clients by the allure of their knowledge and expertise; and ii) maintaining their authority or expert identity through the securing of shared meaning among actors in the situation (Bloomfield & Danieli, 1995). As regards the former, the preexisting links between the Tavistock and the Sarabhais together with the chairman's regard for the nature of the Tavistock's research and work (psychoanalysis) would seem to have been a crucial deciding factor in choosing the Institute for the consultancy project. At root here was a conviction regarding the superiority of Western knowledge and expertise in science and technology. Additionally, the Tavistock had previous experience in dealing with similar situations regarding new technology and production (e.g., in the British coal mines), and Rice himself had worked with Trist and several Tavistock staff on studying absenteeism and labor turnover in a British enterprise applying the tenets of group dynamics (e.g., Rice et al., 1950). With all this expertise and reputation as well as the similarity in the nature of interests and experience between the client and consultant, Rice (and the Tavistock) arguably appeared indispensable to the Sarabhais. In short, Rice's suggestions would naturally carry weight, and given the enrollment of management at the mills to his ideas (translations of the "text" through conversations), they would ensure that it would be followed through.

Turning now to the matter of Rice's perceptions about the labor union and workers, we find from his later writing that he thought "[T]rade unions in India are not . . . , from the Western point of view, strong unions" (1958, p. 18). While conscious of the possibilities of worker resistance in the event of increased external management control due to reorganization, it would appear that Rice did not consider workers' resistance to be a hurdle in reorganizing work along the lines of increasing internal control in the experiment. Even if he did, within the context of the prevailing non-Western caste/religion and supervisor/worker-based hierarchy and organization, the senior managers could have ensured that resistance from workers would not be manifest. Built on Gandhian principles of "self-help, self-education, responsibility, and service to its members" (Kannappan, 1962, p. 86), the workers' union had little bargaining power vis-à-vis management (Rice, 1958). As we have noted earlier, Rice's recommended solution was never proposed in consultation with workers. It is not known from his accounts whether there was actually any resistance, whether workers might have objected but been replaced by other workers or whether the labor union might have intervened. The received account only highlights the point that Rice's proposal had a spontaneous uptake among workers and the experiment proceeded. Rice reports that the outcome was successful: Productivity increased in the mills and there was less damage in the cloth produced. The STS theory of organization that was embodied in the initial coal mine "text" of Trist and Bamforth (1951), translated in the meetings and conversations between Rice and senior management at Ahmedabad and enacted in the loom shed, was thereby (re)produced in the shape of Rice's journal article (1953). The newly (re)produced decontextualized text fixes meaning, universalizes STS theory and provides an image of an efficient "organization". The text (i.e., Rice, 1953) makes the identification of chaos and disorder explicit and ready to be acted upon in a new context of action.

Recontextualizing Rice's Account: Opening Up Meaning to Labor Union and Worker Resistance

As researchers/audience of Rice's received account of STS, our next task is to offer a different translation of this text by considering in further detail some of the social and industrial relations issues that can serve to recontextualize it. Our starting point from our frame of interpretation and background information is the claimed success of the experiment, and consequently the universal appeal of STS theory. Importantly, this hinges on the solitary assumption that the workers at Ahmedabad willingly approved of the approach and reorganized themselves to carry out the experiment.

We know from elsewhere, however, that in the post-independence period (beginning 1947) there was a substantial degree of tension among workers, supervisors and jobbers (Murphy, 1953). This hostility can be understood broadly from two angles: first, a caste-religion-based hierarchy that led to resentment among workers; and second, workers' hostility toward rationalization. Complaints received by the labor union derived mainly from the Spinning department (where workers belonged to the lowliest "untouchable" caste); and from the loom shed (where weavers were mostly Muslims, together with some Hindus). According to Murphy, in a study conducted in the immediate post-independence phase in the Ahmedabad mills, the attitude of the immediate supervisor toward the workers was important in determining the latter's attitude and morale in work. Additionally, he claims that there was a positive connection between workers' earnings and their morale. This is best represented in his explanation of the results of the study:

It is not those who are near the top of the job hierarchy and who take over some middle-class ideas who are actually most restless. It is rather those who are at the very bottom of the wage ladder.

(Murphy, 1953, p. 207)

Those who were at the very bottom of the wage ladder and most discriminated against socially were the spinners. Dissatisfaction was higher among them than among the Muslim weavers. Although they belonged to a completely different religion, Muslims were almost treated as a caste "in the lower-middle region of the caste hierarchy" (Murphy, 1953, p. 208). They therefore enjoyed a better social standing than that of the spinners. Murphy argues from the findings of his study that the low wages just about helped workers meet their ends and left most of them in huge debts. Moreover, their low earning power destroyed their bargaining capabilities on the one hand and led to poor productivity standards on the other. Furthermore, prior to the introduction of new production technology, the low productivity was exacerbated by hugely old-fashioned machinery. The working conditions that resulted from this were characterized by huge levels of noise, dirt and crowding, further affecting morale negatively.

In addition, we are informed that remnants of an old practice in the mills, which enabled the supervisors to exercise the power to hire and fire workers and, moreover, to draw a fraction of workers' salaries, caused a lot of tension between workers and supervisors. Although this practice had been gradually abolished by the time of independence from British rule, an indirect power of firing workers still rested with the supervisors in the sense that they would warn workers for serious failures in production, and three warnings would normally lead to job loss. For workers at the bottom of the ladder it would have been difficult to find a new job in India at that time.

Turning now to another source, we know from Wolcott's (1994) study that tensions and hostility among workers and supervisors were also a product of the employers' effort at rationalization in the mills. In the immediate post-independence period in India, a national drive toward industrialization had resulted in many mills introducing new machinery to automate work, with an aim to increase efficiency and thereby productivity. In the weaving sheds, the owners had been trying for some time to implement a new mechanism that would stop a loom if a warp thread broke and would thereby reduce the production of faulty cloth. However, the weavers were not in favor of the introduction of this mechanism because "their bonus for quantity was greater than the fines for faults" (Wolcott, 1994, p. 311). Interestingly, and importantly, it is noteworthy that these sorts of conflicts related by both Wolcott (1994) and Murphy (1953) are underplayed by Rice. Accordingly, we contend that the basis of the success of the experiment, i.e., Rice's claim of the spontaneous acceptance of proposals among workers, might not have been as straight-forward as he believed or indicated. Additionally, we believe the success of the experiment was partial at best, not just because workers were not consulted in decision-making on reorganization. Of equal importance was the fact that if the spinners had been part of the automatic shed, the possibility of small group formation among workers would have been problematic. Indeed, this issue is germane to the spread of the experiment which we discuss next.

Following the initial success in the experimental shed there was an effort to extend Rice's redesign to other (non-automatic loom) sheds of the Calico Mills. However, our archival research revealed a letter[4] dated 1956 that was written to the chairman of the mills in which the labor union expressed its deep dissatisfaction with management for having spread the experiment to a new department, the Ring-Frame department, where spinners worked. In this letter the union argued that the workers were instructed on "behalf of the Mills to accept the said experiment and to give their co-operation". Having been informed about the facts of the experiment, they, however, had realized soon after that they would not benefit in any way; that it was against their interests and consequently they refused to participate in it. The union had, according to this letter, even "requested" the mills to not proceed with any further experiments: "[I]t is a matter of sorrow that the Mills have decided to go on with the experiment *disregarding the request of the workers*" (Dave, 1956; our emphasis).

This piece of archival evidence sits alongside Roy's (1969) claim that Rice underestimated the cash incentives meted out to the group of vol-unteers in making the experiment work as well as his wider neglect of the labor union in the reorganization of work at Ahmedabad. Generally speaking, Rice's later book (1958) engages rather cursorily with issues of cash incentives (p. 158), negotiations with the labor union (if at all) (p. 152) or worker resistance toward rationalization (pp. 150–151). In none of these aspects is resistance highlighted; they are presented more as inconveniences that could be easily resolved. For example, Rice claims that it was not merely cash incentives that allured workers to the experi-ment, but really the abundance and availability of nonpermanent "badli" (casual) workers that provided ready volunteers. But cash incentives, that according to Roy (from his own experience in mills in Ahmedabad at that time) were the most essential impetus for getting workers to volunteer for an experiment, do not appear at all in the story of success presented through the 1953 journal article. Similarly, resistance toward rationaliza-tion (by not turning up for work) is downplayed by Rice by mentioning that the majority of the workers ignored all hostility toward rationaliza-tion brought on by fellow workers and came to work at the mills (1958, p. 151). Whatever agitation remained was apparently settled by manage-ment's promise toward taking responsibility for workers' wellbeing in the event of injury due to hostility by a small section of workers (Rice, 1958, p. 151). Once again, Rice leaves out the details of worker discontent by mentioning how an abundance of applications came in for volunteering in the "new shed" for non-automatic looms in 1954. He also mentions that an agreement between the labor union and the Calico Mills permitted the smooth spread of experiments to other sheds; and that in spite of agitation by the Communist Party leaders in Ahmedabad "conditions in the mill returned steadily to normal" (Rice, 1958, p. 152).

By 1956 when the experiment had proceeded to the (Ring-)Spinning department, Rice merely mentions that small group working was running in 12 ring frames. Rice's observation in the experimental phase is summed up as "[T]he experiment has not yet continued for sufficiently long to make the results reliable, nor have other workers in the Spinning department yet asked for permission to reorganize themselves in the same way" (Rice, 1958, p. 175). Without Roy's (1969) claims or our archival finding, Rice's observation has little negative impact on the success story of the experiments. Yet, we know from our earlier discussion that participation on the part of workers from the Ring-Frame department was reluctant. Of course, Rice's (1953) account of the experiment's success is the story of the experimental "weaving" shed, but our archival engagement and reading of other contemporary sources led us to question the choice of that particular shed in which the experiments were conducted.

The union and worker perspectives are represented in a very particular way within Rice's prescriptive ideas for the small group organization of work. His partial account of labor conflicts implies an absence, or writing out, of meaning and disorder that has remained in the background and "haunted" the further articulation or conversation/interpretation of his text (Cooren, 2009). In reality, the spinners had resisted further participation regarding the spread of the experiment and it had to be temporarily halted. Yet, due to institutional factors, in the context of a newly independent nation striving for modernization, worker voices were in effect downplayed if not silenced. Again, the locational and cultural specificity of Ahmedabad facilitated the silencing of the lowliest voices—despite the best intentions of the socio-technical reorganization to ensure a fair workplace. As noted by Spivak (1988), a spinner's voice is easy to write out, for they cannot be heard. Devoid of any negotiating power, the "subaltern" spinners were not even represented by the union. With no contentions to consider, worker involvement thereby appeared seamless, resulting in an "efficient organization".

Rice's decontextualized "text" clearly lays down steps toward the potential attainment of efficiency by any enterprise. Devoid of any seriously contentious labor issues it is straightforward and appealing for use by consultants. In contrast, our postcolonial perspective and research into the background context of the experiment inspires an alternative meaning. When the shortcomings of the experiment and the absences about preexisting and ongoing labor-management tensions are juxta-posed alongside Rice's account, they help to recontextualize it. Through the study of absences in the account of STS theory and our follow-up research we have demonstrated how when a text "travels", it may be "both decontextualized and recontextualized" (Vásquez et al., 2016, p. 651). The received meaning or understanding of the experiment at the mills that is conveyed in Rice's decontextualized account from 1953 is opened up by the "absences" from the diagrammatic and textual rep-resentations (Figure 8.1 and Table 8.1) we have brought to attention. This supports Gilbert and Mulkay's (1984) claim that organization is a repository of multiple meanings. The reductive style of text and diagram-matic representations in reporting the Ahmedabad Experiment helped decontextualize information in the account, but outside of the project's context the possibility of alternative or multiple understandings strength-ened. This "reflect(s) the disorderly side of communication" (Vásquez et al., 2016, p. 647). In our case, from a postcolonial viewpoint and associated conversation, we have uncovered absences that haunt Rice's account of STS theory to (re)produce a recontextualized account of the re-organization at Ahmedabad. Of course, a different interpretative lens, one not centered on the study of absences and a postcolonial reading, would lead to a different reading of STS.

Given that texts have inherent disordering properties offering the pos-sibility of multiple interpretations once leaving the initial context of their creation, their meanings transcend the control of the initial authors (Calás & Smircich, 1999). The case presented here is no exception. The post-war and post-independence development contexts at the time of the run-ning of experiments, together with the Tavistock's own agenda of theory development around the promotion of use of small (semi-)autonomous groups (Dicks, 1970), shaped the generalized accounts of STS theory to a notable extent. The locational and postcolonial temporal background of the experiment in India thus provided an excellent opportunity for Tavistock's theory development. Through this opportunity what evolved as the guiding principles of STS theory in the British coal mines got estab-lished broadly through Rice's accounts about the later experiments in India. Yet the precise details of how work reorganization was achieved differed as the location and therefore context of the theory changed from that of its initial inception. The generalization of theory was possible however not just because of the postcolonial opportunity of the exper-iment. More subtly, the success of the theory's development stemmed from postcolonial beliefs about the superiority of the West among the local elites as well as the role of the West itself in legitimizing power dif-ferentials in favor of elites against those of workers whose efforts had made the experiment possible.

STS theory is built on the premise of understanding organizations as "whole systems" (Rice, 1953, p. 297) which are "open" (Bertanlanffy,

1950). Thus, every part (sub-system) of the organization (the whole system) is linked to and dependent upon every other and is of equal importance for the operation of the organization. Accordingly, we might suggest that the labor union, like every sub-system, was also a legitimate part of the system. Indeed, the Spinning or Ring-Frame department was an important part of the entire system—it is through spinning that cotton gets converted to yarn for take up by the weaving looms—and it was the spinners who had proved particularly resistant to rationalization. However, our research indicates that through the writing out of the labor union and worker demands the participatory ethos of STS theory that prevailed through the textual accounts had been claimed on a somewhat partially inclusive experiment (Roy, 1969). Our research might be said to breathe life into absent meanings that "haunted" Rice's accounts (Derrida, 1978; Cooren, 2009) and makes space for a participatory dialogue.

Conclusion

The Ahmedabad Experiment (Rice, 1953, 1958, 1963) tells a story of work reorganization around new technology. It centered on the formation of self-regulatory autonomous groups in order to promote and prescribe internal control (rather than external supervision), raising productivity whilst managing an organization in a more *participative* manner. Given this background, the neglect/absence of the worker demands or labor union negotiations (Roy, 1969) in the accounts of running the weaving shed experiments seemed to be a valid point of inquiry. Focusing on Rice's account of what happened at Ahmedabad, this chapter discusses both the decontextualization of the text as well as its recontextualization. The decontextualization is presented through our analysis of Rice's use of inscriptions (text) that reify and remove reality from its immediate social and political contexts by focusing only on numbers and machines. Decontextualization helped negotiate tensions and highlighted chaos in tangible terms for consultants and managers to work upon. It thereby fixed meanings, producing practicable prescriptions for tidying up disorganization. On the other hand, recontextualization is specifically enacted through an attempt to open up meanings by addressing absences in the decontextualized (received) version (Vásquez et al., 2016) of what happened at Ahmedabad. The absences have offered insights into the concealed contexts of the decontextualized text and provided an alternative reading of the organization. We have discussed the contexts that have influenced the actual running of the experiment, including the interests of the mill owners, the larger agenda of the Tavistock Institute in the development of STS theory and the nature of the labor union at Ahmedabad. We have also touched upon the discourse of development in a post-independence India.

In the Indian weaving sheds we might suggest that the socio-technical organization was "incarnated *in* the texts that [spoke] in its name and *through* the conversations . . . these texts [were] (re)produced" (Ashcraft et al., 2009, pp. 20–21). In this process of universalization of the theory the initial "texts" were Trist and Bamforth's article (1951) and others on socio-technical reorganization experiments written by Tavistock researchers and drawn upon by Rice. Additionally, Rice and Miller, as consultants and experts, were the spokespersons (also "texts" as categorized by Ashcraft et al., 2009) for the socio-technical reorganization around small group work organization—a Tavistock hallmark of the time. Through our analysis we thus uncover how local conversations produced Rice's decontextualized texts and thereby helped to generalize the theory.

Our postcolonial viewpoint helps reveal absences in Rice's partial account. The nature of these absences reflects a specific sensibility that draws on an assumed position of Western superiority and granted Rice (the expert) legitimacy to identify chaos and disorder (represented through Figure 8.1) in local inferior ways of work organization. Additionally, aided by local elites, it helped write out subaltern voices of dissent. Through our postcolonial recontextualization of the account of STS theory, we have thereby broadened the understanding of events and phenomena in the background to the communicative power of a text in constituting organization. This expansion in perspective also suggests the emancipatory potential of our research. Through the opening up of absent meanings haunting Rice's text, we acknowledge the existence of less powerful stakeholders.

Our study resonates with Cooper's (1986) insight concerning the duality of organization/disorganization. The effort to rationalize and re-order production at the Ahmedabad mills was consequent upon the removal or suppression of disorder. But the social, cultural and economic aspects of the prevailing context that Rice's re-ordering ignored, was not cognizant of and certainly did not adequately recognize in his text, nonetheless remained and impacted the longer term fate of the experiments. As we hinted earlier in the chapter, this might be seen as the return of the repressed (de Certeau, 1986), the reassertion of that which was negated by the re-ordering (decontextualization) of Rice's text and the consequent reorganization of work. Rice's account of voluntary self-organization within small work groups in the weaving shed denies the role of monetary incentives (pace Roy, 1969) in the initial success of the experimental reorganization. Any admission of such motives would of course threaten to undermine the very ethos and rationale of STS and the general applicability that was proclaimed for it and thereby represents a source of disorder, an absence that haunts the received story of STS at Ahmedabad.

Our analysis also raises questions about the status of the claimed generalized character of STS theory. In particular, given that not only the actual processes of the experiments that informed the writing of Rice's text, but the text itself (through its representation of "the" problem and its solution) can be said to have reinforced power imbalances rather than removing hierarchies of work organization. In other words, supporting Vásquez et al. (2016), what our research shows is that a text, through its potential for opening up of meanings, might allow the voices of less powerful stakeholders to be recognized. This would be a positive or productive example of the disordering possibilities of a text when absent meanings are brought to the fore. However, additionally, we would argue that the outcome is likely dependent on the context of its application and therefore the meanings that are affirmed and enacted; or, alternatively, those that are dismissed, sidelined and otherwise suppressed. For example, in the case of Ahmedabad, even if the labor union had had an opportunity to read the text (Rice's diagrammatic analysis) or participate in the decision-making around reorganization and disagree and resist, the social and cultural conditions of the experimental site were such that there was no avenue for negotiation of meanings from the workers' or union's side as relevant stakeholders. The workers' social standing and class membership did not allow them access to knowledge about group restructuring and organization and they were therefore unable to voice their concerns—e.g., that the group system could not work because of caste discrimination—in the same register of managerial knowledge.

Grounded in the conviction that organization is born, bred and transformed through communication (Ashcraft et al., 2009; Cooren et al., 2011), we have thus argued that the nature of transformation through the application of socio-technical systems design could vary between worker emancipation or, alternatively, a strengthening of the power imbalance between workers and other powerful organizational stakeholders. The fluidity of outcomes can be explained through the claim that organizations exist in communication through the interpretive actions of their members (Taylor et al., 1996), which though inherently open-ended (Vásquez et al., 2016) are nonetheless subject to the power dynamics of the prevailing context. Using a theory of communication that views the latter as a process of dialectical translations between text and conversation, we have demonstrated through our empirical study that text-conversation translations shape the understanding of organization that emerges out of communication events. But these translations are shaped by contexts, postcolonial in our case. The interpretive, context-related nature of these translations holds the key to the type of social structuring and image of organization that emerges from communication.

Inspired by a need to study democratic/participative forms of organization and new ways of researching the topic, our endeavor has proved useful. In presenting the process of decontextualization and a subsequent recontextualization of a text we have been able to reveal certain (typical) tensions. Although seen through a postcolonial lens, these tensions underpin organizations in general. In our case, in the context of STS theory, perhaps the inclusion of worker voices into Rice's prescriptive solutions could re-fix meanings and take us back to a more participatory form of organization as engendered by Trist and Bamforth's original studies (1951). Thus, our research suggests a need for new theory development around socio-technical systems, but one which is substantively inclusive of those interests and voices all too easily ignored if not actively excluded by those in a better position to exercise power.

Notes

1. Following Prasad (2003), we use the term "postcolonial" (without the hyphen) to suggest a way of thinking about colonialism, its ways of operating and its consequences. Our focus is broadly on processes (in our case communication through organizational texts) that help perpetuate the dominance of the West vis-à-vis the former colonies. In an increasingly de-colonized world, this dominance has involved forms of economic exploitation legitimated in part through postcolonial sensibilities centered on the supposed superiority of Western powers, including their corporations and geo-political institutions. In contrast, the term "post-colonial" (i.e., with a hyphen) is used as a temporal expression referring to the "period" after colonial powers granted independence to their colonies, and all that comes thereafter (Prasad, 2003).
2. In Ahmedabad, STS theory was qualified and strengthened through the claim that in a climate of market competition, it could ensure organizational efficacy through small group work organization that could internalize external shocks and respond through "responsible autonomy" (Trist & Bamforth, 1951, p. 6). Improving on the coal mine studies, this claim was based on the premise that organizations are open systems (Bertanlanffy, 1950) interacting with the environment, and that all subsystems within the organization need to work in tandem with each other and with the environment for organizational efficacy (Rice, 1963).
3. In Figure 8.1, Rice represents a simplified version of the organization of one shift in the automatic loom shed. He admits that "[I]t was not possible to represent all lines of communication and theoretical authority" (Rice, 1958, p. 59).
4. Letter from Textile Labour Association (TLA) to the chairman: "Regarding matter of conducting the experiment of the Group System in the Ring Frame Department of the Calico Mills": dated 17-03-1956. It was then sent to Rice by Gautam Sarabhai "for info".

9 The Paradox of Digital Civic Participation

A Disorganization Approach

Amanda J. Porter and Michele H. Jackson

National and local governments in the United States increasingly adopt participatory programs to give citizens a voice in government decision-making and policy. Digital technologies have enabled governments to inform citizens, gain citizen feedback and support more direct and continuous interaction with citizens (Smith, 2013; Smith, Schlozman, Verba & Brady, 2009). Yet despite the promise of digital tools to transform traditional government decision-making, digital civic participation has also exacerbated many participatory problems. Government experts have increased their power through technologies that value expertise while devaluing citizens' knowledge (Byrne & Pickard, 2016; Leszczynski, 2014). Further, already active citizens are likely to become more engaged through digital tools, while citizens less likely to be traditionally engaged are even further marginalized (Davis, 2010; Smith, 2013). Paradoxically, increased connection through digital technologies proves to also widen the government–citizen divide.

Our aim in this chapter is to answer the question of why and how paradoxes of digital civic participation persist. To accomplish this, we first articulate a communicational lens of disorganization that builds on the "Communication as Constitutive of Organization", or CCO, approaches (Cooren, Kuhn, Cornelissen & Clark, 2011) focused on the indeterminacy of meaning (Kuhn, 2012) and the disordering properties of communication (Vásquez, Schoeneborn & Sergi, 2016). To examine persistent paradoxes more specifically, we draw on literature on multiplicity of objects and practices (Law, 2002; Law & Singleton, 2005) in order to conceptualize digital civic participation as *multiple*, that is, across interconnected communication episodes, meanings open and close in such a way as to interfere with one another and, in so doing, enact a paradoxical practice. Multiplicity usefully positions communication episodes as breeding grounds for contradictions and paradoxes.

We use our communicational approach to disorganization to analyze a digital civic participation project called Mesa Vision 2030. We collected and analyzed qualitative data, consisting of participant observations and in-depth interviews, across three communication episodes in an iterative fashion, guided by the combined analytic tools of situational analysis (Clarke, 2005) and iterative analysis (Tracy, 2013). Our findings detail a controversial "voting incident" in Mesa and show how this controversy emerged from enactments of digital civic participation across two different communication episodes: the planning practices of the Local Advisory Committee (LAC) and the design practices of the funding NGO, the Circle Foundation. We then analyze the multiplicity of the voting incident, showing how the opening and closing of meanings in the LAC and the Circle Foundation interfere with one another to produce paradoxical results (Law, 2002).

Our study makes conceptual and methodological contributions to a communication lens of disorganization. First, the concept of multiplicity, and the disordering dynamic of interference, offers a new analytic dimension for the empirical study of disorganization from a communication lens. We theorize that the push-pull between order and disorder operates in multiple distinct, yet overlapping, communication episodes simultaneously; how these come together shows a third dimension of disorganization: the push-pull for control over which configuration of meaning is in focus. Second, our use of situational analysis (Clarke, 2005) makes a methodological contribution to CCO research by providing tools that open empirical situations to differences and heterogeneities. Situational analysis also aids in making transparent methodological choices (Boivin, Brummans & Barker, 2017) by guiding the analyst in the iterative process of data collection and data analysis. Finally, our study has implications for the practice of digital civic participation. Our findings suggest that participants need to be equipped with robust coping mechanisms that encourage learning from failures (Ferraro, Etzion & Gehman, 2015). Accordingly, civic technology organizations should place greater emphasis on flexible designs of participatory tools that preserve the voices of diverse participants.

In the following section, we begin by reviewing literature on digital technologies in civic participation, and in particular on the paradoxes of digital civic participation. After this, we articulate our communicational lens of disorganization, and the concept of multiplicity, followed by a short description of our research site. We then detail our data collection and analysis methods, followed by a presentation of our main findings. We conclude the chapter with a discussion of contributions for both theory and practice.

The Paradox of Digital Technologies for Civic Participation

Civic participation, or a citizen's voluntary actions in decision-making and problem-solving efforts to improve a community through nonelectoral means, is integral to functioning democratic governments (Kim &

Ball-Rokeach, 2006; Putnam, 2000). Local government decisions that reflect the core values of the community are more likely to be widely accepted (Roper & Muller, 2002) and enhance accountability of government decisions by opening up deliberations to public scrutiny (Plein, Green & Williams, 1998).

However, governments in the US have struggled to engage citizens at the local level due to highly structured modes of bureaucratic organization. Public hearings, used as forums for citizen input, must be scheduled, and fixed at times and locations that limit the involvement of diverse citizen groups (Richards & Dalbey, 2006). Further, public hearings are primarily used by governments to inform citizens, rather than as opportunities for citizens to learn about issues, seek clarification or make thoughtful recommendations (Fischer, 2009; Innes & Booher, 2004). Richards and Dalbey (2006) found that forums limit the involvement of citizens to the final stages of planning and decision-making, dividing communities by foregrounding tense exchanges between supporters and opponents of local planning initiatives. Yet conditions that facilitate involvement depend on citizens' capacity to engage with structured and technical government systems. Vast differences in knowledge between government experts and ordinary citizens can leave citizens participating in these systems feeling their opinion has little actual influence (Gordon, Schirra & Hollander, 2011; Young, 2002).

Amidst the growing recognition that traditional systems of civic participation in local governments fall short, scholars and practitioners have turned to digital technologies that afford opportunities for citizens to voice their opinions. Through computer-supported voting, for example, greater numbers of citizens are able to express their opinions on community matters (Gordon et al., 2011), increasing the legitimacy of civic participation processes (Plein et al., 1998). Brinker, Gastil and Richards (2015) found sharing information online through videos produces knowledge gains for citizens on important civic issues. Further, residents' use of Internet technologies and mobile phones to share information and express opinions about community affairs enhances the civic utility of community storytelling networks (Nah & Yamamoto, 2017).

Digital technologies can also facilitate greater interaction among government planners and citizens. Incompatible expertise between government officials and citizens can be reduced through participatory technology such as geographic information systems (GIS), which provide visual maps of complex issues (Sieber, 2006). GIS computer simulations enable citizens to visualize development in existing community spaces, enabling greater shared understanding of geographic phenomena in relation to community needs (González, Gilmer, Foley, Sweeney & Fry, 2008; Hopfer & MacEachren, 2007). Participating in interactive forums online, citizens interact more with one another, increasing faith in the efficacy of group deliberation (Brinker et al., 2015). Digital technologies facilitate involvement that can lead to better understanding of fellow citizens' needs and desires (Richards & Dalbey, 2006).

Despite the promise of digital technologies in facilitating more informed and widespread civic participation, successful uses of these technologies can paradoxically create greater power imbalances. For example, rather than "leveling the playing field", Leszczynski (2014) found that GIS visualizations give experts in policy-making an upper hand by requiring knowledge of spatial and urban dynamics. Similarly, Jankowski (2009) found that experts in GIS exerted so much influence over the participatory process that the empowerment of participants and their trust in the process outcomes was reduced. Burrows and Ellison (2004) also found that online GIS makes available the informational resources by which strategically inclined social groups are able to find their place within complex and dynamic urban spaces, while leaving others to social exclusion and disengagement. GIS systems can both empower and further marginalize citizens at the same time (Byrne & Pickard, 2016).

Digital technologies themselves become barriers to civic participation by increasing the exclusion of certain groups of actors. Mervyn, Simon and Allen (2014) found that the shift to direct access to local government support and services through mobile information and communication technologies actually undermined traditionally socially excluded participants who lacked literacy and technology skills. Davis (2010) has shown that for citizens already engaged or interested, uses of the Internet make connections that are denser, wider and possibly more inclusive. However, at the same time, unengaged citizens face greater communicative exclusion and experience further disengagement. Paradoxically, increased connection through digital technologies can lead to even greater exclusion.

While many scholars have called attention to the paradoxical impacts of digital technologies on meaningful civic participation, few studies have unpacked how and why such paradoxes persist. One explanation, from a functional perspective on technology, is "misuse" of the tool by the users (Weyers, Burkolter, Kluge & Luther, 2010). However, this explanation falls short because digital technologies are flexible and can be interpreted and used in many different ways (Leonardi, 2011). Another explanation representing a more critical stance toward the role of technology argues that such tools merely give citizens the illusion of meaningful participation (Feenberg, 2002). However, this explanation often overlooks the complex networks of organizations and actors that play a role in realizing citizen participation projects (Ghose, 2005). Alternatively, we argue that rather than ignoring or suppressing paradox, a deeper understanding of the paradoxes of digital technologies in civic participation is needed. Our aim is to understand its persistence and by doing so, offer an explanation of the processes that generate such paradoxes. Understanding these processes is generative for explaining what is lived in organizational settings as misunderstandings or conflict.

Explaining the processes that give rise to paradox can be achieved through a theoretical perspective that foregrounds the precarious and disorderly nature of organizing practices.

A Communicational Approach to Disorganization

To unpack the paradoxes of digital civic participation, we turn to a disorganization ontology that offers a comprehensive portrait of complex organizational phenomenon by challenging widespread assumptions about the stability and determinacy of organizations. Organizational scholars advancing this ontology have conceptualized organizing as a process of appropriating order out of disorder (Chia, 1998; Cooper, 1986; Hassard, Keleman & Cox, 2008). This processual view positions order and disorder as two sides of the same coin, such that organization is always bound with its contrary state of disorganization (Hassard et al., 2008). Common views of organizations as sites of coherence, consistency and consensus give way to a much more dynamic understanding of organization; paradoxes of digital civic participation are not reduced to occasional misuse or ill intent, but rather are an enduring feature of organizational life (Putnam, 1986).

While the disorganization ontology serves an important foundation, in order to explain *how* paradoxes emerge in digital civic participation, we draw on further conceptual insights in the "Communication as Constitutive of Organization", or CCO, perspective. CCO approaches argue that organizations emerge, transform and sustain through interconnected communicative actions (Cooren et al., 2011; Taylor & Van Every, 2000). Communication is thus not the exchange of information between actors, but is defined as "the ongoing, dynamic, interactive process of manipulating symbols toward the creation, maintenance, destruction, and/or transformation of meanings which are axial—not peripheral—to organizational existence and organizing phenomena" (Ashcraft, Kuhn & Cooren, 2009, p. 22). Communication episodes, or sequences of interconnected communication events, form the performative building blocks of organizational reality (Blaschke, Schoeneborn & Seidl, 2012; Cooren et al., 2011). Yet, because language is inherently open-ended, the communication as constitutive of organization is necessarily characterized by a fundamental indeterminacy of meaning (Kuhn, 2012; Porter, 2013, 2014). As organizational actors make use of language and/or texts in communication episodes, meanings will inevitably multiply and exceed the authors' full control (Vásquez et al., 2016). Communication can thus be seen as the "engine" of the dialectic between order and disorder as actors engage in an ongoing process of closing (order) and opening (disorder) meaning (Vásquez et al., 2016). Digital civic participation can thus be understood as complex because the communicative episodes of this practice continually enact the opening and closing of meaning.

In order to explore persistent paradoxes we further conceptualize digital civic participation as *multiple* (Law, 2002, 2004; Law & Singleton, 2005; Mol, 2002). That is, across interconnected communication episodes, meanings open and close in such a way as to interfere with one another and, in so doing, enact a paradoxical practice. For example, Law and Singleton (2005) examined how alcoholic liver disease manifested as different diseases across different sectors of the healthcare system. "In the hospital, it is a lethal condition that implies abstinence. In the substance abuse center, it is a problem that implies regulation and control. In the GP's surgery, it is a reality that is better than hard drugs" (p. 346). They found that what "counted" as the disease in one sector, as manifested in patients, guidelines, forms and rules, was often completely absent in another. As a result, alcoholic liver disease enacted many different realities that by definition could not cohere. This interference between concurrent fixing or closing of meaning (order) and opening of meaning (disorder) across communication episodes produces the breeding grounds for contradictions and paradoxes.

These arguments allow us to give a conceptual answer to why paradoxes persist in digital civic participation. In what follows, we further explore these arguments to show, empirically, how persistent paradoxes constitute the practice of digital civic participation. We ask the following research questions: How is digital civic participation enacted as multiple across interconnected communication episodes? How does this multiplicity implicate the practice of digital civic participation in paradoxical ways? In the next section, we describe the setting of our research in detail.

Research Site

The focus of our study is a community partnership in a small city in a mid-western US state. Beginning in February of 2009, the City of Mesa[1] embarked on a two-year-long community engagement project to create a vision for the city. The project, called "Mesa Vision 2030", involved multiple collaborating actors. A group of planners working for the City of Mesa initiated the participatory engagement project by applying for a grant from a nongovernmental organization, the Circle Foundation, which supports "positive change" in communities through community outreach efforts. The project was steered by a local advisory committee (LAC) of 15 Mesa community members who met monthly to plan the activities of the project, in collaboration with Mesa city planners and Circle Foundation consultants. Additional consultants were also hired who facilitated discussions and integrated technology at community meetings.

Mesa community members participated in a variety of different events in order to co-create community values for the city's new vision. Major events included a series of neighborhood "block parties", community focus groups and community summits. On these occasions, community members and Mesa government planners were co-located and engaged in interactions with each other. The persistent use of keypad polling and geographic information systems to facilitate group interaction and decision-making made Mesa a particularly valuable case for studying digital civic participation. While these tools were designed to get input from large numbers of community members on different scenarios for land use and development, this design for participation led to a host of problems in practice, making Mesa Vision 2030 a fruitful site for gaining insight into the paradoxes of digital civic participation. In the next section, we describe the methods we used to collect and analyze our data.

Method

Our approach to data collection and data analysis proceeded in an iterative fashion over time. We gained access to the Mesa project right before the first LAC meeting and began data collection by conducting participant observations in the monthly LAC meetings. We observed a total of 14 LAC meetings, paying close attention to LAC members' planning of digital technologies in the project. There was also a "demonstration" of a geographic information system at an LAC meeting where we observed LAC members interacting with these tools. In our observations we were careful to remain open to the question of who or what was acting (Cooren et al., 2011). We took careful handwritten notes at each observation, which were later typed up into detailed fieldnotes (Patton, 1990). We also conducted 12 in-depth, open-ended interviews with LAC members (Patton, 1990). We asked LAC members to reflect on their purpose as a group and the role of digital participation in the project. This collection of LAC meetings and interviews, which took place prior to the actual use of the digital technology at community events, comprised the first communication episode in our data set.

But before proceeding with additional data collection, we performed an initial analysis of this data. We engaged in primary cycle, open coding (Tracy, 2013) to familiarize ourselves with the situated practices of the LAC, especially in relation to how digital civic participation was given meaning in this setting. We then used our coded data as a basis to start sketching situational maps (Clarke, 2005). Situational mapping[2] is an analytic tool that starts with the "situation" as the unit of analysis, which in our case was the planning practices of the LAC. Some questions we used to guide the creation of our initial situational map included: Who and what are made present/absent? What discursive constructions are circulating? What cultural symbols were evoked? What were the controversial issues? Answers were written down on paper. The goal is to thoroughly explore a situation by analyzing "all of the analytically pertinent human and nonhuman, material, and symbolic/discursive elements of a particular situation *as framed by those in it and by the analyst*"³ (Clarke, 2005, p. 87, emphasis in original).

Acknowledging the co-constructed nature of communication (Cooren et al., 2011), we started to perform a relational analysis of our map. Specifically, after writing all answers down on paper, we systematically analyzed how each answer (element) related to others on our map, using a mind mapping software to draw lines where there were relations between elements, followed by memoing on the nature of the relations we identified (Clarke, 2005).⁴ We noticed from this relational analysis a link between the LAC's planning of digital civic participation, the emerging construction of technology as a "threat" and the Circle Foundation, the NGO that had partially funded the project. Because our analytic aim was to make our object of study multiple, we concluded from this analysis that we should examine communication episodes of the Circle Foundation for further data collection and analysis.

We thus began data collection focused on tracing the emergence of digital civic participation in the communication of the Circle Foundation, which comprised the second communication episode in our data set. We began by collecting data from the Circle Foundation website and blog, in which we discovered this NGO's extensive involvement in the design and development of civic decision support technology. We then interviewed a Circle Foundation project consultant to learn why technology-enabled decision-making was designed, used and promoted by this NGO. We learned of a conference the Circle Foundation was hosting for other city planners so we attended online portions of this conference, as well as watched a series of videos that were recorded from sessions at this conference. We then interviewed two technology consultants who were regularly hired by the Circle Foundation to facilitate the use of digital technologies for participation, asking them to describe why these tools were used and how this changed the participatory process over the years.

As before, we engaged in primary cycle open coding of this data (Tracy, 2013) in order to familiarize ourselves with the situated practices of the Circle Foundation and their professional network. We used the coded data to begin sketching another situational map (Clarke, 2005), this time focused on the technology development practices of the Circle Foundation. We followed the same procedure of relational analysis as described above. We noticed from this mapping a strong link between the technology designers in this network, technology as a change agent and visions for more effective community decision-making. We then became very curious to know how such community decision-making was constructed not only in design, but in the decision-making practices of citizens. However, we noticed that we had very little in our data set so far about citizens' experiences with technology, an absent presence we wanted to further materialize. We thus decided to follow more closely the Mesa citizens' use of this decision technology.

We then focused on the two large "community summit" events that took place at the end of the Mesa project as the final communication episode comprising our data collection. The purpose of the summits was to decide on the core values that Mesa community members had generated over the last several months using digital voting. We conducted participant observations at these final summit events observing how these technologies were physically used, how community members reacted to using technology for decisions and spatially how the technology structured community members' interactions with each other. We once again took detailed fieldnotes of our observations (Patton, 1990). During the summit we noticed a moment of disruption when Mesa citizens were using the digital voting, which we later refer to in our analysis as the "voting incident". Directly following the summits, we conducted ten in-depth interviews with community members and city planners participating in the summits where we asked participants to critically reflect on this disruption in light of the overall project. As in previous rounds, we openly coded the data from this communication episode (Tracy, 2013) and created more situational maps (Clarke, 2005), where we began to notice the disruption was developing into a controversy. We began to realize the voting incident illuminated relations between many of the actants from our other communication episodes—the LAC and city planners, the Circle Foundation consultants, the citizens, the technology consultants and the technology; the controversy was a communication episode that served as a nexus of the others, a mechanism for surfacing complexity.

We decided to zoom in to "open" the controversy by analyzing it more systematically in relation to the other two communication episodes that comprised our data set. In order to proceed with this analysis, we engaged in secondary coding of the data using a combined inductive and deductive process that involved arranging primary open codes into secondary categories of theoretical significance (Tracy, 2013). We used deductive categories offered for analysis by Clarke (2005).[5] For example, open codes like "confused participant" and "silent city planner" were grouped under Clarke's (2005) category "individual human actors". We then compared all of the codes for each category across the maps of the three communication episodes with the aim to specify difference(s) and variation(s) of all kinds between these episodes.

Comparing the situational maps showed us visually how important elements in one communication episode were present or absent in the others. For example, we noticed that an important actor that emerged in relation to Mesa citizens' experience of using voting technology at the summit was the "confused participant". We noticed this actor was largely absent in the other two communication episodes we analyzed; citizens were instead constructed in relation to digital civic participation as "decisive" and "fun". Multiple meanings across communication episodes were compared in order to create a plausible explanation of the controversial voting incident that occurred at the community summit. In the following section, we detail the findings from our analysis.

Findings

In this section, we first give an in-depth account of the controversial incident that occurred at the Mesa community summit, what we call "the voting incident". Our analysis then proceeds to unpack the voting incident by detailing how it was constituted by two other communication episodes: the planning practices of the LAC and the design practices of the Circle Foundation. We then analyze the multiplicity of the voting incident, specifically showing how paradoxical results of digital voting occurred through interference of meanings across these three communication episodes.

The Voting Incident

One of the most notable moments in the Mesa Vision 2030 process was the final community summit meeting. As the largest single meeting of the process, it was important not only for its size, but also for its significance. Several months of planning by the LAC went into the summit, as it represented the culmination of a year of participatory efforts in Mesa. Over 100 Mesa community participants convened this day to cast digital votes on the most important community values for creating Mesa Vision 2030.

When community members first arrived at the summit, they were immediately greeted by technology throughout the large room. The voluminous space was marked off by five large flat screen televisions positioned at eye level height, in front of which long tables were placed where Mesa citizens sat and viewed 3D visualizations of the city on screens. Centrally positioned in the center of the room was the technology consultant's "central command station", a long table covered in laptops, wires and black boxes that contained the set up for the keypads. Facing the entire set up on the far end of the room was a large white projector screen, where the results of citizens' digital votes would be centrally displayed to the entire room (Fieldnotes, Community Summit).

As Mesa citizens began to take their seats at the tables, they engaged in several minutes of pleasant conversations with their neighbors. Shortly thereafter, the mayor of Mesa made an introductory speech that emphasized the importance of this day for the future of the city. A Mesa city planner joined the speech, explaining the "journey" of the Mesa Vision 2030 process thus far and introducing the activities for today's meeting. Participants were told that they needed to make "critical decisions" about the values that should guide the Mesa government, while also emphasizing that digital voting should be a "fun" experience for everyone.

After introductory speeches, every participant was given a keypad "clicker" for voting. Participants reacted to the clickers with intrigue and curiosity. Each clicker was attached to a long ribbon, so some participants even accessorized by enthusiastically wearing their clickers around their necks. Participants were then directed by technology consultants to use the clickers in several different voting exercises. Voting began with stock questions prepared by the consultants, such as asking the ages and gender of participants, explaining that this was a "warm up" so everyone could get accustomed to using the keypad devices. Each time voting on a question finished, the collective results would immediately display on the large projector screen in the front of the space. We noticed that the loud room became noticeably quiet when results appeared on the screen. Participants were genuinely intrigued to know what their neighbors voted and were noticeably having "fun" so far.

After the practice rounds, voting for the top Mesa community values began. The 11 values that had been distilled from months of community focus groups and block parties were displayed on the TV screens and the large screen in the front of the room. Participants were asked to rank the values in order of their importance, going through each value one-by-one. Immediately after the first value was displayed for a vote, participants seated together at the tables began deliberating. At our table, several participants were giving opinions for their favorite values, relating their choices to planning scenarios displayed on the 3D visualizations. Yet still, a majority of participants expressed being largely unsure about what value should be prioritized.

Despite the obvious discussions still taking place at all tables, after only a minute or so the screen was switched to initiate voting. Many people at our table had not even had the chance to score the first value before the second one appeared for scoring on the screen. It became clear after several rounds that participants would need to pick up the pace significantly if they were going to keep up. We overheard a participant at our table ask another participant next to him, "So what do you think of this whole process?" The other man replied, "I think it is kind of confusing" (Fieldnotes, Community Summit). Several people also noticed that they could not vote for the values they wanted to choose. A participant using a keypad, Dana, recalled:

> The numbering system was off. So the keypads went zero to ten but the values were numbered one to eleven, very confusing. I think a lot of the results I would say were even skewed because there was not that match up.
>
> (Interview)

Though this mistake was brought to the attention of the city planners, they did not stop the technology consultants, who quickly displayed the results on the screen. A participant reflected on the digital vote:

RESEARCHER: What did you think about the keypads stuff?
DARLENE: It was a disaster.
RESEARCHER: Yeah. Do you think that people understood what they were doing?
DARLENE: Not at all. The second summit, no. It was very convoluted. And there was a blind guy in the audience for the second summit. And so he couldn't see the numbers so they had to go through and read them but then the numbering system was off. So, I think it would have been great if it worked differently. I would have liked to see what 80 people in the room thought.

(Interview)

Perhaps the most surprising result of the voting incident was how Mesa city planners chose to promote the results as valid. After the final Vision 2030 report was issued, we asked Mesa city planners and participants to reflect on the process and the final outcome. Most people we spoke to agreed that the digital voting at the summit was a total failure, yet they still adamantly chose to support the results of the vote. A Mesa city planner reflected:

My biggest regret is all of the technology crap at the summits. Even if it had worked I'm not so sure I would have loved it. I have a lot of personal credibility with council and the community. I lost some [credibility] in those summits. In spite of everything, the results that came out of it were very big and I think right on. Right on exactly. So I don't know what that says (laughs). Maybe it says that you can screw up the process quite a bit if you have good information and committed people, you can still get good results.

(Steve, Interview)

The top values that came from this "skewed" vote were featured as the guiding principles of the final Mesa Vision 2030 report.

We walked away from the community summits with ambivalent feelings about the value of "participatory" technologies, which seemed to have almost the opposite effect intended: While digital civic participation enabled community input, it reduced the quality of that input by disregarding the actual choices of the participants. How was it that such a significant error occurred? Why was nothing done to fix the error? Or, perhaps even more importantly, why were Mesa city planners "happy" with results that clearly did not fully reflect the community choice?

The Enactment of the Voting Incident Across Communication Episodes

If we examine how communication episodes in other spaces and times constituted digital voting in that controversial incident, we immediately deepen our understanding of the voting incident. We focus first on the planning of digital voting in the LAC meetings, and secondly on the design of digital voting by the Circle Foundation.

The LAC: Taming a Technological Threat

The voting incident emerged in part through the monthly planning practices of the Mesa Local Advisory Committee (LAC). The LAC was a working group comprised primarily of Mesa city planners and community members who planned the meetings that Mesa used to create and decide upon their community values. Before the actual use of the digital voting in the community summits, these technologies were greatly anticipated and deliberated in the LAC's monthly meetings.

In the beginning of the project, LAC members admitted to feeling somewhat unsure about a long process of citizen engagement focused on something as "fuzzy" as values. After several meetings and block parties, they had already generated hundreds of "value statements", and with so much input it was hard to envision this process ending with a concise community vision. The LAC members frequently engaged in talk to rationalize their rather unique and nontraditional approach of values based decision-making.

Yet over time, we began to notice a shift in the discussion; instead of worrying about the eventual outcomes, we saw that most LAC members started believing in the value of the participatory process itself:

> I know that this [project] is very new, and it might be ambivalent in terms of it being fuzzier or soft. But I want to say that I think it's the most exciting, meaningful thing you could possibly do. So I would like to see us going forward not with any kind of diffidence about this approach, but being very strong and behind it. I personally am and I think the rest of the group is too.
>
> (LAC Meeting Transcript, LAC Member)

We noticed that eventually "the project" began to gain a life of its own in the LAC. "We're on the right path. There is a process taking shape" (LAC Meeting Transcript, LAC member). LAC members were impressed by the dialogue taking place between neighbors at the "block parties" and were keen in monthly meetings to discuss the success of past project meetings and events and plan new ones in upcoming phases of the project.

Given the shift toward valuing the process they had created, many LAC members were initially unsure about digital voting at the summits. In the exchange below, we see this initial ambivalence expressed:

SPEAKER 1: It's [technology] not any magic bullet. But hey, it's interesting. It's a tool I think in the toolbox.

SPEAKER 5: Yeah, it's one tool.

SPEAKER 1: It's one of many, but there is no silver bullet. I'm really so tired that everyone wants to use all of these tools.

SPEAKER 5: When you're a hammer, everything's a nail.

(LAC Meeting Transcript)

After a demonstration by a technology consultant to the LAC, a discussion ensued about possible problems that might arise if they decided to use the digital voting during the summits, as if foreshadowing the voting incident. Keypads that required a forced ranking of values were discussed as a potentially disruptive threat to the process of engagement.

It was expressed that people may feel dissonance in moving from group discussion to keypad polling. It was decided it might be better to end the summit on the feeling of accomplishment in your group instead of ranked voting with keypads.

(Fieldnotes, LAC Meeting)

The digital voting was perceived as imposing too much order, potentially closing down important meanings that were created together with fellow citizens. However, Mesa planners continued to insist they had to use digital voting. A planner explained:

Part of it [using technology] is because the Circle Foundation—part of our obligation to them was to experiment. And to try "stuff." And they are very much into "stuff." And our obligation for the money was actually to look for new ways to engage and to do things.

(Sandler, Mesa Planner, Interview)

Whether the LAC liked it or not, they had an obligation to use the technologies provided by the funding NGO, the Circle Foundation. "Nelda [Mesa City Planner] mentioned that even if they did not use the GIS scenario technology, they needed to use the keypad polling 'for something'" (Fieldnotes, LAC Meeting).

The tension between the potential threat of digital voting to their engagement process and its inevitable presence was something that the LAC spent months diffusing leading up to the final community summit. Specifically, the LAC shifted from discussing the potential threats of digital voting to sharing more ideas about how these tools could possibly be "fun" for community members. LAC members downplayed digital voting as a decision-making tool and instead talked about it as an "interesting", "good hook" to get community members intrigued to come to the summit. In flyers the LAC used to announce the summit, participants are promised "Innovative hands-on tool . . . keypad polling . . . fun and results-oriented activity". A city planner elaborates, "Our traditional processes are boring and not particularly fun. I think people think that's [digital voting] fun. And they're more likely to participate you know, using that" (Tanya, Interview). Since fun was almost never associated with traditional forms of civic participation, the LAC began promoting digital voting as a symbol of their non-traditional approach to planning. The LAC's talk eventually resolved tensions by constructing digital voting as a benign and entertaining tool. Noticeably absent in the language of the LAC is the image of the decisive citizen that we will show in the next section to be so central to the Circle Foundation.

The Circle Foundation: Packaging Technological Solutions

While the LAC played a central role in planning the final summit, the emergence of digital voting at Mesa was tied to the design practices of the funding NGO, the Circle Foundation. In our investigation of the Circle Foundation we found that Mesa Vision 2030 was just one of several dozen "project towns" that adopted the technologies and philosophy of the Circle Foundation. We learned that the Circle Foundation, other professional planners and technology consultants formed a professional network of technology enthusiasts that promoted digital civic participation in projects across the country.

At the heart of this network was the Circle Foundation. The organization was built around early collaborative decision-making technologies. The idea that technology could "level the playing field" between government experts and community members was particularly important to creating the Foundation's early aims and goals. The Circle Foundation website described how decision support technologies were central to their "empowered" approach to community decision-making:

> Under the leadership of Don F., the Foundation's first President, the Foundation began to explore the development of tools and resources to help citizens make better, more informed land use decisions. Over the ensuing eight years, the Foundation invested in the development of Community Biz, its flagship GIS-based 3D visualization and decision-support tool. In communities across the U.S., Community Biz came to represent the Foundation's vision for how innovative

technology could help elevate and inform the planning process while assisting communities in imagining new possibilities for the future.

(Circle Foundation Website)

Civic participation was constructed by the Circle Foundation around the possibilities that decision support technologies afforded.

The central role of decision technologies within the Foundation created a need for specific and more targeted technological expertise. Over a period of many years, the Foundation ramped up its technological efforts into a new partnership with a group of technology consultants. These technology consultants expanded their business over time, working with civic engagement projects across the country. Technology consultants focused on technologies that could be "packaged" as effective solutions to overcome common planning problems. A technology consultant explains how their technology-enabled participatory process was designed to give communities "a recipe for how to harness future growth to arrive at a chosen future" (Sander, Interview). Consultants described how they designed citizen interactions around digital voting to save time and make decision-making more efficient:

> So the keypads allow you to give a structure to this. I mean, the guy that would normally stand up in the back of the room and go into some speech about how wetlands are worthless sees that eighty-five percent of the people in this room think there's value in deferring development from wetlands and he keeps his damn mouth shut. So it really does, it really does help be efficient with your meetings. Literally keypad polling allows you to do like, two meetings at once. I mean you can summarize the results of the first keypad polling questions and then frame some questions around it and ask what you would have normally had to come back a month later to ask. So it becomes much more efficient using the technology. . . . Enabling decisiveness—that's what a lot of this technology does to this process. People can make firm choices.
>
> (Sander, Interview)

Another technology consultant elaborated along similar lines:

> I think as history has progressed, people got more and more sophisticated, using more specialized tools and now comes along the opportunity to use decision support technology. The computer program allows you to come up with more sophisticated plans. They [plans] still aren't perfect but you understand more than you did before and make more informed decisions . . . it's all about having a vivid picture for the future.
>
> (David, Interview)

For technology consultants, decision support technologies and civic participation were joined into a single package for creating future-oriented solutions to planning problems. Noticeably absent in the decisive language of the technology consultants is the dialogue or deliberation between citizens that was so central to the LAC.

The solutions that technologies like digital voting represented were also popular within a network of community planners across the country. Conferences took place in which city planners could engage in trainings and information sharing with the Circle Foundation, technology consultants and other technology enthusiasts. The broader professional movement described itself as "an innovation-action network for people imagining, driving, and creating community change" (Community website). In a keynote speech at the conference, the Circle Foundation's President opened with talk about the "power" of visualization technology, followed by an announcement of a new technology exchange designed to become a central repository for sharing technologies across the practitioner network. The tools and techniques of community planning were featured at the conference, complete with decision-making technology "sandboxes" where conference attendees could play with the visualization tools. City planners supported by this professional network took pride in constructing themselves as different from the "traditional" city planners. Rather than operating from behind closed doors, these city planners had an ethic of experimentation with technology, and much like the technology consultants, this professional network of planners shared a vision for an ideal future. Through innovative technologies, communities could thrive and realize their full potential.

The Voting Incident: An Interference of Meanings

If we return to the voting incident, we can see the interference of meanings occurring between the LAC and the Circle Foundation. The opening and closing of meaning within the LAC and the Circle Foundation enacted what "counts" as an engaged citizen and planner, relations configured in practice by a participatory technology. Certainly, the "misalignment" of the numbering of the Mesa values (1–11) with the numbers on the actual voting keypads (0–10) was a material manifestation of this interference. However, if we attend to the differences in the meanings of digital civic participation, we reveal the more extensive role played by the interference of meaning.

For the LAC, voting technology in the Mesa participatory process was a threat. Sustained engagement required citizens to listen to one another and explore the meanings of held values. The voting technology, in contrast, was an ordering device that threatened premature closure of this open exploration. Reducing the technology to simply a "fun tool", the LAC neutralized the technology and protected against the closure of meaning that such ordering devices might impose. Closing the meaning of technology itself was thus a crucial move for continued exploration and openness of meaning in the engagement process.

For the Circle Foundation, the voting technology was also an ordering device but, unlike the LAC, Circle Foundation planners saw the closure of meaning as an important feature of a participatory process because it produced tangible outcomes. Voting technology quickly gathered and provided feedback on the collective decisions of the citizens, ordering an otherwise "unruly" participatory process. The Circle Foundation, thus, heralded the technology as empowering a truly "decisive" participatory citizen. Unlike the LAC, which reduced the meaning of the technology, the Circle Foundation sought to give it a deep and rich meaning. In so doing, it could claim to provide an open and inclusive process while legitimizing the closure of meaning of the engagement process itself.

Comparing the opening and closing of meaning across these two communication episodes reveals an interference of meaning: The LAC's enactment of digital civic participation reduces the meaning of the voting technology in order to open the participatory process to a greater variety of meanings from the "engaged" citizen, while the Circle Foundation enriches the meaning of voting technology in order to close the participatory process to unruly meanings and empower the "decisive" citizen. Even so this interference does not fully explain the paradoxical nature of the voting incident in Mesa. For that, we need to add a third element: the experience of the citizens themselves in negotiating this interference during the community summit. Mesa citizens experienced significant difficulty in using the technology, beyond what could be attributed to its novelty. It was this additional task, this unstated but critical task of negotiating the interference of meaning, that Mesa citizens simply could not complete successfully. Instead, citizens were largely confused and unable to act coherently. This new persona—the "confused" citizen—was neither the "engaged citizen" of the LAC nor the "decisive citizen" of the Circle Foundation. As a result, simultaneously bound by their constricted meanings of the technology, neither could alleviate, or even acknowledge, Mesa citizens' frustrations. Even in the months following the incident, there was recognition of the interference of these meanings and no serious acknowledgement of the "skewed" results. To do so could potentially expose the entire participatory process at Mesa to unwanted meanings: That the LAC's otherwise genuinely engaging participatory process was subverted when digital voting limited the choices of Mesa residents, or that the Circle Foundation's technological solution could be, in some way, fundamentally flawed. The lack of an appropriate acknowledgement was, we suggest, itself a move to close meaning of the interference itself. The layers of meaning would not be resolved, and digital civic participation—though paradoxical—could persist.

Discussion

The aim of this study was to explain how and why paradoxes of digital civic participation persist. We employed a communicational approach to disorganization in order to analyze the case of digital voting in Mesa. We analyzed a controversial incident, in which citizens' participation through digital voting, paradoxically, resulted in little citizen influence in actual decision-making. Our analysis shows how this incident emerged in the interference of meanings of digital civic participation across interconnected communication episodes. The LAC's enactment of digital civic participation reduced the meaning of the voting technology in order to open the participatory process, while the Circle Foundation deepened the meaning of voting technology in order to close the participatory process. Though Mesa citizens experienced this interference as a confused and unreliable voting process, the LAC and the Circle Foundation supported the voting results, enacting closure on the meaning of the interference itself. In this section of the chapter, we discuss the conceptual and methodological contributions of our analysis for a communicational lens of disorganization as well as implications for the practice of digital civic participation.

Conceptual Contributions to a Communicational Lens of Disorganization

Our study makes an important contribution to frameworks for the empirical study of disorganization using a communication lens. First, our in-depth analysis answers recent calls within CCO research (Cooren et al., 2011; Kuhn, 2012; Porter, Kuhn, & Nerlich, 2017; Vásquez et al., 2016) and organization studies more broadly (Chia, 1998; Clegg, Kornberger, & Rhodes, 2005; Hassard et al., 2008) for research that takes seriously the disorderly character of organization in the "post-bureaucratic" era. We advance this largely conceptual body of research by providing a rigorous in-depth empirical account of why paradoxes of digital civic participation persist.

Second, the concept of multiplicity—the interference of meaning across interconnected communication episodes—offers a new analytic dimension for the empirical study of disorganization. Importantly, disorganization is triggered not only when the indeterminacy of meaning is beyond the author's control to fix (Vásquez et al., 2016); rather, our argument is that certain practices—such as digital civic participation—that are enacted in interconnected communicative episodes across space and time *are inherently multiple* by virtue of the permanent de/re/contextualization of meaning (Vásquez et al., 2016), and thus inhabited by differences (Law & Singleton, 2005). In this view, disorganization is not two-dimensional, swinging like a pendulum between order and disorder, but rather operates at multiple layers simultaneously. In Mesa we see in three episodes—real-time digital civic participation, its planning and its design—the dialectic between order and disorder, each creating a distinct layer of meaning. As meanings open and close within each episode, they in turn interfere with the opening and closing of meanings in the other episodes. How these came together to enact the voting incident shows an important third dimension of disorganization: the push-pull for control over which layer of meaning is in focus. Each layer of meaning masks others such that, regardless of the particular substance of communication, only certain perspectives and values are allowed in view. These layers, then, are communicative resources for negotiation and control. As in Mesa, actors may control the *layer* to close meaning and, therefore, circumvent the demand of understanding differences and bypass significant effort required to come to shared meaning.

Methodological Contributions to a Communicational Lens of Disorganization

Our study also answers calls for advancements of CCO related methodologies. While CCO scholarship has no privileged method, but rather is open to a plurality of methodological approaches (Cooren et al., 2011), the field has been criticized for a lack of methodological transparency (Boivin et al., 2017) and a focus on primarily local communication events (Blaschke et al., 2012). Further, relatively little attention has been given to methods that embody the ontological and epistemological assumptions of a communicational approach to disorganization. We discuss how our use of situational analysis in this study addresses these methodological criticisms and can serve as fruitful tools for analysts to empirically study disorganization from a communication lens.

First, situational analysis is a useful method to study disorganization because it is designed to "open up" empirical situations to differences and heterogeneities (Clarke, 2005). By offering a very broad starting point, taking "the situation" as the unit of analysis, the analyst is initially encouraged to be inclusive of a plurality of communication episodes related to the arena of inquiry. Such inclusivity encourages the analyst to explore the dialectic between order and disorder as a pattern across space and time, linking the here and now of a specific communication episode to the there and then of future, past and simultaneous episodes (Vásquez & Cooren, 2013). Additionally, the variation in the analytic categories of situational maps usefully positions the analyst to interrogate the taken-for-granted in communication episodes. For example, Clarke (2005) offers these questions to provoke the analyst in making a situational map: "What seems present but unarticulated?" and "How might we pursue these sites of silence and ask about the gorillas without putting words in the mouths of our participants?" (p. 85). The result of this analysis is an explicit inquiry into what is made silent and absent in communication practices. Situational analysis is thus a useful tool for making complexity of communication episodes to heighten and refine the analyst's sensitivity to difference and ability to tolerate ambiguity (Hassard et al., 2008).

However, a very inclusive approach means the analyst has an ever-greater burden to be transparent about *when, where and how* to enter the data. Situational analysis, and relational analysis in particular, aids the analyst in making transparent choices by facilitating an iterative process of data collection and data analysis. Because situational maps are tools for thinking rather than final analytic products, mapping and relational analysis begins very early in the process of data collection as an analytic exercise in order to notice tensions, partialities or dominant relations that deserve additional inquiry (Clarke, 2005). For example, early on in our data collection, after relational analysis of the LAC situational map, we noticed a link between the LAC planning practices, the enactment of technology as a threat and the design practices of the Circle Foundation, which helped us in making the choice to begin collecting data specifically on the communication practices of the Circle Foundation. Further, relational analysis is also useful to aid the analyst in making transparent decisions about what to leave out of the analysis. For example, by choosing to follow our object of analysis as it was enacted by the Circle Foundation, we also were making a choice *not* to further explore other potential connections that surfaced in our mapping. Being aware of what we choose not to analyze is important given that the aim of a disorganization analysis is not to derive representative themes from the "whole cloth" of data. Our methods do not simply describe reality, but participate in the enactment of reality (Law, 2004).

Implications for the Practice of Digital Civic Participation

Finally, our study also makes important contributions to the practice of digital civic participation. We offer a strikingly realistic portrayal of the challenges of participatory organizing that serves as a useful alternative to other dominant approaches in practice that tend to tilt toward emphasizing either the "promise" or the "problem" of digital forms of civic participation. Perspectives that focus on the promise of technology often assume technology is a "silver-bullet" to solve participatory problems, a tool of organization (Metamorphosis, 2018; Smith et al., 2009). Perspectives that focus on the problem of technology often assume technology degrades the "gold standard" of face-to-face communication, a tool of disorganization (Smith et al., 2009). Our analysis suggests that both perspectives overlook critical complexities and differences in the participatory setting, and thus technology is better considered a tool for both order and disorder. Though our analysis of Mesa reveals many limitations of digital technology in this setting, a disorganization approach does not imply a fatalistic vision that civic participation through technology is bound to failure. Quite the contrary, we discuss insights from our disorganization perspective of how citizens, government planners and technology organizations can coordinate their efforts in light of inevitable tensions, contradictions and paradoxes.

First, our disorganization approach suggests that participants in digital civic participation develop robust coping mechanisms that encourage greater tolerance and appreciation for the "disorderly" nature of civic participation. Our analysis of Mesa demonstrates how voting technology was employed as an ordering device to force citizens to make decisions without room for discussion and dialogue. While community members in the LAC anticipated this problem, they coped with this threat by communicatively enacting a "fun" and "entertaining" role for the technology. This reactive coping mechanism sought to minimize differences and was swift to restore order (temporarily) while overlooking other important complexities of the setting. Minimizing differences in order to achieve greater alignment between community and governments often ends up with citizens being forced to adopt bureaucratic approaches of the government, overlooking what community members need and how they are already engaged (Eversole, 2011).

Alternatively, our disorganization approach suggests that participants in digital civic participation would benefit from robust communicative coping mechanisms that encourage participants to learn from moments of tension. Such coping mechanisms would, for example, encourage use of technologies that make the diverse practices of both government and community members more visible to one another. Additionally, experimentation with multiple types of participation simultaneously, where participants expect failure and design the participatory process accordingly, could help participants with very diverse interests learn to coordinate without consensus (Ferraro et al., 2015). Our call for more robust coping mechanisms echo recent calls in civic participation to position learning as a focal mechanism for engagement (Gordon & Baldwin-Philippi, 2014). However, future research from a disorganization perspective is needed to better understand exactly what types of coping mechanisms might stimulate learning from tensions, contradictions and paradoxes in digital civic participation.

Second, our analysis suggests that civic technology organizations should develop participatory tools with flexible designs that meet the very diverse needs of the participants. Civic technology organizations are part of the rapidly professionalizing "consultative layer" that serve as a bridge between governments and citizens through the provision of new media technologies (Brabham & Guth, 2017; Ghose, 2005). Because these bridge organizations provide the communicative infrastructure that connects the many diverse actors in this setting, these organizations are a critical point of attention for improving the practice of civic participation. An important implication of our study is that civic technology organizations, such as the Circle Foundation, do not merely serve to facilitate more efficient transactions between governments and citizens, but play a fundamental role in shaping the communicative practices of both governments and citizens. Previous research has shown that the intent of designers of civic technology aligns with democratic ideals "to facilitate progress, to enrich democracy through citizen engagement, and to adapt to client needs in an ongoing way" (Brabham & Guth, 2017, p. 462). Yet our study suggests that even when all parties have good intent, the results can still be quite disappointing. We showed that participatory technology was tied to different practices and thus embodied a diversity of meanings rather than a single normative ideal. Accordingly, rather than designing civic technologies around democratic ideals, technologies of civic participation should be designed and configured to support more fluid movement between different modes of participation: engagement that includes dialogue, fun experiences with fellow citizens and making hard decisions about the future. Shared innovation, or the act of improving the technological design by merging the intention of the designers with feedback from diverse user groups (Brabham & Guth, 2017), seems a reasonable starting point. However, future research from a communicational lens of disorganization is needed to investigate how shared design of participatory technologies can be accomplished when the guiding assumption is not consensus but rather inclusion of differences.

Notes

1. Locations and names of participants are pseudonyms.
2. Situational mapping was conceived by Clarke (2005) as a way to bring grounded theory around the postmodern turn.
3. Situational maps are not meant to be representations of a social reality, rather, they are always partial. Recognizing this actually attunes the analyst to presence/absence, an important shift towards seeing the world in disorderly terms.
4. In relational analysis, the analyst is looking for both where there are connections and where there are not, and how strong or weak are those connections. Memoing these relations can help the analyst to develop theoretical sampling strategies to collect further data and then return to particular relations that were missing, unclear or were particularly strong but taken for granted.
5. Categories include individual human elements/actors, collective human elements/actors, discursive constructions of individual and/or collective human actors, political economic elements, temporal elements, major issues/debates, nonhuman elements/actants, implicated/silent actors/actants, discursive construction of nonhuman actants, sociocultural/symbolic elements, spatial elements and related discourses (historical, narrative and/or visual). You do not need all of these categories in your analysis and can add new ones as fits your situation of concern. The point is to use these categories to examine your situation more thoroughly (Clarke, 2005).

10 Organizing from Disorder: Internet Memes as Subversive Style

Peter Winkler and Jens Seiffert-Brockmann

The insight that contemporary forms of organizing are increasingly dynamic and fluid has turned into a common place in recent organizational scholarship (e.g., Schreyoegg & Sydow, 2010; Tsoukas & Chia, 2002). In line with this insight, scholarly approaches that comprehend organizing as a process that is equally constituted by orderly and disorderly properties have gained considerable attention in recent years. Thirty years ago, in the foundational works of Robert Cooper (e.g., 1986, 1989, 1992) on that topic, scholarly engagement with the disorderly properties of organizing still represented a peripheral and overall critical position that challenged a predominant modernist and functionalist understanding of organizing. Today, this peripheral and critical stance has abated, and gave rise to a growing number of analytically oriented research approaches comprehending organizing as a continuous interplay of order and disorder. This is most prominent in process oriented approaches, such as the concept of organizing as communication (e.g., Brummans, Cooren, Robichaud & Taylor, 2014), organization as becoming (e.g., Tsoukas & Chia, 2002) and organization as practice (e.g., Schatzki, 2005, 2008), which analyze processes of organizing as an ongoing interplay of stabilizing and irritating interpretative, relational or practical order, respectively.

Yet, despite this growing analytic awareness for the circularity of order and disorder in contemporary forms of organizing, one particular aspect has gained only little consideration so far. Disorder is not only an element that challenges and thereby transforms organizational order. Disorder can also be a particular form of organizing *in itself*. The aim of this chapter, hence, is to introduce a unique form of social organizing from disorder to enrich the current debate. Borrowing the label from the general sociology of Harrison White (2008), we christen such a form of organizing from disorder as *style*. The emergence and evolution of a style, and thus organizing from disorder, is understood as a communicative form of organizing that reproduces from irritation of established meaning, relational expectations and sociomaterial affordances.

Styles are ubiquitous empirical phenomena that can, for example, be observed in expressions of jokes and humor (Jarzabkowski & Lê, 2017), cynical forms of breaking role expectations (Suominen & Mantere, 2010), workplace resistance (Mumby, 2005) or brand appropriation (Kornberger, 2015) in the organizational domain. Yet, very often, styles, particularly in the context of formal organization, remain on an ephemeral and clandestine level and vanish soon after they emerge. Thus, to empirically trace the evolution of a style, and to better comprehend its underlying logic of organizing from disorder, we draw on Internet memes as an empirical example.

Internet memes have attracted considerable attention in recent scholarship, particularly in media and political studies (Freelon & Karpf, 2015; Hristova, 2014; Milner, 2016; Miltner, 2014; Shifman, 2013). They are defined as "digital objects that riff on a given visual, textual or auditory form and are then appropriated, re-coded, and slotted back into the Internet infrastructures they came from" (Nooney & Portwood-Stacer, 2014, p. 249). By reassembling professional artifacts initially designed for publicity, branding or entertainment purposes, and by outwitting affordances and algorithms of the social web (Katz & Shifman, 2017; Shifman, 2013), Internet memes are discussed as a novel form of public expression to subtly subvert mass media influence, voice public dissent and activate political movements (e.g., Freelon & Karpf, 2015; Milner, 2016; Mina, 2014). Yet, due to the merits of digital archiving and search, Internet memes also give us the chance to trace the evolution of a style in the making empirically, by reconstructing its logic of reproduction and diffusion from continuous irritation of established meanings, relational expectations and web affordances.

As an empirical example, we choose two highly popular memes, the *Trump's First Order of Business* meme and the *Obama Hope* meme (knowyourmeme, 2017). The former emerged immediately after Donald Trump signed his first executive order on the day of his inauguration on January 20, 2017. The latter evolved out of the artwork of Shepard Fairey, who in early 2008 created a series of three posters with the captions of *hope, progress* and *change*. The posters were later used by the Obama campaign, at which point they began to transform into Internet memes. We apply an integrative framework for the qualitative analysis of visual online communication practices (Schreiber, 2017), which allows for a balanced analytic emphasis on visual content, framing practices and platforms that constitute the visual production and dissemination of Internet memes. This framework follows a documentary analytic approach (Bohnsack, 2008, 2014) and helps to reconstruct Internet memes as subversive visual styles that reproduce from disorder by subverting the visual meaning, relational expectations and sociomaterial affordances of artifacts of professional communication.

In that, this chapter makes both an analytic and empirical contribution. Analytically, the concept of styles contributes to the current advancements in process oriented organizational research, and recent attempts to approximate these streams (Cooren, Bencherki, Chaput & Vásquez, 2015; Ashcraft, Kuhn & Cooren, 2009; Leonardi, 2011), by introducing styles as a genuine form of social organizing from disorder. Further, our research supports recent efforts in organizational studies that encourage a more systematic reflection of contemporary forms of organizing outside the "frontiers" of the classic formal organization (Ahrne & Brunsson, 2011; Cheney & Munshi, 2017) and, in the case of Internet memes, points at fruitful opportunities of mutual exchange between organizational and political communication research. Empirically, we show how the style concept can help form a better understanding of how disorder in terms of irritation and subversion of established meanings, expectations and practices provides a source of a unique form of social organizing in its own right and hence lays the ground for future empirical style-oriented research inside and beyond the organizational domain.

This chapter is structured as follows: In the theoretical part, we first provide a brief overview of the growing emphasis on disorder in process oriented organizational research, starting with the foundational work of Cooper. Secondly, we introduce the general sociology of White and outline how the concept of styles can contribute to these current efforts by presenting a genuine form of social organizing from disorder. In the empirical part of the chapter, we present previous research on Internet memes, our research design and our findings on Internet memes as subversive style. Our chapter closes with a discussion of practical and academic implications of the style concept introduced.

The Growing Emphasis on Disorder in Organization Research

Cooper's Legacy

When it comes to the notion of disorder in organization research, the works of Robert Cooper, and particularly his seminal article "Organization/Disorganization" (1986), are widely considered the foundational contribution. Yet, despite Cooper's prominence in organizational scholarship, it is crucial to note that his analytic emphasis never was on organizations in a narrow sense (Spoelstra, 2005). In his entire work, Cooper was interested in understanding modern forms of organizing in broader sociological terms, whereas modern formal organizations only represented a particularly prominent and symptomatic example (Cooper, 1989, 1992). Further, it is worth noticing that Cooper (2001) promoted a critical stance toward modern forms of organizing by challenging an overemphasis on order in scholarship and practice, while he considers the crucial role of disorder as systematically sidelined. Cooper elaborates this critique building on three premises.

In his first premise, Cooper criticizes that both modern organizational practice and scholarship constantly promote and re-affirm a rational and functional understanding of organizing. He labels this discourse the *organization of organization* (1986), and argues that practitioners and scholars alike stress an orderly reading of social organizing. Disorderly aspects, on the other hand, inherent in the interpretative uncertainty and undecidability of meaning as vital sources of change, get systematically excluded and suppressed (Cooper, 1986).

In his second premise, Cooper argues that our common sense understanding of the world is essentialist by nature. However, modern organization, like any other form of social organizing, cannot be considered a given entity. Such essentialism necessarily represents an illusion that rests on improper observational shortcomings. It considers social identities as "already formed" (Cooper, 1986, p. 304), although they represent the effect of an ongoing and necessarily disorderly "transformation of boundary relationships" (Cooper, 1992, p. 257). Consequently, Cooper emphasizes to shift the observational focus from seemingly orderly social entities to the disorderly relational struggles over boundaries that, in effect, constitute the impression of such entities.

Finally, Cooper articulates a third political premise. As essentialist reasoning and its ongoing communicative re-affirmation do not only shape modern organizations, but also the sociomaterial conditions of everyday life, a stronger analytic emphasis on and political promotion of disorderly forms is crucial on the practical level as well. Otherwise "we are in danger of becoming technical products of the technology we have produced" (Cooper, 2001, p. 334). There are still a few scholars in organizational research that straightforwardly follow Cooper's critical legacy (e.g., Abrahamson, 2002). To a larger extent, however, the contemporary academic debate has developed and diversified into a more analytically oriented direction. Most prominent are process oriented approaches, which we will briefly discuss in the following section.

Process Oriented Approaches

For process oriented approaches to organizations studies, we follow a recent systematization of Schoeneborn, Vásquez and Cornelissen (2016) and differentiate between three prominent concepts: Organization as Communication, Organization as Becoming and Organization as Practice. Yet, while Schoeneborn and colleagues focus on the process-entity-paradox in these approaches, we rather focus on their implied circularity of order and disorder.

The *Organization as Communication* approach, and particularly its promotion by the Montreal school (Brummans et al., 2014; Schoeneborn et al., 2014), chooses a genuine communicative angle to discuss the circularity of order and disorder. Its focus is on the organizing properties of language. Parallels to Cooper's (1986) first premise of an "organization of organization", asking how organizations talk themselves into ordered entities, are evident. Organization as Communication scholars argue that any type of communication inhabits organizational properties, as of the moment it leads to authority claims that transcend the situational expectations of actors involved (Taylor & Cooren, 1997; Cooren & Fairhurst, 2009). If these authority claims consolidate in some sort of textual manifestation, they hold the potential not only to organize the current interaction, but also to become attribute and possessor of future interactions (Bencherki & Cooren, 2011). Yet, while authoritative texts provide certain order, this order is necessarily precarious and contested. This is due to a second property inherent in communication, i.e., its infinite potential of conversational negotiation of meaning, which inevitably brings disorder back in (Taylor & van Every, 2000; Vásquez, Schoeneborn & Sergi, 2016). In doing so, the Organization as Communication approach aims at developing a balanced analytic focus on the ordering and disordering properties of communication. Without the emergence of authoritative text, there is no organization (Dobusch & Schoeneborn, 2015; Taylor & van Every, 2014). Yet such authority is always precarious as it has to be actualized and undergoes continuous reinterpretation in conversation and thus equally builds on disorder (Vásquez et al., 2016).

The *Organization as Becoming* approach echoes Cooper's second premise. It argues that organizational research shall overcome its primary focus on organization as ordered entity and emphasize the relevance of emergent and changing patterns of relations that constitute organizational life (Chia, 1995). Organizing hence means a process of permanent relational transformation. This is why scholars argue for the label of organization as becoming. Yet, despite continuous transformation, scholars also explain how the idea of an organization as a fairly stable and ordered entity maintains. This is achieved by means of mostly retrospective, second order observation and rationalization (Tsoukas, 2015), either in terms of (re)interpreting emergent clusters of relations as expressions of order, or in terms of (re)interpreting continual corrections of relational imbalances as expressions of stability (Chia, 2005; Tsoukas & Chia, 2002).

Ultimately, the *Organization as Practice* approach explains the circularity of order and disorder from yet another analytic angle. Its emphasis is on how sociomaterial practices constitute organizational phenomena (Schatzki, 2005, 2008; Vaara & Whittington, 2012). It corresponds to Cooper's (2001) critical third premise regarding the material dependency of organizational practices. Yet again, this approach argues for a balanced analytic focus on practical order and disorder as circular. Indeed, practice research does not deny that formal prescriptions or material affordances lead to order in terms of roles, strategies or technical routines (Jarzabkowski & Kaplan, 2015; Orlikowski & Scott, 2008). The entire point is, however, that this hardly ever happens in a linear or prescribed way. Rather, what effectively turns out as a viable organizational role, strategy or practice is the outcome of contested sociomaterial exploration, negotiation and enactment. Hence, what appears to be a fairly ordered organizational practice, is in fact equally dependent on ongoing situated tinkering, contestation and thus, disorder.

Current process oriented approaches substantially deepen our analytic understanding of the crucial role of disorder in forms of organizing. They share a circular understanding of the interplay of order and disorder, and they demonstrate that this circularity can be analyzed on a communicative, relational and practical dimension. Yet, the recent analytic orientation and diversification of process oriented approaches comes with a number of obstacles for scholars interested in studying disorder.

First, each of these approaches has a very pronounced analytic focus on either communication, relations or practices. This makes an interrelated argumentation of these dimensions, as initially suggested by Cooper, much aspired (Ashcraft et al., 2009; Cooren et al., 2015; Leonardi, 2011), yet complicated. Second, these approaches apply a predominantly micro-analytic angle when studying forms of organizing, which makes the crucial question of "scaling up" (Cooren & Fairhurst, 2009) from single relational interactions and in-situ praxis to more persistent forms of organizing an analytic challenge. Third, in line with this, these approaches show certain ambivalences when it comes to an ontological definition of organization and organizing and how to distinguish them from other social forms (Sillince, 2010). On the one hand, these approaches welcome a broad and inclusive understanding to analytically grasp recent fluid, networked and clandestine forms of "partial" and "alternative" organization (Ahrne & Brunsson, 2011; Cheney & Munshi, 2017; Schoeneborn & Scherer, 2012). Yet, on the other hand, when it comes to defining constitutive features of "organizationality" (Dobusch & Schoeneborn, 2014), an emphasis on orderly features—authority (Taylor & van Every, 2014), decidability (Dobusch & Schoeneborn, 2014), ex-post-stabilization (Chia, 2005) or practical routines (Vaara & Whittington, 2012)—still prevails. This, ultimately, also has a largely implicit impact on the political stance of process oriented approaches. While these approaches indeed echo Cooper's argument to consider disorder as an integral element of organizing, organizationality is still defined as dependent on orderly features. Cooper's politically more radical claim, however, to consider (and promote) genuine forms of organizing form disorder, remains only little addressed.

To respond to these challenges, in the next section, we introduce the concept of style from the general sociology of White (2008). We present styles as a form of organizing that reproduce and scale up from disorder—concretely the exploitation of the polysemy of meaning, breaking of relational expectations and the subversion of sociomaterial affordances—and in doing so present a genuinely political form of organizing, as they not only irritate existing order, but indeed present a core driver of social change.

Styles as Organizing From Disorder

White's General Sociology

White's early roots lie in an empirically driven, structuralist tradition of Social Network Analysis (Burt, 2004; Granovetter, 1973). Different from most of these scholars, White as of his early writings (1963, 1965) is overtly critical when it comes to essentialist explanations of social networks reduced to attitudes and attributes of actors involved. Rather, White proclaims a radical non-essentialist view to explain both micro-action as well as macro-structures as effects of *relations* (for related work, see Emirbayer, 1997; Fuchs, 2001; Mische, 2008). In his later writings, White is increasingly interested not only to explain the structural, but also cultural foundations that constitute social relations, which leads to a *communicational turn* in his writing inspired by sociolinguist (Godart & White, 2010; Mische & White, 1998) and Luhmannian systems theory (White, Fuhse, Thiemann & Buchholz, 2007a). In his very late writings, White shows awareness for the importance of *material* conditions to explain the emergence and decline of social forms, which leads to yet another redefinition of his theoretical body (White, Godart & Thiemann, 2013).

Comparable to Cooper and process oriented approaches, White's central analytic premise is that there is nothing such as a given social identity. Social identity is the effect of control efforts in social relations. Control is defined as any communicative effort to come to terms with uncertainty (White, 2008, p. 1). To get a better analytic grip of uncertainty, White distinguishes three dimensions of uncertainty, which reveal striking parallels to the analytic perspectives of current process oriented approaches in organization studies. White differentiates between ambiguity, ambage and contingency (White et al., 2013). *Ambiguity* stands for interpretative uncertainty, indicating to what extent meaning of a given communicative content is negotiable. *Ambage* stands for relational uncertainty, indicating to what extent given roles, expectations and frames are negotiable. Finally, *contingency* stands for sociomaterial uncertainty, indicating to what extent practices either affirm or transform a given material context.

Building on these three analytic dimensions, White explains the emergence, maintenance and change of all sorts of social identities. White uses this analytic repertoire to investigate how identities emerge from relational control efforts, and how they scale up to larger social forms of organizing

(White, 2008). He describes this development as a continuous reduction of uncertainty on all three analytics dimensions. Dyadic relationships, as basic building blocks, reduce uncertainty by developing idiosyncratic "stories" that consolidate mutual expectations and stabilize reciprocal practices (White & Godart, 2007). Social networks, then, share a communicative emphasis on particular value logics centered on social purity, instrumental quality or influence, and in doing so regulate internal status relations and practices of inclusion and exclusion (White et al., 2013). Institutions build on a communicative generalization of network values that consolidate unrequested norms, structural stratification and practical routines (for the example of religious and academic institutions, see Mohr & White, 2008). In line with recent partial organizational literature (Ahrne & Brunsson, 2011), modern formal organizations, then, can be explained as evolutionary intermediaries between networks and institutions, which hold the capacity to explicate and instrumentalize both informal network expectations and institutionalized norms by means of decisional communication (Fuchs, 2001; Luhmann, 2003). In sum, all abovementioned forms of social organizing emphasize orderly properties by systematically reducing uncertainty by means of communication. Yet, in his later writings, White adds a fourth basic form of social organizing that follows an inverted logic by reproducing from uncertainty: *styles* (White, 2008, 1993a; White et al., 2007a; White, Godart & Corona, 2007).

Styles

All previously mentioned forms of organizing (relationships, networks, institutions, organizations) share one crucial feature. They block *fresh meaning* in terms of new interpretations and *fresh action* in terms of new relational and material possibilities (Mische & White, 1998; White, 1995; White et al., 2007a). This leads White to the conclusion that social identity cannot be explained by focusing on communicative reduction of uncertainty alone. Rather, sociological inquiry has to consider the emergence of social identity from attempts to increase uncertainty in order to get access to fresh meaning and action as well. He labels such attempts as style.

Styles, in their very early expression, as *alpha styles*, emerge from ephemeral, idiosyncratic and mostly tacit attempts to change existing social order by expanding uncertainty on one or several of the analytic dimensions discussed (Godart & White, 2010). On the dimension of ambiguity, this can be achieved by bringing in irritation via unexpected interpretation, ranging from simple turn taking to subversive deviance. Regarding the dimension of ambage, this can be accomplished by developing specific patterns of *switching*, which stands for all kind of unexpected changes concerning relational expectations (Mische & White,

1998; White, 1995; White et al., 2007a). On the dimension of contingency, this is enacted by challenging and subverting existing sociomaterial affordances (White, 1993b). White argues that liminal events, like carnival or art, represent ideal contexts to observe the emergence of an alpha style in its purest empirical form, simply because these contexts provide generic conditions to challenge and subvert existing social order (White, 1993b; White et al., 2013). Yet, in essence, every personal habitus in terms of idiosyncratic behavior can be interpreted as a style (White, 2008). Alpha styles find expression in spontaneity and novelty, as they foster fresh meaning and action from increasing uncertainty and thus irritate existing order. However, alpha styles often remain tacit and are bound to situated local practices. The full transformative potential of styles lies in their dual nature. Alpha styles irritate existing order, but they do not necessarily change it. Yet, the irritation generates observational sensibility and attention. This very attention by others is the basis for the emergence of *beta styles*, which lead to an explanation of a style and thus contribute to "reach some level of codification and imitability" (Godart & White, 2010, p. 578). Ultimately, beta styles can also lead to shared narrative patterns "used in the process of mobilization, as a tool to convince allies and thwart adverse control attempts, following patterns from the codified type of style" (Godart & White, 2010, p. 579).

In short, the concept of styles represents a counterpart to orderly forms of organizing in social life, be it relationships, networks, formal organizations or institutions. Styles typically start on a micro-analytic and ephemeral level. Due to the irritation they cause, they attract attention and thus induce attempts of imitation, explication in certain codes and contribute to social mobilization. Styles can swiftly spread across social space and time, as their very reproduction is not bound to existing interpretive, relational or practical expectations, but driven by the very opposite: A particular way of irritating established meaning, a codified pattern of switching from relational expectations or a particular way of subverting established practical affordances. According to these reflections, White's sociology also suggests a circularity between social order and disorder, yet on a more general level. On the one hand, styles can be considered as a central driver of social change—ranging from playful irritation to full deconstruction of an existing social order (e.g., Mohr & White, 2008). On the other hand, styles can also represent the breeding ground for new order, which is the case as soon as mutual expectations consolidate in a style, and thus lead to the emergence of new networks, and ultimately even new institutions (e.g., Godart & White, 2010).

During the remainder of this chapter, we place our emphasis on concretizing this abstract concept of styles by drawing on the example of Internet memes and apply a qualitative framework of visual online communication analysis for this purpose. This framework allows for systematic investigation of how Internet memes as subversive style reproduce from disorder by exploiting interpretative ambiguity on the level of visual content, relational ambage on the level of meme production and socio-material contingency by means of outwitting affordances of social networking sites and search algorithms.

Internet Memes as Subversive Style

One feature that has put Internet memes into the focus of academic research in recent years is their subversive nature. Memes spring where authoritative texts (Kuhn, 2008) fall on deaf ears. Their features enable them to undermine mainstream frameworks in mass media (Benkler & Nissenbaum, 2006), to mobilize movements and voice dissent in public discourses (Bennett, 2012; Hristova, 2014; Milner, 2016; Mina, 2014). Memes act as subversive elements in discourses as they undercut the logic of professionalized communication. Their subversive nature stems from three features. First, their authors are usually not known, or only known to a small audience. A prominent counter strategy in the realm of professional communication, to attack the accuser, is thereby doomed to fail. Second, Internet memes spread quickly through the Internet infrastructure, and thus cannot be contained. Professional communicators can try to intervene with news outlets, or even threaten to sue them in order to somehow cap a story. Memes, however, spread through decentralized networks. Taking out one node in the network does not damage the capacity of the network for further spread. Third, through mimicry and remix (Shifman, 2013), memes constantly vary and alter. While classic news cycles prevent a story from developing from a certain point on, Internet memes can vary almost indefinitely and can thus stay alive for a very long time. Today, Internet memes resemble in their function satire and parody in authoritarian regimes (Mina, 2014). Their inherent ambiguity makes it hard for professionalized communication to control them in the public sphere. They are a form of subversive speech, published on "parody accounts, mirror websites, fake usernames, and proxy servers", which allows them to "slip under the watchful radar of state agencies" (Kumar & Combe, 2015, p. 212), as well as press secretaries and public relations professionals. Based on these characteristics, Internet memes inject discourses with new meanings through irritation, and given their persistency, provide these new meanings with a permanent foothold in discourses on Internet platforms. Thereby, Internet memes represent a prime example of a style in the digital society.

If we regard alpha style as "a style that expresses itself in spontaneity and novelty" (Godart & White, 2010, p. 578), Internet memes in a nascent state fit that description. They emerge spontaneously as a reaction to an event and present an irritating, usually subversive and humorous angle on the subject. A beta style then "has reached some level of codification and imitability" (Godart & White, 2010, p. 579), and hence features that are inherent in Internet memes further their diffusion. They are codified in the sense that they are tagged with search terms in order to be found on the Internet, and they are based on templates, which are provided by users to invite imitation, mimicry and remix. Furthermore, Internet memes are ephemeral, idiosyncratic and tacit in the sense that they are initially not available to a mass audience, but to an enclosed group of users, yet can become viral and have subversive impact, particularly if they earn recognition by classic mass media. In the following empirical section, we will now show how Internet memes as subversive styles reproduce from disorder.

Empirical Design

Method

To explore Internet memes as subversive style, we apply a recently introduced integrative framework for qualitative-reconstructive analysis of visual online communication practices (Schreiber, 2017). This framework follows the idea that studying these new communication practices requires a balanced analytic focus on three empirically interrelated, yet analytically distinguishable dimensions that constitute them. The first analytic dimension addresses the visual content and "aims to reconstruct the *meaning* conveyed visually and aesthetically, for example, through composition, perspective, scenic choreography, colors, contrast, etc." (Schreiber, 2017, p. 38; our emphasis). The second dimension analyzes how this visual content is framed toward an audience (Marwick, 2013b; Thiel-Stern, 2012; Hutchby, 2014). It follows questions such as "How do users *'audience'* pictures? Do visual media allow for differentiated tonalities, cultural markers and insider jokes?" (Schreiber, 2017, p. 39; our emphasis). The third analytic dimension focuses on the platforms where these practices are enacted and hence analyzes the Web affordances in terms of the "*material* substratum which underpins the very possibility of different courses of action in relation to an artefact" (Hutchby, 2001, p. 450; our emphasis).

Each of these dimensions finds consideration by following three analytic steps borrowed from documentary analysis (Bohnsack, 2008, 2014), a method that is applied to all sorts of qualitative data such as observations, discussion protocols, interview transcripts, images, videos and other artifacts. The first step of documentary analysis remains on the level of description and reconstructs what can be considered common sense knowledge following questions of *what* is observable. The second step of reflexive analysis, then, focuses on questions of *how* things are expressed and done in a particular way and thereby aims at a reconstruction of the habitual knowledge that implicitly frames expectations, narratives or practices. In a third step, this method follows a logic of comparative sampling, in which iterative comparison of contrasting cases leads to the formation of typologies.

These three analytic dimensions and three methodological steps are particularly useful for our reconstructive analysis of Internet memes as subversive style. First, the three analytic dimensions are useful as they help to reconstruct how an Internet meme visually manipulates the intended meaning of an image (ambiguity), re-contextualizes the framing of audience expectations (ambage), outwits affordances of the Web (contingency) and thereby allows for reconstructing how a style produces and reproduces from disorder. Second, the two analytical steps focusing on a descriptive formulation of common sense knowledge (what) and a reflexive analysis of habitual knowledge (how) help to analytically reconstruct how the reproduction of a style works. The initial cause of disorder is typically rooted in an irritation of common sense knowledge and expectations—be it by deconstructing an established iconographic trope, an expected form of reception or an established affordance of assigning and using search terms. Yet, it needs the second analytic step of reflexive analysis to reconstruct how habitual forms of knowledge guide this process, which helps to understand what concrete associations and beliefs drive the reproduction of an Internet meme as a style in the making. Third, the systematic comparative approach of documentary analysis supports a reflected sampling and analytic creation of meme typologies.

Sampling

For our study, we selected two widely recognized Internet memes, the *Obama Hope* meme and the *Trump's First Order of Business* meme, which we describe in detail below. To collect our data of analysis, for each meme, we drew a fixed term sample, using a Google image search. All memes that were found with the search terms +Obama, +hope, +meme, and +Trump, +signature, +meme within two months after the inauguration of both presidents were collected. Thereby, 146 memes were collected for Donald Trump and 92 for Barack Obama. In a second step, we started to analyze random examples out of this collection on the descriptive and reflexive level. We then systematically searched for other examples that we considered as maximally contrasting to the first examples picked and systematically compared their differences. We repeated this procedure until we reached theoretical saturation.

In both cases, this led to a typology of four clusters of memes with idiosyncratic forms of irritating established meaning and framing audience expectations, which correspond to the analytic dimensions of ambiguity and ambage. To illustrate these typological clusters, we additionally created a visual "memealogy" with examples representing these types and intermediaries for both cases (see Figures 10.3 and 10.4). We explain these typologies for both memes separately in the following section, mainly focusing on central outcomes of our comparative reflexive analysis. Findings on practices that directly irritate Web affordances, and hence represent the dimension of contingency, we discuss for both cases together, as they follow quite similar logics.

Reconstructing the Origins: The Visionary and the Executive Leader

The *Obama Hope* meme originates in artwork created by Shepard Fairey (knowyourmeme, 2017, see Figure 10.1). In early 2008, Fairey created a series of iconic posters, showing Obama with the captions of *hope*, *progress* and *change*. After its initial success, the poster was later used by the Obama campaign as an official image during the Democratic primaries, and, subsequently, during the presidential election campaign. Quickly after the posters became public, the image proved to be highly prolific. The original poster and its further dissemination follow an established iconology and framing logic. The image stylizes Obama as a visionary leader, which is affirmed by his anticipatory countenance in his full frontal profile, the prophetic slogans (*change*, *hope*, *progress*) and the three color stencil aesthetic. This aesthetic refers to at least three originally subcultural, yet today well-established visual vocabularies: pop art, street art and revolutionary art (ambiguity). This form of representation and its timing (a fan art piece turning into an integral element of Obama's campaign for president) create a clear framing regarding audience expectations and reception, namely political *mobilization* (ambage). Ultimately, the idea behind spreading the image online follows a *political campaigning* logic with emphasis on sourcing "shared and earned media" in terms of viral dissemination of the image by Obama supporters and influencers in their own digital networks (contingency).

The second meme, *Trump's First Order of Business*, emerged immediately after Trump took office, starting his tenure with the signing of an executive order on the day of his inauguration, January 20, 2017. The original press photo (see Figure 10.2) shows Trump sitting at his desk, surrounded by staff members and holding the signed order into the camera. The formality of the setting is affirmed by the Oval Office atmosphere and the apparel of all participants, the attentive posture of the staff members and Trump's serious and significant countenance, which affirm the impression of an *executive leader* in charge (ambiguity). This form of representation and the timing of the image (real-time documentation of a legal act) draw on an established frame of immediate exercise and demonstration of *political power* (ambage). The reason for disseminating this image online follows a media logic of *political reporting* and hence public documentation and information, which has, in this particular case right after inauguration, global reach and impact (contingency).

Figure 10.1 Obama's Hope Subject
Source: Fairey (2008); knowyourmeme (2017)

Figure 10.2 Trump's First Order of Business Subject
Source: Reddit; knowyourmeme (2017)

The Initial Irritation: How an Alpha Style Emerges

As stated above, alpha styles depend on the ability to irritate established meaning, role expectations or affordances by expanding ambiguity, ambage or contingency in a substantial way, and thereby potentially create social recognition and trigger further imitation and variation—a beta style (Godart & White, 2010). In the case of the origins of both memes, we can identify this initial irritation on all three analytic levels, which makes them particularly valuable examples of analysis.

In the case of the *Obama Hope* meme, the initial irritation is caused by a particular web application called obamicon.me (a now defunct website). This app allows for uploading random images and applies a filter that transforms this image into the three color stencil aesthetic of the original image. Further, it is possible to insert one of the existing slogans (*hope, change, progress*) or to customize an own slogan with the same font (see Figure 10.3e). The emergence of this very app evidently represents a chance for irritating established meaning, the framing of audience expectations and Web affordances. It allows for exchanging the Obama profile and slogan within an established formal aesthetic, is open for replacement by any random meaning (ambiguity) and contextual reframing (ambage). Further, the app automatically creates a new visual of high quality in a format that can be tagged in various ways and slotted back into the Internet (contingency). While the app is open for creating

sacred   profane

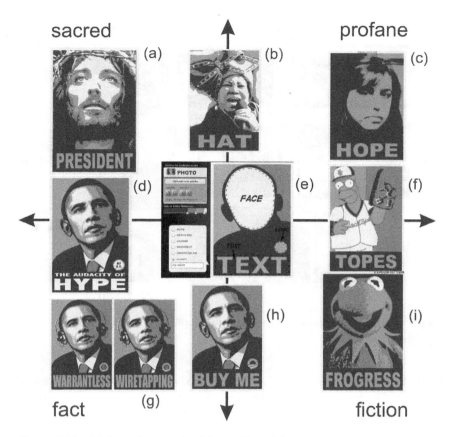

fact   fiction

Figure 10.3a–i Memealogy of the *Obama Hope* Meme
Source: Own creation

all kind of content, ranging from affirmative to nonsensical, subversive memes will be the focus of our further analysis. Thereby, three aspects of the app prove to have a particularly strong impact on the further (re)production dynamic of these memes. First, the opportunity of *ex*changing the Obama profile and slogan obviously allows for another association, which is the *interchangeability* of both leader and vision (ambiguity). Second, the stencil aesthetic, which remains the only stable formal aspect of the meme, allows for foregrounding and subverting implicit *cultural frames* and related audience expectations it inhabits (ambage). Third, the material creation of a new image that is visually close to the original image allows for outwitting filter algorithms, not only on the level of text but also image search (contingency).

In the case of the Trump meme, we can trace the initial irritation back to a *meme template*, which an anonymous user uploaded on the platform

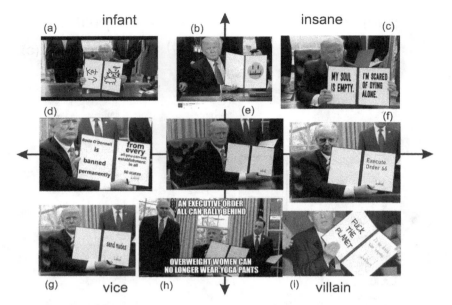

Figure 10.4a–i Memealogy of the *Trump's First Order of Business* Meme
Source: Own creation

imgflip.com right after the first images of the signing ceremony emerged online. The irritating intervention it set by replacing the executive order that Trump holds into the camera with a blank sheet, where only Trump's signature in the bottom right corner remains (see Figure 10.4e). Yet, despite this minimal intervention, the image is now open for endless variations of its original meaning (ambiguity), for decontextualizing and reframing the formal political context it is embedded in (ambage) and for uploading and creative tagging of newly created memes that outwit Web search algorithms (contingency). Again, this initial intervention is not necessarily subversive by nature. However, compared to Obama, in our sampling time of two months, we could identify only one clearly positive meme (affirming Trump in a newly inserted text as a president who does exactly what he promised to do). All other memes are subversive by nature. Further, different expressions of subversion are to a certain extent guided by the initial intervention, the blank order template. First, by blanking the text of the order, the *interchangeability* of this order and its dependency on the leader who signs it becomes apparent (ambiguity). Second, the act of only blanking the order, yet keeping the rest of the setting stable, creates a focus on *who* are the people, and particularly the leader, who constitute this setting (ambage). Third, again, allowing for uploading a meme of quite similar formal content allows for outwitting both text and visual search algorithms (contingency). In the next section, we present our results on the way these initial irritations provide a source for ongoing (re)production and diffusion—and that describes the logic of a beta style.

Organizing From Disorder: How a Beta Style Diffuses

As argued above, beta styles emerge if a style manages to create some sort of codification and imitability (Godart & White, 2010), which is assured by the meme generator and blank order template, and on that basis contributes to some sort of style reproduction and further mobilization by exploiting the initial source of irritation. For both memes, in the two months of observation, we could analytically identify four typological clusters with references to quite distinct visual meanings (ambiguity) and distinct forms of reframing audience expectations (ambage) for each meme.

Barack Obama: How to Subvert a Visionary Leader

In the case of the Obama meme, we have labeled these four types as *sacred, profane, fact* and *fiction* (for exemplary images, see Figures 10.3a, 10.3c, 10.3g and 10.3i, respectively). The *sacred* type of meme (see Figure 10.3a), in its most evident expression, exchanges the Obama profile with a religious leader or martyr figure. These type of memes reference the original *Obama Hope* subject by choosing the same stencil aesthetic and selecting an image that resembles Obama's countenance (which is relatively easy as a glance in the upper corner is codified as dialogue with God in Christian iconography), or by hinting at it in an exchanged slogan. In doing that, the visionary iconography of Obama is made explicit and thereby exaggerated (ambiguity). Though we can only speculate about the intentions that drive this exchange practice (which can range from expression of religious creed to ridiculing the Obama campaign), in any case this exchange aims at an irritation of audience expectations and reconceptualizes the original framing, scrutinizing the adequacy and hubris of the original political image and its aim of voter mobilization (ambage).

On the other end of the spectrum, we identify a *profane* type of meme (see Figure 10.3c), which follows an opposite form of subversion. Instead of exaggerating the visionary appeal of the initial *Obama Hope* subject, it vulgarizes it. A typical form of doing so is by uploading random profile images, yet with a bored, frustrated or turned off countenance, while either keeping, and thereby subverting the initial visionary slogan, or customizing a slogan that supports this slack facial expression (ambiguity). The irritation of audience expectations in this case is to dismantle the original framing of political mobilization by profaning, randomizing and thereby subverting its singularity and visionary appeal (ambage).

Between these poles of sacred and profane, we could further identify a considerable number of clearly affirmative memes that use the Obama subject and slogan to cherish a leader figure from another domain—sport trainers, entertainers or public protest leaders. Yet, we also find some more ambivalent to subversive memes of this genre, which portray famous people of color, yet comment on random features of their look or everyday culture (e.g., the customized slogan "hat" under a profile of Aretha Franklin wearing an elaborated headscarf in Figure 10.3b) (ambiguity). This form of reframing decontextualizes Obama as political leader and creates a connection to his ethnic background and community. It reintroduces a distinction, which is absent in the original campaign, by referring to other prominent persons and leading figures of color, yet ambiguously leaves open if this represents a positive accentuation or attempt of public schism (ambage).

Though the typological poles of sacred and profane are contrasting, memes within their range have one thing in common. They avoid commenting on Obama as a *political* leader. This attempt is rather represented by the two poles in the lower left and lower right of Figure 10.3, which we have labeled as fact and fiction, respectively.

Memes representing *fact* typically address and subvert in a more or less subtle way Obama's campaign communication. One recurring expression of this type is represented by memes that keep the original profile of Obama unchanged, yet critically comment on his campaigning logic in a customized slogan (e.g., the slogan questioning the "audacity of the hype" under the Obama profile in Figure 10.3g) (ambiguity). This form of visual manipulation irritates the existing frame by directly addressing the media hype around Obama, and thus directs audience attention toward what can be considered the *factual* political situation (ambage). An even more explicit expression can be found in memes that directly address issues and scandals of his "realpolitik", most prominently symbolized by a meme that portrays Obama with headphones and a customized slogan of "warrantless wiretapping" (ambiguity). In this case, the very manipulation of the image deconstructs the affirmation of a visionary leader by drawing audience attention to the NSA surveillance scandal, which substantially overshadowed Obama's first term (ambage).

Complementary to the *fact* type, we identify a *fiction* type of meme at the other end of the spectrum, which exaggerates and thereby subverts the promotional character of the Obama campaign. While a number of memes again express this by customizing the slogan (see the slogan of "buy me" in Figure 10.3h), a larger number of memes portray fully fictional characters from the entertainment industry, and particularly cartoons. Most memes of this type tend to remain on a subtle and inoffensive level. They often build on a pun between the portrayed fictional character and a clever variation of the initial Obama slogans (see the customized slogan of "frogress" with an image of Kermit the Frog, and the slogan "topes" combined with an image of Homer Simpson in Figure 10.3i and 10.3f, respectively). Yet, we also find memes that picture famous villains of entertainment culture (e.g., the Joker from Batman with the slogan "Joke"), and thereby give the meme a more offensive tonality (ambiguity). In each of these cases, however, we can identify a clear decontextualization of the initial political mobilization frame and a direction of audience attention to its promotional and entertainment-driven character (ambage).

To conclude, our study reveals that this meme, though in effect infinitely open toward irritation attempts, tends to reproduce and diffuse in recurring visual and framing patterns. They typically subvert the visionary and singular appeal of Obama as a leader. As we will show in our second case, the subversive potential of Internet memes as style can also develop into a very different direction, depending on its original source of reference and its original source of irritation.

Donald Trump: How to Subvert an Executive Leader

We have argued above that the original press photo of Trump portrays him as an executive leader (ambiguity) and follows the established news frame of a demonstration and documentation of political power (ambage). The initial irritation goes back to a meme template that blanks the focal order, and thereby sets free a plethora of new meanings and framings of audience expectations. Our reflexive comparative analysis of these memes leads to the formation of four typological clusters, which we have labeled as *infant, insane, vice* and *villain*.

Infant is the by far most prominent type of meme which we could identify in our two-month sample. It uses the blank space and fills it with doodles of animals, buildings and everyday objects, often accompanied by misspelled descriptions in infantile writing (see Figure 10.4a). Further, memes are popular that displace the executive order with Pokemon cards, a popular card game. In both cases, the initial meaning of the image and particularly the status of Trump as executive leader is subverted by means of infantilizing and thereby devaluating meaning and relevance (ambiguity). Yet, this very deconstruction of the meaning of the executive order is in line with a substantial reframing of audience expectations, as Trump as a leader is not only ridiculed. More than that, his very personal constitution and capacity to hold public office is subtly attacked (ambage).

These attacks become increasingly explicit if we approximate to memes that represent the type *insane*. A still quite subtle intermediary form cites psychedelic iconography in the blanked order, either referring to kaleidoscope, paradox or fractal visuals, or citing symbols from rave culture such as the Acid Head Smiley carrying Trump's signature instead of a smile (ambiguity) (see Figure 10.4b). Though highly codified, these memes subvert the existing frame and abduct audience expectations into "altered states", and evidently propose some connection to Trump as focal character of the image (ambage). While these intermediary psychedelic memes remain ambiguous, memes of the type insane are very explicit when it comes to eroding the condition and capacity of Trump as political leader. They do so by hijacking the blank order and redefining it as a personal cry for help, or moments of introspection and epiphany (e.g., "My soul is empty. I don't want to die alone" in Figure 10.4c) (ambiguity). The initial political framing is thereby radically subverted and transformed into a setting wherein Trump uses public attention to confess his inability and incapacity as a leader (ambage). The two polar types infant and insane, hence, use the blank order template to erode the reputation of Trump as a person, while the initial meaning of the order as order does not play a major role.

In the two other types of memes, vice and villain, the content of the order and its exertion of power are central. Memes that represent the type *vice* address Trump as a political leader who abuses orders for personal gains. These memes either show Trump presenting an executive order that immediately serves his personal satisfaction (e.g., the meme with the order "bring nudes" in Figure 10.4g, which refers to allegations of sexual harassment and misogyny against Trump). Alternatively, the memes depict executive orders in terms of bans toward particular groups and persons with whom Trump is considered to be hostile, e.g., ethnic and sexual minorities or celebrities who have publicly voiced criticism against Trump (e.g., Figure 10.3d decreeing a permanent ban on Rosie O'Donnell from all-you-can-eat-restaurants in the US) (ambiguity). In any case, in memes of the *vice* type, a switching of the expectation frame is reached by directing audience attention to two suggested deficiencies of Trump as a leader: Trump's excessive and erratic self-interest when it comes to executing orders, and the assertive way this interest is pursued (ambage).

Memes of the type *villain*, on the other hand, directly address assumed consequences of Trump's politics. These memes either construct exaggerated parallels between Trump and random real or fictional tyrants and their most detrimental orders (e.g., the "Order 66" from *Star Wars*, causing the extermination of all Jedi knights, in Figure 10.4f, additionally exchanging Trump's head with that of Supreme Chancellor Palpatine from that series). Alternatively, again, the blank order is transformed into a device of public confession of Trump, admitting his indifference with regard to detrimental consequences of his politics (e.g., "Fuck the planet. I will be dead soon anyway" in Figure 10.4i).

Hence, the diffusion of *Trump's First Order of Business* memes mirrors quite a different logic of subversion than that of Obama. This has to do with both the original source of the reference, the first order signing ceremony and the blank order template as initial source of irritation. It is the co-dependency of political leader and executive order, which only in combination create a frame of political power, and hence become central

objects of subversion. Subversion, then, is either achieved by fully decontextualizing the order from its political context, and transforming it into
a confession statement on the (inept) personal condition of the leader.
Or the order remains political, as it expresses some sort of edict or ban.
Yet in this case, it is the content and tonality of the very order that question and subvert the capacity of the leader. In both cases, the personal
condition of Trump as leader becomes the focal object of subversion. In
Obama's case, in turn, it is the singularity, hubris and promotional attitude of his visionary claim.

How to Subvert Affordances of Power

In this final part of our empirical analysis, we show how memes as styles
subvert Web affordances, understood as intended ways of using the socio-
technical infrastructure of the Web. As our findings regarding this last analytic dimension of contingency are quite similar for both cases, we present
the four major forms of sociomaterial subversion in one joint section.

The first and most crucial socio-technical intervention of both memes
is rooted in their initial irritation: the obamicon.me web application
(among others), and the blank executive order template uploaded on img-
flip.com (among others). Both interventions create a common domain for
further meme production and provide a material basis that commodifies
an easy creation of memes. In both cases, these memes remain formally
very similar to the initial visual source, and hence systematically support
confusion with the original in case of user search.

This similarity further contributes to a second intervention, which is
the outwitting of search algorithms by means of *"subversive tagging"*.
Memes created by using such an app or template can be tagged freely
and uploaded everywhere on the Web. This openness for assigning the
tags Obama, Hope, Trump, Order to subversive memes does not only
contribute to "slipping" memes into official search threads of particular
social media platforms such as Twitter, Facebook or Instagram. Further,
if memes have reached certain digital recognition, they also make it on
the first pages of meta-search engines such as Google's image query. On
this level, then, the similarity of both textual tag and visual resemblance
allow for outwitting crawlers and bots of meta-search engines, which are
programmed to filter and rank down obviously misleading content, yet
unable to distinguish memes from the original in case of similar search
terms and visual similarities.

A third prominent form to subvert the initial intent of Internet affordances is to *create own threads and pages* for particularly popular types
of memes to boost reproduction and dissemination. One example from
our case is the Twitter page twitter.com/trumpdraws, counting over
437,000 followers, which has specialized in ridiculing any documentation of Trump signing documents by replacing the content with a goofy

child doodle and misspelled descriptions (see meme type *infant* in Figure 10.4a).

A fourth and last form of outwitting affordances of the Web are memes that implement *a re-entry of the infrastructure* of reproduction and dissemination into the content. This is achieved by promoting Web-links to meme creation and sharing sites directly in the meme, in the case of Obama in a customized slogan or an additionally applied heading. In the case of Trump, they are typically embedded as a part of his order, either by "ordering" people to subscribe to a certain site or by ironically spelling a "ban" on a site, and thereby boosting traffic.

In each of these examples, the infrastructure of the Web is creatively outwitted in order to subvert its official use by the two presidential leaders, be it for means of online campaigning, or a demonstration and documentation of power. Hence, Internet memes provide a prime example to study a style in the making. Their digital traceability over time allows for longitudinal study on how irritation, and in our case subversion, of established meanings (ambiguity), role expectations (ambage) and Web affordances (contingency) contribute to the emergence and diffusion of a genuine form of social organizing from disorder.

Discussion

In this chapter, we have introduced White's (2008) concept of styles to organizational communication research. Styles represent a genuine form of social organizing from disorder, understood as reproduction from the irritation of established meaning (ambiguity), relational role expectations (ambage) and affordances inscribed into the material infrastructure (contingency). The concept contributes to recent attempts in organizational scholarship, and process oriented approaches in particular, which promote a balanced focus on the interplay of order and disorder. It suggests a reintegration of increasingly diversified analytic efforts in recent process oriented scholarship, by analyzing organizing from disorder following an integrated perspective on communication, relations and sociomaterial practices. Further, the concept revives an explicitly political reading of disorder that harkens back to the foundational work of Cooper (1986), arguing to go beyond a balanced focus on order and disorder, but to acknowledge disorder as a genuine form of organizing *in itself*. We consider this reflection particularly fruitful for recent research on fluid, partial and alternative forms of organizing that are of equal interest to organizational (Ahrne & Brunsson, 2011; Cheney & Munshi, 2017) and political communication scholarship (Bennett, Segerberg & Walker, 2014).

Empirically, however, the study of styles is a challenging endeavor (White et al., 2007a), as styles are notoriously futile and particularly prosper in informal and clandestine environments. We thus referred to the empirical example of Internet memes, which due to the merits of digital archiving and tracking, are relatively easy to access. We applied a recently introduced integrative framework for studying online visual practices (Schreiber, 2017) and, on this basis, investigated the emergence and diffusion of two of the world's most famous Internet memes, the *Obama Hope* meme and *Trump's First Order of Business* meme, as examples of styles in the making. Though echoing very different tonalities, both show analytic commonalities in the way they irritate established meanings, relational expectations and affordances of the Web, which are not only of interest to research on styles in organization studies, but further point at promising opportunities of exchange with political communication research.

On the dimension of ambiguity—understood as uncertainty in meaning— our study on Internet memes expands our existing understanding of the organizing properties inherent in the polysemy of communication (Cooren & Sandler, 2014). The style concept makes evident that polysemy does not only drive organizing in terms of a constant interplay of authoritative text and its conversational negotiation (Taylor & van Every, 2000). Rather, styles represent a form of organizing that reproduces from ongoing "resistant readings" (Ceccarelli, 1998), which do not aim at a transformation, but a fundamental deconstruction of authoritative texts. As our empirical study on Internet memes exemplifies, this is typically achieved by explicating meanings that are suppressed and "silenced" by the authoritative text. Forms of humor, irony and other paradoxical speech acts are ephemeral expressions of such a style and find growing consideration in recent organizational research (e.g., Jarzabkowski & Lê, 2017; Suominen & Mantere, 2010). Similar phenomena can also be observed in political communication, for example in the case of the use of parody and satire to dismantle political authoritative texts (Kumar, 2015), which invites for stronger exchange. Further, our research shows that, in order to achieve maintenance, styles over time require certain codification and imitability— which, in our case, manifested in recurrent visual patterns of "resistant readings" in meme types and only then bear the potential of broader social mobilization and change.

On the dimension of ambage—understood as relational uncertainty— our findings advance the current understanding of organizing as ongoing relational negotiation and ex-post-rationalization of authority claims (Tsoukas & Chia, 2002). Styles, however, do not rationalize, but systematically irrationalize authority claims and their implied relational expectations. They do not aim at negotiating relational positioning within a given setting, but provoke a "switching" from and devaluation of this very setting. In the case of Internet memes, this finds expression in systematic attempts to disenchant political authorities by exposing features "beneath" the official role of the two presidential candidates. Research on public subversion of politicians, particularly in authoritarian regimes, knows such tactics well (Mina, 2014). Yet, organizational scholarship on micropolitical forms of subversion and denial reveal similar tactics (Burns, 1961) as well, which equally draw on informal and intimate resources to undermine official prescriptions and procedures, and in doing so can unfold substantial transformative effects.

Ultimately, on the dimension of contingency—that is sociomaterial uncertainty—our study allows for an advanced understanding of the role of disorder in practice oriented approaches to organizing (Schatzki, 2008). While recent literature indeed promotes a view that considers organizing as flexible adaption and imbrication of social routines and material affordances (Leonardi, 2011), the style concept sensitizes us for forms of organizing that systematically *manipulate* affordances in order to unsettle underlying routines. The focus, hence, is not on how to enhance practices by creative adaption of routines or affordances, respectively, but to fundamentally question and redirect the practices as such. In the case of Internet memes, this is accomplished by irritating customized and commodified user practices of Web search and sharing, by slotting back manipulated content and outwitting search algorithms. And once again, related forms of resistance to affordances do not only mirror in the organizational domain (Mumby, 2005), but on a more general level present genuine and "productive" expressions of political subversion, particularly in high surveillance contexts such as the digital sphere (Ettlinger, 2018).

Taken together, the style concept introduced in this chapter provides a fresh lens on the organizing properties of disorder. Due to its multidimensional approach and conceptual inclusivity, it does not only provide a promising perspective for process oriented organizational scholarship, but, beyond that, also points at opportunities for exchange with recent political communication scholarship on disorderly forms of public organizing.

11 Extreme Context as Figures of Normalcy and Emergency

Reorganizing a Large-Scale Vaccine Campaign in the DR Congo

Frédérik Matte

One early morning in the city of Bunia in RD Congo, I was accompanying the vaccination teams to a nearby location on the outskirts of town. After only ten minutes on the road, the MSF radio operator announced that prisoners from the nearby prison had escaped and that the convoy should return to the base immediately. Suddenly all five vehicles did a quick u turn and sped up in order to get back to the MSF compound as fast as possible. Everyone seemed to know what to do in this kind of situation as it was apparently done in accordance with the MSF security guidelines. No one rushed nor panicked. It was almost business as usual for the MSF teams—significantly more than myself I have to admit—even if the situation was considered somehow a bit unusual by the local staff. Nevertheless and after about an hour of an additional coffee back at the compound, the logistical coordinator in charge of security gave us the green light to resume the vaccine campaign as the arrest of the prisoners was confirmed. We all took the road again back on track to vaccine more than a thousand people that day.

(Ethnographic notes, Bunia, DR Congo)

Extreme sports (Wacquant, 2004), extremists and hidden organizations (Stohl & Stohl, 2011), extreme weather, extreme makeovers, etc.—the word seems to be on all lips nowadays (Spencer, 2014). Defined as "exceeding the ordinary, usual or expected and as situated at the farthest point of the center" (Merriam-Webster, 2018), the notion of extreme represents for many a supposed state of exception involving an unusually high degree of risk. In sports and adventures for instance, it is as if it was a *real* made human choice, a proper decision that looks to be taken in the name of passion, belief, fear, boredom and individualistic matter (Hällgren, 2016). It thus appears to be a buzzword among Westerners or said-to-be moderns (Latour, 2012), allowing for bouts of intensity in a land of monotony. But what about the many places around the world or in particular situations where this notion of extreme is *imposed* by the broader context, thus making it far more ambiguous and to some extent less qualified as such? What are the implications for organizations working in these said-to-be extreme contexts and how can this framing of extremeness be mobilized and negotiated to manage possible (dis) organizing effects daily?

With this chapter, I wish to explore these questions by showing how alleged extreme contexts represent sites of emerging disorders (i.e., unexpected events, surprising outcomes, unsettled features, up-to-the-minute knowledge, disruptive situations, ambiguous occurrences, etc.) that serve as discursive apparatuses for organizational actors working in these settings. More specifically, I will illustrate how these discursive tokens (i.e., through figures, to be explained later) of extremeness are mobilized to reorganize and manage emerging disorders. With this portrayal of extremeness in hand, organizational actors are better equipped—discursively speaking—to claim what is supposedly required in a situation or what might be needed according to this world view (Taylor & Van Every, 2010). Nevertheless and as we will see with the analysis, the evocation or depiction of extremeness by some organizational actors working in these contexts does not mean that other representatives, partners or collaborators agree on the implication of such an interpretation, on the contrary.

For this case study, I will illustrate how representatives from the humanitarian aid organization *Doctors Without Borders/Médecins sans frontières* (hereafter, MSF)—who constantly face emerging disorder brought by the contexts in which they operate (Fox, 2014)—evoke extremeness through discourse and interactions in order to push for a specific medical agenda. More precisely, I will empirically show how MSF representatives speak this notion of extremeness to attempt to temporarily enroll collaborators to cooperate for the planning of a large-scale vaccine campaign. In turn, because of MSF's enrollment process, the collaborators—the local health authorities in this case study—depict the situation as mostly being ordinary and mundane by evoking logics of normalcy and routines. By partially resisting this depiction of extremeness or emergency, collaborators thus make the so-called extreme context speak in terms of "endemic crisis" where a long-term planning motto is privileged. Accordingly, I argue that the extreme contexts in which MSF implements medical programs make emerge various and sometimes contradictory readings, and the very implicit or explicit evocation of matters, interests or preoccupations play a defining role in how representatives into the field get organized (Langley & Tsoukas, 2017). In other words, I contend that such said-to-be extreme contexts (Barton, Sutcliffe, Vogus & DeWitt, 2015) trigger both organizing as well as (dis)organizing processes, a performative understanding that is mostly accomplished through cooperation and collaboration (Kapucu, 2005; Simo & Bies, 2007; Weick & Sutcliffe, 2015).

To orient my discussion on (dis)organizing in extreme contexts, I will first show the ways the literature has only partially engaged with this notion. This will allow me to introduce an approach that sees emerging disorders (i.e., actual disorganizing effects) as "business as usual" albeit framed in many ways, thus representing a key aspect for organizing. In this sense, paying attention to what the situation calls for can be envisaged as a constitutive mode of being for MSF or any other organization working in allegedly extreme contexts. After that, I will introduce the ventriloqual approach to communication mobilized for this study as well as the ethnographic perspective developed. A thorough and detailed discursive analysis will follow with a focus on a specific meeting that occurred in the Democratic Republic of Congo. Finally, I will conclude by discussing the implication of this specific portrayal of extreme contexts as key figure for (dis)organizing.

Extreme Contexts as Constitutive of Organizing

A significant bulk of the literature about organizations and organizing addressing extreme contexts, unstable environment or natural disasters opts for a managerial and discursive-oriented perspective (Hällgren, Rouleau & De Rond, 2018). For instance, we find studies that highlight emotional labor faced by organizational actors on 911 calls (Tracy & Tracy, 1998), resilience mechanisms at play for inter-organizational relationship after a disaster (Doerfel, Chewning & Lai, 2013; Agarwal & Buzzanell, 2015; Buzzanell, 2010) and attitude of expatriates toward performance facing terrorism-related stressors (Bader & Berg, 2013). Some studies also address topics and matters related to leadership (Geier, 2016; Tempest, Starkey & Ennew, 2007; Hannah, Uhl-Bien, Avolio & Cavarretta, 2009), storytelling (Linden & Klandermans, 2007), decision-making (Ludvig, Madan & Spetch, 2014), intergovernmental response to terrorism (Comfort, 2002) and High Reliability Organizations (Weick & Sutcliffe, 2015). These themes have been explored to show manners in which organizational actors act, react, talk, think or feel about unexpected events and extreme contexts and the many ways these volatile environments influenced their world in terms of organizing and sensemaking (Boddy, Miles, Sanyal & Hartog, 2015).

Accordingly, Lyng (2005) coined the term "edgework" to refer to any voluntary activities that imply risk taking as an exploration of "edges" (p. 4). Edges "can be defined in various ways: the boundary between sanity and insanity, consciousness and unconsciousness, and the most consequential one, the line separating life and death" (p. 4). Edgework is described as being any out of the ordinary situation and is epitomized in the leisure and adventure business (Holyfied, Jonas & Zajicek, 2005). Drawing on Girin's (1990) management-based definition of extreme situations, Bouty et al. (2012) state that extreme refers to a situation that is evolving (rapidly), uncertain and highly risky. It is said to be dangerous, intense, powerful, risky and so on. In the literature, extreme contexts are thus typically envisaged as constituted of unexpected and chaotic events

(Cunha, Clegg & Kamoche, 2006) but fall short in tackling directly its mundane and ordinary characteristics while neither addressing straightforwardly the process of disorganizing. Said differently, extreme context as a construct—and the implication for disorganizing—seems already at play and reified in many studies, somehow missing the point of letting organizational actors tell us what are the daily and usual outcomes of such a social construct and the many ways it can be enacted, appropriated, translated or even rejected as is.

Exceptionally and as mentioned above, studying the ways High Reliability Organizations (HRO) manage to generate less accident or mishap than common organizations on a daily basis permitted the emergence of normative characteristics (Sutcliffe, 2006) achieved by actors. Some authors have also highlighted the day-to-day process of getting organized and the ways this specific disposition (i.e., HRO) is shaped, constructed and *performed* (Brown, Colville & Pye, 2017), allowing to show "the practices and how they play out in everyday life (and its productive sets of intuitions, cultures, habits)" (Helin, Hernes, Hjorth & Holt, 2014, p. 14). With the same performativity lens yet not directly related to extreme context nor to HRO, Pullen and Knights (2007) highlight "how gender gets done and undone in organizations and through organizing, and with what consequences" (p. 506). Building on Judith Butler's work, these authors engage by "rethinking gender as a lived experience and textual practice, and empirically to explore gender doing and undoing in everyday organizational and work practices" (p. 507).

For this study and particularly related to the performativity of (dis) organizing, I build on Cooren (2015) by recognizing that if the very process of organizing is a performance, disorganizing is also what people (or things) do (p. 138). Purposely, it is argued that disorganizing is the flip side of organizing since "the organizational world is, by definition, an alienating world, but it is also a world of cooperation and co-construction. Organizing is thus always at the price of disorganizing (a meeting, a relationship or other potential activities), hence its polemical dimension" (p. 165). With a similar logic, Latour (2013b) suggests that is it merely impossible to distinguish organization and *dis*organization from the very perspective of actors involved in the process, as scripts are continuously variable and alterable:

> In the thick of being an organizer . . . , there is no way to make a distinction between being organized and being disorganized, or between being well-organized and badly organized—which has no meaning for those who are in the middle of it.
>
> (p. 41)

For organizational actors, being "in the middle of it" means coming up with plans, scripts or thoughts about how things *must* evolve in an ideal world. It is therefore continuously a somehow becoming world that we live in (Khandker, 2016). Following these authors, I contend that to organize is always a way to get *reorganized*, similarly Tsoukas (2013) proposes with his three components of any organizational process: a process of representation, a process of meaning making and a process of improvisation. Accordingly, "disorganization occurs when any of these processes displace the others" (p. 64), an ontology of becoming where change is seen as "normal" rather than an exception (Bjerregaard & Jonasson, 2014) and where organizational actors seem to constantly appeal for what a situation might call for.

Reorganizing to Respond to What the Situation Calls For

As mentioned above, there are many places around the world or in particular situations where this notion of extreme is *imposed* by the broader context, thus making it far more ambiguous and to some extent less qualified as such. I thus with this study look to highlight the practical implications for organizations working in these said-to-be extreme contexts and how this framing of extremeness can be mobilized and negotiated to manage possible (dis)organizing effects daily. As such, organizational actors who work in extreme contexts ought to 1) get reorganized and 2) make speak and express what a situation calls for according to someone or something. Hence, any situation or organizational phenomena emerging from allegedly extreme contexts can be viewed as an ontological site of inquiry where cooperation as well as negotiation are crucial, as this location makes various interests, matters and concerns that potentially make a difference emerge (Schatzki, 2005). By adding layers of what counts or matters (in a relation, a situation or a context), we can also take into account the plenum of agencies—i.e., what/who makes a difference and what matters and counts for actors—that constitute them (Cooren, 2016). Envisaging the world as various agencies or a plenum of (possible) scripts represents a fruitful avenue for letting organizations or situations talk to us (or "us" being talked to) and let us know what might be an accurate reading of it (and "us" being read by it). In other words, the main traction of agency is here given to a situated and performative site (i.e., extreme context as what the situation calls for) albeit packed with emerging disorders and possible (dis)organizing effects. As we will see through the analysis, considering what a situation *requires* (Follett, 1926) generates an ongoing negotiation about whom and what has the authority, legitimacy (and credibility) to speak in its name.

This negotiation process appears to represent an almost never-ending process with an unlikely closure attached to it (Taylor & Robichaud, 2007), unless someone or something has a privileged position of power without any possibility of resistance (Mumby, Thomas, Martí & Seidl,

2017). Thus, to state that a situation requires something poses the problem of reification and plain power, a moment in time and space that would be fixed and dominated by someone or something, at least temporarily. To counter this predicament, a plausible conceptual argument resides in the proposal that a situation must always require something *in the name* of what counts and matters to the representatives, a mattering that should always be accounted for (Cooren, 2016).

I therefore argue that organizations' representatives in such extreme contexts have to evoke as well as negotiate "what the situation or context calls for" on a daily basis, in order to reorganize these possible emerging disorders. This calling of a situation or a context will generate various readings from organizational actors involved—sometimes in contradiction—prompting different voices, matters, interests and preoccupations that appear to count and matter for them. Hence, the calling or the reading of a situation—or an organization or a said-to-be extreme context for instance—must always be incarnated, channeled, reflected upon and materialized, whether it is through artifacts, languages, relations, signs or symbols. It does not have to be explicit or obvious, but any situation or context that wishes to stay salient needs representatives that speak in its name. It is never a whole situation that speaks for itself; it is a situation that expresses many agents or representatives that are trying to come up with a consensus or a temporary agreement on what should/could/might be done to keep things going and make speak, in our case at study here, an extreme context through its evoked emerging disorders.

Hence, if emerging disorders from extreme contexts might at first be seen as disorganizing sites, they can also be envisaged as constitutive and central for some organization operating in these settings. Alas, even if disorganization is characterized by chaos or disorder, it can be nonetheless considered as being part and parcel of organizing processes. As Vásquez, Bencherki, Cooren and Sergi (2018) suggest, organizing "embraces disorder as the characterizing ethos of organizations by directly challenging the order/disorder dualism" (p. 632). From this perspective, extreme contexts call for organizational actors to discursively engage with disorder, disruption or eventfulness while still ensuring that the organization's mission is being accomplished.

To illustrate this phenomenon, I mobilize a ventriloqual approach to communication (Cooren, 2010, 2015) that offers an analytical toolbox to address what the situation calls for. This approach accounts for discourses and agencies arising from the daily activities of an organization (or any social phenomenon) as it invites us to observe how "various forms of reality (more or less material) come to do things and even express themselves in a given interaction" (Cooren, Fairhurst & Huët, 2012, p. 296).

A Ventriloqual Approach to Communication

A ventriloqual approach to communication highlights the various discursive and material features (i.e., figures) that populate organizational actors' conversations and actions (Cooren, 2012). The notion of figure refers to what *drives* these logics of action, that is, any preoccupation, value, interest, concern or matter on behalf of which an actor speaks or acts (Cooren, 2010). By shedding light on the figures *ventriloquized* by organizational actors, it is possible to draw attention to what preoccupies them, their actual matters of concern, that is,

> the cultivation of a *stubbornly realist attitude*—to speak like William James—but a realism dealing with what I will call *matters of concern*, not *matters of fact*. . . . Matters of fact are only very partial and, I would argue, very polemical, very political renderings of matters of concern and only a subset of what could also be called *states of affairs*.
> (Latour, 2004, p. 4, emphasis in original)

In a nutshell, Cooren argues that a multitude of "effects" will be produced by these figures through interactions such as authority, presence, representation, intelligibility or dislocality. Consequently, a ventriloqual approach permits us to reveal any practices that emerge from the very mundane discourses and actions of organizational actors. Figures themselves, taken as sole agents who can act beyond or independently of their authors' "intentions" (Brummans, 2007), have the ability to incarnate many things such as ideas, other actors, principles, facts, desires, reasons of the past or future events. What counts ultimately is that these figures are staged up, that is to say, they are both mentioned and/or invoked by actors. Figures can be expressed explicitly, but they can also be implied, allowing someone to speak and act on behalf of someone or something in filigree. This double movement of oscillation between figures and actors implies that both can be acted upon according to what is put forward. Said differently, people make figures speak through discourses and interactions on their behalf, and figures can also speak in their names just like the ventriloquists do (Craig, 2015). As Keenoy and Oswick (2004) suggest: "all discourse analysis can be treated as a 'textscape': a socially constructed account of some phenomena, which for its multitude of possible meanings, embodies continual (and often covert) reference to a wide variety of other texts and other possible texts" (p. 140). In other words, the broader environment in which the discursive apparatuses are produced—here, extreme context—must be reflexively mobilized and conjured by organizational actors in order for them to get organized. Accordingly, ventriloquism allows for a discursive and agential investigation that gives the analyst a way to consider the situation (or context) as a text (a figure) that is taking an active part in the interactional scene.

To exemplify how extreme contexts are evoked as well as negotiated in terms of both normalcy and emergency at MSF—and how this same evocation enacts the reality in which actors are—I will focus my analysis on one key inter-organizational meeting taken from a longitudinal ethnographic approach to this organization. Hence, I will show how the interactional work of MSF representatives and local health delegates leads to the emergence of various figures that allow for both parties to get reorganized. In the next section, I will briefly introduce the ethnographic approach developed for this study, an approach that allowed me to take part in MSF's field operations, thus "providing uniquely privileged opportunities to enter into and to share the everyday lives of other people" (Atkinson, 2014, p. 3).

Ethnography of MSF and the DR Congo Fieldwork

To better understand how such figures of extremeness are talked into being at MSF, it seems productive to closely look at what is happening through key moments or interactions, echoing both a becoming and a grounded in action perspective. Putnam and Fairhurst (2015) have suggested that adopting a process view toward preoccupations and matters "captures the ongoing flows of experience that orders and disorders routines as well as connects and reconnects the mutual constitution of organization and disorganization" (p. 386). To do so, I opted for an "embedded ethnographic" approach (Atkinson, 2014) implying not only a presence from researchers in the field but a posture that explores in this study the mundane ethos embodying the performativity of extreme contexts and emergency. As Morrill (2008) suggests:

> Scholars using ethnographic and case-study methods moved beyond human relations to reveal a complex "underlife" (Goffman, 1961) in organizations containing conflicting values and interests that both subverted and facilitated the achievement of formal goals (Selznick, 1948). In this context, scholars focused on the institutionalization of social values, as well as the day-to-day negotiation of meaning by organizational members.
>
> (p. 16)

This embedded ethnographic posture, like a view from the inside while being from the outside—a look that is both analytical and reflective—has given me the chance over the past ten years to draw a portrait of MSF that I deem to be both revealing and representative of the daily operating mode of this organization. There is no pretension on my part to prescribe any method of operation. It is only a matter of being a faithful witness of the "typical" activities of the organization, and this, with the help of video recordings that are part of a shadowing method (Meunier & Vásquez, 2008). For each of the 12 research fieldworks I completed—including the DR Congo, chosen for this study—I used the same data collection method that consisted in following with a video camera one or more MSF representatives in their daily work, whether during their meetings with politicians, local health delegates or other NGOs. In short, shadowing MSF involved trailing organizational representatives, as they got busy with their respective tasks, alternating filmed observation and reflective questioning about their work. As Vásquez, Brummans and Groleau (2012) suggest, "shadowing presents a particular way for researchers to move through actual organizational contexts/situations in order to understand people's sensemaking in interaction" (p. 148).

In exploring the data collected, I was mainly interested in what seemed to animate the different positions and decisions of MSF representatives and their collaborators; in other words, I wanted to better understand the principles, values and norms that seemed not only to be incarnated, but also making a difference in MSF's everyday life so that I could capture them in action (Bencherki, Matte & Pelletier, 2016). Once these data were selected (I will explain shortly how this selection was made), I transcribed in detail "key" moments or situations from the recordings in which some figures emerged and seemed to matter to organizational actors. I thus sought to better understand how MSF representatives proceeded to organize and reorganize themselves through key moments, mainly involving emerging disorders for this study. This sensitivity allowed me to uncover how actions and decision-making were "put into action" and to get a better idea of what these medical interventions actually consisted of, whether in terms of planning, coordination, negotiation, logistics or even improvisation. More concretely, I attended MSF weekly operational meetings on each mission, as well as meetings for logistic, medical departments or with partners and collaborators.

Broadly speaking, MSF is "an international, independent medical organization that provides medical assistance to people affected by conflicts, epidemics, disasters, or exclusion from healthcare" and that "observes neutrality and impartiality in the name of universal medical ethics and the right to humanitarian assistance" (Médecin Sans Frontières, 2018). Around one-third of MSF's projects are devoted to delivering assistance to people living in areas of war and armed conflict such as in South Sudan, Central African Republic, Iraq and DR Congo among many others (MSF website, 2018). Whether it is political unrest, a civil and ethic war or an extremely remote area to cover, DR Congo is considered a highly unpredictable country to intervene in as has been regularly the case for the past 30 years.[1] Cultural, social, political or geographical aspects have to be taken into account on a daily basis (Brauman, 2006) as teams into the field encounter numerous situations where it is a real challenge to assess what is happening or to come up with a proper analysis of the whole picture. During this fieldwork completed in 2010, MSF operated a 100-bed hospital with a focus on maternity needs and pediatrics while also doing outreach for vaccinations in the Ituri province.

Concretely, I gathered more than ten hours of video recordings, dozens of pages of notes and several ethnographic thoughts over a period of one month. These recordings were then viewed and analyzed during data analysis sessions where I focused my attention on situations and moments that seemed to make emerge questions related to emerging disorders and the explicit or implicit evocation of extreme contexts as both an ordinary and emergency phenomenon. I noted all preoccupations, interests and matters (i.e., figures) that MSF representatives and collaborators referred to. This allowed me to identify patterns and ways of doings, lending to the emergence of these figures. In the meeting chosen for this analysis, two MSF representatives gather with the Congolese local health delegate based in Bunia (Ituri province). The MSF coordinator reveals that the organization calls for the introduction of a new type of vaccine (i.e., *Pentavallin*) for this yet-to-be announced large-scale vaccination campaign for children under three years.

Vaccination coverage for large-scale matter is a real challenge in DR Congo—and a real matter of life and death for many people—due to the numerous remote areas to cover and to the borderless territories either under the rebels' or army faction's control or caught up in fighting with the regular army. According to the organization, epidemic outbreaks like measles, yellow fever or cholera are recurrent and periodic due to poor surveillance and infrastructure. In 2017, MSF teams into the field, with the collaboration of DR Congo local health authorities, reached about 330,000 patients in the country with medical issues related to malaria, typhoid fever, cholera or displaced people (Médecins Sans Frontières, 2018).[2] For instance, 869,067 patients were vaccinated against measles in response to an outbreak in 2016 for the whole country. These numbers show the magnitude of the tasks to be undertaken daily and the apparent indisputable yet negotiable extremeness of this context.

Extremeness as Both Figures of Emergency and Normalcy

As we will see in detail, two different worldviews or readings of the situation seems at play in this meeting, yet both displayed in the name of the patients to be treated. Broadly speaking and on one hand, MSF representatives seem to envisage the situation regarding this "new" vaccination campaign for children as an emergency that is critically time bounded. Thus, they translate the figure of extreme context or extremeness in terms of swiftness, large coverage, up-to-date medicine as well as a quite blunt attitude, representing numerous organizational features that animate them. This view appears to normalize extreme context in the sense that it is always there to be managed and taken upon no matter what. On the other hand, local health authorities seem to foresee this said-to-be extreme context in terms of mundane and usual, downplaying the scale of such an emergency reading from MSF. Hence, they translate this reading of the situation with figures related to continuity, supply, long-term and rational as well as with a more composed manner. If MSF representatives normalize the extremeness of the context by its prompted actions—*this is what we do all the time as we are primarily an emergency organization*—the local health delegates in return also normalize the situation by deflating its attribution as supposedly extreme or being solely an emergency.

In particular, let's see how the beginning of the meeting illustrates these different yet complementary readings of the situation (for the complete transcript of the interaction see the Appendix). The MSF coordinator reveals to start with that an "immunization for children up to three years of age is initiated with *Pentavallin*" (lines 1–2). He follows immediately with an interrogative formulation by asking his Congolese counterpart, "I do not know if you were told about it?" (line 3). The MSF coordinator seems to call for an immediate and already effective "new" way of doing things according to what he considers the situation requires, a justification for such a requirement that will only come later in the meeting. But for now and by asking a rhetorical question after announcing this "new" vaccination plan, the MSF coordinator appears to feign surprise of a supposedly shared view with his counterpart about this planning already set in motion. He does so by using the present tense with the verb "is initiated" (line 2), a declarative term that instantiates the program of action set up by MSF. In other words, it is like the health delegate *should have known* beforehand about this use of *Pentavallin*, the new vaccine apparently already effective in the emergency planning to come. Here, we could argue that the MSF coordinator might have inquired *first* about the situation for the whole vaccination approach in the region or what might have been already put in place at the hospital since vaccines have been administered for decades in the region. After all, MSF is on the health delegate's turf, as he is officially in charge of public health issues in Bunia.

This quite blunt way of doing things—positioning the situation as an almost *fait accompli* without a proper contextualization—a contextualization that will come only later in the meeting—seems like a usual trait at MSF albeit not always cordial. Indeed, the organization, with its considerable means, resources and ways of doing—extremeness as emergency is the norm not the exception—seems prone to "authorizing itself" to paint a portrait of the situation as generally critical, precarious or already set in motion. This depiction or reading of what the situation calls for thus prompted the apparent immediate need for a new vaccine without any explanation or justification to the local collaborators. In other words, MSF seems to display this world view by implicitly evoking the figure of emergency—a token of extremeness—in order to make things go forward *now* and forthrightly pushing for the introduction of this "new" vaccine to be distributed.

After this first utterance from the MSF coordinator, the health delegate answers directly the rhetorical question about the knowledge of such a new campaign with a laconic "no" while nodding his head. The MSF coordinator thus seemed obliged to better explain the reasons for an unannounced and time bounded new approach for this large-scale vaccination. To do so, he puts into context the MSF planning by letting the health delegate know, according to him, what the situation calls for. He divulgates that the organization is moving its pediatric wards into a new building,[3] giving a chance, according to his reading of the situation, to "unclog the hospital and for children to be better immunized" (lines 8–9), implicitly saying that children might not be fully protected in the region. This relocation into a new building is not explicitly justified in the conversation but it can undoubtedly be considered as an emerging disorder as the organization was *forced* to move out of the infrastructures due to security reasons, according to the MSF logistical manager.[4]

The MSF coordinator then goes on by revealing the exact months where the vaccination campaign shall happen, a strategy he legitimizes by discursively mobilizing a plan. He says, "we put our plan of action for the year to come" (lines 10–11). By evoking this plan of action, he appears to share the authority of the decision—*it is not I personally but the plan itself that is telling us that we need to put up a new and up-to-date vaccine campaign*—a decision that is being materialized in an official MSF document stating that children must be "better immunized". Again, we could argue that MSF is displaying an emergency motto regarding the situation—*we need to go faster now and to do better for children just like the plan indicated to us*.

After that and in a somewhat backtracking mode—perhaps the MSF coordinator senses that the boldness of the announcement might have hampered is counterpart's authority?—he goes on to conclude his turn of talk by saying "but we also wanted to talk about it before to see with you" (lines 13–14). The health delegate, after a few seconds of silence, a silence that seems to express his reluctance regarding this reading of the situation or what is allegedly required, that is, the introduction of a new vaccine *now*, puts into doubt the plan and its actual value. He asks, "if there is an added value to this, because vaccination is a routine activity here?" (lines 15–16). With this rebuff posture, the health delegate calls into question the rightfulness of this proposed vaccination campaign by questioning its added value. To justify his logic, he puts the emphasis on the routine characteristic of vaccination in the Bunia region, a counterpoint to this apparent urgency from MSF that somehow disrupts local ways of doing. The health delegate seems to argue on the contrary that vaccination is a routine activity implemented in a well-organized and long-term approach, thus not requiring this new vaccine. In other words, he does not seem to read the situation as being extraordinary nor exceptional but as mostly mundane and under control.

Continuing with his argument that this vaccination represents an added value, the MSF coordinator respond by saying "with *Pentavallin* I am not sure" (line 17), putting forward the specific and more up-to-date type of vaccine MSF plan to use and by doing so implying that the health delegate does not do so in his routine activity. The delegate's response is interesting in many ways as it gives us a glimpse into what the situation calls for according to his reading of the situation. He says:

> Yes, because you have not introduced the vaccines we have here. We must be sure that these vaccines arrive because there is no point in vaccinating people with a vaccine that will not continue. . . . At the level of each health center, children are vaccinated regularly. Especially here in Bunia, there is no concern because there is no epidemic that threatens and coverage is already quite high.

(lines 18–26)

With this reply, the delegate seems to put the responsibility of the possible disruption of vaccination activities on MSF for bringing a "new" vaccine (*Pentavallin*) that is not always available, thus leaving the local health authorities with the burden of a continuous coverage without it. In other words, the delegate implies that MSF disorganizes or disrupts "usual" vaccination campaigns by introducing "new" vaccines without the necessary continuity for such a planning. He seems to criticize this approach by stating, "there is no point in vaccinating people with a vaccine that will not continue" (lines 21–22). We thus could argue that the Congolese delegate speaks in the name of the figure of continuity where the MSF coordinator, in turn, talks in the name of the figure of "actual needs and up-to-date medicine" as well as the figure of scale as we will see later in the meeting.

The Congolese health delegate then reminds the two MSF representatives that "children are vaccinated regularly" and that "the coverage is quite high", a way to reestablish his authority regarding the continuity and stability of vaccination and to counter the need for a change put forward by MSF. In other words, the Congolese delegate frames or makes the situation speak by putting the emphasis on the fact, according to him, that there is "no epidemic that threatens" (line 25) the region, a reading that is far less alarming and extreme than MSF's reading, as we will witness in the coming turns of talks.

Perhaps sensing that he might have gone too far too fast, the MSF coordinator replies by saying: "Hum (3 seconds). Well, I do not know, Laurence [the Head of Mission], she did not tell you about this phase of vaccination?" (lines 30–33), going back to his initial argument about the fact that the health delegate should have known about the planning, a presupposition that was put forward by the coordinator himself. The health delegate answers straightforwardly by saying "no, this is the first piece of information I receive" (lines 34–35), thus enabling him to close the door to any further pushing into this allegedly accomplished fact of a vaccine campaign to come with *Pentavallin*.

In order to frame the situation from a medical perspective yet still with an emergency dictum, the MSF health representative intercedes by putting forward arguments backing up the medical added value for the vaccination campaign, a way to reply to the doubts cast by the health delegate at line 15. He states that the use of *Pentavallin* "would be to my knowledge the first campaign here compared to the country in relation to this antigen" (lines 46–48), arguing that it would be an innovative approach from a nationwide perspective. After that, he goes on by claiming, "it is therefore through this campaign that we will be able to reduce infant mortality, which is very high in the country, as you know. The figures we have at the hospital are a bit scary" (lines 55–59).

With this intervention, the MSF health representative mobilizes both figures—literally with numbers and metaphorically with the medical one— looking for a way to return to the overall aim of this new campaign, that is, to reduce infant mortality, a goal that seems improbable to be against. Implying that the Congolese delegate also knows that mortality rates are very high in the country by making him speak directly ("as you know" [lines 57–58]), the MSF health representative suggests that numbers at the MSF hospital are a bit scary. Putting the emphasis on these "scary numbers" represents a way to frame the situation in a somehow more serious and "extreme" term than the Congolese delegate does. To conclude his argument, the MSF health representative claims that the organization is trying to raise awareness to the national authorities and to sensitize the doctors, "and now we also want to discuss with you how we could go forward" (lines 63–65). By mentioning that MSF is apparently raising awareness to the national health authorities, the health representative seems to counter the continuity and local figures evoked by the Congolese health delegate at lines 15 and 30. He does so by mobilizing the figure of scale, allowing him to enlarge the reading of the situation to the entire country. In other words, the whole situation in the country is telling MSF that the issue regarding the use of *Pentavallin* is not only a matter of continuity and a local preoccupation but also a matter of scale, as the nationwide coverage exceeds what is happening in Bunia. In this sense, MSF seems to tell the health delegate that without the use of *Pentavallin* here in Bunia, the situation might worsen across the country, as this antigen targeted might proliferate elsewhere in an apparent extreme case scenario yet to be materialized but in becoming. Nonetheless, MSF is also reiterating that the health delegate is a fully fledged partner in the equation because "we also want to discuss with you", a somehow late inclusion given the fact that MSF seems to have already planned the campaign and has previously talked to the national health authorities about it.

Shortly after this during the meeting, the Congolese health delegate seems to come to terms with the argument put forward by MSF about the scaling up of the vaccination campaign including *Pentavallin*. This suspected submission from the health delegate—now seemingly adhering to this more extreme/emergency reading of the situation that would need the use of *Pentavallin*—could certainly be analyzed as a power struggle. The health delegate does so by directly going back to potential emerging disorders for his hospital by saying, "But then hum, who brings the vaccine? Because it is also a problem. If this is the stock we have here, this stock is already intended for children up to 11 months" (lines 67–69). Building on the argument made by MSF about its willingness to vaccine children up to three years old (i.e., the figure of the scale), the health delegate implicitly agrees to do so but claims that he cannot supply for children older than 11 months. Thus, he implicitly tells MSF that they should themselves provide for *Pentavallin* or with the support of national health authorities. Seeming not sure what to respond, the MSF coordinator says, "ok. But already we can see what we can do, what you can do" (lines 73–74), putting the emphasis on both organizations' roles to play by the use of an ambiguous "we" followed by a "you", like if the two organizations would work together hand in hand and contribute equally.

The Congolese health delegate does not seem to buy in with this suggestion of an allegedly equal collaboration (and contribution), a partnership that would share the same reading of the situation (extremeness as emergency). Instead, he argues MSF should continue its discussion with national authorities, a claim already made by the MSF health representative at line 61. To do so, the Congolese health delegate stresses, "it is really necessary to contact Kinshasa [the capital] first to increase the quantity" (lines 82–83). After that, he conjures another emerging disorder, that is, the problem of bringing the vaccines from the capital Kinshasa. He underlines this struggle by saying, "I am not sure how easy it is because we have huge difficulties with the transport of vaccines so far" (lines 83–85). This utterance seems to open the door to the MSF coordinator for a way to both mitigate this emerging disorder and to "help out" his counterpart. He goes on by saying "no no but we in terms of transport, maybe we can still try to relieve you, because there is an MSF plane in Kinshasa" (lines 89–90), suggesting that this emerging disorder might be resolved with the use of an MSF plane. This reading from the MSF coordinator seems to imply that it would also *relieve* the Congolese health delegate as if this was *his* problem of transport with the use of the sentence "*to relieve you*".

However, the delegate does not seem to take this attributed burden of the transport for more *Pentavallin* on its own, his apparent main motto figure being about continuity and normalcy, not scale and emergency. He thus replies with the use of an ambiguous "us" in order to share the weight of this emerging disorder on both organizations. He asserts "that's why I said it could be a problem for us. So, Kinshasa must be very aware. Otherwise, they will consider it a loss. If we do not agree, it will happen to us" (lines 93–96).

The MSF coordinator seems to play on the ambiguity about which organization could be responsible to tackle this problem of supply by saying, "No but we'll see, we can already ask them and then we'll see how we can get organized" (lines 97–98). In order to push the responsibility of supply to MSF—and to build on the coordinator's openness to take the lead to ask the national authorities—the Congolese health delegate proposes several strategies to convince these authorities to supply them with more *Pentavallin*.

The closing of the meeting somehow rebalances the authorities at play as well as the two readings of the situation regarding the degree of extremeness put forward and how it can be envisaged as both normalcy and emergency for getting reorganized. The Congolese health delegate indeed seems to have reestablished his authority regarding what the situation seems to need for the vaccination campaign—both from a scale and a continuity perspective—and on how to concretely get reorganized by overcoming emerging disorders. Hence, he "suddenly" appears to represent a resourceful ally to MSF as it looks like the health delegate knows how to play the game with the national authorities in DR Congo. Accordingly, the MSF coordinator seems to be in a posture where he is somehow obliged to ask how to proceed in order to put his reading of the situation into motion, a reading that foresees an emergency without the immediate use of *Pentavallin* for the whole country. The MSF coordinator says, "Hum hum. Okay okay. So how do we make a request here or directly in Kinshasa? How it's working?" (lines 112–114).

These questions raised by the coordinator at the end of the meeting exemplify with great accuracy the contradicting yet complementary readings of what an extreme context calls for according to MSF (and collaborators to a certain extent). By both playing on the normalizing of extremeness, that is, an emergency situation that *has* to be managed swiftly in a somehow blunt matter; as well as by rending normalcy of this said-to-be extreme context by taking into account the situated ways of doing from local authorities—in a more composed manner that incorporates the negotiation with national health authorities and the supplying reality of the whole health system—MSF seems to adopt a logic of action favoring a "both/and" approach instead of an "and/or" one in regards to what extremeness seems to call for and what it can do to make things happen.

Discussion

When MSF disembarks with plenty of resources and means in a broken country like DR Congo, it certainly allows teams into the field and collaborators to swiftly manage the many emerging disorders such an extreme context bring. Nevertheless, and considering these same resources, it seems the organization fails to develop a more thorough understanding of "local" ways by not fully taking into account usages, customs and local authorities. With the empirical case, we saw that by not knowing "how it's working" with the national authorities, the MSF coordinator appears to have disclosed a deficiency toward local (and national) knowledge—as well as a more subtle and to some extent a less extreme way to frame the context—a lack that was partially hidden behind the bravado attitude put forward at the beginning of the meeting.

As we also witnessed in the analysis, this collaborative effort between MSF and local health authorities in a setting such as DR Congo makes various, and sometimes contradicting, figures in regard to the appreciation of the context, emerge. Through discourses and interactions, we saw coming to light figures incarnating matters of 1) continuity *and* swiftness, 2) up-to-date medicine *and* supplying, 3) collaboration *and* resistance, and 4) national/scale *and* local realities, just to name a few. Those figures translated in numerous ways both readings of this said-to-be extreme context, readings that varied from normalcy to emergency on a gradation spectrum. These appreciations of what the situation was apparently calling for allowed MSF and the local health authorities to get reorganized by addressing emerging disorders like transport, limits of medicine or failed infrastructures. This reorganizing of emerging disorders thus generated continuous negotiations about how to make speak the situation and the context in which they were as well as authorities and responsibilities.

Thus, this somehow ambiguous view about extreme context—both as normalcy and emergency—ought to engender different types of relations between order and disorder: If we have the need to suppress disorder to get organized, which entails a form of routinization of disordering (or chaos), it appears that there is an inverse logic at play where disorder is also indispensable for organizing. Paying attention to what the situation or context calls for thus entails organizational actors to fully embrace the unsettled, ambiguous and sometimes unexpected dimensions of it and what is required to make it speak accordingly. Hence, emerging disorders become "business as usual" for organizations that operate in these environments, foreseeing these social constructs as opportunities to get reorganized rather than something to get rid of.

Conclusion

With this study, I contributed to the literature about organizations and organizing addressing extreme contexts in two ways. First, a performativity lens allowed me to show how organizational actors themselves actively enact on a daily basis this social construct that is extreme context. Thus, instead of taking for granted that organizational actors were "only" getting organized within such a said-to-be context, I showed how discourses and interactions played a constitutive role for MSF representatives and their temporary collaborators, both making the figure of extremeness in order to put forward a specific view of how to set up a vaccine campaign.

Second, and by highlighting what seems to animate organizational actors—translated into the utterance "what the situation calls for"—I was able to underline the constant interplay of negotiations and interpretations occurring while planning this vaccine campaign in a said-to-be extreme context of DR Congo. Hence, it appears that such a context must always be incarnated, channeled, reflected upon and materialized, whether it is through artifacts, languages, relations, signs or symbols in order to be considered as a matter of concern.

More specifically and epitomizing an enduring matter of concern for MSF, the figure of the patient's care is considered as the center of MSF's *"raison d'être"* as it is explicitly stated in its chart and mission statement (MSF website, 2018). But this textual inscription does not mean that representatives are free from representational work and discussion among local and national partners; far from it (Cooren, Brummans & Charrieras, 2008). As we witness in the excerpt taken from the meeting analyzed, there is a constant need to re-present, that is, render present, medical imperatives the organization is enhancing, as these extreme contexts tend to "disorganize" inter-organizational cooperation or more broadly the delivery of medical aid. Yet, and as we also saw with the analysis, MSF itself tends to disorganize the very delivery of aid by imposing medical standards (i.e., *Pentavallin*), giving rise to an ongoing negotiation on how to get things done within a collaborative framework but also to the attribution and appropriation of responsibilities and authorships.

Hence, this meeting between two representatives of health organizations allowed us to observe the ongoing authority games at play through language when collaborative work is accomplished under a temporary partnership. As Taylor and Van Every (2000) put it, "an instrument, language has intrinsic properties that give it an active role in the construction of social and organizational reality. In other words, language is a script for organizing" (p. 133). As we saw, a key figure in MSF's action and discourse, if not the tutelary figure, that is, the patient and the quality of the care provided, animate the discussions, whether with partners or between MSF actors themselves. Again, its centrality translates into an attitude of reluctance toward collaboration, which makes the organization's coordinators say they are, for example, willing to push forward specific types of drugs (i.e., *Pentavallin*) that foster quality over what is available for the partner. We also noted that it is often in the name of the quality of care and (well-being) of patients that some tensions arise with partners, particularly when it comes to questioning their own practices.

Everything happens as if the patient was acting as a catalyst for the action of the organization, a catalyst in the name of which local practices of often well-established medical interventions can be interrogated. To some extent, it is this constant concern for patients that leads MSF to be criticized for a position that some would consider a neocolonialist one. In the name of the health of the patient, one can, in fact, shake up local medical and hospital practices by trying to impose (and imposing de facto) what one considers as being the "right way to treat" patients. Dispositions such as lassitude and burnout, ill-conceived procedures, work overload, events (e.g., rumors), missing artifacts (medicine) and people (attacks against a hospital by rebels) are the nitty-gritty of MSF when representatives organize missions into the field. These emerging disorders have therefore the capacity to create plenty of lacks: lack of resources, lack of personnel, lack of resilience, lack of effective procedures and lack of time. It thus seems that extreme contexts are contexts in which *lacks are constantly felt* and are disorganizing the aid more broadly. Resources are rare or unstable and we deal with conditions in which the means of our action can be jeopardized at any moment. In such contexts, a certain level of disorganization is something that tends to be *taken for granted*. It is, so to speak, *business as usual*.

Practically speaking for MSF and in said-to-be extreme contexts, things that could be destabilizing are in the long run treated as small perturbations and somehow normalized. Members of the personnel are sick? "Well, we'll do without them. It will take more time, patients won't receive their treatment as quickly as usual, but we will ago about our business anyway. We are used to it". Even if such contexts tend to represent a somehow unstable and ambiguous place, I showed how the mundane and uneventful also constituted a core facet of these settings. "*Polé-polé*", as the Congolese say ("slow and steady" in Swahili). But does *slow and steady* always win the race, as the fable says? MSF constantly fights against this effect of normalization (see Cooren et al., 2012) while trying not to look like they are imposing their protocols and rules even if they do so in many ways. Nevertheless, and as we saw with the empirical data, a blunt attitude pushed forward by the coordinator seems to constitute a communicative approach at MSF to make sure that the reorganizing of the large-scale vaccine campaign got materialized.

Appendix
Transcription, MSF Meeting, Bunia, DR Congo

1	MSF COORD:	Immunization for children up to three years
2		of age is initiated with *Pentavallin*. I do not
3		know if you were told about it?
4	BUNIA DOC:	No
5	MSF COORD:	No. Well, we plan to transfer some activities
6		in July with pediatrics. Before the transfer of
7		children from one place to another, we wanted
8		to organize this vaccination to unclog the hos-
9		pital and for children to be better immunized.
10		And so we put our plan of action for the year
11		to come to be able to make the vaccination in
12		three times. We wanted to start organizing in
13		May, June and July, but hey, we also wanted to
14		talk about it before to see with you.
15	BUNIA DOC:	Is there any added value to this because vac-
16		cination is a routine activity here?
17	MSF COORD:	With *Pentavallin*, I am not sure.
18	BUNIA DOC:	Yes, because you have not introduced the vac-
19		cines we have here. We must be sure that these
20		vaccines arrive because there is no point in
21		vaccinating people with a vaccine that will not
22		continue. . . . . At the level of each health center,
23		children are vaccinated regularly. Especially
24		here in Bunia, there is no concern because
25		there is no epidemic that threatens and cover-
26		age is already quite high.
27	MSF COORD:	Hum hum.
28	BUNIA DOC:	There are all the vaccination services right
29		here downstairs.
30	MSF COORD:	Hum hum [silence for 3 seconds]. Well, I do
31		not know, Laurence [the Head of Mission],
32		she did not tell you about this phase of
33		vaccination?

34	BUNIA DOC:	No, this is the first piece of information I
35		receive.
36	MSF COORD:	Ah okay.
37	MSF DOC:	The added value is what, it's . . . [silence for 2
38		seconds]. Well, first of all, the antigen in ques-
39		tion, the *Pentavallin*, that's the national policy,
40		that's what's used now. The added value is,
41		first of all, it's a new antigen because, in fact,
42		we started using this antigen last year. Well,
43		here in Bunia as a whole I do not know, I don't
44		think so. Well, the added value just like I said
45		first, if we agree with the authorities, it would
46		be to my knowledge the first campaign here
47		compared to the country in relation to this
48		antigen. . . . Another added value is in relation
49		to age because we still widen the plate because
50		we pick up anyway children up to three years
51		and some of these children have never been
52		vaccinated compared to these antigens. We
53		are catching up. The ideal and if the means
54		were there, it would have been to go up to five
55		years. It is therefore thought that this cam-
56		paign we will be able to reduce infant mortal-
57		ity, which is very high in the country, as you
58		know. The figures we have at the hospital are
59		a bit scary. That's what we're aiming for any-
60		way. Of course, we are also discussing with
61		the authorities to see at the operational level.
62		We are also trying to raise the awareness of
63		the authorities. We sensitized the doctors and
64		now we also want to discuss with you how we
65		could go forward.
66	BUNIA DOC:	But then hum, who brings the vaccine?
67		Because it is also a problem. If this is the stock
68		we have here, this stock is already intended for
69		children up to 11 months.
70	MSF COORD:	Up to 11 months? Okay.
71	BUNIA DOC:	Ah yes. We cannot go beyond. If we go beyond,
72		we lose programming. There you go.
73	MSF COORD:	Okay. But already we can see what we can do,
74		what you can do.
75	BUNIA DOC:	We cannot go to the file and add children over
76		11 months; otherwise, they are considered
77		"losses". We call it "losses" because our pro-
78		gram does not target these children.

79	MSF COORD:	Hum.
80	BUNIA DOC:	If it is necessary to find an extra vaccine for
81		these children beyond 11 months, it is really
82		necessary to contact Kinshasa [the capital] first
83		to increase the quantity. I'm not sure how easy
84		it is because we have huge difficulties with the
85		transport of vaccines so far. The coordination
86		did not turn well all year long which created
87		breaks and lacks.
88	MSF COORD:	No no but we in terms of transport, maybe
89		we can still try to relieve you, because there is
90		an MSF plane in Kinshasa. So, there are pos-
91		sibilities anyway. If in Kinshasa they can make
92		vaccines available to us, we can do it.
93	BUNIA DOC:	That's why I said it could be a problem for us.
94		So, Kinshasa must be very aware. Otherwise,
95		they will consider it a loss. If we do not agree,
96		it will happen to us.
97	MSF COORD:	No but we'll see, we can already ask them and
98		then we'll see how we can get organized.
99	BUNIA DOC:	Perhaps an another avenue, a good way to
100		convince them would be to, if you charter the
101		plane, you can say we bring not only these
102		vaccines, but we could also bring other vac-
103		cines. Then there, they will perhaps bent and
104		be more malleable.
105	MSF COORD:	Other vaccines than *Pantavallin*?
106	BUNIA DOC:	Oh yes yes.
107	MSF COORD:	Well, after—
108	MSF DOC:	Other antigens—
109	BUNIA DOC:	Other antigens yes. Maybe here they will feel
110		a little relieved with the transport by putting
111		other things too.
112	MSF COORD:	Hum hum. Okay okay. So how do we make a
113		request here or directly in Kinshasa? How's it
114		working?
115	BUNIA DOC:	Well, there is the hierarchical issue huh—
116	MSF COORD:	Hum hum.
117	BUNIA DOC:	But it's up to you to apply. I know they will
118		respond more easily to Kinshasa.
119	MSF COORD:	Alright alright.
120	BUNIA DOC:	If MSF in Kinshasa can go directly to the per-
121		son in charge.
122	MSF COORD:	Okay okay we will try then.

Notes

1. Human Rights Watch produces a report every year on the country's political situation highlighting its many flaws: www.hrw.org/world-report/2018/country-chapters/democratic-republic-congo.
2. See https://www.msf.org/international-activity-report-2017.
3. At the time, MSF had been already in the region for many years and decided to build a new ward for children, a ward that would be passed over to the local health authorities; in any case, the organization would leave the place.
4. I did an interview with the logistical coordinator who expressed his view about the situation, putting the emphasis on the "normalcy of being obliged to move quickly" in those contexts where infrastructures are very weak.

Contributors

Oana Brindusa Albu is Associate Professor in the Department of Marketing and Management at the University of Southern Denmark, Odense. Her research focuses on organizational communication, information and communication technologies, and alternative forms of organizing in the Middle East and North Africa region.

Karen Lee Ashcraft is Professor in the Department of Communication at the University of Colorado Boulder, USA. Her research examines how relations of difference—such as gender, race and sexuality—shape various scenes of work and organization. Her work appears in such venues as the *Academy of Management Review*, *Communication Theory*, *Administrative Science Quarterly* and *Management Communication Quarterly*. Most recently, she coauthored a book called *The Work of Communication* (2017, Routledge), where she considers how occupational identities arise and circulate through affective economies.

Anindita Banerjee is Temporary Lecturer in the Department of Organization, Work & Technology at Lancaster University, UK. Her research interests include evolution of theories and practices of organization and management; the scope of archival research methodology in management and organization studies; and embodiment and digital health technologies.

Brian Bloomfield is Professor of Technology and Organization in the Department of Organization, Work & Technology at Lancaster University, UK. His research interests include social imaginaries and technoscientific innovations; human enhancement technologies and the discourse of the posthuman; and the neglect of organized destruction within organization studies.

Pascale Caïdor is a doctoral student at the Université de Montréal, Canada. Her primary research interests include communication and diversity in organizations. She earned, in 2015, her master's degree in communication at the Université de Montréal. She teaches and conducts research on communication theory and organizational diversity.

She is scheduled to graduate with her Ph.D. in organizational communication in 2019.

François Cooren is Professor at the Université de Montréal, Canada. His research focuses on organizational communication, language and social interaction, and communication theory. He is a past president of the International Communication Association (ICA, 2010–2011), president of the International Association for Dialogue Analysis (IADA, 2012–2019) and former editor-in-chief of *Communication Theory* (2005–2008). He is also an ICA fellow since 2013 and an NCA distinguished scholar since 2017.

Gail T. Fairhurst is Distinguished University Research Professor of Organizational Communication at the University of Cincinnati, USA. She specializes in organizational and leadership communication processes, including those involving paradox, problem-centered leadership and framing. She is a Fellow of the International Communication Association, Distinguished Scholar of the National Communication Association, and a Fulbright Scholar.

Michael Grothe-Hammer is a postdoctoral researcher at the Institute of Social Sciences of the Helmut Schmidt University Hamburg, Germany. His current research focuses on characteristics and consequences of new forms of organization, the relationship between organization and society, and organization and digitalization. His works have been published in various outlets such as *Current Sociology, European Management Journal, Organizational Research Methods* and the *Journal of Public Administration Research and Theory*.

Michele H. Jackson is Professor and Dean of the Lyman Briggs College at Michigan State University, USA. Her research examines the interplay of communication technology with collaboration and group processes and has been published across disciplines, including communication, management, computer science and education.

Timothy Kuhn is Professor in the Department of Communication at the University of Colorado Boulder, USA. His research addresses the constitution of authority and agency in organizational action, with particular attention to how knowledge, identities and conceptions of value emerge in sociomaterial, power-laden communication practices. His research has been published in *Organization Studies, Academy of Management Review, Academy of Management Annals, Organization, Management Communication Quarterly* and *Communication Monographs*, among others.

Frédérik Matte is Assistant Professor of Communication at the University of Ottawa, Canada. He studies tensions in the extreme and emergency situations faced by international nongovernmental organizations (INGOs). He has published in the *Journal of Communication, Communication Monographs, Discourse and Communication* and *Pragmatics & Society*.

Dennis K. Mumby is the Cary C. Boshamer Distinguished Professor of Communication at the University of North Carolina at Chapel Hill, USA. His research focuses on the communicative dynamics of organizational control and resistance under neoliberalism. He is a Fellow of the International Communication Association and a National Communication Association Distinguished Scholar. He has authored or edited seven books and over 60 articles in the area of critical organization studies.

Amanda J. Porter is Assistant Professor in the KIN Center for Digital Innovation at the Vrije Universiteit Amsterdam, the Netherlands. Her research investigates how digital technologies play a role in tackling grand challenges in multi-stakeholder contexts. Publications include work in journals such as *Organization Studies, Journal of Computer Mediated Communication, The International Journal of Communication* and *Management Communication Quarterly*.

Linda L. Putnam is Distinguished Research Professor Emerita in the Department of Communication at the University of California, Santa Barbara, USA. Her current research interests include organizational tensions, materiality and space, and organizational conflict. She is the co-editor of *Building Theory of Organization: The Constitutive Role of Communication* (2009) and a constitutive approach to the study of contradictions and paradoxes in *The Academy of Management Annals* (2016).

Dennis Schoeneborn is Professor of Organization, Communication and CSR at Copenhagen Business School, Denmark, and Visiting Professor of Organization and Management at Leuphana University Lüneburg, Germany. His current research is concerned with the communicative constitution of new, alternative and rudimentary forms of organizing. His work has been published in the *Academy of Management Review, Human Relations, Journal of Management Studies, Management Communication Quarterly* and *Organization Studies*, among others.

Jens Seiffert-Brockmann is Senior Researcher at the Corporate Communication Research Group at the Department of Communication at the University of Vienna, Austria. His research interests are evolutionary psychology in strategic communication, gamification in organizational communication and memes in discourses, particularly Internet memes.

Mathew L. Sheep is Acting Associate Dean and Associate Professor of Management at Florida Gulf Coast University, USA. His research focuses on discursive perspectives of paradoxical tensions that dynamically construct and constrain organizational and individual identity work, innovation and change, and the navigation of work-home boundaries. His research has won several awards from the Academy of Management, the Society for Industrial and Organizational Psychology and the British Academy of Management.

Consuelo Vásquez is Associate Professor in the Département de Communication Sociale et Publique at the Université du Québec à Montréal, Canada. Her research interests include ethnography, project organizing, volunteering and the communication as constitutive of organizations. Her work appears in such venues as *Communication Theory*, *Human Relations* and *Qualitative Research in Organizations and Management*.

Peter Winkler is Professor at the FHWien—University of Applied Science for Management & Communication, Vienna, and Visiting Professor of Organizational Communication at the University of Salzburg, Austria. He is interested in sociological approaches to organizational and strategic communication research. His articles have appeared in such journals as *Business & Society*, *International Journal of Strategic Communication* and *Management Communication Quarterly*, among others.

References

Abbott, A. (2014). The problem of excess. *Sociological Theory*, *32*, 1–26.

Abdallah, C., Denis, J. L. & Langley, A. (2011). Having your cake and eating it too: Discourses of transcendence and their role in organizational change dynamics. *Journal of Organizational Change Management*, *24*(3), 333–348.

Abrahamson, E. (2002). Disorganization theory and disorganizing behavior: Towards an etiology of messes. *Research in Organization Behavior*, *24*, 139–180.

Acker, J. (1990). Hierarchies, jobs, bodies: A theory of gendered organizations. *Gender and Society*, *4*, 139–158.

Acker, J. (2006). Inequality regimes: Gender, class, and race in organizations. *Gender & Society*, *20*, 441–464.

Ackroyd, S. & Thompson, P. (1999). *Organizational misbehaviour*. London: Sage Publications.

Agarwal, V. & Buzzanell, P. M. (2015). Communicative reconstruction of resilience labor: Identity/identification in disaster-relief workers. *Journal of Applied Communication Research*, *43*(4), 408–428.

Ahmed, S. (2014). *Willful subjects*. Durham, NC: Duke University Press.

Ahmed, S. (2010a). Happy objects. In M. Gregg & G. J. Seigworth (Eds.), *The affect theory reader* (pp. 29–51). Durham, NC: Duke University Press.

Ahmed, S. (2010b). Killing joy: Feminism and the history of happiness. *Signs*, *35*(3), 571–594.

Ahmed, S. (2010c). *The promise of happiness*. Durham, NC: Duke University Press.

Ahmed, S. (2006). *Queer phenomenology: Orientations, objects, others*. Durham, NC: Duke University Press.

Ahrne, G. & Brunsson, N. (2011). Organization outside organizations: The significance of partial organization. *Organization*, *18*(1), 83–104.

Ahrne, G. & Brunsson, N. (2008). *Meta-organizations*. Cheltenham, UK: Edward Elgar.

Ahrne, G., Brunsson, N. & Seidl, D. (2016). Resurrecting organization by going beyond organizations. *European Management Journal*, *34*(2), 93–101.

Albu, O. B. & Etter, M. (2016). Hypertextuality and social media: A study of the constitutive and paradoxical implications of organizational Twitter use. *Management Communication Quarterly*, *30*(1), 5–31.

Alvesson, M. & Willmott, H. (2002). Identity regulation as organizational control: Producing the appropriate individual. *Journal of Management Studies*, *39*, 619–644.

Andersen, N. A. (2003). The undecidability of decision. In T. Bakken & T. Hernes (Eds.), *Autopoietic organization theory: Drawing on Niklas Luhmann's social systems perspective* (pp. 235–258). Oslo: Abstrakt.

Andrejevic, M. (2014). Surveillance in the big data era. *Emerging Pervasive Information and Communication Technologies (PICT)*, 11, 55–69.

Andriopoulos, C. & Lewis, M. W. (2009). Exploitation-exploration tensions and organizational ambidexterity: Managing paradoxes of innovation. *Organization Science*, 20(4), 696–717.

Apelt, M., Besio, C., Corsi, G., von Groddeck, V., Grothe-Hammer, M. & Tacke, V. (2017). Resurrecting organization without renouncing society: A response to Ahrne, Brunsson and Seidl. *European Management Journal*, 35(1), 8–14.

Apprich, C., Slater, J., Iles, A. & Schultz, O. (2014). *Plants, androids and operators: A post-media handbook*. Luneburg: PML Books.

Arvidsson, A. (2006). *Brands: Meaning and value in media culture*. London: Routledge.

Arvidsson, A. & Peitersen, N. (2013). *The ethical economy: Rebuilding value after the crisis*. New York: Columbia University Press.

Ashcraft, K. L. (2017). "Submission" to the rule of excellence: Ordinary affect and precarious resistance in the labour of organization and management studies. *Organization*, 24(1), 36–58.

Ashcraft, K. L. (2013). The glass slipper: "Incorporating" occupational identity in management studies. *Academy of Management Review*, 38(1), 6–31.

Ashcraft, K. L. & Kuhn, T. R. (2017). Agential encounters: Performativity and affect meet communication in the bathroom. In B. H. J. M. Brummans (Ed.), *The agency of organizing: Perspectives and case studies* (pp. 170–193). New York: Routledge.

Ashcraft, K. L., Kuhn, T. R. & Cooren, F. (2009). Constitutional amendments: "Materializing" organizational communication. *The Academy of Management Annals*, 3(1), 1–64. London: Routledge.

Ashcraft, K. L. & Mumby, D. K. (2004). *Reworking gender: A feminist communicology of organization*. Thousand Oaks, CA: Sage Publications.

Atkinson, P. (2014). *For ethnography*. London: Sage Publications.

Bader, B. & Berg, N. (2013). An empirical investigation of terrorism-induced stress on expatriate attitudes and performance. *Journal of International Management*, 19(2), 163–175.

Bakhtin, M. M. (1984). *Rabelais and his world*. Bloomington: Indiana University Press.

Bakker, R. M. (2010). Taking stock of temporary organizational forms: A systematic review and research agenda. *International Journal of Management Reviews*, 12(4), 466–486.

Bakker, R. M., De Fillippi, R. J., Schwab, A. & Sydow, J. (2016). Temporary organizing: Promises, processes, problems. *Organization Studies*, 37(12), 1703–1719.

Banerjee, A. (2015). *Writing silences into sociotechnical systems theory: The historiography of the Tavistock Institute's "Ahmedabad Experiment"*. (PhD Thesis). Lancaster: Lancaster University.

Banet-Weiser, S. (2012). *Authentic: The politics of ambivalence in a brand culture*. New York: New York University Press.

Barad, K. (2007). *Meeting the universe halfway: Quantum physics and the entanglement of matter and meaning*. Durham/London: Duke University Press.

Barad, K. (2003). Posthumanist performativity: Toward an understanding of how matter comes to matter. *Signs: Journal of Women in Culture and Society*, 28(3), 801–831.

Barsade, S. G. (2002). The ripple effect: Emotional contagion and its influence on group behavior. *Administrative Science Quarterly, 47*(4), 644–675.

Barton, M. A., Sutcliffe, K. M., Vogus, T. J. & DeWitt, T. (2015). Performing under uncertainty: Contextualized engagement in wildland firefighting. *Journal of Contingencies and Crisis Management, 23*(2), 74–83.

Bateson, G. (1972). *Steps to an ecology of mind.* New York: Ballatine Books.

Baudrillard, J. (1996). *The system of objects* (J. Benedict, Trans.). London: Verso.

Baxter, L. A. (2011). *Voicing relationships: A dialogic perspective.* Thousand Oaks, CA: Sage Publications.

Bean, H. & Buikema, R. J. (2015). Deconstituting al-Qa'ida: CCO theory and the decline and dissolution of hidden organizations. *Management Communication Quarterly, 29*(4), 512–538.

Becker, G. (1976). *The economic approach to human behavior.* Chicago: University of Chicago Press.

Beer, D. & Burrows, R. (2013). Popular culture, digital archives and the new social life of data. *Theory, Culture & Society, 30*(4), 47–71.

Bencherki, N. (2016). How things make things do things with words, or how to pay attention to what things have to say. *Communication Research and Practice, 2*(3), 272–289.

Bencherki, N. & Cooren, F. (2011). Having to be: The possessive constitution of organization. *Human Relations, 64,* 1579–1607. https://doi.org/10.1177/0018726711424227

Bencherki, N. (2009). Avoir ou ne pas être: Le langage et le matériel. In C. Lonneux & B. Parent (Eds.), *Actes du colloque international Jeunes chercheurs et recherches récentes* (pp. 101–106). Rennes, France. http://org-co2009.lescigales.org/ACTES-COLLOQUES.pdf

Bencherki, N., Matte, F. & Pelletier, É. (2016). Rebuilding Babel: A constitutive approach to Tongues-in-use. *Journal of Communication, 66*(5), 766–788.

Benkler, Y. & Nissenbaum, H. (2006). Commons-based peer production and virtue. *Journal of Political Philosophy, 14*(4), 394–419.

Bennett, J. (2012). Powers of the hoard: Further notes on material agency. In J. J. Cohen (Ed.), *Animal, vegetable, mineral: Ethics and objects* (pp. 237–269). Washington, DC: Oliphaunt.

Bennett, W. L. (2012). The personalization of politics: Political identity, social media, and changing patterns of participation. *The Annals of the American Academy of Political and Social Science, 644*(1), 20–39.

Bennett, W. L. & Segerberg, A. (2013). *The logic of connective action: Digital media and the personalization of collective action.* New York: Cambridge University Press.

Bennett, W. L., Segerberg, A. & Walker, S. (2014). Organization in the crowd: Peer production in large-scale networked protests. *Information, Communication & Society, 17*(2), 232–260.

Benoit-Barné, C. & Cooren, F. (2009). The accomplishment of authority through presentification: How authority is distributed among and negotiated by organizational members. *Management Communication Quarterly, 23*(1), 5–31.

Benson, J. K. (1977). Organizations: A dialectical view. *Administrative Science Quarterly, 22*(1), 1–21.

Bertanlanffy, L. V. (1950). The theory of open systems in physics and biology. *Science, 3,* 23–29.

Beynon, H. (1973). *Working for Ford.* London: Allen Lane.

Bisel, R. S. (2009). On a growing dualism in organizational discourse research. *Management Communication Quarterly, 22*(4), 614–638.

Bjerregaard, T. & Jonasson, C. (2014). Managing unstable institutional contradictions: The work of becoming. *Organization Studies, 35*(10), 1507–1536.

Blaschke, S. (2015). It's all in the network: A Luhmannian perspective on agency. *Management Communication Quarterly, 29*(3), 463–468.

Blaschke, S., Schoeneborn, D. & Seidl, D. (2012). Organizations as networks of communication episodes: Turning the network perspective inside out. *Organization Studies, 33*(7), 879–906.

Bloomfield, B. P. & Danieli, A. (1995). The role of management consultants in the development of information technology: The indissoluble nature of sociopolitical and technical skills. *Journal of Management Studies, 32*(1), 23–46.

Bloomfield, B. P. & Vurdubakis, T. (1997). Visions of organization and organizations of vision: The representational practices of information systems development. *Accounting, Organizations and Society, 22*(7), 639–668.

Bloomfield, B. P. & Vurdubakis, T. (1994). Re-presenting technology: IT consultancy as textual reality constructions. *Sociology, 28*(2), 455–478.

Boddy, C., Miles, D., Sanyal, C. & Hartog, M. (2015). Extreme managers, extreme workplaces: Capitalism, organizations and corporate psychopaths. *Organization, 22*(4), 530–551.

Böhm, S. & Land, C. (2012). The new "hidden abode": Reflections on value and labour in the new economy. *The Sociological Review, 60*, 217–240.

Bohnsack, R. (2014). Documentary method. In U. Flick (Ed.), *The sage handbook of qualitative data analysis* (pp. 217–233). London: Sage Publications.

Bohnsack, R. (2008). The interpretation of pictures and the documentary method. *Forum Qualitative Social Research, 9*(3), 1–24.

Boivin, G., Brummans, B. H. J. M. & Barker, J. R. (2017). The institutionalization of CCO scholarship: Trends from 2000 to 2015. *Management Communication Quarterly, 31*, 331–355.

Boltanski, L. & Chiapello, E. (2005). *The new spirit of capitalism* (G. Elliott, Trans.). London: Verso.

Bouchikhi, H. (1998). Living with and building on complexity: A constructivist perspective on organizations. *Organization, 5*(2), 217–232.

Bouty, I., Godé, C., Drucker-Godart, C., Lièvre, P., Nizet, J. & Pichault, F. (2012). Coordination practices in extreme situations. *European Management Journal, 30*(6), 475–489.

Brabham, D. C. & Guth, K. L. (2017). The deliberative politics of the consultative layer: Participation hopes and communication as design values of civic tech founders. *Journal of Communication, 67*(4), 445–475.

Brauman, R. (2006). Les liaisons dangereuses du témoignage humanitaire et des propagandes politiques. In *Crises extrêmes* (pp. 188–204). Paris: La Découverte.

Braverman, H. (1974). *Labor and monopoly capital: The degradation of work in the twentieth century*. New York: Monthly Review Press.

Brayne, S. (2017). Big data surveillance: The case of policing. *American Sociological Review, 82*(5), 977–1008.

Brewer, M. M. (1995). *Claude Simon: Narrativities without narrative*. Lincoln, NE: University of Nebraska Press.

Brighenti, A. (2010). *Visibility in social theory and social research*. New York: Palgrave Macmillan.

Brinker, D. L., Gastil, J. & Richards, R. C. (2015). Inspiring and informing citizens online: A media richness analysis of varied civic education modalities. *Journal of Computer-Mediated Communication, 20*(5), 504–519.

Bromley, P. & Powell, W. W. (2012). From smoke and mirrors to walking the talk: Decoupling in the contemporary world. *Academy of Management Annals, 6*(1), 483–530.

Brophy, E. (2017). *Language put to work: The making of the global call centre work force*. London: Palgrave MacMillan.

Brown, A. D., Colville, I. & Pye, A. (2017). Storytelling, mindfulness and high-reliability organizing. *Academy of Management Proceedings, 1,* 15235.

Bruch, E. & Feinberg, F. (2017). Decision-making processes in social contexts. *Annual Review of Sociology, 43*(1), 207–227.

Brummans, B. H. J. M. (2007). Death by document: Tracing the agency of a text. *Qualitative Inquiry, 13*(5), 711–727.

Brummans, B. H. J. M., Cooren, F., Robichaud, D. & Taylor, J. R. (2014). Approaches in research on the communicative constitution of organizations. In L. L. Putnam & D. Mumby (Eds.), *The Sage handbook of organizational communication* (3rd ed., pp. 173–194). Thousand Oaks, CA: Sage Publications.

Brunton, F. & Nissenbaum, H. (2015). *Obfuscation: A user's guide for privacy and protest.* Boston, MA: MIT Press.

Burawoy, M. (1979). *Manufacturing consent: Changes in the labor process under monopoly capitalism.* Chicago: University of Chicago Press.

Burnes, B. & Cooke, B. (2012). Review article: The past, present and future of organization development: Taking the long view. *Human Relation, 65*(11), 1395–1429.

Burns, T. (1961). Micropolitics: Mechanisms of institutional change. *Administrative Science Quarterly, 6*(3), 257–281.

Burrell, G. & Morgan, G. (1979). *Sociological paradigms and organizational analysis.* London: Heineman.

Burrows, R. & Ellison, N. (2004). Sorting places out? Towards a social politics of neighbourhood informatization. *Information Communication & Society, 7*(3), 321–336.

Burt, R. (2004). Structural holes and good ideas. *American Journal of Sociology, 110,* 349–399.

Butler, J. (1993). *Bodies that matter: On the discursive limits of "sex".* New York: Routledge.

Butler, J. (1990). *Gender trouble.* New York: Routledge.

Buzzanell, P. M. (2010). Resilience: Talking, resisting, and imagining new normalcies into being. *Journal of Communication, 60*(1), 1–14.

Byrne, D. & Pickard, A. J. (2016). Neogeography and the democratization of GIS: A metasynthesis of qualitative research. *Information, Communication & Society, 19*(11), 1505–1522.

Calás, M. & Smircich, L. (1999). Past postmodernism? Reflections and tentative directions. *Academy of Management Review, 24*(4), 649–671.

Callon, M. (2002). Writing and (re)writing devices as tools for managing complexity. In J. Law & A. Mol (Eds.), *Complexities: Social studies of knowledge practices* (pp. 191–218). Durham, NC: Duke University Press.

Callon, M. & Latour, B. (1981). Unscrewing the big Leviathan: How actors macro-structure reality and how sociologists help them to do so. In A. V. Cicourel & K. Knorr-Cetina (Eds.), *Advances in social theory and methodology: Towards an integration of micro-and macro-sociologies* (pp. 277–303). Boston, MA: Routledge/Kegan Paul.

Ceccarelli, L. (1998). Polysemy: Multiple meanings in rhetorical criticism. *Quarterly Journal of Speech, 84*(4), 395–415.

de Certeau, M. (1986). *Heterologies: Discourse on the other.* Manchester: Manchester University Press.

Cheney, D. & Munshi, D. (2017). Alternative forms of organizing and organization. In C. R. Scott & L. Lewis (Eds.), *The international encyclopedia of organizational communication.* Hoboken, NY: Wiley-Blackwell.

Chia, R. C. H. (2005). Organization theory as a postmodern science. In H. Tsoukas & C. Knudsen (Eds.), *The Oxford handbook of organization theory* (pp. 113–140). Oxford: Oxford University Press.

Chia, R. C. H. (1998). *In the realm of organization: Essays for Robert Cooper*. London: Routledge.

Chia, R. C. H. (1995). From modern to postmodern organizational analysis. *Organization Studies*, 16(4), 579–604.

Chia, R. C. H. & Kallinikos, J. (1998). Interview with Robert Cooper. In R. C. H. Chia (Ed.), *Organized worlds: Explorations in technology and organization with Robert Cooper* (pp. 121–165). London: Routledge.

Chia, R. C. H. & Tsoukas, H. (2003). Everything flows and nothing abides. *Process Studies*, 32(2), 196–224.

Ciote, C. S. (2012). Complexity theory and Hayekian natural order. *Economics, Management, and Financial Markets*, 7(4), 459–465.

Claes, L., Muller, A. & Luyckx, K. (2016). Compulsive buying and hoarding as identity substitutes: The role of materialistic value endorsement and depression. *Comprehensive Psychiatry*, 68, 65–71.

Clarke, A. (2005). *Situational analysis: Grounded theory after the Postmodern turn*. Thousand Oaks, CA: Sage Publications.

Clegg, S. R. (1975). *Power, rule, and domination*. New York: Routledge/Kegan Paul.

Clegg, S. R., Kornberger, M. & Rhodes, C. (2005). Learning/becoming/organizing. *Organization*, 12(2), 147–167.

Cohen, P. (2017, May 31). Steady jobs, with pay and hours that are anything but. *The New York Times*. Retrieved from www.nytimes.com/2017/05/31/business/economy/volatile-income-economy-jobs.html

Collinson, D. (1994). Strategies of resistance: Power, knowledge and resistance in the workplace. In J. M. Jermier, D. Knights & W. R. Nord (Eds.), *Resistance and power in organizations* (pp. 25–68). London: Routledge.

Collinson, D. (1992). *Managing the shop floor: Subjectivity, masculinity, and workplace culture*. New York: De Gruyter.

Comfort, L. K. (2002). Managing intergovernmental responses to terrorism and other extreme events. *Publius: The Journal of Federalism*, 32(4), 29–50.

Cooley, C. H. (1924). *Social organization: A study of the larger mind*. New York: Charles Scribner's Sons.

Cooper, R. (2001). Un-timely mediations: Questioning thought. *Ephemera*, 1(4), 321–347.

Cooper, R. (1992). Formal organization as representation: Remote control, displacement and abbreviation. In M. Reed & M. Hughes (Eds.), *Rethinking organization* (pp. 252–272). London: Sage Publications.

Cooper, R. (1990). Organization/disorganization. In J. Hassard & D. Pym (Eds.), *The theory and philosophy of organizations: Critical issues and new perspectives* (pp. 167–197). London: Routledge.

Cooper, R. (1989). Modernism, postmodernism and organizational analysis 3: The contribution of Jacques Derrida. *Organization Studies*, 10(4), 479–502.

Cooper, R. (1986). Organization/disorganization. *Social Science Information*, 25(2), 299–335.

Cooren, F. (In press). Materializing communication: Making the case for a relational ontology. *Journal of Communication*.

Cooren, F. (2018). Materializing communication: Making the case for a relational ontology. *Journal of Communication*, 68(2), 278–288.

Cooren, F. (2016). Ethics for dummies: Ventriloquism and responsibility. *Atlantic Journal of Communication*, 24(1), 17–30.

Cooren, F. (2015). *Organizational discourse: Communication and constitution*. London: Polity Press.

Cooren, F. (2012). Communication theory at the center: Ventriloquism and the communicative constitution of reality. *Journal of Communication*, 62, 1–20.

Cooren, F. (2010). *Action and agency in dialogue: Passion, incarnation, and ventriloquism.* Amsterdam/Philadelphia: John Benjamins.

Cooren, F. (2009). The haunting question of textual agency: Derrida and Garfinkel on iterability and eventfulness. *Research on Language and Social Interaction, 42*(1), 42–67.

Cooren, F. (2006). The organizational world as a plenum of agencies. In F. Cooren, J. R. Taylor & E. J. Van Every (Eds.), *Communication as organizing: Practical approaches to research into the dynamic of text and conversation* (pp. 81–100). Mahwah, NJ: Lawrence Erlbaum.

Cooren, F. (2004). Textual agency: How texts do things in organizational settings. *Organization, 11*(3), 373–393.

Cooren, F. (2000). *The organizing property of communication.* Amsterdam/Philadelphia: John Benjamins.

Cooren, F., Bencherki, N., Chaput, C. & Vásquez, C. (2015). The communicative constitution of strategy-making: Exploring fleeting moments of strategy. In D. Golsorkhi, L. Rouleau, D. Seidl & E. Vaara (Eds.), *Cambridge handbook of strategy as practice* (2nd ed., pp. 365–388). Cambridge, UK: Cambridge University Press.

Cooren, F., Brummans, B. H. J. M. & Charrieras, D. (2008). The coproduction of organizational presence: A study of Médecins Sans Frontières in action. *Human Relations, 61*(10), 1339–1370.

Cooren, F. & Fairhurst, G. T. (2009). Dislocation and stabilization: How to scale up from interactions to organization. In L. L. Putnam & A. M. Nicotera (Eds.), *Building theory of organization: The constitutive role of communication* (pp. 117–152). London: Routledge/Taylor & Francis.

Cooren, F., Fairhurst, G. T. & Huët, R. (2012). Why matter always matters in (organizational) communication. *Materiality and Organizing: Social Interaction in a Technological World*, 296–314.

Cooren, F., Kuhn, T., Cornelissen, J. P. & Clark, T. (2011). Communication, organizing and organization: An overview and introduction to the special issue. *Organization Studies, 32*(9), 1149–1170.

Cooren, F., Matte, F., Benoit-Barné, C. & Brummans, B. H. J. M. (2013). Communication as ventriloquism: A grounded-in-action approach to the study of organizational tensions. *Communication Monographs, 80*(3), 255–277.

Cooren, F. & Robichaud, D. (2010). Les approches constitutives. In S. Grosjean & L. Bonneville (Eds.), *la communication organisationnelle* (pp. 140–175). Montreal, Canada: Chenelière.

Cooren, F. & Sandler, S. (2014). Polyphony, ventriloquism, and constitution: In dialogue with Bakhtin. *Communication Theory, 24*(3), 225–244.

Costanza-Chock, S. (2004). The whole world is watching: Online surveillance of social movement organizations. In P. N. Thomas & Z. Nain (Eds.), *Who Owns the media* (pp. 271–292). London: Zed Books.

Costas, J. & Grey, C. (2014). Bringing secrecy into the open: Towards a theorization of the social processes of organizational secrecy. *Organizational Studies, 35*(10), 1–25.

Couldry, N. & Turow, J. (2014). Advertising, big data and the clearance of the public realm: Marketers' new approaches to the content subsidy. *International Journal of Communication, 8*, 1710–1726.

Craig, R. T. (2015). The constitutive metamodel: A 16-year review. *Communication Theory, 25*(4), 356–374.

Cruz, J. (2017). Invisibility and visibility in alternative organizing: A communicative and cultural model. *Management Communication Quarterly, 31*(4), 614–639.

Cunha, M. P., Clegg, S. R. & Kamoche, K. (2006). Surprises in management and organization: Concept, sources and a typology. *British Journal of Management, 17*(4), 317–329.

Cunha, M. P. & Gomes, J. F. S. (2003). Order and disorder in product innovation models. *Creativity and Innovation Management, 12*(3), 174–187.

Curran, J., Fenton, N. & Freedman, D. (2012). *(Mis)understanding the Internet.* New York: Routledge.

Currie, G. & Kerrin, M. (2004). The limits of a technological fix to knowledge management: Epistemological, political and cultural issues in the case of intranet implementation. *Management Learning, 35*(1), 9–29.

Dahlgren, P. (2013). *The political web: Media, participation and alternative democracy.* Basingstoke: Palgrave Macmillan.

Dalhuisen, J. (2015, June). *Expulsion throws spotlight on Morocco human rights.* Retrieved from www.amnesty.org/en/latest/news/2015/06/expulsion-throws-spotlight-on-morocco-human-rights/

Dave, S. P. (1956). *Regarding matter of conducting the experiment of the Group System in the Ring Frame Department of the Calico Mills.* [Letter] Folder: "Calico Mills 1956 visit. Working Notes 1956 & 1958", Box: 205802435 Eric Miller A.K. Rice Calico Mills (1) EJM. London: TIHR Archives.

Davis, A. (2010). New media and fat democracy: The paradox of online participation. *New Media & Society, 12*(5), 745–761.

Dawkins, C. E. & Barker, J. R. (2018). A complexity theory framework for issue movement. *Business & Society.* https://doi.org/10.1177/0007650318762404

Dean, J. (2014). Communicative capitalism: This is what democracy looks like. In J. S. Hanan & M. Hayward (Eds.), *Communication and the economy: History, value, and agency* (pp. 147–164). New York: Peter Lang.

Dean, J. (2012). *The communist horizon.* London: Verso.

Dean, J. (2009). *Democracy and other neoliberal fantasies: Communicative capitalism and left politics.* Durham, NC: Duke University Press.

Deetz, S. (2003). Reclaiming the legacy of the linguistic turn. *Organization, 10,* 421–429.

Deetz, S. (1992). *Democracy in an age of corporate colonization: Developments in communication and the politics of everyday life.* Albany, NY: State University of New York Press.

Deleuze, G. & Guattari, F. (1987). *A thousand plateaus* (B. Massumi, Trans.). Minneapolis: University of Minnesota Press.

Den Hond, F. & De Bakker, F. G. (2007). Ideologically motivated activism: How activist groups influence corporate social change activities. *Academy of Management Review, 32*(3), 901–924.

Derrida, J. (2002). *Negotiations: Interventions and interviews, 1971–2001.* Stanford, CA: Stanford University Press.

Derrida, J. (1988). *Limited Inc.* Evanston, IL: Northwestern University Press.

Derrida, J. (1981). *Dissemination.* London: The Athlone Press.

Derrida, J. (1978). *Of grammatology.* Baltimore, MD: Johns Hopkins University Press.

de Saussure, F. (1974). *Course in general linguistics.* London: Fontana/Collins.

Dicks, H. V. (1970). *Fifty years of the Tavistock clinic.* London: Routledge/Kegan Paul.

Dirksen, V., Huizing, A. & Smit, B. (2010). "Piling on layers of understanding": The use of connective ethnography for the study of (online) work practices. *New Media & Society, 12*(7), 1045–1063.

Dobusch, L. & Schoeneborn, D. (2015). Fluidity, identity, and organizationality: The communicative constitution of Anonymous. *Journal of Management Studies, 52*(8), 1005–1035.

Doerfel, M. L., Chewning, L. V. & Lai, C. H. (2013). The evolution of networks and the resilience of interorganizational relationships after disaster. *Communication Monographs*, *80*(4), 533–559.

Doherty, N. F. (2014). The role of socio-technical principles in leveraging meaningful benefits from IT investments. *Applied Ergonomics*, *45*(2), 181–187.

Duffy, B. E. (2017). *On (not) getting paid to do what you love: Gender, social media, and aspirational work*. New Haven, CT: Yale University Press.

Duffy, B. E. (2015). The romance of work: Gender and aspirational labour in the digital culture industries. *International Journal of Cultural Studies*, *19*(4), 441–457.

Duffy, B. E. & Hund, E. (2015). "Having it all" on social media: Entrepreneurial femininity and self-branding among fashion bloggers. *Social Media & Society*, 1–11.

Du Gay, P. (1996). *Consumption and identity at work*. London: Sage Publications.

Eason, K. (2014). Afterword: The past, present and future of sociotechnical systems theory. *Applied Ergonomics*, *45*(2), 213–220.

Ebbers, J. J. & Wijnberg, N. M. (2017). Betwixt and between: Role conflict, role ambiguity and role definition in project-based dual-leadership structures. *Human Relations*, *70*(11), 1342–1365.

Eddy, C. (2014). The art of consumption: Capitalist excess and individual Psychosis in *hoarders*. *Canadian Review of American Studies*, *44*(1), 1–24.

Edwards, R. (1979). *Contested terrain: The transformation of the workplace in the twentieth century*. New York: Basic Books.

ElementsBehavioralHealth. (2013). *DSM-V: Hoarding new mental-disorder diagnoses*. Retrieved from www.elementsbehavioralhealth.com/mental-health/dsm-v-hoarding-new-mental-disorder-diagnoses/

Emirbayer, M. (1997). Manifesto for a relational sociology. *American Journal of Sociology*, *103*, 281–217.

Endrissat, N., Kärreman, D. & Noppeny, C. (2017). Incorporating the creative subject: Branding outside-in through identity incentives. *Human Relations*, *70*, 488–515.

Ettlinger, N. (2018). Algorithmic affordances for productive resistance. *Big Data & Society*, *5*(1).

Eversole, R. (2011). Community agency and community engagement: Re-theorising participation in governance. *Journal of Public Policy*, *31*(1), 51–71.

Fairhurst, G. T. & Sheep, M. L. (In press). 'If you have to say you are, you aren't': Paradoxes of Trumpian identity work knotting in a post-truth context. In A. D. Brown (Ed.), *The Oxford Handbook of Identities in Organizations*. Oxford University Press.

Fairhurst, G. T. & Putnam, L. L. (In press). An integrative methodology for organizational oppositions: Aligning grounded theory and discourse analysis. *Organizational Research Methods*. DOI.org/10.1177%2F1094428118776771

Farjoun, M. (2010). Beyond dualism: Stability and change as a duality. *Academy of Management Review*, *35*(2), 202–225.

Fassauer, G. (2017). Organization as communication and Honneth's notion of struggles for recognition. In S. Blaschke & D. Schoeneborn (Eds.), *Organization as communication: Perspectives in dialogue* (pp. 27–44). New York: Routledge/Taylor & Francis.

Feenberg, A. (2002). *Transforming technology: A critical theory revisited*. Oxford: Oxford University Press.

Ferraro, F., Etzion, D. & Gehman, J. (2015). Tackling grand challenges pragmatically: Robust action revisited. *Organization Studies*, *36*(3), 363–390.

Fischer, F. (2009). *Democracy and expertise: Reorienting policy inquiry*. Oxford: Oxford University Press.

Fleming, P. (2017). The human capital hoax: Work, debt and insecurity in the era of Uberization. *Organization Studies, 38*, 691–705.

Fleming, P. (2014). When "life itself" goes to work: Reviewing shifts in organizational life through the lens of biopower. *Human Relations, 67*, 875–901.

Fleming, P. & Sewell, G. (2002). Looking for the good soldier, Svejk: Alternative modalities of resistance in the contemporary workplace. *Sociology, 36*, 857–873.

Florida, R. (2003). *The rise of the creative class: And how it's transforming work, leisure, community and everyday life*. New York: Basic Books.

Flyverbom, M. (2016). Transparency: Mediation and the management of visibilities. *International Journal of Communication, 10*, 110–122.

Flyverbom, M., Leonardi, P., Stohl, C. & Stohl, M. (2016). The management of visibilities in the digital age. *International Journal of Communication, 10*, 98–109.

Follett, M. P. (1926). The giving of orders. *Scientific Foundations of Business Administration*, 29–37.

Fortes, M. (1955). Radcliffe-Brown's contributions to the study of social organization. *The British Journal of Sociology, 6*(1), 16–30.

Foucault, M. (2008). *The birth of biopolitics: Lectures at the Collège de France, 1978–1979* (G. Burchell, Trans.). Basingstoke: Palgrave Macmillan.

Foucault, M. (1980). *Power/knowledge: Selected interviews and other writings 1972–1977* (C. Gordon, L. Marshall, J. Mepham & K. Soper, Trans.). New York: Pantheon.

Foucault, M. (1979a). *Discipline and punish: The birth of the prison* (A. Sheridan, Trans.). New York: Vintage.

Foucault, M. (1979b). Governmentality. *Ideology and Consciousness, 6*, 5–21.

Foucault, M. (1970). *The order of things: An archaeology of the human sciences*. New York: Pantheon.

Fox, R. C. (2014). *Doctors without borders: Humanitarian quests, impossible dreams of medecins sans frontieres*. Baltimore, MD: Johns Hopkins University Press.

FPU. (2016, January 20). *Hicham Mansouri released after 10 months in prison*. Retrieved from www.freepressunlimited.org/en/news/hicham-mansouri-released-after-10-months-in-prison

Frank, L. K. (1944). What is social order? *American Journal of Sociology, 49*(5), 470–477.

Freelon, D. & Karpf, D. (2015). Of big birds and bayonets: Hybrid Twitter interactivity in the 2012 Presidential debates. *Information, Communication & Society, 18*(4), 390–406.

Friedman, G. (2014). Workers without employers: Shadow corporations and the rise of the gig economy. *Review of Keynesian Economics, 2*(2), 171–188.

Frost, R. O. & Hartl, T. L. (1996). A cognitive-behavioral model of compulsive hoarding. *Behaviour Research and Therapy, 34*, 341–350.

Frost, R. O., Hartl, T. L., Christian, R. & Williams, N. (1995). The value of possessions in compulsive hoarding: Patterns of use and attachment. *Behaviour Research and Therapy, 33*, 897–902.

Frost, R. O. & Steketee, G. (2010). *Stuff: Compulsive hoarding and the meaning of things*. Boston, MA: Houghton Mifflin Harcourt.

Fuchs, S. (2001). *Against essentialism: A theory of culture and society*. Cambridge, UK: Harvard University Press.

Geier, M. T. (2016). Leadership in extreme contexts: Transformational leadership, performance beyond expectations? *Journal of Leadership & Organizational Studies, 23*(3), 234–247.

Gelfand, M. (2018). *Rule makers, rule breakers: How tight and loose cultures wire our world*. New York: Scribner.

Ghose, R. (2005). The complexities of citizen participation through collaborative governance. *Space and Polity, 9*(1), 61–75.

Giddens, A. (1979). *Central problems in social theory: Action, structure and contradiction in social analysis*. Berkeley: University of California Press.

Gilbert, G. N. & Mulkay, M. J. (1984). *Opening Pandora's box: A sociological analysis of scientists' discourse*. Cambridge, UK: Cambridge University Press.

Gill, R. & Pratt, A. (2008). In the social factory? Immaterial labour, precariousness and cultural work. *Theory, Culture & Society, 25*(7–8), 1–30.

Gillespie, T. (2014). The relevance of algorithms. In T. Gillespie, P. Boczkowski & K. Foot (Eds.), *Media technologies: Essays on communication, materiality, and society* (pp. 167–194). Cambridge, MA: MIT Press.

Girin, J. (1990). Analyse empirique des situations de gestion: Éléments de théorie et de méthode. In A. C. Martinet (Ed.), *Epistémologie et sciences de gestion* (pp. 141–182). Paris: Economica.

Godart, F. C. & White, H. C. (2010). Switchings under uncertainty: The coming and becoming of meanings. *Poetics, 38*, 567–586.

Goffey, A. (2008). Algorithm. In M. Fuller (Ed.), *Software studies: A Lexicon* (pp. 15–20). Cambridge, MA: MIT Press.

Goffman, E. (1961). *Asylums: Essays on the social situation of mental patients and other inmates*. New York: Basic Books.

González, A., Gilmer, A., Foley, R., Sweeney, J. & Fry, J. (2008). Technology-aided participative methods in environmental assessment: An international perspective. *Computers, Environment and Urban Systems, 32*(4), 303–316.

Gordon, E. & Baldwin-Philippi, J. (2014). Playful civic learning: Enabling lateral trust and reflection in game-based public participation. *International Journal of Communication, 8*(28), 759–786.

Gordon, E., Schirra, S. & Hollander, J. (2011). Immersive planning: A conceptual model for designing public participation with new technologies. *Environment and Planning B: Planning and Design, 38*(3), 505–519.

Gornostaeva, G. & Pratt, A. (2005). Digitisation and face-to-face interactions: The example of the film industry in London. *International Journal of Technology, Knowledge and Society, 1*(3), 101–108.

Gorz, A. (2010). *The immaterial: Knowledge, value and capital*. London: Seagull Books.

Gramsci, A. (1971). *Selections from the prison notebooks* (Q. Hoare & G. N. Smith, Trans.). New York: International Publishers.

Granovetter, M. (1973). The strength of weak ties. *American Journal of Sociology, 78*, 1360–1380.

Greenberg, A. (2015). *Hacking Team Breach Shows a Global Spying Firm Run Amok*. Retrieved November 16, 2018 from https://www.wired.com/2015/07/hacking-team-breach-shows-global-spying-firm-run-amok/

Grossberg, L. (2018). *Under the cover of chaos: Trump and the battle for the American right*. London: Pluto Press.

Grothe-Hammer, M. (2017). Preparing for the field by topics: A systems theory inspired strategy for improving social access. *Systems Research and Behavioral Science, 34*(1), 41–50.

Grothe-Hammer, M. (2015). "You watch that the maniac finishes in time": On the balance of power between the director and production manager in film projects. *SCM Studies in Communication\Media, 4*(3), 189–247.

Grothe-Hammer, M. (In press). Membership or contributorship? Managing the inclusion of individuals into organizations. In G. Ahrne & N. Brunsson (Eds.),

Organization outside organizations. Cambridge, UK: Cambridge University Press.

Gumprecht, H.-P. (2002). *Ruhe bitte! Aufnahmeleitung bei Film und Fernsehen* (2nd ed.). Konstanz: UVK.

Habermas, J. (1987). *The theory of communicative action: Lifeworld and system* (Vol. 2, T. McCarthy, Trans.). Boston, MA: Beacon Press.

Hall, S. & O'Shea, A. (2013). Common-sense neoliberalism. *Soundings: A Journal of Politics and Culture, 55*, 1–18.

Hällgren, M. (2016). Situated teams: Dropping tools on Mount Everest. *Project Management in Extreme Situations: Lessons from Polar Expeditions, Military and Rescue Operations, and Wilderness Exploration, 171*.

Hällgren, M., Rouleau, L. & De Rond, M. (2018). A matter of life or death: How extreme context research matters for management and organization studies. *Academy of Management Annals, 12*(1), 111–153.

Hannah, S. T., Uhl-Bien, M., Avolio, B. J. & Cavarretta, F. L. (2009). A framework for examining leadership in extreme contexts. *The Leadership Quarterly, 20*(6), 897–919.

Hänska Ahy, M. (2014). Networked communication and the Arab Spring: Linking broadcast and social media. *New Media and Society, 18*(1), 1–18.

Harvey, D. (1989). *The condition of postmodernity: An enquiry into the origins of cultural change*. Oxford: Basil Blackwell.

Hassard, J. (2012). Rethinking the Hawthorne Studies: The Western Electric research in its social, political and historical context. *Human Relations, 65*, 1431–1461.

Hassard, J., Kelemen, M. & Cox, J. W. (2008). *Disorganization theory: Explorations in alternative organizational analysis*. London: Routledge.

Hegel, G. W. F. (1969). *The philosophy of history* (J. Sibree, Trans.). New York: Wiley-Blackwell.

Helin, J., Hernes, T., Hjorth, D. & Holt, R. (Eds.). (2014). *The Oxford handbook of process philosophy and organization studies*. Oxford: Oxford University Press.

Heller, N. (2017, May 15). Is the gig economy working? *The New Yorker*. Retrieved from www.newyorker.com/magazine/2017/05/15/is-the-gig-economy-working

Hernes, T. (2008). *Understanding organization as process: Theory for a tangled world*. New York: Routledge.

Herring, S. (2011a). Collyer curiosa: A brief history of hoarding. *Criticism, 53*(2), 159–188.

Herring, S. (2011b). Material deviance: Theorizing queer objecthood. *Postmodern Culture, 21*(2), 1–15.

Hine, C. (2015). *Ethnography for the Internet: Embedded, embodied, and everyday*. London: Bloomsbury.

Hobday, M. (2000). The project-based organisation: An ideal form for managing complex products and systems? *Research Policy, 29*(7), 871–893.

Hoffmann, J. (2018). Talking into (non) existence: Denying or constituting paradoxes of corporate social responsibility. *Human Relations, 71*(5), 668–691.

Holt, D. B. (2002). Why do brands cause trouble? A dialectical theory of consumer culture and branding. *Journal of Consumer Research, 29*, 70–90.

Holyfield, L., Jonas, L. & Zajicek, A. (2005). Adventure without risk is like Disneyland. In S. Lyng (Ed.), *Edgework: The sociology of risk-taking* (pp. 173–186). New York: Routledge.

Honneth, A. (1997). Recognition and moral obligation. *Social Research, 64*(1), 16–35.

Honneth, A. (1996). *The struggle for recognition*. Cambridge: Polity Press.

Hopfer, S. & MacEachren, A. M. (2007). Leveraging the potential of geospatial annotations for collaboration: A communication theory perspective. *International Journal of Geographical Information Science, 21*(8), 921–934.

Hristova, S. (2014). Visual memes as neutralizers of political dissent. *Journal for a Global Sustainable Information Society*, 12(1), 265–276.

Hudson, J. (2012, June 8). The Muppet theory that explains humanity. *The Atlantic*. Retrieved from www.theatlantic.com/entertainment/archive/2012/06/muppet-theory-explains-humanity/327133/

Husserl, E. (1948). *Erfahrung und Urteil: Untersuchungen zur Genealogie der Logik*. Hamburg: Claassen & Goverts.

Hutchby, I. (2014). Communicative affordances and participation frameworks in mediated interaction. *Journal of Pragmatics*, 72, 86–89.

Hutchby, I. (2001). Technologies, texts and affordances. *Sociology*, 35(2), 441–456.

Illouz, E. (2007). *Cold intimacies: The making of emotional capitalism*. Cambridge: Polity Press.

Innes, J. E. & Booher, D. E. (2004). Reframing public participation: Strategies for the 21st century. *Planning Theory & Practice*, 5(4), 419–436.

James, W. (1912/1976). *Essays in radical empiricism*. Cambridge, MA: Harvard University Press.

Jankowski, P. (2009). Towards participatory geographic information systems for community: Based environmental decision-making. *Journal of Environmental Management*, 90(6), 1966–1971.

Jarzabkowski, P. A. & Kaplan, S. (2015). Strategy tools-in-use: A framework for understanding "technologies of rationality" in practice. *Strategic Management Journal*, 36(4), 537–558.

Jarzabkowski, P. A. & Lê, J. K. (2017). We have to do this *and* that? You must be joking: Constructing and responding to paradox through humor. *Organization Studies*, 38(3–4), 433–462.

Jarzabkowski, P. A., Lê, J. K. & Van de Ven, A. H. (2013). Responding to competing strategic demands: How organizing, belonging, and performing paradoxes coevolve. *Strategic Organization*, 11(3), 245–280.

Jayyusi, L. (1984). *Categorization and the moral order*. Boston, MA: Routledge/Kegan Paul.

Jeffcutt, P. & Thomas, M. (1998). Order, disorder and unmanageability of boundaries in organizational life. In R. Chia (Ed.), *In the realm of organization: Essays for Robert Cooper* (pp. 67–87). London: Routledge.

Kannappan, S. (1962). Gandhian model of unionism in a developing economy: The TLA in India. *Industrial and Labor Relations Review*, 16(1), 86–110.

Kapucu, N. (2005). Interorganizational coordination in dynamic context: Networks in emergency response management. *Connections*, 26(2), 33–48.

Katz, Y. & Shifman, L. (2017). Making sense? The structure and meanings of digital memetic nonsense. *Information, Communication & Society*, 20(6), 825–842.

Kavada, A. (2016). Social movements and political agency in the digital age: A communication approach. *Media and Communication*, 4(4), 8–12.

Keenoy, T. & Oswick, C. (2004). Organizing textscapes. *Organization Studies*, 25(1), 135–142.

Kellett, S., Greenhalgh, R., Beail, N. & Ridgway, N. (2010). Compulsive hoarding: An interpretative phenomenological analysis. *Behavioural and Cognitive Psychotherapy*, 38, 141–155.

Kellett, S. & Holden, K. (2014). Emotional attachment to objects in hoarding: A critical review. In R. O. Frost & G. Steketee (Eds.), *The Oxford handbook of hoarding and acquiring* (pp. 120–138). Oxford: Oxford University Press.

Keyton, J. (2011). *Communication & organizational culture: A key to understanding work experiences* (2nd ed.). Thousand Oaks, CA: Sage Publications.

Khandker, W. (2016). Henri Bergson: Toward a philosophy of becoming. *The SAGE Handbook of Process Organization Studies*, 43.

Kim, Y. C. & Ball-Rokeach, S. J. (2006). Civic engagement from a communication infrastructure perspective. *Communication Theory, 16*(2), 173–197.

Kings, C. A., Moulding, R. & Knight, T. (2017). You are what you own: Reviewing the link between possessions, emotional attachment, and the self-concept in hoarding disorder. *Journal of Obsessive-Compulsive and Related Disorders, 14*, 51–58.

Knox, H., O'Doherty, D. P., Vurdubakis, T. & Westrup, C. (2015). Something happened: Spectres of organization/disorganization at the airport. *Human Relations, 68*(6), 1001–1020.

Knox, H., O'Doherty, D. P., Vurdubakis, T. & Westrup, C. (2007). Rites of passage: Organization as an excess of flows. *Scandinavian Journal of Management, 23*, 265–284.

Koch, J. (2017). Organization as communication and the emergence of leadership: A Luhmannian perspective. In S. Blaschke & D. Schoeneborn (Eds.), *Organization as communication: Perspectives in dialogue* (pp. 121–140). New York: Routledge.

Kornberger, M. (2015). Think different: On studying the brand as valuation device. *International Studies of Management & Organization, 45*(2), 105–113.

Kornberger, M. (2010). *Brand society: How brands transform management and lifestyle.* Cambridge, UK: Cambridge University Press.

Kreiner, G. E., Hollensbe, E. C., Sheep, M. L., Smith, B. R. & Kataria, N. (2015). Elasticity and the dialectic tensions of organizational identity: How can we hold together while we're pulling apart? *Academy of Management Journal, 58*(4), 981–1011.

Kristeva, J. (1984). *Revolution in Poetic language.* New York: Columbia University Press.

Kuhn, T. (2017). Developing a communicative imagination under contemporary capitalism: The domain of organizational communication as a mode of explanation. *Management Communication Quarterly, 31*, 116–122.

Kuhn, T. (2012). Negotiating the micro-macro divide: Communicative thought leadership for theorizing organization. *Management Communication Quarterly, 26*, 543–584.

Kuhn, T. (2008). A communicative theory of the firm: Developing an alternative perspective on intra-organizational power and stakeholder relationships. *Organization Studies, 29*(8–9), 1227–1254.

Kuhn, T., Ashcraft, K. L. & Cooren, F. (2017). *The work of communication: Relational perspectives on working and organizing in contemporary capitalism.* London: Routledge/Taylor & Francis.

Kumar, S. (2015). Contagious memes, viral videos and subversive parody: The grammar of contention on the Indian web. *International Communication Gazette, 77*(3), 232–247.

Kumar, S. & Combe, K. (2015). Political parody and satire as subversive speech in the global digital sphere. *International Communication Gazette, 77*(3), 211–214.

Kunda, G. (1992). *Engineering culture: Control and commitment in a high-tech corporation.* Philadelphia: Temple University Press.

Kushner, D. (2016, April 26). Fear this man. *Foreign Policy.* Retrieved from http://foreignpolicy.com/2016/04/26/fear-this-man-cyber-warfare-hacking-team-david-vincenzetti/

Land, C. & Taylor, S. (2010). Surf's up: Work, life, balance and brand in a new age capitalist organization. *Sociology, 44*, 395–413.

Langenmayr, F. (2016). *Organizational memory as a function: The construction of past, present, and future in organizations.* Wiesbaden: Springer VS.

Langley, A. & Tsoukas, H. (2017). Introduction: Process thinking, process theorizing and process researching. In *The Sage handbook of process organizational studies* (pp. 1–25). Los Angeles, CA: SAGE.

Latour, B. (2013a). *An inquiry into modes of existence: An anthropology of the moderns.* Cambridge, MA: Harvard University Press.

Latour, B. (2013b). "What's the story?" Organizing as a mode of existence. In D. Robichaud & F. Cooren (Eds.), *Organization and organizing: Materiality, agency, and discourse* (pp. 37–51). New York: Routledge.

Latour, B. (2012). *We have never been modern.* Cambridge, MA: Harvard University Press.

Latour, B. (2005). *Reassembling the social: An introduction to actor-network-theory.* Oxford: Oxford University Press.

Latour, B. (2004). Why has critique run out of steam? From matters of fact to matters of concern. *Critical Inquiry, 30*(2), 225–248.

Latour, B. (1999). On recalling ANT. *The Sociological Review, 47*(S1), 15–25.

Latour, B. (1996). On interobjectivity. *Mind, Culture, and Activity, 3*(4), 228–245.

Latour, B. (1987). *Science in action.* Milton-Keynes: Open University Press.

Law, J. (2004). *After method: Mess in social science research.* New York, NY: Routledge.

Law, J. (2002). *Aircraft stories.* Durham, NC: Duke University Press.

Law, J. (1994). *Organizing modernity.* Oxford: Blackwell.

Law, J. & Singleton, V. (2005). Object lessons. *Organization, 12*, 331–355.

Lazzarato, M. (2009). Neoliberalism in action: Inequality, insecurity and the reconstitution of the social. *Theory, Culture & Society, 26*(6), 109–133.

Lazzarato, M. (2004). From capital-labour to capital-life. *Ephemera, 4*(3), 187–208.

Leonardi, P. M. (2017). Methodological guidelines for the study of materiality and affordances. In M. Raza & S. Jain (Eds.), *Routledge companion to qualitative research in organization studies* (pp. 279–290). New York: Routledge.

Leonardi, P. (2011). When flexible routines meet flexible technologies: Affordance, constraint, and the imbrication of human and material agencies. *MIS Quarterly, 35*(1), 147–167.

Leonardi, P. M., Nardi, B. A. & Kallinikos, J. (2012). *Materiality and organizing: Social interaction in a technological world.* Oxford, UK: Oxford University Press on Demand.

Lepselter, S. (2011). The disorder of things: Hoarding narratives in popular media. *Anthropological Quarterly, 84*(4), 919–948.

Leszczynski, A. (2014). On the neo in neogeography. *Annals of the Association of American Geographers, 104*(1), 60–79.

Lewis, M. W. (2000). Exploring paradox: Toward a more comprehensive guide. *Academy of Management Review, 25*(4), 760–776.

Lewis, M. W. & Smith, W. K. (2014). Paradox as a metatheoretical perspective: Sharpening the focus and widening the scope. *Journal of Applied Behavioral Science, 50*(2), 127–149.

Lincoln, Y. S. & Guba, E. G. (1986). But is it rigorous? Trustworthiness and authenticity in naturalistic evaluation. In D. D. Williams (Ed.), *Naturalistic evaluation* (pp. 73–84). San Francisco, CA: Jossey-Bass.

Lindebaum, D. & Gabriel, Y. (2016). Anger and organization studies: From social disorder to moral order. *Organization Studies, 37*(7), 903–918.

Linden, A. & Klandermans, B. (2007). Revolutionaries, wanderers, converts, and compliants: Life histories of extreme right activists. *Journal of Contemporary Ethnography, 36*(2), 184–201.

Lindlof, T. R. & Taylor, B. C. (2010). *Qualitative communication research methods*. Thousand Oaks, CA: Sage Publications.

Lithwick, D. (2012, June 8). Chaos theory: A unified theory of Muppet types. *Slate*. Retrieved from www.slate.com/articles/life/low_concept/2012/06/what_kind_of_muppet_are_you_chaos_or_order_.html

Lorey, I. (2015). *State of insecurity: Government of the precarious* (A. Derieg, Trans.). London: Verso.

Ludvig, E. A., Madan, C. R. & Spetch, M. L. (2014). Extreme outcomes sway risky decisions from experience. *Journal of Behavioral Decision Making*, 27(2), 146–156.

Luhman, J. T. & Cunliffe, A. L. (2013). *Key concepts in organization theory*. London: Sage Publications.

Luhmann, N. (2018). *Organization and decision*. Cambridge, UK: Cambridge University Press.

Luhmann, N. (2013). *Introduction to systems theory*. Cambridge, UK: Polity Press.

Luhmann, N. (2006). System as difference. *Organization*, 13(1), 37–57.

Luhmann, N. (2003). Organization. In T. Bakken & T. Hernes (Eds.), *Autopoietic organization theory: Drawing on Niklas Luhmanns social systems perspective* (pp. 31–52). Copenhagen, DK: Copenhagen Business School Press.

Luhmann, N. (2002). How can the mind participate in communication? In N. Luhmann & W. Rasch (Eds.), *Theories of distinction: Redescribing the descriptions of modernity* (pp. 169–184). Stanford: Stanford University Press.

Luhmann, N. (1996). Membership and motives in social systems. *Systems Research*, 13(3), 341–348.

Luhmann, N. (1995). *Social systems*. Stanford, CA: Stanford University Press.

Luhmann, N. (1993). Ecological communication: Coping with the unknown. *Systems Practice*, 6(5), 527–539.

Luhmann, N. (1992). What is communication? *Communication Theory*, 2(3), 251–259.

Lundin, R. A. & Söderholm, A. (1995). A theory of the temporary organization. *Scandinavian Journal of Management*, 11(4), 437–455.

Lyng, S. (2005). Edgework and the risk-taking experience. In S. Lyng (Ed.), *Edgework: The sociology of risk-taking* (pp. 3–16). New York: Routledge.

Maguire, M. (2000). Policing by risks and targets: Some dimensions and implications of intelligence-led crime control. *Policing and Society*, 9(4), 315–336.

Manning, S. (2017). The rise of project network organizations: Building core teams and flexible partner pools for interorganizational projects. *Research Policy*, 46(8), 1399–1415.

Manning, S. & Sydow, J. (2007). Transforming creative potential in project networks: How TV movies are produced under network-based control. *Critical Sociology*, 33(1–2), 19–42.

Martin, J., Feldman, M., Hatch, M. J. & Sitkin, S. J. (1983). The uniqueness paradox in organizational stories. *Administrative Science Quarterly*, 28, 438–453.

Marwick, A. (2015). Instafame: Luxury selfies in the attention economy. *Public Culture*, 27, 137–160.

Marwick, A. E. (2013a). *Status update: Celebrity, publicity and attention in the social media age*. New Haven, CT: Yale University Press.

Marwick, A. E. (2013b). Online identity. In J. Hartley, J. Burgess & A. Bruns (Eds.), *A companion to new media dynamics* (pp. 355–364). Oxford, UK: Wiley-Blackwell.

Marx, K. (1867/1906). *Capital: A critique of political economy* (Vol. 1, S. Moore & E. Aveling, Trans.). New York, NY: Modern Library.

Mas, A. & Pallais, A. (2016). Valuing alternative work arrangements (22708). *National Bureau of Economic Research.*

Matamoros, C. A. (2018, February 17). *Internet research agency: Russian "troll farm" that "defrauded the US".* Retrieved from www.euronews.com/2018/02/17/the-internet-research-agency-the-russian-troll-farm-that-meddled-with-2016-us-elections

Mathews, J. (2010). Lachmannian insights into strategic entrepreneurship: Resources, activities and routines in a disequilibrium world. *Organization Studies, 31*(2), 219–244.

McCurdy, P. & Uldam, J. (2014). Connecting participant observation positions: Toward a reflexive framework for studying social movements. *Field Methods, 26*(1), 40–55.

McKelvey, B. (1999). Avoiding complexity catastrophe in coevolutionary pockets: Strategies for rugged landscapes. *Organization Science, 10*(3), 294–321.

McRobbie, A. (2016). *Be creative: Making a living in the new culture industries.* Cambridge, UK: Polity Press.

Médecins Sans Frontières. (2018). Retrieved from https://www.msf.org

Mercea, D., Iannelli, L. & Loader, B. D. (2016). Protest communication ecologies. *Information, Communication & Society, 19*(3), 279–289.

Merriam-Webster. (2018). Extreme. Retrieved from https://www.merriam-webster.com/dictionary/extreme

Mervyn, K., Simon, A. & Allen, D. K. (2014). Digital inclusion and social inclusion: A tale of two cities. *Information, Communication & Society, 17*(9), 1086–1104.

Metamorphosis. (2018). *Mission.* Retrieved from www.metamorph.org/

Meunier, D. & Vásquez, C. (2008). On shadowing the hybrid character of actions: A communicational approach. *Communication Methods and Measures, 2*(3), 167–192.

Meyer, J. W. & Rowan, B. (1977). Institutionalized organizations: Formal structure as myth and ceremony. *American Journal of Sociology, 83*(2), 340–363.

Miller, E. J. (1975). Socio-technical systems in weaving, 1953–1970: A follow-up study. *Human Relations, 28*(4), 349–386.

Miller, P. & O'Leary, T. (1987). Accounting and the construction of the governable person. *Accounting, Organizations and Society, 12,* 235–265.

Miller, P. & Rose, N. (2008). *Governing the present.* Cambridge, UK: Polity Press.

Miller, P. & Rose, N. (1995). Production, identity, and democracy. *Theory and Society, 24,* 427–467.

Milner, R. M. (2016). *The world made meme: Public conversations and participatory media.* The Information Society Series. Cambridge, MA: The MIT Press.

Miltner, K. M. (2014). "There's no place for lulz on LOLCats": The role of genre, gender, and group identity in the interpretation and enjoyment of an Internet meme. *First Monday, 19*(8).

Mina, X. (2014). Batman, Pandaman and the Blind Man: A case study in social change memes and Internet censorship in China. *Journal of Visual Culture, 13*(3), 359–375.

Mir, R., Mir, A. & Upadhyaya, P. (2003). Toward a postcolonial reading of organizational control. In A. Prasad (Ed.), *Postcolonial theory and organizational analysis: A critical engagement* (pp. 47–74). New York: Palgrave.

Mische, A. (2008). *Partisan publics: Communication and contention across Brazilian youth activist networks.* Princeton, NY: Princeton University Press.

Mische, A. & White, H. C. (1998). Between conversation and situation: Public switching dynamics across network-domains. *Social Research*, 65(3), 695–724.

Mohe, M. & Seidl, D. (2011). Theorizing the client-consultant relationship from the perspective of social-systems theory. *Organization*, 18(1), 3–22.

Mohr, J. & White, H. C. (2008). How to model an institution. *Theory and Society*, 37, 485–512.

Mol, A. (2002). Cutting surgeons, walking patients. Some complexities involved in comparing. In *Complexities: Social studies of knowledge practices* (pp. 218–257). Durham and London: Duke University Press.

Moreland, J. & Apker, J. (2016). Conflict and stress in hospital nursing: Improving communicative responses to enduring professional challenges. *Health Communication*, 31(7), 815–823.

Morgner, C. (2014). The theory of love and the theory of society: Remarks on the oeuvre of Niklas Luhmann. *International Sociology*, 29(5), 396–404.

Morozov, E. (2009). Iran: Downside to the "Twitter Revolution". *Dissent*, 56(4), 10–14.

Morrill, C. (2008). Culture and organization theory. *The Annals of the American Academy of Political and Social Science*, 619(1), 15–40.

Mumby, D. K. (2018). Targeting Alex: Brand as agent in communicative capitalism. In B. H. J. M. Brummans (Ed.), *The agency of organizing: Perspectives and case studies* (pp. 98–122). New York: Routledge.

Mumby, D. K. (2016). Organizing beyond organization: Branding, discourse, and communicative capitalism. *Organization*, 23(6), 884–907.

Mumby, D. K. (2005). Theorizing resistance in organization studies. *Management Communication Quarterly*, 19(1), 19–44.

Mumby, D. K. (1988). *Communication and power in organizations: Discourse, ideology, and domination*. Norwood, NJ: Ablex.

Mumby, D. K., Thomas, R., Martí, I. & Seidl, D. (2017). Resistance redux. *Organization Studies*, 38(9), 1157–1183.

Muñiz, A. M. & Schau, H. J. (2005). Religiosity in the abandoned apple newton brand community. *Journal of Consumer Research*, 31, 737–747.

Munro, R. (2003). Disorganization. In R. Westwood & S. Clegg (Eds.), *Debating organization: Point-counterpoint in organization studies* (pp. 283–297). Malden, MA: Blackwell.

Munro, R. (2001). Unmanaging/disorganization. *Ephemera*, 1, 395–403.

Munro, R. (1998). Belonging on the move: Market rhetoric and the future as obligatory passage. *The Sociological Review*, 46(2), 208–243.

Murphy, G. (1953). *In the minds of men: The study of human behavior and social tensions in India*. New York: Basic Books, Inc. Publishers.

Nagourney, A., Perez-Pena, R. & Goodman, J. D. (2015, December 15). Los Angeles and New York differ in their responses to a terrorism threat. *The New York Times*. Retrieved from www.nytimes.com/2015/12/16/us/los-angeles-schools-bomb-threat.html

Nah, S. & Yamamoto, M. (2017). Civic technology and community building: Interaction effects between integrated connectedness to a storytelling network (ICSN) and Internet and mobile uses on civic participation. *Journal of Computer-Mediated Communication*, 22(4), 179–195.

Nassehi, A. (2005). Organizations as decision machines: Niklas Luhmann's theory of organized social systems. *Sociological Review*, 53(1), 178–191.

National Public Radio (NPR). (2015). *Diane Rehm show of 17 December 2015*. https://dianerehm.org/shows/2015-12-17/assessing-violent-threats-against-our-schools

Neave, N., Jackson, R., Saxton, T. & Hönekopp, J. (2015). The influence of anthropomorphic tendencies on human hoarding behaviours. *Personality and Individual Differences, 72*, 214–219.

Neave, N., Tyson, H., McInnes, L. & Hamilton, C. (2016). The role of attachment style and anthropomorphism in predicting behaviours in a non-clinical sample. *Personality and Individual Differences, 99*, 33–37.

Neff, G. (2012). *Venture labor: Work and the burden of risk in innovative industries.* Cambridge, MA: MIT Press.

Neilson, B. & Rossiter, N. (2008). Precarity as a political concept, or, Fordism as exception. *Theory, Culture & Society, 25*(7–8), 51–72.

Neumayer, C. & Svensson, J. (2014). Activism and radical politics in the digital age: Towards a typology: Convergence. *The International Journal of Research into New Media Technologies, 22*(2), 131–146.

Newell, S., Bresnen, M., Edelman, L., Scarbrough, H. & Swan, J. (2006). Sharing knowledge across projects: Limits to ICT-led project review practices. *Management Learning, 37*(2), 167–185.

Nooney, L. & PortwoodStacer, L. (2014). One does not simply: An introduction to the special issue on Internet memes. *Journal of Visual Culture, 13*(3), 248–252.

Norton, T. & Sadler, C. (2006). Dialectical hegemony and the enactment of contradictory definitions in a rural community planning process. *Southern Communication Journal, 71*(4), 363–382.

Obar, J. A., Zube, P. & Lampe, C. (2012). Advocacy 2.0: An analysis of how advocacy groups in the United States perceive and use social media as tools for facilitating civic engagement and collective action. *Journal of Information Policy, 2*(1), 1–25.

Olins, W. (2000). How brands are taking over the corporation. In M. Schultz, M. J. Hatch & M. H. Larsen (Eds.), *The expressive organization: Linking identity, reputation, and the corporate brand* (pp. 51–65). Oxford, UK: Oxford University Press.

Orlikowski, W. J. (2007). Sociomaterial practices: Exploring technology at work. *Organization Studies, 28*(9), 1435–1448.

Orlikowski, W. J. & Scott, S. V. (2008). Sociomateriality: Challenging the separation of technology, work and organization. *Academy of Management Annals, 2*(1), 433–474.

Paragi, B. (2017). Contemporary gifts. *Current Anthropology, 58*(3), 317–339.

Patton, M. Q. (1990). *Qualitative evaluation and research methods.* Thousand Oaks, CA: Sage Publications.

Peters, T. (1988). *Thriving on chaos: Handbook for a management revolution.* New York: Knopf.

Peters, T. & Waterman, R. M. (1982). *In search of excellence.* New York: Harper & Row.

Piezunka, H. & Dahlander, L. (2015). Distant search, narrow attention: How crowding alters organizations' filtering of suggestions in crowdsourcing. *Academy of Management Journal, 58*, 856–880.

Plein, L. C., Green, K. E. & Williams, D. G. (1998). Organic planning: A new approach to public participation in local governance. *The Social Science Journal, 35*(4), 509–523.

Plowman, D. A., Solansky, S., Beck, T. E., Baker, L., Kulkami, M. & Travis, D. V. (2007). The role of leadership in emergent, self-organization. *The Leadership Quarterly, 18*(4), 341–356.

Poole, M. S. (2013). *Paradoxes of collaboration.* The Carroll C. Arnold Distinguished Lecture of the National Communication Association. Washington, DC: National Communication Association (NCA).

Porter, A. J. (2014). Performance as (dis)organization: The case of discursive material practices in academic technologies. *Canadian Journal of Communication, 39*, 639–650.

Porter, A. J. (2013). Emergent organization and responsive technologies in crisis: Creating connection or enabling divides? *Management Communication Quarterly, 27*(1), 6–33.

Porter, A. J., Kuhn, T. R. & Nerlich, B. (2017). Organizing authority in the climate change debate: IPCC controversies and the management of dialectical tensions. *Organization Studies, 39*(7), 873–898.

Postill, J. (2008). Localizing the Internet beyond communities and networks. *New Media & Society, 10*(3), 413–431.

Prasad, A. (Ed.). (2003). The gaze of the other: Postcolonial theory and organizational analysis. In *Postcolonial theory and organizational analysis: A critical engagement* (pp. 3–43). New York: Palgrave.

Pullen, A. & Knights, D. (2007). Undoing gender: Organizing and disorganizing performance. *Gender, Work & Organization, 14*(6), 505–511.

Putnam, L. L. (1986). Contradictions and paradoxes in organizations. *Organization-Communication: Emerging Perspectives, 1*, 151–167.

Putnam, L. L. & Fairhurst, G. T. (2015). Revisiting "organizations as discursive constructions": 10 years later. *Communication Theory, 25*(4), 375–392.

Putnam, L. L., Fairhurst, G. T. & Banghart, S. (2016). Contradictions, dialectics, and paradoxes in organizations: A constitutive approach. *The Academy of Management Annals, 10*(1), 65–171.

Putnam, L. L., Nicotera, A. M. & McPhee, R. D. (2009). Introduction: Communication constitutes organization. In L. L. Putnam & A. M. Nicotera (Eds.), *Building theory of organization: The constitutive role of communication* (pp. 1–19). London: Routledge/Taylor & Francis.

Putnam, L. L. & Pacanowsky, M. (Eds.). (1983). *Communication and organizations: An interpretive approach*. Beverly Hills, CA: Sage Publications.

Putnam, R. (2000). *Bowling alone: The collapse and revival of American community*. New York: Simon & Shuster.

Radhakrishnan, R. (1994). Postmodernism and the rest of the world. *Organization, 1*(2), 305–340. Rane, H. & Salem, S. (2012). Social media, social movements and the diffusion of ideas in the Arab uprisings. *The Journal of International Communication, 18*(1), 97–111.

Rehn, A. & O'Doherty, D. (2007). Organization: On the theory and practice of excess. *Culture and Organization, 13*, 99–113.

Rennstam, J. (2012). Object-control: A study of technologically dense knowledge work. *Organization Studies, 33*(8), 1071–1090.

Rheingold, H. (1994). *The virtual community: Finding connection in a computerised world*. London: Secker and Warburg.

Rhodes, C. (2001). D'Oh: The Simpsons, popular culture, and the organizational carnival. *Journal of Management Inquiry, 10*(4), 374–383.

Rice, A. K. (1963). *The enterprise and its environment: A system theory of management organization*. London: Tavistock Publications.

Rice, A. K. (1958). *Productivity and social organisation: The Ahmedabad Experiment*. London: Tavistock Publications.

Rice, A. K. (1953). Productivity and social organisation in an Indian weaving shed: An examination of the socio-technical systems of an experimental automatic loom shed. *Human Relations, 6*(4), 297–329.

Rice, A. K., Hill, J. M. M. & Trist, E. L. (1950). The representation of labour turnover as a social process. *Human Relations, 3*(4), 349–372.

Richards, L. & Dalbey, M. (2006). Creating great places: The role of citizen participation. *Community Development, 37*(4), 18–32.

Robichaud, D., Giroux, H. & Taylor, J. R. (2004). The metaconversation: The recursive property of language as a key to organizing. *Academy of Management Review, 29*(4), 617–634.

Robins, J. A. (1993). Organization as strategy: Restructuring production in the film industry. *Strategic Management Journal, 14*(S1), 103–118.

Robinson, A. (2011, September). In theory Bakhtin: Carnival against capital, carnival against power. *Ceasefire.* Retrieved from https://ceasefiremagazine.co.uk/in-theory-bakhtin-2/

Roethlisberger, F. J. (1953). The administrator's skill: Communication. *Harvard Business Review, 31*(3), 55–62.

Romanelli, E. & Tushman, M. (1994). Organizational transformation as punctuated equilibrium: An empirical test. *Academy of Management Journal, 37*(5), 1141–1666.

Roper, W. & Muller, B. H. F. (2002). Envisioning rural futures: Using innovative software for community planning. In J. N. Levitt (Ed.), *Conservation in the Internet age: Threat and opportunities* (pp. 218–241). Washington, DC: Island Press.

Rorty, R. (1995). A spectre is haunting the intellectuals. *European Journal of Philosophy, 3*(3), 289–298.

Rose, N. (1999). *Governing the soul: The shaping of the private self* (2nd. ed.). London: Free Association Books.

Ross, A. (2003). *No-collar: The humane workplace and its hidden costs.* New York: Basic Books.

Roster, C. A. (2015). "Help, I have too much stuff!": Extreme possession attachment and professional organizers. *Journal of Consumer Affairs, 49*(2), 303–327.

Roy, S. K. (1969). A re-examination of the methodology of A.K. Rice's Indian Textile Mill work reorganisation. *Indian Journal of Industrial Relations, 5*(2), 170–191.

Sacks, H. (1992). *Lectures on conversation* (Vol. 1 & 2). Oxford, UK: Blackwell.

Salge, C. & Karahanna, E. (2016). Protesting corruption on Twitter: Is it a bot or is it a person? *Academy of Management Discoveries, 4*(1), 32–49.

Sandberg, S. (2013). *Lean in: Women, work and the will to lead.* New York: Alfred A. Knopf.

Sathe, V. (1983). Implications of corporate culture: A manager's guide to action. *Organizational Dynamics, 12*(3), 5–23.

Schatzki, T. R. (2008). On organizations as they happen. *Organization Studies, 27*(12), 1863–1873.

Schatzki, T. R. (2005). The sites of organizations. *Organization Studies, 26*(3), 465–484.

Schoeneborn, D. (2013a). The pervasive power of PowerPoint: How a genre of professional communication permeates organizational communication. *Organization Studies, 34*(12), 1777–1801.

Schoeneborn, D. (2013b). PowerPoint und die Einkapselung von Prozessualität im projektübergreifenden Lernen. *Managementforschung, 23*, 127–156.

Schoeneborn, D. (2011). Organization as communication: A Luhmannian perspective. *Management Communication Quarterly, 25*(4), 663–689.

Schoeneborn, D. (2008). *Alternatives considered but not disclosed: The ambiguous role of PowerPoint in cross-project learning.* Wiesbaden: VS Verlag für Sozialwissenschaften.

Schoeneborn, D., Blaschke, S., Cooren, F., McPhee, R. D., Seidl, D. & Taylor, J. R. (2014). The three schools of CCO thinking: Interactive dialogue and systematic comparison. *Management Communication Quarterly*, 28(2), 285–316.

Schoeneborn, D. & Dobusch, L. (In press). Alternating between partial and complete organization: The case of Anonymous. In G. Ahrne & N. Brunsson (Eds.), *Organization outside organizations*. Cambridge, UK: Cambridge University Press.

Schoeneborn, D., Kuhn, T. R. & Kärreman, D. (In press). The communicative constitution of organization, organizing, and organizationality. *Organization Studies*.

Schoeneborn, D. & Scherer, A. G. (2012). Clandestine organizations, al-Qaeda, and the paradox of (in)visibility: A response to Stohl and Stohl. *Organization Studies, 33*, 963–971.

Schoeneborn, D. & Vásquez, C. (2017). Communication as constitutive of organization. In C. R. Scott & L. K. Lewis (Eds.), *International encyclopedia of organizational communication*. Hoboken, NJ: Wiley.

Schoeneborn, D., Vásquez, C. & Cornelissen, J. (2016). Imagining organization through metaphor and metonymy: Unpacking the process-entity paradox. *Human Relations, 69*(4), 915–944.

Schön, D. A. (1983). *The reflective practitioner: How professionals think in action*. New York, NY: Basic Books.

Schradie, J. (2018). Moral Monday is more than a hashtag: The strong ties of social movement emergence in the digital era. *Social Media + Society, 4*(1).

Schreiber, M. (2017). Showing/sharing: Analysing visual communication from a praxeological perspective. *Media and Communication, 5*(4), 37–50.

Schreyoegg, G. & Sydow, J. (2010). Organizing for fluidity? Dilemmas of new organizational forms. *Organization Science, 21*(6), 1251–1262.

Scott, C. R. (2015). Bringing hidden organizations out of the shadows: Introduction to the special issue. *Management Communication Quarterly, 29*, 503–511.

Scott, C. R. (2013). *Anonymous agencies, backstreet businesses, and covert collectives: Rethinking organizations in the 21st century*. Stanford, CA: Stanford University Press.

Searle, J. (1995). *The construction of social reality*. New York: Free Press.

Seidl, D. (2005). *Organisational identity and self-transformation: An autopoietic perspective*. Aldershot, UK: Ashgate.

Seidl, D. & Becker, K. H. (2006). Organizations as distinction generating and processing systems: Niklas Luhmann's contribution to organization studies. *Organization, 13*(1), 9–35.

Seidl, D. & Schoeneborn, D. (In press). Niklas Luhmann: Une perspective systémique des organisations. In O. Germain (Ed.), *Les grands inspirateurs de la théorie des organisations* (Vol. 2). Colombelles: Editions Management et Société.

Seigworth, G. J. & Gregg, M. (2010). An inventory of shimmers. In M. Gregg & G. J. Seigworth (Eds.), *The affect theory reader* (pp. 1–25). Durham, NC: Duke University Press.

Selznick, P. (1948). Foundations of the theory of organization. *American Sociological Review, 13*(1), 25–35.

Sheep, M. & Fairhurst, G. T. (2016, July). *Exploring disequilibrium in paradox: Power and context in the case of school shooting threats in New York and Los Angeles*. Paper presented as part of Sub-Theme 35: Theorizing (or Exploring) Disequilibrium in Paradox, European Group and Organization Studies (EGOS) Conference, Naples, Italy.

Sheep, M. & Fairhurst, G. T. (2015, July). *Accounting for disequilibrium in knotted systems of paradoxical tensions*. Paper presented as part of Sub-Theme 52: Paradoxes and Unreason: Provoking Greater Examination into Organizational

Life Rethinking Order and Disorder, European Group and Organization Studies (EGOS) Conference, Athens, Greece.

Sheep, M., Fairhurst, G. T. & Khazanchi, S. (2017). Knots in the discourse of innovation: Investigating multiple tensions in a reacquired spin-off. *Organization Studies, 38*, 463–488.

Sheremata, W. A. (2000). Centrifugal and centripetal forces in radical new product development under time pressure. *Academy of Management Review, 25*(2), 389–408.

Shifman, L. (2013). Memes in a digital world: Reconciling with a conceptual troublemaker. *Journal of Computer Mediated Communication, 18*(3), 362–377.

Sieber, R. (2006). Public participation geographic information systems: A literature review and framework. *Annals of the Association of American Geographers, 96*, 491–507.

Sillince, J. A. A. (2010). Can CCO theory tell us how organizing is distinct from markets, networking, belonging to a community, or supporting a social movement? *Management Communication Quarterly, 23*(1), 132–138.

Simo, G. & Bies, A. L. (2007). The role of nonprofits in disaster response: An expanded model of cross-sector collaboration. *Public Administration Review, 67*(S1), 125–142.

Singh, A. (2017, January 10). Citizen lab research on hacking team in NY Times. *The Citizen Lab.* Retrieved from https://citizenlab.ca/2017/01/new-york-times-article-features-citizen-lab-research-hacking-team/

Smith, A. (2013). Civic engagement in the digital age. *Pew Research Center.* Retrieved from www.pewinternet.org/2013/04/25/civic-engagement-in-the-digital-age/

Smith, A., Schlozman, K. L., Verba, S. & Brady, H. (2009). The current state of civic engagement in America. *Pew Research Center.* Retrieved from www.pewinternet.org/2009/09/01/the-current-state-of-civic-engagement-in-america/

Smith, D. (1974). The social construction of documentary reality. *Sociological Inquiry, 44*, 257–268.

Smith, J. H. (1998). The enduring legacy of Elton Mayo. *Human Relations, 51*, 221–249.

Smith, W. K. & Lewis, M. W. (2011). Toward a theory of paradox: A dynamic equilibrium model of organizing. *Academy of Management Review, 36*(2), 381–403.

Spencer, D. C. (2014). Sensing violence: An ethnography of mixed martial arts. *Ethnography, 15*(2), 232–254.

Spencer Brown, G. (1972). *Laws of form.* New York: The Julian Press.

Spivak, G. C. (1988). Can the subaltern speak? In C. Nelson & L. Grossberg (Eds.), *Marxism and the interpretation of culture.* London: Palgrave.

Spoelstra, S. (2005). Robert Cooper: Beyond organization. *The Sociological Review, 53*, 106–119.

Srnicek, N. (2017). *Platform capitalism.* Cambridge, UK: Polity Press.

Stacey, R. D. (1995). The science of complexity: An alternative perspective for strategic change processes. *Strategic Management Journal, 16*(6), 477–495.

Starkey, K., Barnatt, C. & Tempest, S. (2000). Beyond networks and hierarchies: Latent organizations in the UK Television industry. *Organization Science, 11*(3), 299–305.

Stewart, K. (2007). *Ordinary affects.* Durham, NC: Duke University Press.

Stohl, C. & Stohl, M. (2011). Secret agencies: The communicative constitution of a clandestine organization. *Organization Studies, 32*(9), 1197–1215.

Storper, M. (1989). The transition to flexible specialisation in the US film industry: External economies, the division of labour, and the crossing of industrial divides. *Cambridge Journal of Economics, 13*(2), 273–305.

Sullivan, K. & Delaney, H. (2017). A femininity that "giveth and taketh away": The prosperity gospel and postfeminism in the neoliberal economy. *Human Relations, 70*, 836–859.

Suominen, K. & Mantere, S. (2010). Consuming strategy: The art and practice of managers' everyday strategy usage. In J. Baum & J. Lampel (Eds.), *The globalization of strategy research* (pp. 211–245). New York, NY: Emerald.

Sutcliffe, W. (2006). *Managing the unexpected: Assuring high performance in an age of complexity.* New York: John Wiley & Sons.

Swan, J., Scarbrough, H. & Newell, S. (2010). Why don't (or do) organizations learn from projects? *Management Learning, 41*(3), 325–344.

Sydow, J. & Windeler, A. (Eds.). (2004). *Organisation der Content-Produktion.* Wiesbaden: VS Verlag für Sozialwissenschaften.

Taekke, J. (2011). Digital panopticism and organizational power. *Surveillance & Society, 8*(4), 441–459.

Taylor, F. W. (1911/1934). *The principles of scientific management.* New York: Harper & Brothers.

Taylor, J. R. (1988). *Une organisation n'est qu'un tissu de communications. Cahiers de recherches en communication* (Working Paper). Montréal: Universite de Montréal.

Taylor, J. R. (1999). What is "organizational communication"? Communication as a dialogic of text and conversation. *Communication Review, 3*(1–2), 21–63.

Taylor, J. R. & Cooren, F. (1997). What makes communication "organizational"? How the many voices of a collectivity become the one voice of an organization. *Journal of Pragmatics, 27*(4), 409–438.

Taylor, J. R., Cooren, F., Giroux, N. & Robichaud, D. (1996). The communicational basis of organization: Between the conversation and the text. *Communication Theory, 6*(1), 1–39.

Taylor, J. R. & Robichaud, D. (2007). Management as metaconversation: The search for closure. In F. Cooren (Ed.), *LEA's communication series: Interacting and organizing: Analyses of a management meeting* (pp. 5–30). New York: Taylor & Francis Group/Lawrence Erlbaum Associates.

Taylor, J. R. & Van Every, E. J. (2014). *When organization fails: Why authority matters.* New York, NY: Routledge.

Taylor, J. R. & Van Every, E. J. (2010). *The situated organization: Case studies in the pragmatics of communication research.* Abingdon, UK: Routledge.

Taylor, J. R. & Van Every, E. J. (2000). *The emergent organization: Communication as its site and surface.* Mahwah, NJ: Lawrence Erlbaum.

Tempest, S., Starkey, K. & Ennew, C. (2007). In the death zone: A study of limits in the 1996 Mount Everest disaster. *Human Relations, 60*(7), 1039–1064.

Thiel-Stern, S. (2012). Collaborative, productive, performative, templated: Youth, identity and breaking the fourth wall. In R. A. Lind (Ed.), *Produsing theory in a digital world* (pp. 87–103). New York, NY: Peter Lang.

Thompson, M. (2008). *Organising and disorganizing.* London: Triarchy.

Tilly, C. (2005). *Identities, boundaries and social ties.* Boulder, CO: Paradigm Publishers.

Timpano, K. R. & Shaw, A. M. (2013). Conferring humanness: The role of anthropomorphism in hoarding. *Personality and Individual Differences, 54*, 383–388.

Thompson, J. B. (2005). The new visibility. *Theory, Culture & Society, 22*(6), 31–51.

Tolentino, G. (2017, March 17). The gig economy celebrates working yourself to death. *The New Yorker.* Retrieved from www.newyorker.com/culture/jia-tolentino/the-gig-economy-celebrates-working-yourself-to-death

Tracy, K. & Tracy, S. J. (1998). Rudeness at 911 reconceptualizing face and face attack. *Human Communication Research, 25*(2), 225–251.

Tracy, S. J. (2013). *Qualitative research methods: Collecting evidence, crafting analysis, communicating impact*. Wessex, UK: John Wiley & Sons.

Trethewey, A. & Ashcraft, K. L. (2004). Practicing disorganization: The development of applied perspectives on living with tension. *Journal of Applied Communication Research, 32*, 81–88.

Trist, E. L. (1981). The evolution of sociotechnical systems as a conceptual framework and as an action research program. In A. H. Van de Ven & W. F. Joyce (Eds.), *Perspectives on organization design and behavior*. New York: John Wiley & Sons.

Trist, E. L. & Bamforth, K. (1951). Some social and psychological consequences of the long wall method of coal-getting. *Human Relations, 4*(1), 3–38.

Tronti, M. (2012). Our operaismo. *New Left Review, 73*, 119–139.

Trottier, D. & Fuchs, C. (2015). *Social media, politics and the state: Protests, revolutions, riots, crime and policing in the age of Facebook, Twitter and YouTube*. New York: Routledge.

Tsoukas, H. (2015). Practice, strategy-making and intentionality: A Heideggerian onto-epistemology for strategy as practice. In D. Golsorkhi, L. Rouleau, D. Seidl & E. Vaara (Eds.), *Cambridge handbook of strategy as practice* (2nd ed., pp. 58–78). Cambridge, UK: Cambridge University Press.

Tsoukas, H. (2013). Organization as chaosmos. In F. Cooren & D. Robichaud (Eds.), *Organization and organizing: Materiality, agency and discourse* (pp. 52–65). New York: Routledge.

Tsoukas, H. (1998). Introduction: Chaos, complexity and organization theory. *Organization, 5*(3), 291–313.

Tsoukas, H. & Chia, R. (2002). On organizational becoming: Rethinking organizational change. *Organization Science, 13*(5), 567–582.

Tunc, T. (2009). Role conflict, role ambiguity, and burnout in nurses and physicians at a university hospital in Turkey. *Nursing & Health Sciences, 99*(4), 410–416.

Uldam, J. (2018). Social media visibility: Challenges to activism. *Media, Culture & Society, 40*(1), 41–58.

Uldam, J. & Hansen, H. K. (2017). Corporate responses to stakeholder activism: Partnerships and surveillance. *Critical Perspectives on International Business, 13*(2), 151–165.

Vaara, E. & Whittington, R. (2012). Strategy-as-practice: Taking social practices seriously. *The Academy of Management Annals, 6*(1), 285–336.

Vallas, S. P. & Cummins, E. R. (2015). Personal branding and identity norms in the popular business press: Enterprise culture in an age of precarity. *Organization Studies, 36*, 293–319.

Vallas, S. P. & Prener, C. (2012). Dualism, job polarization, and the social construction of precarious work. *Work and Occupations, 39*, 331–353.

Van De Donk, W. B. H. J., Loader, B., Nixon, P. & Rucht, D. (Eds.). (2004). *Cyberprotest: New media, citizens, and social movements*. Berkley, CA: California University Press.

Vásquez, C. (2016). A spatial grammar of organizing: Studying the communicative constitution of organizational spaces. *Communication Research and Practice, 2*(3), 351–377.

Vásquez, C. (2013). Spacing organization or how to be here and there at the same time. In D. Robichaud & F. Cooren (Eds.), *Organization and organizing: Materiality, agency, and discourse* (pp. 127–149). New York: Routledge.

Vásquez, C., Bencherki, N., Cooren, F. & Sergi, V. (2018). From "matters of concern" to "matters of authority": Studying the performativity of strategy from a communicative constitution of organization (CCO) approach. *Long Range Planning*, *51*(3), 417–435.

Vásquez, C., Brummans, B. H. & Groleau, C. (2012). Notes from the field on organizational shadowing as framing. *Qualitative Research in Organizations and Management: An International Journal*, 7(2), 144–165.

Vásquez, C. & Cooren, F. (2013). Spacing practices: The communicative configuration of organizing through space-times. *Communication Theory*, 23(1), 25–47.

Vásquez, C., Schoeneborn, D. & Sergi, V. (2016). Summoning the spirits: Organizational texts and the (dis)ordering properties of communication. *Human Relations*, 69(3), 629–659.

Virno, P. (2004). *A grammar of the multitude: For an analysis of contemporary forms of life*. Los Angeles, CA: Semiotext(e).

von Foerster, H. (1992). Ethics and second-order cybernetics. *Cybernetics & Human Knowing*, 1(1), 9–19.

Wacquant, L. (2004). Following Pierre Bourdieu into the field. *Ethnography*, 5(4), 387–414.

Weick, K. E. (2001). *Making sense of the organization*. Oxford: Blackwell.

Weick, K. E. (1995). *Sensemaking in organizations*. Thousand Oaks: Sage Publications.

Weick, K. E. (1993). The collapse of sensemaking in organizations: The Mann Gulch disaster. *Administrative Science Quarterly*, 38(4), 628–652.

Weick, K. E. (1979). *The social psychology of organizing*. New York: Random House.

Weick, K. E. (1969). *The social psychology of organizing*. Reading, MA: Addison-Wesley.

Weick, K. E. & Sutcliffe, K. M. (2015). *Managing the unexpected: Sustained performance in a complex world*. New York: John Wiley & Sons.

Weick, K. E., Sutcliffe, K. M. & Obstfeld, D. (2005). Organizing and the process of sensemaking. *Organization Science*, 16(4), 409–421.

Weick, K. E., Sutcliffe, K. M. & Obstfeld, D. (1999). Organizing for high reliability: Processes of collective mindfulness. In B. M. Staw & L. L. Cummings (Eds.), *Research in organizational behavior*. (Vol. 21, pp. 81–123). Stamford, CT: JAI Press.

Weil, D. (2014). *The fissured workplace*. Cambridge, MA: Harvard University Press.

Weyers, B., Burkolter, D., Kluge, A. & Luther, W. (2010). *User-centered interface reconfiguration for error reduction in human-computer interaction*. Advances in Human-Oriented and Personalized Mechanisms, Technologies and Services (CENTRIC), 2010 Third International Conference on (pp. 52–55), IEEE.

White, H. C. (2008). *Identity and control: How social formations emerge* (2nd ed.). Princeton, NJ: University Press.

White, H. C. (1995). Network switchings and Bayesian forks: Reconstructing the social and behavioral sciences. *Social Research*, 62, 1035–1063.

White, H. C. (1993a). Values come in styles, which mate to change. In M. Hechter, L. Nadel & R. Michad (Eds.), *The origin of values* (pp. 63–91). New York, NY: de Gruyter.

White, H. C. (1993b). *Careers and creativity: Social forces in the arts*. Boulder, CO: Westview.

White, H. C. (1965). Notes on the constituents of social structure. Soc. Rel. 10— Spring Lecture '65 at the Harvard University. First published in *Sociologica*, 1, 1–15.

White, H. C. (1963). *An anatomy of kinship*. Englewood Cliffs, CA: Prentice-Hall.

White, H. C., Fuhse, J., Thiemann, M. & Buchholz, L. (2007a). Networks and meaning: Styles and switchings. *Soziale Systeme*, 13, 534–555.

White, H. C. & Godart, F. (2007). Stories from identity and control. *Sociologica*, 3, 1–17.

White, H. C., Godart, F. & Corona, V. P. (2007). Mobilizing identities: Uncertainty and control in strategy. *Theory, Culture & Society*, 24(7–8), 181–202.

White, H. C., Godart, F. & Thiemann, M. (2013). Turning points and the space of possibles: A relational perspective on the different forms of uncertainty. In F. Dépelteau & C. Powell (Eds.), *Applying relational sociology* (pp. 137–154). New York, NY: Palgrave Macmillan.

Whitworth, B. & de Moor, A. (Eds.). (2009). *Handbook of research on sociotechnical design and social networking systems*. Hershey, New York: IGI Global.

Wikileaks. (2016). *Spectre of ISIS used to erode rights in Morocco*. Retrieved from https://wikileaks.org/hackingteam/emails/emailid/156704

Willmott, H. (1993). Strength is ignorance; slavery is freedom: Managing culture in modern organizations. *Journal of Management Studies*, 30, 515–552.

Windeler, A. (2004). Organisation der TV-Produktion in Projektnetzwerken: Zur Bedeutung von Produkt-und Industriespezifika. In J. Sydow & A. Windeler (Eds.), *Organisation der Content-Produktion* (pp. 55–76). Wiesbaden: VS Verlag für Sozialwissenschaften.

Wirth, C. (2010). *Reflexive Arbeitskräftewirtschaft: Strukturation, Projektnetzwerke und TV-Content-Produktion*. München: Hampp.

Wheatley, M. J. (1999). *Leadership and the new science: Discovering order in a chaotic world* (2nd ed.). San Francisco: Berrett-Koehler Publishers.

Wolcott, S. (1994). The perils of lifetime employment systems: Productivity advance in the Indian and Japanese Textile Industries, 1920–1938. *The Journal of Economic History*, 54(2), 307–324.

Woodside, A. G. (2014). Embrace•perform•model: Complexity theory, contrarian case analysis, and multiple realities. *Journal of Business Research*, 67(12), 2495–2503.

Wrong, D. H. (1994). *The problem of order: What unites and divides society*. New York: Macmillan.

Young, I. M. (2002). *Inclusion and democracy*. Oxford: Oxford University Press.

Zaid, B. (2016). Internet and democracy in Morocco: A force for change and an instrument for repression. *Global Media and Communication*, 12(1), 1–18.

Zyman, S. (2002). *The end of advertising as we know it*. New York: John Wiley and Sons.

Zwick, D., Bonsu, S. K. & Darmody, A. (2008). Putting consumers to work: "Co-creation" and new marketing govern-mentality. *Journal of Consumer Culture*, 8, 163–196.

Index